NATIONAL GEOGRAPHIC

TRAVELER

beijing
& shanghai

D980211

NATIONAL GEOGRAPHIC
TRAVELER

beijing
& shanghai

Paul Mooney & Andrew Forbes
photography by
Catherine Karnow & David Butow

National Geographic
Washington, D.C.

CONTENTS

TRAVELING WITH EYES OPEN 6

CHARTING YOUR TRIP 8

History & Culture 15
Feature: Dangerous Beauty 34
Feature: In Style in Shanghai 48

BEIJING

Dongcheng District 61
Introduction & Map 62
Walk Among the *Hutongs* 74
Feature: Confucius: The Comeback Kid 80

Xicheng District 83
Introduction & Map 84
Bicycle Tour Around the Forbidden City 88
Feature: *Hutongs* 92

Chongwen District 95
Introduction & Map 96
Feature: Legation Quarter 102
Legation Quarter Walking Tour 104

Xuanwu District 107
Introduction & Map 108
Qianmen Dajie & Dashilan Walk 112
Feature: Gods & Goddesses 116

Chaoyang District 121
Introduction & Map 122

Haidian District 129
Introduction & Map 130
A Walk Around Peking University 134
Feature: Dancing in the Streets 138

Excursions North to the Great Wall 143
Introduction & Map 144
Feature: The Disappearing Wall 150

Excursions South 157
Introduction & Map 158
Feature: Chinese Temples 166

SHANGHAI

The Bund to People's Square 177
Introduction & Map 178
Walk the Bund 182
Feature: Shanghai's "Yellow Creek" 188

Nanshi: The Old Town 201
Introduction & Map 202
Walk Shanghai's Old Town 206
Feature: Shikumen Architecture—
Twilight of a Tradition 210

Fuxing Road to Huaihai Road 213
Introduction & Map 214
Walk Around Xintiandi 220
Feature: The Original Power Couple 224

Pudong 227
Introduction & Map 228
Cruise the Huangpu River 234

North Shanghai 237
Introduction & Map 238
Jewish Shanghai Walk 242
Feature: Chinese Ceramics 247

West Shanghai 249
Introduction & Map 250
Feature: Western Architecture
in Shanghai 256

Excursions From Shanghai 259
Introduction & Map 260
Feature: Grand Canal 266
Feature: Water Towns 274

TRAVELWISE 281
Hotels & Restaurants 294
Beijing Shopping 317
Beijing Entertainment 318
Shanghai Shopping 323
Shanghai Entertainment 324
Language Guide 328
Menu Reader 329

INDEX 334   **CREDITS** 342

Pages 2–3: The Summer Palace at night, Beijing
Opposite: Boys performing lion dance, Shanghai

TRAVELING WITH EYES OPEN

Alert travelers go with a purpose and leave with a benefit. If you travel responsibly, you can help support wildlife conservation, historic preservation, and cultural enrichment in the places you visit. You can enrich your own travel experience as well.

To be a geo-savvy traveler:

- Recognize that your presence has an impact on the places you visit.

- Spend your time and money in ways that sustain local character. (Besides, it's more interesting that way.)

- Value the destination's natural and cultural heritage.

- Respect the local customs and traditions.

- Express appreciation to local people about things you find interesting and unique to the place: its nature and scenery, music and food, historic villages and buildings.

- Vote with your wallet: Support the people who support the place, patronizing businesses that make an effort to celebrate and protect what's special there. Seek out shops, local restaurants, inns, and tour operators who love their home—who love taking care of it and showing it off. Avoid businesses that detract from the character of the place.

- Enrich yourself, taking home memories and stories to tell, knowing that you have contributed to the preservation and enhancement of the destination.

That is the type of travel now called geotourism, defined as "tourism that sustains or enhances the geographical character of a place—its environment, culture, aesthetics, heritage, and the well-being of its residents." To learn more, visit National Geographic's Center for Sustainable Destinations at *www.nationalgeographic.com/travel/sustainable*.

beijing
& shanghai

ABOUT THE AUTHORS & THE PHOTOGRAPHERS

Paul Mooney, who wrote the Beijing part of the guidebook, is an American freelance journalist. He has reported on China, Taiwan, and Hong Kong since 1985. Mooney is the author and editor of more than a dozen travel books on China and Taiwan. He has lived in Beijing since 1994.

Damien Harper wrote the "Beijing Today" part of the guidebook, and **Christopher Pitts** wrote the "Beijing Architecture" and "Arts & Culture" sections.

Andrew Forbes, who wrote the Shanghai part of the guidebook, is the author of more than a dozen books on East and Southeast Asia. He has contributed to numerous international publications. Forbes is also editor of *CPA Media* in Chiang Mai, Thailand.

Peter Holmshaw, author of the Shanghai Travelwise, first lived in China in 1988. He has since traveled extensively throughout the country and now divides his time between Chiang Mai, Thailand, and China's Yunnan Province.

Catherine Karnow, who photographed the Beijing part of the guidebook, is a San Francisco–based photographer. She was born and raised in Hong Kong, the daughter of an American journalist. Karnow has photographed for the National Geographic Society and numerous international publications.

David Butow, who covered Shanghai for this guidebook, is a photojournalist based in Los Angeles. In addition to Shanghai, his assignments have taken him to Asia, Africa, Europe, the Middle East, and South America.

Gary Bowerman is an Asia-based travel, business, and lifestyle writer, researcher, and editor specializing in China, the Far East, and Southeast Asia. He is co-founder of Scribes of the Orient, a Shanghai- and Hong Kong–based content and editorial services agency. He divides his time between Shanghai and Kuala Lumpur.

Charting Your Trip

Distinct in landscape, form, and personality, Beijing and Shanghai offer compelling contasts. Beijingers take pride in the capital's history, its revered temples, palaces, and proximity to the Great Wall. This historic appeal is enlivened with creative dining and nightlife, and an edgy contemporary art scene. Younger, brasher, more hedonistic, Shanghai is often defined by its futuristic skyline. The view from the ground, however, reveals fine heritage and art deco architecture alongside China's most eclectic and progressive fashions, restaurants, and clubs.

Getting Around

There is plenty to pack in, as China's public transport systems have improved immeasurably in the past five years. Flight access is world class; Beijing Capital International Airport and Shanghai Pudong International Airport are among the best served in Asia. Shanghai also has a second airport, Hongqiao International Airport, and a second Beijing airport is due to open later this decade. Frequent flights are offered between Shanghai and Beijing, and all airports offer train and/or metro access plus buses and taxis connecting with the city centers.

Increasingly popular is China's high-speed train link (*www.travelchinaguide.com/china-trains*), which opened in late 2011, connecting Beijing South Railway Station and Shanghai Hongqiao Railway Station in five and a half hours (trains can take up to eight hours, as some services have more en route stops). These daily trains run frequently from early morning until late evening. Both rail stations are connected to the metro network for easy access to/from downtown Beijing and Shanghai. Beijing and Shanghai also serve as hubs for frequent high-speed rail routes to cities across China. For example, Beijing–Tianjin takes just 27 minutes, while Shanghai connects with Nanjing (one hour),

A colorful Chinese dragon adds decorative drama to a Beijing wall.

Hangzhou (50 minutes), and Suzhou (35 minutes).

Wherever you are traveling to, booking accommodations and onward flights is made simpler by the Ctrip *(www.ctrip.com)* and ELong *(www.elong.net)* online booking sites. Widely used by locals, expats, and travelers, both have English-language portals and secure credit card booking engines, and they offer a large number of hotel and flight options throughout China each day.

Travel around Beijing and Shanghai is best undertaken underground, as traffic congestion is common. The metro networks of both cities *(see Travelwise pp. 284, 286–287, www.explorebj.com & www .exploreshanghai.com)* have undergone expansions in recent years, and both are clean, efficient, and cheap. Metro stations are located within walking distance of most city attractions. Taxis can be hailed on the street and are good value, but you'll need to speak to the driver in Chinese or have your destination written in Chinese characters. Another tip is to carry a local mobile phone with the number of the venue you are visiting, so the cab driver can speak to the receptionist or concierge for directions.

If You Only Have One Week in Beijing

On **Days 1 and 2** visit some of the city's signature attractions, such as the Forbidden City, Tiananmen Square, and Drum and Bell Towers. Take a rickshaw around the lakes at Houhai. Rise early on **Day 3** for a tour to the Great Wall of China at Badaling (see p. 148), 43 miles (70 km) northwest of Beijing, taking in the Ming Tombs (see p. 153). If you have time, book lunch or enjoy

NOT TO BE MISSED:

IN & AROUND BEIJING

A stroll through Beijing's Forbidden City 64–69

Beijing from above: the view from the Drum Tower 73

Exploring Beijing's famous 798 Art District 126

The scenic beauty of the Great Wall of China 144–152

IN & AROUND SHANGHAI

The Bund's neoclassical architecture 178–184

Sipping cocktails in Shanghai's legendary Long Bar 181

Nanjing Road's buzz 185–187

Pudong's soaring skyline 228–229

Taking a boat trip along the Huangpu River 234–235

Visitor Information

Beijing and Shanghai have tourist information offices, but their use is limited, and you may be pushed toward joining tours. Branches of **China International Travel Service** or CITS, operate in Beijing *(1 Dongdan Beidajie, tel 010/8522 8445, www.cits.net)* and in Shanghai *(Beijing Xi Lu 1277, Guolu Dasha, tel 021/6289-4510, www.cits.net)*. **China Travel Service** *(www.chinatravelservice .com)* or CTS, also has offices throughout the country. Alternatively, you can ask for travel advice from the front desk at your hotel or at any expat bar.

Useful terms are *lu* or road, *jie* or street (used in Beijing, not Shanghai), *dadao* or avenue, and *xiang* or lane. These are often subdivided according to the cardinal directions (see p. 286).

As Shanghai upgraded all local signage in 2010 with street signs, metro stations, and public notices in both English and Chinese characters, its main roads are listed in English in this guidebook. In Beijing, Chinese characters and pinyin are used on street signs and metro stations.

sundowner drinks on the terrace of Commune by the Great Wall (see p. 152) with views over the Shuiguan Valley. On **Day 4** explore the numerous contemporary art and photography galleries at 798 Art District. Later, enjoy the nightlife and dining vibe of Sanlitun and Nali Patio. On **Day 5** visit Beijing's revered temples, including the Temple of Heaven, Lama Temple, and Confucius Temple, with dinner at Temple Restaurant Beijing *(www.temple-restaurant.com)*, housed in a restored Tibetan temple

Neon-lit buildings on bustling Nanjing East Road signal Shanghai's ultramodern future.

complex. Head out of the city on **Day 6** to wander the surrounds of the Summer Palace and the ruins of the Old Summer Palace. Start **Day 7** with a leisurely tour of the National Museum of China, then head south of Tiananmen Square to the Dashilan and Liulichang *hutongs* and sample the capital's most famous dish, roasted Peking duck.

If You Only Have One Week in Shanghai

Shanghai may lack Beijing's imperial legacy, but there is lots to explore and experience in China's most vibrant modern city. **Day 1** inevitably means being drawn to the Bund to relish its fine heritage buildings, riverside landscapes, and the Pudong skyline. Enjoy an evening dinner in a Bund restaurant with dramatic views of the river and neon lights. On **Day 2,** explore the backstreets behind the Bund and the modern and ancient buildings of People's Square. Allow a couple of hours to take in the vast Shanghai Museum. Make time on **Day 3** to visit the M50 galleries, Shanghai's contemporary arts hub, followed by an evening out in the hip Sinan Mansions party district. On **Day 4,** catch the Puxi to Pudong river ferry and take the elevator to the 100th level observatory of the Shanghai World Financial Centre for bird's-eye panoramas. Back on terra firma explore Pudong's riverside attractions, including the Oriental Pearl TV Tower. Take a trip on **Day 5** to either the ancient gardens of Suzhou or Hangzhou's West Lake. Both make easy one-day round-trips by train. Head into the old city on **Day 6** to explore Yuyuan Gardens and sip tea at the Huxinting Teahouse and eat Shanghai's cherished *xiao long bao* dumplings at the nearby Nanxiang Steamed Dumplings restaurant.

Climate

Your itinerary should be determined not just by how much time you have but also by the season. The climate in Shanghai and Beijing differs considerably, especially in winter. Summer (July and August) is best avoided in both cities, as the weather is extremely hot and, particularly in Shanghai, uncomfortably humid. The months either side of summer (April–June and September–October) are the best times to visit with clear skies and temperate weather. Winter (late November–March) in Shanghai is gray, wet, and cool, although temperatures can drop to around freezing in January and early February. Beijing is much colder; temperatures dip well below zero throughout December to early February, with bitter winds and heavy and prolonged snowstorms.

Money Matters

The currency of the People's Republic of China is the yuan renminbi (people's currency), denoted as RMB. It is commonly referred to as yuan and, in Shanghai, kuai. One RMB is divided into 10 jiao (mao). One jiao is divided into 10 fen. Paper RMB bills come in denominations of 1 (though this is being phased out in favor of the 1RMB coin), 2, 5, 10, 20, 50, and 100. The RMB is not yet internationally convertible, so you cannot buy currency in advance of your arrival, and you should spend everything you exchange while in China. If you are headed onward to Hong Kong or most Southeast Asian countries (including Thailand, Malaysia, and Thailand), you will be able to change a small amount of Chinese money (notes only) into the local currency of your destination.

Cultural Etiquette & Tipping

The Chinese are less open and gregarious than many Southeast Asian peoples, but they are always communicative if you make an effort in the local language. Learn to say *ni hao* (hello) and *ni hao, ma?* (how are you?). Politeness is also appreciated, so saying *xie xie* (thank you) and *zaijian* (goodbye) with a smile to taxi drivers, hotel and wait staff will prompt a similar response. You will often be asked *Ni cong nar lai?* (Where are you from?) and replying *Wo shi meiguo ren/jia'nada ren* (I am American/Canadian) will raise a smile of recognition. Traditionally, tipping has been frowned upon in China, but most restaurant and hotel staff now accept tips, although taxi drivers don't expect to be tipped and usually refuse an offer.

If You Have More Time

Beijing is a large, widely spread city, and seven days can easily get eaten up exploring the marquee attractions, which are dispersed over a wide area, and the Great Wall. With more time, the magnificent **Bird's Nest Olympic Stadium** is reachable by metro, and excursions can be made to the ancient **Qing Tombs,** the palatial imperial retreats and hunting lodges at Chengde, or the **Daobatai Western Han Tombs.** Athletic and adventurous travelers might want to plan a hike across unreconstructed "wild wall" sections of the Great Wall. Taking a 27-minute, high-speed train from Beijing to explore the fine city of **Tianjin**–nicknamed the "Shanghai of the North"–is another option. Tianjin offers plentiful European heritage architecture, and it boasts excellent hotels for a deluxe overnight stay.

    Shanghai's compulsive urban buzz can make time vanish, but to escape the rush, head from downtown to the magnificent **Guilin Park** and the **Longhua Martyrs Memorial,** both in the southeast. In the north, the **Shanghai Glass Museum** and, in the east, the **Shanghai Science and Technology Museum,** both offer interactive and educational experiences that will appeal to children.

    Excursion options include staying overnight to better explore the myriad

Language

Mandarin is the official language of the People's Republic of China and it is spoken in both Beijing and Shanghai—although you will note a distinct difference in accent. In Beijing, words are pronounced slowly with a heavy burr, whereas in Shanghai speech is faster and more clipped. Shanghai locals also speak their own dialect, Shanghainese, which is very different to Mandarin, and often impenetrable even to northern Chinese. If you do not speak either Mandarin or Shanghainese, do not worry—English is increasingly widespread, especially by younger people in both cities. Hotel, restaurant, store, and airline staff always speak some English, and all street and public signage is written in English. Taxi drivers and railway and metro staff rarely speak English, so have your destination written in Chinese characters. If your efforts fail, ask a young Chinese person behind you in the line for assistance, they are usually keen to use the opportunity to practice their English.

Giant pandas are the main attraction at the Beijing Zoo.

attractions of **Suzhou,** 66 miles (106 km) west of Shanghai, and **Hangzhou,** 124 (200 km) southwest of Shanghai, or climbing the revered **Mount Huangshan** for the picturesque valley mists made famous in Chinese landscape paintings.

    The former Chinese capital of **Nanjing** is just one hour west of Shanghai on the Shanghai–Beijing high-speed rail route, but it is often overlooked. The city boasts well restored ancient city walls, the tomb of Dr. Sun Yat-Sen, and the extremely moving Memorial Museum dedicted to victims of the 1937 massacre of up to 300,000 locals by the invading Japanese army. ∎

History & Culture

Beijing & Shanghai Today   16–23

Food & Drink   24–27

Experience: Learn How to Cook
    Chinese Style   26

Beijing & Shanghai History   28–39

Feature: Dangerous Beauty   34–35

Arts & Culture   40–51

Feature: In Style in Shanghai   48–49

Religion & Philosophy   52–53

Festivals   54–57

A Confucius statue resides beneath the restored eaves of Nanshi's Wen Miao temple in Shanghai.
Opposite: Student musicians perform on the Great Wall near Beijing.

Beijing & Shanghai Today

Though Beijing is not at the geographic center of China, many believe that the former imperial capital is at the heart of China's past, present, and future. Others look to Shanghai, the nation's richest, brashest, most progressive, stylish, and modern metropolis. Perhaps the least Chinese city in China, Shanghai has been molded since the mid-1900s by the cosmopolitan influence of European, American, and Japanese residents. Beijing's hosting of the 2008 Olympics and Shanghai's staging of the 2010 World Expo were opportunities to upgrade infrastructure, transport systems, and tourism facilities. The legacy of multibillion-dollar investment is evident in both cities today.

Beijing

Beijing was the capital of China as early as the 13th century, when imperial commands were issued from the Forbidden City and sent to the remotest outposts of the Chinese Empire. Today, China's ponderous political directives are composed in neighboring Zhongnanhai, not Beijing. But stroll through the cavernous Tiananmen Square and you will instantly sense the continual significance of what is arguably China's greatest city.

Compared to Shanghai, Beijing culture is more considered and less showy, but this is not to say that the city lacks finesse. Beijing provides access to both reconstructed and "wild" portions of the Great Wall, superior opera companies, the most delectable roast duck, the finest palaces in China, and one of the world's largest public squares, to name just a few of its rich historical and cultural treasures. And even though China ranges through several geographic time zones, the whole nation—officially at least—sets its clocks to Beijing time.

Beijing folk (Beijingren) are dependable and forthright, with a pleasing wholesomeness and an honest appreciation of life's simple pleasures.

Beijing folk (Beijingren) are dependable and forthright, with a pleasing wholesomeness and an honest appreciation of life's simple pleasures. They also carry with them wherever they go a sense of pride about their city and its long history, while their unique elongated accent sets them apart from other Chinese. Beijingers speak Beijinghua, the highly distinctive language spoken for centuries in the city's *hutongs* (alleys). To them, the rest of China rattles away in outlandish dialects. Mandarin—officially called Putonghua and China's official language—is itself based on Beijinghua, minus much of its quirky slang.

Beijingers are notably amiable and generous, down-to-earth even. Famously bookish and well read, they talk far more about politics than their fellow countrymen. Political action these days may be theoretical at best, but Beijing's instinct for protest has frequently translated into action—from the May Fourth Movement of 1919 to the pivotal

Strolling along Beijing's Wangfujing

student-led disturbances of 1989. And unlike in other Chinese cities, being an artist is more acceptable in Beijing, where a large number of galleries and small art spaces cluster in the city's celebrated 798 Art District, attracting artists from across the nation.

Despite its modern facade, today's Beijing is a huge, arid, dusty, polluted, and flat metropolis infused with a potent sense of timelessness. Unlike Shanghai, with its east and west parts separated by the Huangpu River, no geographical feature splits Beijing. If a partition does exist, then the city cleaves into old Beijing—the archaic, hutong-riddled region surrounding the Forbidden City—and new Beijing, the recently fashioned area outside the confines of the old city walls razed under Mao's regime. But such a division is just a mirage; large-scale construction projects, a preponderance of abstract modern architecture, and the disappearance of historic hutongs have left the city an often bewildering mix of old and new.

Old Beijing: The original Ming-dynasty conception of the city survives in part, and although its narrative is patchy and inconsistent, historic Beijing can still be found—as long as you are adventurous and willing to explore.

The grounds of the former imperial capital envelop the Forbidden City, which is also surrounded by the true soul of Beijing: the city's grid of charming hutongs. Lose yourself in these narrow old alleyways—where whole communities still thrive—and you will see

The Giant Glass Egg, China's National Center for the Performing Arts, stands in stark contrast to Beijing's Forbidden City in the foreground.

Life in Modern Beijing

Beijing has fast become the place to be. Migrants stream into the city from all over China in search of jobs. Hordes of foreigners are also suddenly everywhere to *zuo shengyi* (do business), act, teach English, study in Chinese universities, or edit expat magazines.

Here, as in other parts of China, material gain has replaced socialist altruism as the dominant creed, and a preoccupation with money has taken hold. Famously hardworking, Beijingers are putting in even longer hours to afford living space in a city where prices have spiraled upward.

Hopes that political evolution will accompany economic liberalization have so far been dashed. Middle-class Chinese keep their heads down, focused primarily on fuel prices, health care, mortgage payments, education, and employment.

These days, the average Beijinger may not give a foreigner a moment's thought. Yet the novelty of foreigners in Beijing has yet to fully wear off, and you will be exploring a city that has—in sum—had minimal contact with the outside world. At heart, this is what makes Beijing such a unique and remarkable destination.

Beijing at its most authentic. The low-rise, one-story Qing-dynasty courtyard houses of Xicheng and Dongcheng Districts typify old Beijing; these are modest but attractive, gracious, and delightful. Many former residents may have moved out of the hutongs into the modern housing springing up all over the suburbs, but the alleys still ring with the laughter of children and the cries of peddlers, where old folks in *laotoushan* and *laotouxie* (white T-shirts and black cloth shoes) hunch over chess sets while cyclists weave down ancient lanes thick with the aroma of roast lamb kebabs.

The constant tussle between the old and new has found new areas of conflict. In 2000, a branch of the popular coffeehouse chain Starbucks opened in the Forbidden City to the rear of the Hall of Preserving Harmony, but it was replaced by a local copycat café in 2007, much to the unmistakable delight of local traditionalists. Some Beijingers are also understandably indignant at the cavorting parties that rock fragile sections of the Great Wall in summer.

Several pages of Beijing's history may have been shredded, but people everywhere try to glue them back together. The great gate of Yongding Men has been rebuilt from scratch, but like much else in town, it's only a modern reconstruction of what was once a priceless historical treasure.

More and more recently, the city is making efforts to retain some of its proud history, declaring some hutongs protected sites, remodeling or rebuilding courtyard houses in a few areas, and collecting the bricks of the original city wall in order to rebuild a small section. A number of citizens have also banded together, forming nongovernmental organizations dedicated to the preservation of the city's past.

New Beijing: After the communists came to power in 1949, Beijing experienced its most dramatic redesign since the Ming-dynasty Emperor Yongle laid out his plan of the capital in the 15th century. Beijing's architectural mishmash follows the lurching twists and turns of the Communist Party—from builders of a socialist utopia (Great Hall of the People) and champions of nationalist aspirations (China Millennium Monument) to, more latterly, champion capitalists (Oriental Plaza) and governmental urban planners (Bird's Nest National Stadium).

Under the communists, the vast city walls and most of their splendid gates, along with numerous old temples, were destroyed and replaced with graceless socialist buildings. Narrow hutongs made way for wider roads, shopping malls, and apartment blocks; Beijing as a modern city of high-rises and shimmering towers began to take shape.

More recently, China has proven itself to be a significant player on the global economic stage as its economy surges to newfound heights, a fact that has fueled boundless growth in major cities, especially Beijing. This, along with the city's hosting of the 2008 Summer Olympic Games, has turned Beijing's architectural narrative increasingly topsy-turvy. Huge swaths of old hutongs and courtyard houses have been razed to make way for new housing, business complexes, hotels, and Olympic venues. Estimated to cost more than $20 billion, the preparations for the Summer Games altered the city's layout in a manner that hasn't been seen in this city since imperial times. Glassy new skyscrapers, highways, metro lines, an extra airport, and sidewalks paved with shiny new tiles all combine to create the look of a sophisticated modern city.

Shanghai

Originally a sleepy fishing port on the west bank of the Huangpu River, Shanghai—which means "on the sea" in Chinese—has always been associated with water. To the east sprawls the East China Sea, while to the north, just 15 miles (24 km) distant, the vast Yangtze River draws a decisive geographic dividing line between north and south China. To the south lie the tidal waters of Hangzhou Bay, and to the west are the scattered canals, lakes, and marshlands around Lake Tai.

The Chinese government has set a target date of 2020 for Shanghai to overtake Hong Kong as China's largest financial center.

Over the centuries, this watery setting has brought Shanghai prosperity as a port, especially after the establishment of the International Settlement in the city following the First Opium War in 1842. Yet its location has also brought the city serious problems in the form of foreign invaders, including Western opium dealers, monopoly capitalists, and the soldiers of Imperial Japan. Today, after 40 years of communist austerity between 1949 and 1990, the city is once again booming, having surpassed Singapore in 2005 to become the largest cargo port in the world.

Shanghai is still very much on the sea. But it is also the driving force behind a massive and increasingly high-tech industrial complex centered on the city and the neighboring Yangtze River Delta. The delta covers a relatively small area—in Chinese terms at least—of 38,650 square miles (100,100 sq km), or about 2 percent of the national territory. Yet this area is also home to more than 10 percent of China's population—approaching 150 million people—and accounts for almost 25 percent of China's gross domestic product and around 25 percent of national revenues, while handling a staggering 28.5 percent of the country's import and export volume.

Pavilions, rockeries, ponds, and cloisters add tranquility and beauty to Yuyuan Gardens, which was finished in 1577. Such traditional gardens abound in the Shanghai region.

Shanghai remains the single major engine driving Chinese economic expansion. The city's own economy has continued to expand each year at rapid rates since 1992, when Beijing gave the green light to unrestricted economic development. Quite simply, Shanghai today is a Pacific Rim prodigy that rivals, and may soon surpass, Tokyo. The Chinese government has set a target date of 2020 for Shanghai to overtake Hong Kong as China's largest financial center.

A Citywide Face-lift: When Deng Xioaping, China's leader from 1981 to 1992, permitted the economic opening of Shanghai in 1990, the city responded with gusto. In 1988, the city's tallest building was the 275-foot-tall (84 m) Park Hotel, built in 1934; by 1993, the striking 1,535-foot-tall (468 m) Oriental Pearl Tower, a television tower, rose up in Pudong, across the river from the Bund, changing forever the Shanghai skyline and ushering in a new era of construction.

By 1998, Pudong boasted the tallest building in China, the 1,379-foot (420 m) Jinmao Tower, and an estimated one-quarter of all the high-rise construction cranes in the world were busy transforming the Shanghai skyline. Today 4,000–plus buildings stand more than 330 feet (100 m) tall, a statistic matched by no other megalopolis on Earth. These will include the Shanghai Tower in Pudong, which will stand 2,075 feet (632 m) high when completed in 2014. The city and its environs also boast engineering marvels such as Pudong International Airport; the Maglev train line, connecting the airport to the city; Nanpu Bridge, which was the first bridge across the Hangzhou River when it opened in 1991; Lupu Bridge, the world's longest arched bridge at 5.1 miles (8.3 km); and the Hangzhou Bay Bridge, the longest transoceanic bridge in the world at 22 miles (36 km).

Even as Shanghai blazes the way through the 21st century, the increasingly affluent middle class appreciates the city's former glories. Buildings that date from colonial times, especially along the Bund and in the Fuxing Park area, are being renovated and adapted: Buddhist, Taoist, and even Confucian temples are being painstakingly restored; Nanshi, the center of the Old Town, has been carefully re-created in Ming- and Qing-dynasty styles; and areas of traditional *shikumen* housing are now also being preserved and restored, or rebuilt as trendy shopping and restaurant areas, such as Xintiandi and Sinan Mansions. Another notable recent trend has been the conversion of large, old warehouses in the Zhabei area and along Moganshan Road into art galleries and artist studios. Across town, from Pudong in the east to Xujiahui and Hongqiao in the west, spectacular skyscraper architecture continues to rise almost monthly.

Yangjingbang Style: Shanghainese differ from most other Chinese in having been exposed for so long and so completely to foreign—especially Western—ideas and influences. Only Hong Kong has experienced a longer and more intense—though less interrupted—relationship with the West. Even before the advent of colonialism, the seaport of Shanghai welcomed sailors from many nations. This open face to the outside world was massively reinforced with the establishment of the International Settlement and French Concession in the mid-19th century.

> Even as Shanghai blazes the way through the 21st century, the increasingly affluent middle class appreciates the city's former glories.

A willingness to embrace foreign culture—or at least to take from it that which seems good, useful, or attractive—first developed in the late 19th century. It was popularly styled Yangjingbang, after the name of the stream that separated the International Settlement and French Concession from the old Chinese city of Nanshi. (The stream was filled and paved over in 1915; the thoroughfare Yan'an Donglu now follows its course.) Yangjingbang style referred to something uniquely Shanghainese in terms of dress (see pp. 48–49) and, above all, attitude. It also blended Chinese with Western tradition, often in the trendiest of ways, and it was anathema to the hard-line communists who took over Shanghai in 1949.

Yangjingbang also referred to a pidgin especially popular among colonial-era traders that combined elements of Chinese and English. Today, pidgin English is making a comeback, especially among young people, partly for convenience, partly to show off their educational background, and partly just for fun. However, this has triggered a hot debate about how to maintain the purity of the Chinese language without hindering the drive for openness. Yet Shanghai is now an increasingly bilingual city. Since the 2010 World Expo, all road, rail, metro, and official signs show both Chinese characerters and English lettering.

Cultural Forefront: The Shanghainese are great fans of consumer culture, and nowhere is this more apparent than among the young and upwardly mobile. Foreign products—especially Western—are considered desirable, and all over the city giant, air-conditioned shopping malls and covered markets feed the consumer rush. The fashion-conscious seek out designer labels: Giorgio Armani and Yves Saint Laurent clothing, Calvin Klein and Givenchy shoes, Gucci sunglasses, Christian Dior perfumes, and Burberry handbags. Such trendsetters compare notes using Apple iPhones and iPads. Shanghai is a cultured, sophisticated city and its citizens prefer to compare their city with Paris, London, Tokyo, or New York than with other Chinese cities. Most Shanghainese see themselves as China's cultural and commercial trailblazers, the most internationally oriented people in China, a view vindicated in their eyes by record attendances at the 2010 World Expo. The Shanghainese like to stay a step ahead of other Chinese, whom they often refer to as *waidiren* (outsiders) or (in Shanghainese) *xiangwonin* (provincials).

For more than 150 years, the women of Shanghai have been at the forefront of China's women's rights issues. Whether as 19th-century farm girls escaping rural poverty or as progressive socialites rejecting archaic traditions like foot binding and concubinage, Shanghai's strong-willed and opinionated women have been obliged to stand tall and to compete for a living in a great industrial city for longer than their sisters elsewhere in China.

Growing Pains: Change is sweeping across Shanghai perhaps faster than any other city on Earth. The skyline has altered beyond recognition, and the city enjoys a prosperity unimaginable during the colonial period or under Mao's scornful regime. But affluence is far from ubiquitous. With increased political freedom and spiraling wealth, some of the vices of Old Shanghai—prostitution, drugs, gambling, and corruption—have reappeared. Young, relatively affluent *diaomazi*, or fishing girls, prostitute themselves in dive bars seeking the wherewithal to purchase the latest mobile phone, while poor girls from the countryside are again falling victim to predatory brothel keepers. Drugs, virtually banished under Mao Zedong, are also back, although it's much easier to find ecstasy or even cocaine at a downtown disco than it is to find a genuine opium parlor. Gamblers continue to place bets on card games, but more perniciously they participate in online gambling. And many locals are racking up serious losses on the celebrated Stock Exchange. Having excised the ghosts of its sleazy past, the city is making every effort to prevent a recurrence. Its leaders are cracking down on brothels and the risks of playing the stock market are becoming more apparent as house prices and mortgage payments continue to rise.

The city remains a paradigm, displaying much that is most impressive, as well as some aspects that are less appealing, about the New China. Long the nation's most go-ahead metropolis, Shanghai is still a thriving, noisy, polluted city, overflowing with humanity—and, above all, it is a modern, vibrant, and compelling destination. ■

Speaking Shanghainese

The Shanghainese speak a variant of Wu, the second largest Chinese language group, yet even in the city itself Mandarin is used as the everyday lingua franca. In fact, the central government would like everyone in Shanghai to speak Mandarin; Shanghainese is not taught in schools, and its use is discouraged in media and entertainment. Despite these pressures, there has been some resurgence of the use of Shanghainese by Wu speakers. This is particularly true of the city's vibrant underground music scene, where vernacular Shanghainese offers an alternative to the Mandarin and Cantonese music that dominate most of the Chinese music industry.

Food & Drink

Chinese cuisine is diverse and complicated, with each province and city boasting its own unique flavors and style of cooking. All coalesce in Beijing and Shanghai, including regional cuisines like spicy Sichuan. As a result, it's possible for you to make a culinary tour of China without ever leaving the confines of either city.

Beijing Cuisine

Because of its harsh and cold climate, the northern region—which includes the cities of Beijing and Tianjin—features typically hearty fare. Most dishes rely on wheat flour, and no meal is complete without dumplings or steamed breads *(mantou)*.

While Peking duck is a hallmark of Beijing cuisine, there is a plethora of good dishes virtually unknown to outsiders, such as incredibly tasty *ma doufu*, made from the dredges of mung beans that are then stir-fried with mutton fat and accented with soy beans and pickled *xuelihong* (greens). Equally grand is *zhajiang mian*, Beijing's signature noodle dish.

A chef prepares food to go at a popular night stall in Xujiahui near Shanghai's consular district.

Wheat flour is kneaded to the right consistency then combined with a delectable sauce that has been cooked with pork and topped with multicolored vegetables, including bean sprouts, sliced red radish, and cucumber: a wholesome and satisfying meal.

Beijing food has been influenced greatly by Chinese-speaking Muslims (Hui), whose dishes are an integral part of the city's cuisine. Sour bean juice, boiled tripe, rinsed mutton or hotpot *(shuan yangrou),* skewered mutton kebabs *(chuan),* mutton scrap soup *(yang zasui),* and doornail meat pies are all local favorites.

Culinary Revolution: In recent years, a growing number of Beijing's chefs have begun to experiment with different ingredients. Contemporary, or fusion, cuisine pairs Chinese and Western ingredients with traditional methods of cooking. The result is frequently a fantastic, palate-pleasing experience for everyone.

The variety today is even more impressive when you consider that just two decades ago the city was a culinary desert, the result of anticapitalist policies developed by Mao Zedong during the 1950s. The policies led many private restaurants, including *laozihao,* and other brand-name favorites, to close.

> **Beijing food has been influenced greatly by Chinese-speaking Muslims (Hui), whose dishes are an integral part of the city's cuisine.**

In 1980, Yuebin Fanzhuang became the first *getihu,* or private, restaurant to reopen in Beijing, ending the long hiatus and offering markedly better food and service than the primarily lethargic state-run restaurants. Thousands of simple restaurants followed, providing the capital with a variety of eateries from which to choose.

In 1999, the Red Capital Club opened in a restored courtyard house, sparking a trend that has seen courtyard restaurants springing up across the city, each offering diners the pleasant opportunity of eating outside beneath the trees and stars. Restaurants have been moving into parks, and the city has also witnessed a wave of restaurants opened by artists. Most recently, a growing number of chic restaurants with ultracontemporary designs have opened in Beijing, particularly around Nali Patio and The Village in trendy Sanlitun.

Red lanterns line Guijie, or Ghost Street, where more than a hundred restaurants stand shoulder to shoulder. This crowded all-night dining boulevard—about 1 mile (1.6 km) long—is best known for its hot and mouth-numbing crayfish *(mala xiao longxia),* spicy duck's neck, and hot-and-sour fish stew.

The past few years have also seen a foreign invasion as restaurants from all over the world have set up shop and changed the culinary face of the city. In addition to American, European, and Asian venues, the city now also offers Iranian, Turkish, Israeli, Tunisian, Cuban, and Greek restaurants, all run by natives of those countries, including top-name chefs like Daniel Boulud.

It's hard to imagine where the next culinary trend will take Beijing, but one thing is certain—dining out here will never again be a dull affair.

Shanghainese Cuisine

The Shanghainese have developed a delicious, homey, hybrid cuisine called *hu cai.* The fare is most readily identifiable by the use of alcohol to prepare drunken, or *jiaohu,* dishes, as well as by a liberal use of sugar in combination with soy sauce to create savory dishes, most notably sweet-and-sour pork spareribs.

Most forms of meat are available in the city, especially pork, duck, beef, and—in halal (Islamic permissable) Muslim establishments—lamb. Poultry is less popular in Shanghai than elsewhere in China, but *jiaohua ji* (beggar's chicken) is an exception. This local creation involves chicken wrapped in lotus leaves before being covered with clay and oven-baked until it is literally fall-from-the-bone tender.

Seafood is an obvious Shanghai favorite, given the city's seaside location, followed closely by freshwater fare. Popular fish dishes include *huang yu* (yellow croaker), *lu yu* (Songjiang perch), and *gui yu* (Mandarin fish), all delicious steamed or stir-fried, but perhaps best when cooked with corn and pine nuts. The most celebrated seafood dish is the Chinese mitten crab or *dazhaxie,* also known as the Shanghai hairy crab. The steamed crabs are served with a mixture of raw ginger, soy sauce, and black vinegar, and accompanied by Shaoxing wine. These are a fall delicacy, usually enjoyed late September to early December.

Dumplings: The Shanghainese love dumplings, available from street stalls and small restaurants at any time of day. Dumplings may be filled with pork, beef, chicken, fish, or shrimp (plus lamb in halal Muslim restaurants) that is mixed with cabbage, scallions, chives, and other vegetables and then steamed, panfried, or boiled. They are served with a soy-based dipping sauce. Exclusively vegetarian versions are also widely available or can be made to order; ask for *shucai* in Mandarin. The most popular dumplings are small steamed buns, called *xiao long bao* in Mandarin or *sho lonpotsi* in Wu. Steamed in bamboo baskets, these tasty snacks are stuffed with minced meat and soup, with variations of seafood and vegetarian fillings.

Red Cooking: *Hong shao,* or red cooking, is claimed by locals as a hu cai invention. This popular Shanghainese style involves slowly simmering meat and vegetables in a stock flavored with soy sauce, star anise or five spice powder, alcohol (a local cooking

EXPERIENCE: Learn How to Cook Chinese Style

Beijing is the heart of northern Chinese cooking. Tucked away off Nanluogu Xiang along the Heizhima Hutong is the **Black Sesame Kitchen** *(3 Heizhima Hutong, Dongcheng, tel 1369 147-4408, www .blacksesamekitchen.com),* a restaurant and cooking school founded by Jen Lin-Liu, author of *Serve the People: A Stir-Fried Journey Through China.* Take one class or attend a series, and learn how to *bao jiaozi* (wrap dumplings) the local way. Fry up Chongqing spicy chicken or learn the secret of perfect *mapo doufu* (grandma's tofu). Hands-on classes *($$$$)*, with English instruction, cook up on Thursdays

(11 a.m.–1:30 p.m.) and on Saturdays *(1 p.m.–4 p.m.).* Attend a Friday evening *(7 p.m.–10 p.m.)* Wine 'n' Dine event *($$$$)*, and watch the preparation of a ten-course gourmet dinner. Less well known outside China than Cantonese or Sichuan cuisine, Shanghai cooking uses a lot of fish and seafood. Stir-frying is used as well as steaming, the latter employed in signature dishes like *xiaolong bao.* **The Kitchen at Cooking Studio** *(383 South Xiang Yang Rd., Bldg. 20, 3rd Floor, tel 021 6433-2700, www.thekitchenat.com)* runs courses *($$$$–$$$$$)* on Shanghai and other cuisines on Tuesdays and Saturdays.

Deep-fried crickets are a popular local treat in Beijing.

sherry or rice wine), and sugar. The name derives from the deep red-brown hue the sauce gives the meat, which is often pork, especially pig's knuckle.

Other Regional Cuisines

The most popular regional food is Cantonese, for its refined seafood dishes, double-boiled soups, and lunchtime dim sum. This is followed in popularity by peppery Sichuanese, whose spicy hotpots are devoured in both Beijing and Shanghai, especially in winter. Earthy Yunnanese fare is popular, with its recipes originating from the fertile alpine areas of southwest China. Fresh and mellow Zhejiang cuisine is also outstanding, with a focus on tender foods. The cuisine of Jiangsu Province, known for its fertile lands and abundant waterways, features only the freshest ingredients. Suzhou cuisine has a tendency to be sweet, while Wuxi cuisine focuses on different varieties of congee, or rice porridge, eaten as a savory dish.

Uighur Fare: Uighur Muslim restaurants, or *ashkana,* serve spicy delights from Xinjiang, which spans the steppes and deserts of Central Asia. These establishments serve such delicious dishes as *laghman* (stir-fried noodles with mutton, eggplant, tomatoes, potatoes, and hot green peppers), *poluo* (rice pilaf), *samsa* (samosas with mutton, beef, or vegetables), *chushira* (dumpling soup with spicy peppers), nan (bread with garlic or salt-and-sesame toppings), and kebabs.

Tea & Other Drinks

The most popular drink in China is, of course, tea, with green tea being the most common. Hangzhou's Longjing tea, which has long been produced near Shanghai, is considered one of China's best teas (see sidebar p. 264). Look also for flower tea (jasmine, for example), which mixes green tea with flower petals; black tea; red tea; and the highly prized oolong tea. Beer is popular with meals and China is now the world's largest brewer. Shanghai's breweries produce many decent lagers. Chinese spirits, a centuries-old tradition, can be tame or deadly; be forewarned! ∎

Beijing & Shanghai History

Contrasting hugely in terms of history, culture, and traditions, these two cities are spearheading China's economic and societal transformation. Despite the disparate genesis of north and east China, Beijing and Shanghai share a common dynastic history. Yet the residents of each claim their own megacity's superiority.

Early Beijing

Humans have lived in or near modern-day Beijing for more than 3,000 years. Even prehistoric Peking Man made his home in caves not far from the city. However, the city of Beijing owes its early existence not to indigenous populations but to non-Chinese tribes from northern Asia who first built the city and made it their capital.

Chinese records first mention a settlement in the area of modern Beijing during the Western Zhou dynasty (ca 1122–771 B.C.), when a walled village was built in the general area of present-day Xuanwu District. In 907, the Khitans, a non-Chinese nomadic tribe, founded the Liao dynasty and set up their capital in Yanjing, today a poetic name for Beijing. The city they built—which was encircled by 30-foot-high (9 m) walls—had a circumference of 12 miles (20 km) and an impressive imperial palace. From this base, the Khitans began to make inroads into the heartland of China, which was not brought under control until the Song dynasty in 960.

Humans have lived in or near modern-day Beijing for more than 3,000 years.

In 1120, the Jurchen, a Manchu tribe, formed an alliance with the Song dynasty, and five years later they set up their own Jin ("gold") dynasty to the southwest of present-day Beijing and turned the ruins of Yanjing into a larger walled city called Zhongdu, or Middle Capital. The Jurchen then expanded quickly into central China.

The Mongol troops of Genghis Khan attacked Zhongdu in 1215 and almost completely destroyed the Jin capital. In 1267, Kublai Khan made the city the capital of what would become the Yuan dynasty. He called his new city Khanbalik, or City of the Great Khan. In Chinese, it was known as Dadu ("great capital").

Dadu was a grand city, built with evenly spaced rectilinear streets and centered on a north–south axis. It was designed in the shape of a square bounded by four walls, each more than 3 miles (4.8 km) long and divided by three gates. Nine roads connected the whole city from east to west and from north to south. About a century after establishing their dynasty, the once nomadic Mongolians, softened by city life, suffered defeat at the hands of rebels from the south led by an itinerant Chinese monk. The Yuan dynasty crumbled and the capital was torched, although the basic layout of the city survived.

The new Ming dynasty moved its capital south to Nanjing, near Shanghai, in 1368, and Beijing was reduced to a simple prefecture called Beiping Fu. The dynasty's founding emperor gave the city to his fourth son, Zhu Di, who immediately began to

Portrait of Qianlong, the emperor who presided over Beijing's golden age

change the way it looked. In 1403, Zhu Di usurped the throne from his young nephew and adopted the reign name of Yongle. He moved the imperial capital from Nanjing to his own power base in the north: Beiping Fu. In 1405, Emperor Yongle began to rebuild the city, a massive project that took 15 years to complete and was intended to inspire awe and fear in his subjects. Dubbed the "architect of Beijing," Emperor Yongle is also credited with building the Rear Lakes, the Temple of Heaven, and the Altar of Earth.

Early Shanghai

Originally a small fishing village on the west bank of the Huangpu River, Shanghai was generally overshadowed by its larger and more eminent neighbors, Hangzhou and Suzhou. It gradually grew in size, from town to market town and then, in 1292, to regional capital of Shanghai County under Kublai Khan.

China's Dynasties

Xia: ca 2205–1766 B.C.
Shang: ca 1766–1122 B.C.
Zhou: Western ca 1122–771 B.C.,
   Eastern ca 771–221 B.C.
Qin: 221–206 B.C.
Han: Western 206 B.C.–A.D. 9,
   Xin (Wang Mang) A.D. 9–25,
   Eastern A.D. 25–220
Three Kingdoms period: 220–265
Jin: Western Jin 265–316,
   Eastern Jin 317–420
Northern: Northern Wei 386–534,
   Eastern Wei 534–550, Western Wei
   535–557, Northern Qi 550–577,
   Northern Zhou 557–581
Southern: Song 420–479, Qi 479–
   502, Liang 502–557, Chen 557–589
Sui: 581–618
Tang: 618–907
Five Dynasties: Later Liang 907–923,
   Later Tang 923–936, Later Jin
   936–947, Later Han 947–950,
   Later Zhou 951–960
Song: Northern 960–1127,
   Southern 1127–1279
Yuan: 1279–1368
Ming: 1368–1644
Qing: 1644–1911
Republic of China: 1911–1949
   (maintained in Taiwan)
People's Republic of China:
   1949–present

In 1404, shortly after the establishment of the Ming dynasty (1368–1644), Shanghai's commercial importance had increased sufficiently for the new government to order the Huangpu dredged and developed into the major waterway of the southern Yangtze River Delta, thus ensuring Shanghai's eventual supremacy as a regional port.

The emerging port's prosperity attracted the unwanted attention of the *wokou*, Japanese pirates who began raiding the coast around 1350. By 1550 these raids prompted the construction of a 3-mile-long (4.8 km), 27-foot-tall (8 m) defensive wall around Shanghai. Completed in 1553, a date generally accepted as the foundation of the present city, these fortifications survived until the early 20th century, when they were torn down by the Nationalist authorities as part of a modernization program—only the restored Dajing Tower remains. The area once enclosed is now known as Nanshi, or Southern City. This is generally referred to in English as Shanghai Old Town.

Qing Dynasty (1644–1911)

As with previous dynasties, China's Ming dynasty soon fell victim to apathetic and inefficient rulers, corruption, and natural disasters that fueled public dissatisfaction and rebellions. The government was already in serious decline when in April 1644 a peasant rebel leader named Li Zicheng took over the capital, facing little resistance. Abandoned by his aides and officials, and with the rebels at the city gates, the last Ming-dynasty emperor killed himself, bringing the dynasty to a tragic end.

Manchurian Rise: While Li Zicheng's army was knocking at the gates, Manchu soldiers were gathering in the north, preparing to take advantage of the chaos. They slipped through an opening in the Great Wall and poured into the capital, pushing Li's army out, and established the Qing dynasty (1644–1911). This power shift occured without the destruction that typically followed changes in rule. However, the new Qing rulers, who were keen to retain their unique Manchu traits, ordered that Manchus and Chinese live separately. The Han were relegated to the southern part of Beijing.

Keen to project a sense of continuity, the Qing dynasty rulers built on the legacy established by the Ming dynasty. The government expanded the Forbidden City, and built garden retreats in the western suburbs, as well as a number of wonderful mansions.

Shanghai, which by this time had developed into the most important port in the lower Yangtze region, also continued to prosper. Its fortunes increased further when the great Qing emperor Kangxi (1661–1722) lifted a late 14th-century ban on overseas trading, allowing Shanghai to become the main trade port for regional maritime shipping as well as for commerce along the Yangtze River. By the middle of the reign of Emperor Qianlong (1735–1796), the city had emerged as the largest port in East Asia.

Emperor Qianlong's long reign is considered by many to have been Beijing's golden era. The emperor added military forces while also promoting literature and the arts. He was also interested in Tibetan Buddhism and supported the construction of lamaseries in the capital. While he forbade Chinese from converting to Roman Catholicism, he welcomed the skills of foreign priests in the service of the court.

Yuan Shikai (1859–1916), first president of the Republic of China

Opium Trade: Disturbed by the rising tide of opium arriving on Western ships and the corresponding depletion of the national treasury, Qianlong restricted all foreign trade to Canton (Guangzhou) in 1760. Seeing their trading companies' profits sink, the Western powers, especially Britain, pressured Qianlong to rescind the legislation. Qianlong famously refused and warned that vessels putting ashore at any point other than Canton would be immediately expelled.

In reality, the restrictions proved little more than a formality: Shanghai continued to function as a major port, albeit in a more clandestine fashion, and the traffic in opium continued to increase at an unchecked rate. By the end of the 18th century, there were millions of addicts in China, and the country's drug habit was disastrously depleting the Qing treasury. Clearly, from the Chinese perspective, something had to be done.

In 1838, an official sent by Emperor Daoguang confiscated and destroyed more than 20,000 chests of opium and blockaded Shanghai's port to foreign shipping. The opium merchants loudly demanded compensation and pressed for military retaliation. European military superiority ensured the First Opium War (1840–1842) was short, sharp, and one-sided. The British bombarded from the sea and seized control of Canton and sailed up the Yangtze to intercept tax barges carrying grain to the imperial court at Beijing. In June 1842, they also sailed up the Huangpu, storming and easily capturing the walled city of Shanghai.

Signed in August 1842, the Treaty of Nanking transferred Hong Kong Island to the British, awarded Britain compensation for the seized opium, and opened five ports to foreign trade and residents, including Shanghai. From this time until the fall of the dynasty in 1912, Shanghai may have remained notionally a part of the Qing empire, but in reality it was on the way to becoming a new kind of economic international colony.

Western Encroachment: The British took possession of a small section of muddy riverbank to the north of Shanghai Old Town; this area, centered on the Bund and Suzhou Creek, would soon become the heart of the British Settlement. It wasn't long before other Western nations anxious for a share in the rich China trade

Puyi

There is probably no more tragic figure in 20th-century Chinese history than Puyi, China's famed last emperor, who was a victim throughout his life.

Puyi was born in 1906, and he assumed the throne two years and ten months later upon the death of his cousin, who was likely poisoned by their aunt, Empress Dowager Cixi. Cixi had appointed the young boy emperor while she was on her deathbed. Eunuchs pulled the small Puyi away from his family kicking and scream-ing, and they placed the toddler in the Forbidden City, where he was kept under the care of eunuchs and consorts.

His reign was a short one. The boy emperor was forced to abdicate in 1912 following the revolution, but the new Republican government allowed him to keep his imperial title and to continue to be treated as a foreign monarch. Never-theless, his life was a cruel comedy.

Six years after the abdication, a Qing loyalist general, Zhang Xun, known as the Pigtail General because he ordered his men to retain their Qing-dynasty braids, attempted to restore Puyi to the throne. The move sent men scurrying to find fake braids to replace the ones they'd cut off in 1912. But the restoration lasted just days until another warlord dropped bombs by hand from an airplane flying over the Forbidden City. In 1924, Puyi was forced to vacate the palace by Feng Yuxiang, dubbed the Christian General because he baptized his men with a fire hose.

After his expulsion from the palace, Puyi moved to the Japanese Conces-sion in Tianjin, but in 1932 his Japanese benefactors moved him to the northeast and crowned him reluctant emperor of a puppet state called Manchukuo, a former Manchu territory to the north.

Puyi was captured at the end of World War II and held by the Soviets. He pleaded with Stalin not to send him back to China. At the urging of the Soviets, he testified against the Japanese at the Tokyo war crimes trial, but that didn't save him. In 1950, Stalin sent him back to China, where he spent a decade in a reeducation camp before Mao Zedong declared him reformed. When the Cultural Revolution rolled around, Puyi became a target of rampaging Red Guards who saw him as a symbol of feudalism.

made their appearance. China signed similar treaties with France and the United States, and new concessions were parceled out at Shanghai. Over the next 50 years, both the British Settlement and the French Concession expanded substantially to the west; in 1863, the British and American Settlements united to create the International Settlement. As in the French Concession, Qing law and authority did not apply there, although Chinese nationals were allowed to reside within the foreign concessions.

As Shanghai grew increasingly wealthy and more detached from Qing rule, the city's foreign residents gradually began to adopt and adapt the foreign settlements to suit their increasingly sophisticated requirements. Eventually Shanghai was transformed into the least Chinese but most progressive city in China, with architectural trends—still evident today—imported from the chic cities of the era like New York, London, and Paris.

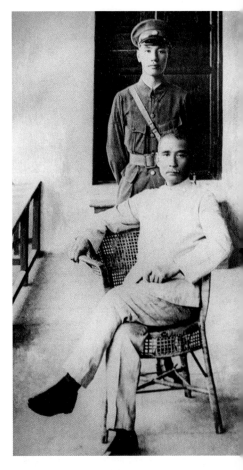

In Beijing, the government had no choice but to cave to foreign demands for a permanent presence. Soon the foreign Legation Quarter sprang up just southeast of the Forbidden City, ushering in irrevocable changes and a new style of Western architecture.

By the mid-1890s, the Harmonious Fists (Yihequan), a secret martial society known in English as the Boxers, had emerged. The Boxers, who claimed to be able to withstand blows by swords and bullets, began to attack foreign missionaries and Chinese converts to Christianity. In 1900, the group laid siege to the Legation Quarter, home to much of the foreign community in Beijing, but made no move against the foreign settlements in Shanghai.

The siege ended after a multinational force, made up of troops from eight allied nations, marched into Beijing, scattering the Boxers and causing the imperial court to flee to the safety of Xi'an in Shaanxi Province. The foreign troops remained in Beijing and the surrounding area for a year, harassing Chinese citizens and looting cultural artifacts. The ancient capital would never be the same again.

Because the foreign powers held them responsible for the rebellion of the Boxers, the Qing-dynasty rulers were forced to agree to an indemnity, payable over several decades to the nations that had helped quell the disturbance. After the foreign troops withdrew, the emperor and empress quietly returned to the capital. The

(continued on p. 36)

President Sun Yat-sen (seated) appointed Chiang Kai-shek commandant of Guangzhou's Whampoa Military Academy in 1924.

Dangerous Beauty

The lovely, delicate opium poppy flourishes in the cool, nutrient-poor hills of southwest China and in Central Asia on China's Western borders. A plant of eastern Mediterranean origin, it was probably introduced to China and India about a thousand years ago by Arab traders. At first the Chinese prized the plant for its medicinal values—in the raw state it is an antidote for pain, diarrhea, and coughing, and it was widely used as an anaesthetic.

But the situation changed in the 18th century, when Great Britain began to pay for Chinese tea shipments with opium from India, rather than with silver. With the added increase in supply, thousands grew addicted to the narcotic, creating an unprecedented social problem in China. Shanghai played a pivotal role in the drug's distribution.

The Qing emperors recognized the substance's rising use and its effect on their people. They made the importation of opium illegal. However, after the Second Opium War (1856–1860)—fought against France and Britain—they were forced to sign unequal treaties that opened China to the opium trade. In 1870, opium accounted for 43 percent of China's total imports. By 1890, about 10 percent of China's total population were opium smokers.

During this time, there were literally hundreds of opium dens in Shanghai, many located in the backstreets behind the riverside Bund—the entry point for opium shipments. Here people came to smoke opium, or *tu* (earth), as it was usually called. Most opium dens were clustered in Nanshi and Zhubei, along the waterfront and Fuzhou Road, as well as in the Great World. The dens were generally very basic: Patrons were given a hard, wooden bunk or board to lie on, a wooden pillow, and a pipe. The smoke-filled dens tended to be quiet, since users were likely to doze while drugged.

The Europeans didn't seem overly concerned about their contribution to the growing addiction problem. The Jardine, Matheson Co. made the following statement in the 1800s in response to the opium question: "The use of opium is not a curse but a comfort to the

hard-working Chinese; to many scores of thousands it has been productive of healthful sustention and enjoyment." Due to fierce competition, compounded by a growing anti-opium lobby, the trading houses pulled out of the

opium trade in the late 1800s and Shanghai's last legal opium shop closed in 1917. This merely forced the drug trade underground. The opium trade then became a driving force behind the gangsterism that plagued Shanghai in the 1920s and 1930s.

Enter "Pockmarked" Huang Jinrong, a corrupt senior Chinese officer in the French police force, and "Big Ears" Du Yuesheng, the city's top gangster and the head of the Green Gang. Together, the two controlled the illicit opium trade in the French Concession (where laws were more lax). Meanwhile, the growth of opium production in China grew exponentially. In 1904, opium poppies occupied 13 percent of the total acreage of arable land; by 1930 this number was 20 percent. The arrival of the Communists in 1949 brought an end to the problem, as they closed Shanghai's illegal opium dens and forced operators to flee abroad. The opium scourge returned in the 1990s, this time in a different guise—heroin.

Opium smokers at an upscale Shanghai opium den, circa 1905. The city's fortunes were largely founded on such illicit operations as drug trafficking.

incident had shocked the imperial court and resulted in a last-minute attempt to carry out reforms, but it was too late.

The Qing failure to deal with foreign encroachment fueled growing public resentment against the Manchu court, which was already reeling from an array of internal problems. Peasant rebellions sprang up around the country. Emperor Guangxu, who had been placed under house arrest in the Hall of Jade Ripples in the Summer Palace after he tried to implement radical reforms in 1898, died in 1908, one day before the death of the Empress Dowager. In October 1911, a revolution brought the imperial system to an end, and the Manchus readily agreed to abdicate, ending 267 years of unpopular Qing rule.

Early Chinese Republic (1912–1927)

In 1912, the Qing dynasty finally collapsed, giving way to the Chinese Republic (1912–1949). This was ruled by the Kuomintang (KMT), or Nationalist Party, which still rules breakaway Taiwan today. Nationalist politician Sun Yat-sen led the revolution, but power passed instead to the ambitious and powerful Yuan Shikai (1859–1916), a former general in the Manchu army. Forced out of Beijing, Sun eventually found refuge in Shanghai's French Concession. The imperial court was permitted to remain within the Forbidden City and Summer Palace in Beijing.

A victim of a succession of rulers, the grand old capital didn't fare well during the next few decades. However, it was also a period of excitement. Leading intellectuals, scholars, and artists flocked to Beijing, where they passionately debated China's sad state of affairs. The most outspoken called for science and democracy to take the place of the Great Sage, Confucius. There was also a movement away from the highly stylized, classical tradition to a vernacular and more accessible form of written Chinese.

In 1912, the Qing dynasty finally collapsed, giving way to the Chinese Republic (1912–1949).

The years of Western supremacy in Shanghai—by now the largest financial center in the Far East—were fast drawing to an end, although the Shanghainese didn't yet know it. In fact, this period was colonial Shanghai's heyday, a period of sybaritic indulgence and revolutionary intrigue.

In 1921, a group of intellectuals, influenced by the Russian Revolution, met in Shanghai to establish the Communist Party of China. From these small beginnings, the Communist movement began to gradually take hold among people throughout the country. After Sun Yat-sen died in 1925, Commander Chiang Kai-shek emerged as the new leader of the Republic of China, launching a purge of the Communists in the KMT. He also married into the influential, and very wealthy, Shanghai-based Soong family.

In 1928, the KMT government moved the capital of China back to Nanjing (now the capital of Jiangsu Province) and changed the name of Beijing ("northern capital") to Beiping ("northern peace"). During this period, the city suffered greatly from both neglect and vandalism.

In 1937, Japan used the pretense of a Chinese attack against Japanese troops to justify opening fire on nationalist troops on the Marco Polo Bridge (Lugou Qiao) in southwest Beijing. The event, known as the Marco Polo Bridge Incident (see p. 164), was the beginning of a brutal eight-year occupation of the city, which was once again named Beijing. The Japanese surrender in 1945 was followed by bitter civil war, which would end with

October 1, 1949: At the entrance to the Forbidden City Mao Zedong, Chairman of the Chinese Communist Party, speaks at a ceremony marking the establishment of the People's Republic of China.

Chiang Kai-shek fleeing with boatloads of ancient Chinese relics to Taiwan, and Mao Zedong assuming power in China in 1949.

New China

After a prolonged battle with nationalist forces, the Red Army marched into Beijing on January 31, 1949, and Shanghai on May 25. Beijing became the capital of the People's Republic of China on October 1, 1949.

Between 1949 and 1954 the Communist Party leadership gradually nationalized all private businesses. Factories went up all over Beijing, each a walled compound, where the workers worked, lived, and took part in party functions. For the average Beijinger, there was little need to step out of one's own work unit. No doubt the most traumatic part of the Communist Party's renewal of Beijing was the dismantling of its city walls, which came down to make way for a metro system, broad central boulevards, and highways ringing the city. Over the next few decades, the city underwent wrenching changes. Ancient structures made way for bland, Soviet-style architecture and boxlike urban factories.

Meanwhile, money from Shanghai's relatively profitable industries was being sent to Beijing for use elsewhere in the country, and class enemies—in fact, anyone who disagreed with the new policies or just got in the way—were sent for reeducation in distant parts of the country. At the same time, stringent campaigns were introduced to banish drugs, prostitution, and gambling.

Cultural Revolution: In 1966, the Gang of Four, the political faction led by Mao Zedong's last wife Jiang Qing, together with three Shanghai radicals, made the city their power base and launched the much vaunted Great Proletarian Cultural Revolution (1966–1976).

> The new economy—
> an intriguing mix of
> capitalist practices
> and party regulations—
> sparked profound
> change in China.

This mad and ultimately doomed campaign promoted continuous revolution across the country to eliminate Mao's opponents from the party. For the next decade, Red Guards patrolled the streets of Shanghai and Beijing, as they did throughout the rest of the country, looking for signs of bourgeois decadence, persecuting tens of thousands of people, and destroying or defacing buildings associated with either Western colonial domination or past imperial regimes. The nightmare did not end until after the death of Chairman Mao in 1976, the arrest of the Gang of Four soon after, and the subsequent rise of Deng Xiaoping to paramount leader of China.

Capitalism With Chinese Characteristics

Deng Xiaoping quickly called for the modernization of China. The new economy—an intriguing mix of capitalist practices and party regulations—sparked profound change in China. In Beijing, large-scale investment was encouraged, while businesses formerly run by the state ceded ownership to local, private companies. Small, family-run businesses also developed, as did the black-market economy, which continues to thrive today. The city's population also grew during the 1980s, as migrants from rural areas poured into the capital in search of jobs.

But economic growth brought rising prices for staple foodstuffs, and bred popular dissatisfaction. In the summer of 1989, thousands of Chinese students—with the hearty support of the people of Beijing—occupied Tiananmen Square to express their frustration with runaway corruption and spiraling inflation. The People's Liberation Army forcefully cleared the square, and the government launched a crackdown against dissent that brought the short-lived open period to a crashing halt.

Beijing rebounded in the 1990s, however, and started to fulfill its promise of becoming an international economic leader. Private ownership and investment exploded, while the city's consumer economy thrived.

Along with the boom came a newfound confidence, culminating in Beijing's successful hosting of the 2008 Summer Olympic Games.

In 1990, Shanghai was chosen to become the nation's new economic powerhouse, and Pudong, the area to the east of the Huangpu River, was declared a special economic zone. Deng Xiaoping hoped the ensuing growth would help Shanghai overtake Hong Kong as China's leading financial center. The city's rapid growth was key to its hosting of the 2010 World Expo, or the "Economic Olympics," as it was dubbed by local media.

After Deng ostensibly retired in 1992, his successors, Jiang Zemin (1992–2004) and Hu Jintao (2004–), made their own substantial contributions to China's spectacular economic development. However, societal conflicts caused by corruption, inflation, and increasing disaffection with Communist Party hemegony look set to be pivotal features of the "next generation" to rule China. ■

Students gather in Beijing's Tiananmen Square in April 1989 to mourn the death of popular Communist Party leader and liberal reformer Hu Yaobang. Bloodshed soon followed.

Arts & Culture

Proud of their city's greater cultural depth and artistic diversity, Beijingers like to berate their Shanghainese counterparts for a hedonistic and faddish approach to life. But in a rapidly changing society, both cities are witnessing great changes in the consumption of the cultural arts, as ancient traditions give way to globalized influences.

Music

Beijing Opera: Chinese opera traces its roots back to the Pear Garden opera troupe of Emperor Xuanzong of the Tang dynasty (618–907). The dramatic art form grew increasingly complex and sophisticated through the Yuan, Ming, and Qing dynasties, diversifying into no fewer than 368 different forms. The most popular and best known, by far, is Beijing opera, which had developed into its present form by the mid-19th century. Most Chinese opera performances staged in China are of this genre.

In Chinese, Beijing opera is styled *jingxi*, or opera of the capital. It incorporates elements of traditional Chinese opera from the Anhui and Hubei Provinces and is sung in Mandarin. The entire process is allusive. Hand gestures, footwork, general body movements, and posture all play a significant role; acrobatic movements indicate violent action, usually accompanied by loud use of clapper drums and cymbals; heavy makeup indicates mood, personality, and even morality. Costumes are colorful and richly lavish. Traditionally, all jingxi roles, regardless of gender, have been played by males; only in the latter part of the 20th century were female actors introduced.

> Beijing opera has a vast repertoire of more than a thousand operas, mainly derived from historical events and novels.

Beijing opera has a vast repertoire of more than a thousand operas, mainly derived from historical events and novels. These largely concern political intrigues and military struggles. Though it's impossible for foreigners to follow the plot (common themes are mythical stories, battles, and love stories driven by ethical conflicts), it's possible to keep track of the characters. Musicians are another integral part of the performance. Operas use a standard (and comparatively small) repertoire of instruments. Melodies are played on the *huqin* or *erhu*, two-stringed violins, and accompanied by the *ruan* or *yueqin* (a plucked four-string lute). Traditional percussion instruments provide a powerful rhythmic background to the singing and acting. The person who plays the *ban* (a wood block or clapper) directs the orchestra and gives the actors their cues.

Traditional: There is an enormous variety of Chinese instruments; the most common include: the *guqin* and *guzheng* (zithers), erhu and huqin, *pipa* (lute), *yangqin* (hammer dulcimer), and *dizi* and *sheng* (flutes). Northern Chinese processions (typical of weddings and funerals) feature the *suona*, a type of

A performer acts in a Beijing opera staged at Shanghai's popular Yifu Theater.

Chinese Opera

Opera emerged from popular theater, an art form that flourished in the Mongol Yuan dynasty. There are many regional forms of Chinese opera, with their own stories, costumes, makeup, and music. The most famous of the regional operas, the Beijing opera (*jingxi*), reached its apex during the Qing dynasty.

Chinese opera has little relation to Western opera. The popular stories are shrilly sung to a clashing of cymbals by heavily made-up performers. The roles can be demanding, with leaping, jumping, and other energetic routines requiring flexibility and endurance. In this sense, Beijing opera is closer to Western ballet, although the choreography is very

different. Characters are identified by their makeup, and the color of their clothing. The roles are generally divided into male (*sheng*), female (*dan*), warriors and heroes (*jing*), and clowns (*chou*). For Westerners, the language is sadly a major hurdle to comprehension. Shanghai, Beijing, and Hong Kong have the best venues for Chinese opera.

Training for the Beijing opera is severe, and it was usually reserved for orphans. The 1993 movie *Farewell My Concubine* delivers a vivid account of the hardships endured by young opera students. Martial arts supremos Jackie Chan, Samo Hung, and Yuan Biao learned their moves through training in Beijing opera.

high-pitched clarinet—you'll know it when you hear it.

Shanghai and the surrounding region—perhaps most especially in Suzhou—is noted for *pingtan,* a form of *shuochang* (spoken song) associated particularly with Jiangsu Province. Two people—usually a man and a woman—tell stories to music played on string instruments like the pipa, accompanied by bursts of song and lively facial expressions. Good places to hear authentic Suzhou pingtan are the Shen Residence in the town of Luzhi and the Pingtan Museum in Suzhou.

Classical: China's most brilliant musicians are pursuing classical Western music with unanticipated enthusiasm and have begun dazzling the West. Performers such as pianists Lang Lang and Xu Zhong have played with many of the world's leading orchestras and many aficionados believe that the future of classical music will, to a certain extent, be determined by Chinese talent.

Shanghai takes pride in its Western-style orchestras, most notably the Shanghai Symphony Orchestra, based at the stunning Shanghai Grand Theater on People's Square. Established in 1879, it originally was called the Shanghai Municipal Band. Since those early days, it has gone from strength to strength, and today it puts on regular world-class performances and is generally judged the best in China.

Visiting orchestras (including the Hong Kong Philharmonic and Philadelphia Chamber Orchestra) frequently perform at Shanghai Concert Hall on Yan'an East Road, while farther to the west, in the Fuxing area, the Shanghai Conservatory of Music holds classical music concerts each Sunday night.

Two of the best places to hear classical music concerts in Beijing include the Lao She Teahouse and the Sanwei Bookstore, with classical recitals frequently held at the National Center for the Performing Arts. The city's leading talent studies at the Central Conservatory of Music.

Pop & Rock: A self-styled underground alternative rock movement parallels its Western roots, embracing elements of grunge, heavy metal, and punk, together with moderated forms of dress to suit the genre. Today, the authorities seem to be finally turning a blind eye to such manifestations of individualism and opting out.

In the U.S. and the West, the power of rock-and-roll to shock and provoke change has long been absorbed into the mainstream. In China rock music is still seen as a dangerous, youthful snarl against a repressive and paternalistic power structure.

Known as *yaogun,* Chinese rock music has charted a tortuous path bedeviled by heavy-handed government censorship and official red tape. Relatively young in global terms, this raw guitar-based sound was born in the mid-1980s, when Cui Jian—the father of Chinese rock—wrote "Nothing to My Name," a seminal song about disaffection in China's transformative society. The hit became an anthem for the Tiananmen Square student protesters in 1989, and the subsequent crackdown by the authorities forced Cui Jian and other artists into hiding in the provinces.

His "New Long March" tour brought further censure when Cui Jian donned a red blindfold over his eyes to perform his political anthem, "A Piece of Red Cloth."

Since then, yaogun—whose heartbeat remains largely in Beijing—has become recognized for producing stirring, multilayered critiques of life and society in urban China. The trials and tribulations of those who rebel through rock music are documented in the fascinating 2012 book, *Red Rock: The Long, Strange March of Chinese Rock & Roll,* written by Canadian author Jonathan Campbell.

> **China's most brilliant musicians are pursuing classical Western music with unanticipated enthusiasm and have begun dazzling the West.**

Most modern-day Chinese pop/rock bands have yet to find success outside China, but there are a few of note: The band Banana Monkey produces a danceable funk sound. As lead singer, Miss Tan provides the sweet, sad vocals of Booji, a Shanghai rock band. Xiao Yao sings lead for the eponymous band that plays hard-beat electronics.

Literature

Although Confucius himself was no poet, his emphasis on education and his legendary status as compiler of *The Book of Songs* (ca 600 B.C.), China's first anthology of poetry, undoubtedly paved the way for the enormous influence of literature on Chinese society. Formal poetry was the style of choice for over a millennium, and once the bureaucratic exam system was introduced in the seventh century, composing verse became an essential component in securing a government position.

In terms of artistic achievement, poetry lost its edge to drama during the 13th century, and drama was in turn succeeded by fiction in the 14th century. Nevertheless, despite this rich tradition, up until a century ago, literature in China had one major drawback—it was written in classical Chinese and thus could only be read by a select few. This changed with the reform-minded May Fourth Movement (1919). A handful of writers—notably Lu Xun, Mao Dun, Guo Moruo, and Bing Xin—set out to make literature more accessible by writing in *baihua,* or common speech.

The writer with the deepest attachment to Beijing is Lao She (1899–1966), another May Fourth writer. His first and most famous novel, *Rickshaw* (1936), describes the life of

Titles of poems, books, and essays of Lu Xun (1881–1936) adorn a wall in Beijing's Lu Xun Museum.

a peasant who comes to Beijing to work as a rickshaw driver, tracing a tragic arc of physical exhaustion and poverty that culminates in a solitary death. Lao She is also famous for the play *Teahouse* (1957), which follows the events in a Beijing teahouse over a 50-year period. He was heavily criticized during the Cultural Revolution, and he eventually died, perhaps by suicide.

Communist rule understandably did little to encourage individual creativity, and until the 1980s there was little real literary output. One of the first voices to break the silence was Wang Meng, a Beijing native born in 1934. Like many writers of his generation, Wang wrote stories, such as "The Butterfly" (1983), that deal with the lives of those who were reeducated by the party and sent to work on communal farms. (Wang was sent to the northwestern province of Xinjiang for seven years.) He served briefly as the minister of culture before resigning after the Tiananmen Square protests in 1989.

Zhang Jie paved the way for female authors with her novels *Love Must Not Be Forgotten* (1979) and *Leaden Wings* (1980), which challenged social mores and the traditional roles of women within marriage. Despite a mere 25-year gap, Zhang's idealism and quiet provocation seem centuries removed from today's sensationalist voices like Chun Sue, who evokes the rock-and-roll lifestyle of Beijing's youth in *Beijing Doll* (2004), and Annie Wang, who mixes sex with gender politics in *The People's Republic of Desire* (2006).

Sex and drugs notwithstanding, Beijing's most famous contemporary author remains Wang Shuo, a prolific novelist who tackles urban slackers, political satire, and the murder-mystery genre all at once. Only two of his many books have been translated into English: *Playing for Thrills* (1998) and *Please Don't Call Me Human* (2000).

Although the capital is home to most major book publishers, one of the main obstacles for Chinese authors remains censorship. Consequently, many writers are only able to publish complete editions of their works in Taiwan. More recently, the rise of the

Internet and blogging has given the younger generation an outlet for publishing.

Other major writers who previously studied or lived in Beijing include Su Tong (*Raise the Red Lantern, Rice*), Jiang Rong (*Wolf Totem*), and the dissident voices of Gao Xingjian (*Soul Mountain*) and Ma Jian (*Red Dust, The Noodle Maker*). Gao, a resident of France since 1987, won the Nobel Prize for literature in 2000. His work has been banned in China since 1989. More recently, Paul French's evocative re-creation of the unsolved murder of a British teenager in Beijing in 1937, *Midnight in Peking*, has become a global bestseller, and is set to become a five-part TV series.

Shanghai is not closely linked with traditional Chinese literature, but it certainly emerged as a center of literary excellence during the first half of the 20th century. The city's vibrancy provided inspiration for both revolutionary socialist writers, like Lu Xun, whose most celebrated work is *The True Story of Ah Q* from the 1920s, and Mao Dun, author of *Midnight,* and more romantic bourgeois writers, like Eileen Chang and Shao Xunmei. The northern district of Hongkou, in particular, is associated with Lu Xun, the father of modern Chinese literature, and his League of Left-wing Writers. Today considerable space is devoted to Lu Xun in and around the area's Duolun Road. In modern Shanghai, stirringly independent writers have given accounts of the city's sex, drugs, and party scene, most notably Wei Hui in *Shanghai Baby*.

Besides its ties with such famous Chinese writers, Shanghai is also linked with the names of several well-known foreign writers and playwrights. Noel Coward (1899–1973) wrote his novel *Private Lives* (1930) while staying at the Cathay Hotel. J. G. Ballard's autobiographical novel of a young boy's experiences during the Japanese occupation of Shanghai, *Empire of the Sun,* was made into a movie by Steven Spielberg. More recently, Japanese novelist Kazuo Ishiguro set the first part of his novel *When We Were Orphans* (2000) in Shanghai.

Martial Arts Shows

Often associated with all-action movie stars like Bruce Lee and Jackie Chan, *wushu,* or marital arts, encompass a range of self-defense styles that developed across several centuries. Popular in Chinese moviemaking, *gongfu* (kungfu) has become synonymous with the warrior Buddhist monks of the Shaolin Temple (*www.shaolin.org .cn*), in Henan Province, whose version of kungfu is rooted in the Chan school of Buddhism. The monks' captivating touring shows can often be enjoyed in theaters in Beijing and Shanghai.

Calligraphy

The most common form of art in China, calligraphy appears everywhere: above entrances to temples, adorning the doorways and walls of homes and restaurants, as decoration on teapots and paintings, and inscribed on stone steles at important monuments. In Beijing, it's not unusual to come across men practicing water calligraphy on the ground in public places.

The dual nature of Chinese characters, which are both conceptual (as a word) and visual (as a stylized image), lends calligraphy its particular form of expression. The leap from simply writing a character as a word to wanting to endow it with aesthetic qualities seems only natural. Yet this leap wasn't instantaneous; Chinese writing dates back to at least the Shang dynasty (1600–1045 B.C.), but calligraphy did not begin its long evolution as an art form until the Spring and Autumn period (770–476 B.C.).

There are five main calligraphic styles, each developed during a different era: seal script (Zhuan Shu), clerical script (Li Shu), semicursive script (Xing Shu), cursive script (Cao Shu), and standard script (Kai Shu). The "chops" or seals dipped in red ink and used as personal signatures are traditionally in seal script, the oldest and most complex form of Chinese characters. Despite the various styles that have evolved over the centuries, the emphasis has remained consistently on the brush strokes that make up each character. These lines convey personal feeling.

Traditional Painting

Traditional painting, which uses the same media—brush, ink, and paper or silk—is inseparable from both poetry and calligraphy. Artists trained in calligraphy from an early age, and this training provided the basis for many of the brush techniques they developed. There are deep connections between the three arts—paintings generally contain at least one line of poetry written by the owner, artist, or master calligrapher—but painting conveys a different realm of concepts and emotions.

One of the fundamental artistic principles of ink painting is *qi*. In most contexts, qi is translated as "energy." In painting, however, qi has a more figurative meaning. It is the inner spirit or underlying essence of whatever is depicted, animate and inanimate objects alike. Chinese artists weren't nearly as concerned with capturing the exact likeness of something as they were with expressing its qi or underlying reality.

Early artists painted aristocratic portraits and religious parables or figures; the most unique style of Chinese painting, landscape painting, developed later. This genre, which shifted the focus of visual art from human activities to the natural world, began in the

A scene from Zhang Yimou's visually spectacular 2004 film *House of Flying Daggers*

fifth century and gained importance with the works of the eighth-century poet and intellectual Wang Wei (699–761). Heavily influenced by the philosophies of Taoism and Chan (Zen) Buddhism, landscape painting reached full maturity during the Song and Yuan dynasties. The most sophisticated works portrayed visual representations of the tao, or underlying force of the universe.

One of the unique characteristics of landscape painting is its temporal dimension. Such paintings weren't meant simply to be viewed; they were intended to be experienced. Mounted on scrolls, landscapes were often unrolled from right to left, adding an element of time: seasons changed, rivers flowed, voyages taken. Ideally, landscape painting was a spiritual experience as the imagination conveyed otherwise inexpressible ideas. Sadly, many of China's masterpieces were looted by foreign powers in the early 1900s, shipped to Taiwan by nationalists decades later, or destroyed in the Cultural Revolution. Today the Capital Museum is the best place to view traditional artworks in Beijing.

Contemporary Art

In the blink of an eye, Chinese artists have begun fetching six-figure sums for their paintings, creative photography, and satirical illustations. More and more collectors now travel to China to invest in contemporary art. While some critics have likened the situation to an economic bubble, others claim that the contemporary art market is still in its nascent stages—Chinese and international collectors have just begun to take interest, and that interest is sure to grow in the coming decades.

Poetic Painting

Poetry and painting developed in harmony in China, a trend maybe best exemplified by the work of the Tang-dynasty poet-painter Wang Wei (699–759). Wang's frequently snow-filled landscapes evoke poetic concepts while his poetry is alive with the vivid images of nature. The Song dynasty further nurtured this marriage of the two arts. Ma Yuan (1165–1225) was a master of the technique of leaving large areas of the picture blank, giving the impression of vast space and depth and light.

Of course, economic success is hardly indicative of artistic merit—it's only one factor among many that have helped fuel the community's growth. The country's artistic movement has been evolving since Chairman Mao's death, slowly growing from a handful of subversive figures to the array of trendy galleries and exhibition spaces scattered around Beijing and Shanghai today. Even if there wasn't such a sudden demand for Chinese art, the massive social upheavals of the 21st century have given artists plenty of material to work with, not to mention the constantly looming threat of political repression and the excitement of working with media previously unknown in China—video installations, abstract oil painting, performance pieces.

When it all began back in the 1980s, life as an artist was a precarious existence. Some of the luckier figures, such as Ai Weiwei (who founded the influential avant-garde group The Stars in 1979), managed to move abroad and work in freedom for extended periods. More recently, he has endured arrest and censorship since moving back to Beijing. After the student protests at Tiananmen Square in 1989, the Chinese art world took a decisive turn, ushering in the movement known as cynical realism. Two of the most prominent names in Chinese art, Fang Lijun and Yue Minjun, developed their

(continued on p. 50)

In Style in Shanghai

In the early 1990s, after four decades of austerity—in which all were forced to wear blue, gray, or black Mao suits and peaked caps, and women were denied makeup or fashion accessories of any kind—Shanghai once again reclaimed the top spot in China's fashion scene. Prior to the communist seizure of power in 1949, Shanghai had introduced to China the figure-hugging modern *qipao* (long dress), silk stockings, high-heeled shoes, and the permanent wave.

The figure-hugging silk *qipao* is enjoying a fashionable renaissance.

It has long been said (and chiefly by the Shanghainese themselves) that "Everybody imitates Shanghai, but never success-fully—by the time they imitate one style, Shanghai fashion has already progressed to the next level." Today the Shanghai fashion industry is in full swing, living up to that saying. Designers are striving to turn the city into China's Paris or Milan—and with considerable success. There's at least one show a day somewhere in the city, with slender Shanghailander models strutting in everything from 21st-century qipao designs to creative fusion designs of East and West to international haute couture. Two couture designers gaining international recognition are the innovative Lu Kun and the more traditional Wang Yi Yang.

The stylish stores and boutiques of Huaihai Lu already set the fashion trend in China, and the city's couturiers and style aficionados seem set to transform the city into a world fashion center. Western fashion magazines such as *Marie Claire, Harper's Bazaar, Elle,* and *Vogue* are widely available at newsstands throughout the city, while the *Shanghai Tatler* casts an informed and very contemporary eye across the city's fashion scene each month. One trend to watch is Shanghai fusion fashion, which combines contemporary Chinese and Western styles. Luxury brand Hermes has gone even further. In late 2010 it launched a new brand, Shang Xia, specifically created for Chinese customers.

> One trend to watch is Shanghai fusion fashion, which combines contemporary Chinese and Western styles.

Shanghai Qipao

The most recognizable fusion of Eastern and Western fashion styles has been the transformation of the traditional qipao, a woman's long dress. Long Chinese dresses with high collars first became familiar to Westerners in Hong Kong, where they are known as *cheongsam,* the name now generally applied in English. In fact cheongsam more correctly should be applied to a man's mandarin-style robe, while a woman's long dress is called qipao *(zanshi* in the Shanghainese dialect).

The earliest qipao tended to be wide, loose, and baggy—comfortable, practical, and not too revealing, since it covered most of the female body, except the head, hands, and feet. Over time, the dress became more formfitting and revealing. The modern qipao—or at least the prototype thereof—first appeared in Shanghai around 1900. Slender, with an elegant high-cut collar, it was definitely designed to be sensual, in marked contrast to the original qipao. By the 1920s and '30s, Shanghai-style qipao were everywhere: in dance halls and restaurants, on the ubiquitous cigarette girl and calendar girl images (now widely for sale as reproductions), and in the city's infamously decadent den, the Great World, where the higher the floor, the more revealing the qipao became, until on the fifth floor "dresses were slit to the armpits."

In true Yangjingbang style, Western cultural influences also crept in. By the 1940s, the Shanghai qipao featured high-necked sleeveless dresses, bell-shaped sleeves, and black lace hems. Later came the transparent black look, beaded bodices, and velvet capes. This new, body-hugging qipao could easily be worn under a Western overcoat and scarf, adding a further frisson of modernity to the stylish extravagance of Shanghai society. When the hard-line communists came to power in 1949, they banned the qipao as frivolous and exploitative. When rules were relaxed in the 1990s, the qipao returned with a vengeance. Today it graces Shanghai's catwalks and sidewalks; more stylish, more hybrid, and more sensual than ever.

Beijing's Modern Fashion

Times are changing in Chinese fashion. While superstars like Alexander Wang, Jason Wu, and Vera Wang left to establish successful labels overseas, the next generation of fashionistas—trained at the world's top fashion academies—are returning to work in China's booming fashion industry. Xiamen-born womenswear designer Vega Zaishi Wang studied at the London College of Fashion and worked with Alexander McQueen before opening a studio in Beijing. Menswear designer Zhang Chi studied at Milan's Istituto Marangoni, and has also returned home, as have emerging talents like Xander Zhou and Qiu Hao. Other names to watch for are Yifang Wan, a L'Oreal Professionnel Young Designer Award-winner, and haute couture designers Shuting Wang and Yiqing Yin.

Using water, an artist expresses his thoughts in Beijing's Beihai Park—"Dragon Dancing, Phoenix Flying."

styles during this time. Cynical realism was succeeded by pop art, a response to growing consumerism and Western influence on Chinese culture and industry.

Independent Venues: Independent galleries remain the best places for visitors to experience the energy of the Beijing art scene. The Redgate Gallery at the Dongbianmen Watchtower recently celebrated 20 years as an independent gallery. The 798 Art District (Dashanzi), founded in 2001, is a renovated industrial zone that has flourished as a subculture in its own right, with cafés, bars, bookshops, and more than a hundred art galleries. Some of the top galleries here include Ullens Center for Contemporary Art, Faurschou Gallery, and the enormous 798 Art Space.

Caochangdi Village, founded by Ai Weiwei in 2000, is a 30-minute ride from central Beijing and draws a more cutting-edge crowd. In addition to the artist's own gallery, the China Art Archives and Warehouse, the enclave is home to the curator Pi Li's gallery, Universal Studios Beijing, White Space China, and Pékin Fine Arts.

Established artists who have become big names in international circles include Fang Lijun, who depicts disillusionment and angst among China's youth; Zhang Xiaogang, who paints surrealist, family-style portraits; Wu Guanzhong, who mixes traditional styles with European impressionism; Liu Xiaodong, a haunting figurative painter who also collaborates with the independent film movement; Liu Wei, who works primarily with

installations, sculpture, and painting; Zhang Peili, a video installation artist; Zhu Wei, who marries modernism with traditional ink paintings; and Huang Rui, an abstract painter. The high points of the year take place in May during the Art Beijing contemporary art festival and the Affordable Art Fair, which run concurrently, and in October, the month of both the China International Gallery Exposition and the Beijing Biennale.

Today the Shanghai art scene is also booming, with many galleries and studios opening across the city, particularly in the M50 cluster at 50 Moganshan Road. SH Contemporary, held each June at the Convention Center is the city's most celebrated art fair.

Contemporary artists of note include Han Lei (ink brush paintings), Xu Zhen (photography), Jin Shan (contemporary video art), Yang Fudong (photography), and Zhu Yu (performance art). The best places to experience the Shanghai art scene, both traditional and contemporary, are the Shanghai Museum of Contemporary Art, in the People's Park area; and larger galleries such as Eastlink and ShanghArt at M50.

Cinema

Shanghai was the birthplace of Chinese cinema. The country's first short film, *The Difficult Couple (Nanfu nanqi),* was made here in 1913, as was its first full-length feature film, *Orphan Rescues Grandfather (Gu'er jiu zuji)* in 1923. By the 1930s, Shanghai was firmly established as the center of China's filmmaking industry. The most infamous actress to come out of Shanghai was Jiang Qing who, later as wife of Mao Zedong and leader of the Gang of Four, dealt a virtual deathblow to all aspects of art and culture in China during the Cultural Revolution (1966–1976). Inevitably, Shanghai cinema suffered under the austere regime of hard-line communism, but the city has gradually been reclaiming its cinematic birthright since the mid-1980s.

Following the loosening of censorship, the unique and lavish imagery of Chinese cinema suddenly began to make headlines. The "fifth generation" directors—the first crop of students to graduate from the Beijing Film Academy following the Cultural Revolution—led the charge. Directors Zhang Yimou *(Red Sorghum, Ju Dou, Raise the Red Lantern, To Live)* and Chen Kaige *(Yellow Earth, Farewell My Concubine, Temptress Moon),* and Tian Zhuangzhuang *(The Horse Thief, The Blue Kite, Springtime in a Small Town)* have produced some of China's most widely acclaimed movies.

Independent galleries remain the best places for visitors to experience the energy of the Beijing art scene.

As Zhang Yimou and Chen Kaige have moved away from political themes toward more commercial ventures *(Hero, House of Flying Daggers,* and *The Promise),* a new group of independently minded graduates from the Beijing Film Academy and the Central Drama Academy—the sixth generation—has sprung up. The films of Wang Xiaoshuai *(Beijing Bicycle),* Zhang Yuan *(East Palace West Palace),* and Jia Zhangke *(Xiao Wu, Still Life)* are low budget and offer an unglamorous yet compelling vision of life in contemporary China. More recently, foreign directors have also started shooting movies at the Beijing Film Studio, including Ang Lee *(Crouching Tiger, Hidden Dragon).* ■

Religion & Philosophy

China is a deeply religious country, and Beijing and Shanghai follow the country's lead, with three main faiths: Taoism, Buddhism, and, to a lesser extent, Confucianism. Confucianism is not strictly a religion but more a philosophy, while Buddhism was imported from India, leaving Taoism as the only true indigenous Chinese faith.

Taoism *(daojiao)* is essentially more mystical than religious, although certain strains are presided over by deities. Supposedly founded in the seventh century B.C. by Laozi, who wrote the *Daodejing (Classic of the Way of Power),* Taoism aims to cultivate a philosophical awareness of life. It seeks revelation of "the Way"—the term used to describe the dynamism of nature and the operating force behind the universe. Taoists believe in achievement through inaction *(wu wei),* allowing things to develop and occur of their

Buddhist monks clad in traditional saffron robes pray at Beijing's Source of Law Temple.

own accord. Those who wish to experience the Way can peruse Laozi's classic, a book that has, as closely as is humanly possible, captured the feeling of the Tao. The Way is also experientially revealed through the practice of *tai ji quan,* a martial art that draws on the Taoist precepts of softness, heightened awareness, and avoidance of conflict.

Most temples in China are Buddhist. Founded by an Indian prince named Siddhartha Gautama (563–483 B.C.), **Buddhism** *(fojiao)* migrated to China from the third through the sixth centuries A.D. The faith seeks to cure suffering through the neutralization of desire. Only by following the eight-fold path can a Buddhist reach nirvana, a transcendent state of freedom.

Confucianism *(rujia sixiang),* named after the sage Confucius, is a paternalistic philosophy of social behavior that has given the Chinese people their codes, rules, and norms of conduct. Many Chinese consider genuflecting to one's elders as ordained by Confucianism a thankless task, yet the philosophy has spread through the soul of the nation. Over the centuries, Confucianism has been loaded with all the trappings of religion and even turned into a national institution, despite being a very human philosophy that offers real answers to suffering and bad governance.

Christianity in Today's China

Catholicism was introduced into China in the 7th century, with Protestantism arriving in the mid 19th-century. Despite religion being decreed "poison" by Chairman Mao, Christian worship has flourished since the 1980s, with congregations expanding fast: Government figures show around 18 million churchgoing Protestants and 6 million Catholics in China, with approximately 58,000 Protestant and 6,000 Catholic churches. These figures don't include the informal "house churches" springing up across China.

Arab merchants along the Silk Road brought **Islam** *(yisilan jiao)* to China. The Muslim community of Beijing speaks Chinese and is considered a group distinct from the Muslims of the Middle East. Beijing's oldest mosque dates from well over a thousand years ago.

Judaism *(youtai jiao)* in China can be traced back to the seventh or eighth century A.D. Although the Jews played an important role in the area's history, there was no Jewish community in Beijing until recently.

Religion & Politics

With mixed success, the Chinese Communist Party tried to replace religion with devotion to Marxism-Leninism *(makesilieningzhuyi)* and reacted strongly to any creed offering an alternative vision to that bequeathed by Karl Marx. Recent riots involving Chinese Christians point to the growing influence of Christianity in an increasingly capitalist-oriented society, where spiritual well-being often seems of secondary importance to material accumulation. Falun Gong (which means "art of the wheel of the law"), a quasi-Buddhist "cult," was outlawed due to fears that it challenges the primacy of the Communist Party. Banning Falun Gong hasn't solved the problem of spiritual emptiness in China; indeed, it may simply have exacerbated it. ∎

Festivals

China, like much of East Asia, follows two calendars when it comes to marking and celebrating festivals. Traditional Chinese holidays and indigenous religious festivals follow the Chinese lunar calendar, while modern secular holidays and imported Christian religious holidays follow the Gregorian calendar.

Traditional Festivals

Chinese New Year/Spring Festival: This traditional holiday, beginning on the first day of the first lunar month (usually January or February), is the most important date on the Chinese calendar.

Temple Fairs: A unique Beijing tradition, these colorful street fairs, with performances, snack foods, arts, and culture, take place in the streets around the main Buddhist temples during the Chinese New Year Festival.

Lantern Festival: Celebrated on the 15th day of the first lunar month, the Lantern Festival (Yuanxiao Jie) marks the official end of winter and the coming of a new spring.

A day dedicated to the respect and memory of the deceased, Qingming occurs in early April. "Ghost money" is burned at the graves to be used by the deceased in the afterlife.

Tomb-sweeping Festival of Qingming: A day dedicated to the respect and memory of the deceased, Qingming occurs in early April. "Ghost money" is burned at the graves to be used by the deceased in the afterlife. Families ritually cleanse their loved ones' gravesites and give offerings of food, wine, and flowers.

Dragon Boat Festival: Generally held each May or June, this festival (Duan Wu) brings to life the compelling sport of Chinese dragon-boat racing. The festival, meant to commemorate the death of Qu Yuan, a third-century B.C. poet-official, involves competing teams racing in traditional long, narrow, rowing boats. The sport is more than 2,000 years old and recognized worldwide.

Mid-Autumn Festival: This family-oriented festival falls on the 15th day of the eighth lunar month (generally September or October), when the moon is full. The shape of the moon represents reunion. During the festivals families get together, forgive old grudges, watch fireworks displays, and eat moon cakes.

Birthday of Confucius: Held annually on the 27th day of the eighth lunar month, typically October, this festival celebrates the life of this renowned philosopher at the numerous Confucian temples throughout the city and country.

A canopy of lanterns hangs in Shanghai's Yuyuan Gardens for the Spring Festival.

The Dragon Boat Festival, seen here in Shanghai, is celebrated nationally to honor the patriotic poet Qu Yuan.

Secular Festivals

Anting Kite Festival: This annual kite-flying festival and competition is held in Anting, in Jiading District in the northwestern suburbs of Shanghai, in the middle of April. Kite-flying is an enduring popular pastime in the city, and any given evening enthusiasts fly their kites along the banks of the Suzhou Creek. At the festival, competitors strive to see who can reach the greatest heights.

Midi Music Festival: Held annually in late April, this festival, inaugurated in 1997, pays tribute to China's burgeoning rock scene. Drawing musicians from around the world to the Shunyi Olympic Rowing Park outside Beijing, it is China's largest rock festival, with more than 30,000 attendees and 50 bands.

May Day: Beijing and Shanghai burst with tourists during the May Day Holiday, which celebrates the International Labor Day, and according to a government ordinance, all parks, gardens, streets, and resorts are elaborately decorated. Parks, gardens, and shopping malls are heavily crowded.

Youth Day: Held on May 4, this festival (Qingnian Jie) commemorates the student demonstrations in Tiananmen Square on that day in 1919. The

demonstrations heralded an upsurge of Chinese national-ism, and today Chinese youths are encouraged to contribute their wisdom to the continued building of the country. Particular to Beijing is the May Fourth Medal, which is awarded to the top Chinese youths of the year.

International Art Festival: A relative newcomer to Beijing festivals, the 798 International Art Festival occurs in September. Put together by 798 Factory, the annual arts extravaganza of Dashanzi offers music, dance, art openings, theater performances, lectures, and gallery receptions. In Shanghai, the SH Contemporary Art Festival at the Shanghai Convention Center each June attracts some of the world's top galleries and collectors.

Beijing Jazz Festival: The first and largest jazz event held in China, the Beijing Jazz Festival originated in 1993. It suffered a seven-year hiatus from 1999 to 2006 but returned in 2007, promising a revival of the annual September celebration. Three days of outdoor concerts—including artists from both China and abroad—mark the festival, which takes place in Haidian District, located in the northwestern portion of Beijing. American performers from previous years include the likes of Grammy-winning trumpet player Wynton Marsalis and pianist Jon Jang.

National Day: This secular festival—and one-week national holiday—marks the creation of the People's Republic of China on October 1, 1949. Each year, millions of Chinese jump on trains and planes to head home and spend this holiday with family. Beijing in particular is ornately beautified with flowers, flags, and buntings lining the streets, red lanterns dangling from shops and official buildings, and elaborate lights illuminating the city by night. The main congregating takes place at the Great Hall of the People, where the official festival reception is held. During every fifth and tenth year, a grand parade takes place in Tiananmen Square. ■

Literary Festivals

Each May, the three-week-long Shanghai International Literary Festival (www.facebook.com/shanghai.literaryfestival) is hosted at M on the Bund restaurant. Among the writers who have spoken at the festival are Amy Tan, Matt Groening, Cheryl Tan, and Ouyang Yu. A spin-off festival is simultaneously hosted at sister restaurant Capital M in Beijing.

An international Literary Festival (www.bookwormfestival.com) is also held each March at the Bookworm, a popular café, library, and bookstore in Sanlitun District. Jonathan Fenby, Paul French, Justin Hill, Han Dong, and Xiong Liang have all been among the literary guests in previous years.

beijing

Dongcheng District 60–82 ■ **Xicheng District** 83–94 ■ **Chongwen District** 95–106 ■ **Xuanwu District** 107–120 ■ **Chaoyang District** 121–128 ■ **Haidian District** 129–142 ■ **Excursions North to the Great Wall** 143–156 ■ **Excursions South** 157–173

The heart of "Old Peking," with idyllic *hutongs,* or alleyways, and rich glimpses of Beijing's proud imperial past

Dongcheng District

Introduction & Map   62–63

Forbidden City   64–69

Tiananmen Square   70–72

Drum & Bell Towers   73

Experience: Culture in the
  Temple   73

Walk Among the *Hutongs*   74–77

Confucius Temple & the Imperial
  Academy   78

Lama Temple   79

Feature: Confucius: The Comeback
  Kid   80–81

More Places to Visit in Dongcheng
  District   82

Hotels & Restaurants   295–298

Pages: 58–59: Age-old Chinese pastimes endure in the Forbidden City.
Above: Soldiers stand at attention in Tiananmen Square.
Opposite: The Ming-dynasty granaries of Nanxincang

Dongcheng District

Dongcheng, or the East District, was formally established in 1958, but humans have lived here since ancient times. During the Yuan, Ming, and Qing dynasties, Beijing was the imperial capital, and this area flourished as the political, economic, and cultural heart of the city.

In busy Wangfujing, modern merchants mix comfortably with shops dating back a century.

NOT TO BE MISSED:

The timeless allure of the
Forbidden City 64–69

Historic Tiananmen Square 70–72

Whizzing through history on the
Road of Rejuvenation tour at the
National Museum of China 71

Marking time, the Chinese way, at
the Drum & Bell Towers 73

A wander through the *hutongs*
of Beijing 74–77

Tranquility in the Lama Temple 79

Shopping on the 700-year-old street
of Nan Luogu Xiang 82

Beijing runs on an invisible north–south axis that cuts right through the spine of the city, from the Temple of Heaven in Chongwen District in the south, through Tiananmen Square, the Forbidden City, and Jingshan Park, all the way up to the Drum Tower and Bell Tower in the north. Other worthwhile sights in Dongcheng include the Lama Temple and the Confucius Temple, as well as the city's colorful alleyways known as *hutongs*.

The area also boasts some of Beijing's best restaurants, from romantic old courtyard venues serving traditional food to sleek high-end venues, where the emphasis is on fusion and nouveau cuisine.

Because of all there is to see and do, you'll need at least two or three days to properly visit the major sights in Dongcheng District. ■

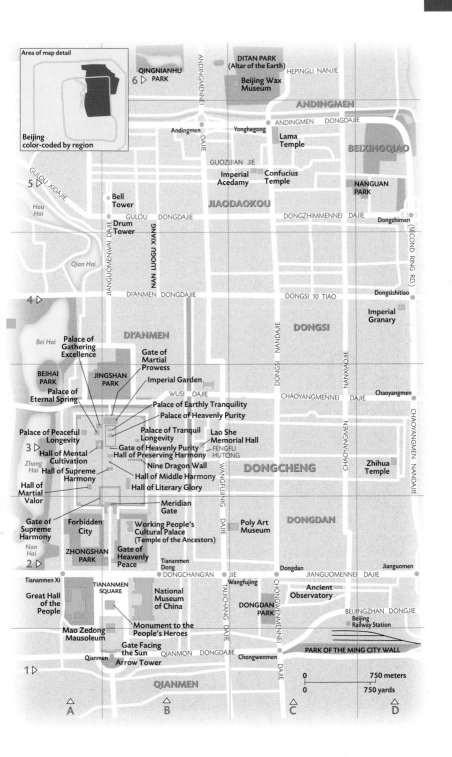

Area of map detail

Beijing color-coded by region

QINGNIANHU PARK   6 ▷

DITAN PARK (Altar of the Earth)

HEPINGLI NANJIE

Beijing Wax Museum

ANDINGMEN

ANDINGMENNEI

ANDINGMEN DONGDAJIE

Andingmen   Yonghegong

Lama Temple

BEIXINGQIAO

GULOU XIDAJIE   5 ▷

GUOZIJIAN JIE

Imperial Acedamy   Confucius Temple

NANGUAN PARK

Hou Hai

Bell Tower

JIAODAOKOU

GULOU   DONGDAJIE

DONGZHIMMENNEI DAJIE

Dongzhimen

Drum Tower

JIANGUOMENWAI DAJIE

NAN LUOGU XIANG

DI'ANMEN   DONGDAJIE

DONGSI 10 TIAO

Dongsishitiao

(SECOND RING RD.)

Qian Hai

4 ▷

Imperial Granary

Bei Hai

Palace of Gathering Excellence

DI'ANMEN

DONGSI

DONGSI NANDAJIE

Gate of Martial Prowess

BEIHAI PARK   JINGSHAN PARK

Imperial Garden

WUSI DAJIE

NANXIAOJIE

Palace of Eternal Spring

Palace of Earthly Tranquility

CHAOYANGMENNEI DAJIE

Chaoyangmen

Palace of Heavenly Purity

Palace of Peaceful Longevity

Palace of Tranquil Longevity

Lao She Memorial Hall

3 ▷

Hall of Mental Cultivation

Gate of Heavenly Purity

FENGFU HUTONG

CHAOYANGMEN NANDAJIE

Zhong Hai

Hall of Preserving Harmony

Hall of Supreme Harmony

Nine Dragon Wall

DONGCHENG

CHAOYANGMEN

Zhihua Temple

Hall of Middle Harmony

Hall of Martial Valor

Hall of Literary Glory

Meridian Gate

WANGFUJING DAJIE

Gate of Supreme Harmony

Forbidden City

DONGDAN

Nan Hai

Working People's Cultural Palace (Temple of the Ancestors)

Poly Art Museum

ZHONGSHAN PARK

Gate of Heavenly Peace

Tiananmen Dong

2 ▷

Tiananmen Xi

DONGCHANG'AN   JIE

Dongdan   JIANGUOMENNEI DAJIE   Jianguomen

TIANANMEN SQUARE

Wangfujing

Ancient Observatory

Great Hall of the People

National Museum of China

TAIJICHANG DAJIE

CHONGWENMENNEI

DONGDAN PARK

BEIJINGZHAN DONGJIE

Beijing Railway Station

Mao Zedong Mausoleum

Monument to the People's Heroes

Gate Facing the Sun

Qianmen   QIANMON DONGDAJIE

Chongwenmen

PARK OF THE MING CITY WALL

1 ▷   Arrow Tower

CHONGWENMENNEI DAJIE

0   750 meters
0   750 yards

QIANMEN

△   △   △   △
A   B   C   D

Forbidden City

One of the most alluring and magnificent treasures in China, the Forbidden City (Zijin Cheng), completed in 1421, was a 78-acre (32 ha) pied-à-terre for emperors of the Ming and Qing dynasties. The Chinese name, which translates literally as "purple forbidden city," is not an allusion to the color of the walls but to two imperial symbols: the Polar Star, located at the center of the celestial world, and purple, a color associated with royalty.

Looking north toward the Drum Tower from the top of Coal Hill

Forbidden City

- 🅰 63 A1–A4, B1–B4
- ✉ 4 Jingshan Qianjie
- ☎ 010/8500-7421
- 💲 $$; Treasure Gallery & Clock Gallery addl. $
- 🚇 Metro: Tiananmen Xi/ Tiananmen Dong; Bus: 1, 4, 52, or 57 to Tiananmen

www.dpm.org.cn

Entering the Forbidden City

The entrance to the Forbidden City is north of **Tiananmen Square,** accessible via the underground walkway that runs under Dongchang'an Dajie. The **Gate of Heavenly Peace** (Tiananmen), the entrance to the Forbidden City, is marked by the monumental portrait of the late Chairman Mao Zedong.

The white characters on the red background to the left of the portrait signify the official mantra of China's government, "Long Live the People's Republic of China." To the right the characters proclaim: "Long Live the United People of the World." It was from atop this gate that Mao Zedong authoritatively announced the founding of New China on October 1, 1949. For a fee, you can climb up an inner staircase through the gate for views over the square.

It was at this ceremonial gate that imperial edicts were proclaimed to citizens via a scroll, which was lowered from the high tower by a sash pulled through the beak of a gilded phoenix.

Walking through the gate brings you into a large courtyard lined by souvenir stalls and restaurants. West of the courtyard is the attractive **Zhongshan Park** (Zhongshan Gongyuan), where the emperor used to make sacrifices in spring and autumn to ensure a fruitful harvest. To the east is the **Working People's Culture Palace** (Laodong Renmin Wenhuagong), the former site of the Temple of the Ancestors (Tai Miao), the most sacred temple after the Temple of Heaven during the Qing dynasty.

The Outer Court

Passing through the next gate leads you to the fortress-like **Meridian Gate** (Wu Men), which marks the actual entrance into the Forbidden City. The gate was reserved for the sole use of the emperor, with drums and bells sounding his passage as he approached the Hall of Supreme Harmony. The 170-foot-wide (52 m) moat begins its circuit here, where the walls, standing a massive 28 feet (8.5 m) wide at the base, create colossal silhouettes at twilight.

Through the Meridian Gate you will enter a huge paved courtyard with five marble bridges straddling a central strip of water.

Imperial Architecture

The finest example of imperial architecture in China, the Forbidden City was the nucleus of the Middle Kingdom—the source from which all imperial dictates were issued. Considerably restored and embellished since the Ming dynasty (most of what you see today dates from the 18th century or later), the Forbidden City signified the distant and unapproachable emperor. The complex is not one stately building as was the Western practice (for example, at Versailles or Buckingham Palace), but rather a series of halls and buildings separated by passages like a small, labyrinthine city. Since traditional Chinese architecture extends horizontally rather than vertically, the buildings in the Forbidden City are not tall, but the space around them is breathtaking.

Beyond lies the **Gate of Supreme Harmony** (Taihe Men), its ceiling a blaze of emerald green and gold. This gate was built in 1420, destroyed by fire in 1888, and rebuilt the following year. As you walk through the gate, you will see to the east the **Hall of Literary Glory** (Wenhua Dian), which contained the imperial library; to the west is the **Hall of Martial Valor** (Wuying Dian).

Ahead of you stand the three Harmony Halls, each of which had a designated ritual use. Grand audiences, New Year's celebrations, the emperor's birthday, and enthronements were all held in the imposing **Hall of Supreme Harmony** (Taihe Dian). Built at the beginning of the 15th century, but destroyed by fire during the Ming and Qing dynasties, the hall was the first and largest of the three Harmony Halls. The

HOW TO VISIT:
It is ideal to approach the Forbidden City from the south, which gives you the chance to admire the port-red walls that thrust out from either side of the Meridian Gate (Wu Men). You can enter from the northern gate early in the morning and escape the throngs coming from the south, but the audio handset tour guides you from the south. Obtain your ticket (and tour guide handset) from the booths to the left and right of the Meridian Gate.

structure that stands today dates from 1695, but it has been renovated many times since then.

Raised on a three-tier carved marble platform, the hall was for many years the tallest building in Beijing, and a law forbade commoners to construct anything higher. Twin sets of stairs ascend to the hall, divided by a decorated stone slab over which the emperor's sedan chair would have been conveyed. Inside sits the imperial throne, as well as a sun dial and grain measure, reminders of the emperor's responsibility to assess the passage of time and determine the correct time of year for sowing and reaping. The large bronze and iron vats outside supplied water for fighting fires.

Tucked behind the Hall of Supreme Harmony is the **Hall of Middle Harmony** (Zhonghe Dian), the smallest of the three halls. Each spring the new agricultural year was celebrated here with a ritual examination of plows and seeds. This is also where ministers from the Ministry of Rites were received and where the emperor would get ready for rituals held in the Hall of Supreme Harmony.

The rectangular **Hall of Preserving Harmony** (Baohe Dian) is where the emperor oversaw the final stages of the civil

Forbidden City

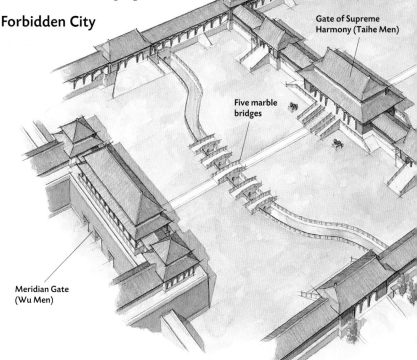

Gate of Supreme
Harmony (Taihe Men)

Five marble
bridges

Meridian Gate
(Wu Men)

service examinations (see sidebar p. 78). This is also the place where the imperial court received foreign envoys and where Ming-dynasty emperors changed their clothing before and after taking part in ceremonies in other parts of the palace.

The first building, the **Palace of Heavenly Purity** (Qianqing Gong), served as the emperor's bedchambers during the Ming and early Qing dynasties. Later emperors moved to the Hall of Mental Cultivation (Yangxin Dian; see sidebar p. 68).

Gate of Heavenly Purity (Qianqing Men)

Hall of Preserving Harmony (Baohe Dian)

Hall of Supreme Harmony (Taihe Dian)

Hall of Middle Harmony (Zhonghe Dian)

The Inner Court

The **Gate of Heavenly Purity** (Qianqing Men) divided the Outer Court from the Inner Court. The courtyard behind the gate marks the entrance to the heart of the Forbidden City, access to which was limited to eunuchs, maids, and the emperor's own relatives.

Behind the palace is the smaller **Hall of Union** (Jiaotai Dian), where the empresses slept during the Ming dynasty. This hall is also where Qing-dynasty empresses received high-ranking civil and military officials on their birthdays.

North of the Hall of Union lies the **Palace of Earthly Tranquility** (Kunning Gong), where Manchu shamans once held sacred rituals. A number of Qing-dynasty emperors and empresses slept in the heated chamber connected to the

Hall of Mental Cultivation

The Forbidden City's Hall of Mental Cultivation served as the living area for Qing-dynasty emperors beginning with the reign of Yongzheng in the 1730s. This was also the place where emperors dealt with important affairs of state and where Puyi abdicated his throne in 1912.

The hall's courtyard has two sections: The south part was used for ceremonies and the north part as the living area. The emperors Tongzhi and Guangxiu held meetings in the hall itself. Because the Empress Dowager Cixi ruled China from "behind a screen" (a term for a regency supervised by a woman), she also attended meetings in the hall, sitting to one side and separated from the public area by a large curtain.

The imperial bedroom was located in the heated chamber in the east of the hall. Here the emperor frolicked with his concubines. Imperial eunuchs stood just steps away, offering warnings to the emperor to be careful.

east side of the hall while on their three-day honeymoon. This is also where the last emperor, Puyi, was married in 1922.

Immediately behind is the **Gate of Earthly Tranquility** (Kunning Men), which leads to the **Imperial Garden** (Yuhua Yuan), some portions of which date as far back as the Ming dynasty. Enjoy the garden's delightful collection of green pines, exotic flowers, rare stones, pavilions, and small houses.

If you wish, you can leave the Forbidden City through the Gate of Martial Prowess (Shenwu Men; see p. 69), which opens to a bridge over the moat that rings the walled city. Or proceed to the two corridors flanking the Forbidden City. First head down the corridor to the west of the Palace of Heavenly Purity.

In 1861, the Empress Dowager Cixi gave birth in the **Palace of Concentrated Beauty** (Chuxiu Gong) to the boy who was eventually to become Emperor Tongzhi. Just to the southwest stands the **Palace of Eternal Spring** (Changchun Gong), once the living quarters for imperial concubines. The palace houses the theater where Cixi often enjoyed performances of Peking opera.

To the southeast lies the most important building in this part of the Forbidden City: the **Hall of Mental Cultivation** (Yangxin Dian; see sidebar above). To the south of the Hall of Mental Cultivation is the **Imperial Kitchen** (Yushanfang), which had more than a hundred stoves, each operated by three chefs.

From here, walk to the northeast side of the Forbidden City, cross in front of the Gate of Heavenly Purity, and continue on to the **Hall of Worshiping Ancestors** (Fengxian Dian), which housed the spirit tables of dead emperors and empresses. Continue west where the next corridor leads to the **Palace of Tranquil Longevity** (Ningshou Gong), which served as the home of the emperor's parents. This building has an excellent collection of paintings, stone rubbings, and personal effects of the Qing royal family. Directly to the south is the

Nine Dragon Screen (Jiulong Bi), similar to one of the same name in Beihai Park (see p. 87).

Turning back to the north you will pass through the **Gate of Imperial Supremacy** (Huangji Men), which will bring you to the **Hall of Imperial Supremacy** (Huangji Dian). The **Treasure Gallery** (Zhenbao Guan) here has an impressive collection of ceremonial and religious objects.

The **Pavilion of Pleasant Sounds** (Changyin Ge) is in a courtyard to the northeast of the Palace of Tranquil Longevity, which has a three-tier opera stage and an array of props and costumes. Cut across the courtyard to the **Garden of the Palace of Tranquil Longevity** (Ningshou Gong Huayuan), a traditional Suzhou garden, and continue to the **Qianlong Garden** (Qianlong Huayuan). Just north of the garden stand three halls, the **Hall of Nourishing Heavenly Nature** (Yangxing Dian), the **Hall of Joyful Longevity** (Leshou Tang), and the **Pavilion of Peace and Harmony in Old Age** (Yihe Xuan).

Finish your tour at the **Well of the Pearl Concubine** (Zhenfei Jing), tucked away in the northeast corner of the Forbidden City. It's said that Zhenfei, Guangxu's favorite concubine and a force behind the emperor during the Reform Movement of 1898, was stuffed down the well by a eunuch after she had angered the Empress Dowager Cixi.

To exit the Forbidden City, walk west to the **Gate of Martial Prowess,** the north gate. This part of the Forbidden City was reconstructed in 2007; tours of the gate's tower can be arranged for an extra fee. Cross the road to **Jingshan Park,** climb the hill, and marvel at the Forbidden City stretched out below you. ∎

Members of the People's Armed Police march through the Forbidden City.

Tiananmen Square

The sweeping square of the Gate of Heavenly Peace—Tiananmen Square—is the symbol of China. This vast expanse of paving stones, scene of the 1989 student demonstrations and their gory climax, is an ordered microcosm of the communist universe and a colossal statement of state power. Chairman Mao is interred here, and the monolithic Chinese Parliament overlooks the square.

A guard stands at attention in front of the Gate of Heavenly Peace.

Tiananmen Square

 63 A2–B2

 $ for Arrow Tower

 Metro: Tiananmen East/Qianmen

Tiananmen Square (Tiananmen Guangchang) was the scene of exultation at the launch of the Cultural Revolution in 1966. Today, it is a favorite destination for the hordes of both local and foreign tourists, who crowd just about every inch of the square on a daily basis, eager to soak up its history.

Despite the authoritarian design, the square has become a battleground in the lopsided tussle between government and disaffected groups. In May 1919, disgruntled Chinese university students and intellectuals marched here to protest the unequal Versailles Treaty, which stipulated that China cede territories to Japan. On April 4, 1976, hundreds of thousands of Beijing residents gathered to mourn the death of Premier Zhou Enlai. Wreaths laid to commemorate his passing

INSIDER TIP:

Try to catch the National Flag Ceremony, which occurs exactly at sunrise, when soldiers march through the gate of Tiananmen Tower and raise the flag.

—BARBARA A. NOE
*National Geographic
Travel Books senior editor*

vanished, leading to a massive riot (the Tiananmen Incident), which was branded a counterrevolutionary plot by some.

Democracy protests in the spring of 1989 were similarly molded from public grief (on this occasion, the death of reformer Hu Yaobang). Sadness again smoldered to anger when the authorities rebuffed the people. Bizarrely, the government sent tanks against unarmed workers and students, rather than using riot police and tear gas.

Since then, the square has become a tempting forum for dissent and is perennially patrolled by plainclothes police. In recent times, middle-aged followers of a banned spiritual exercise system, the Falun Gong, frequently assembled in the square, only to be arrested and bundled into waiting vans of the Public Security Bureau. In April 2010, a Chinese protestor was arrested for hurling a bottle of ink at Mao's portrait.

October 1 is China's National Day, when half of Beijing descends on the square (see p. 57).

Visiting the Square

The square, one of the largest public squares in the world, is also a huge park, where couples stroll languidly hand in hand, children play, and elderly men enthusiastically fly their colorful kites. At twilight on a clear day the view here can be astonishing. In the early evening, soldiers of the PLA march out to lower the Chinese flag, attracting an

Charting Modern Chinese History

Most visitors to Tiananmen Square take a photo of the monumental **National Museum of China** (*www.chnmuseum.cn, $*). Inside, this cavernous building offers an insight into culture and arts officially sanctioned by the Chinese government. Originally founded in 1912, the museum underwent several moves before relocating—as two separate entities, the National Museum of Chinese History and the National Museum of Chinese Revolution—to its current locale in 1959. The two museums merged in 2003, but closed for major refurbishments in 2007. Reopened in 2011, it features five floors of galleries and exhibition rooms. The centerpiece is the Road of Rejuvenation, a well-curated visual journey overlaid with nationalistic sentiment and political nostalgia documenting the achievements of China—and predominantly, the Chinese Communist Party—from the Opium War in 1840 through Mao's revolution, opening up under Deng Xiaoping, the hosting of the 2008 Olympics, through to the current-day space exploration program.

A sculpted page from China's revolutionary history

Mao Zedong Mausoleum

📍 63 B1–B2

🕐 Closed Mon.

🚇 Metro: Tiananmen East/Qianmen

National Museum of China

📍 63 B2

✉️ 16 Dongchang'an Dajie

☎️ 010/6511-6400

💲 $

🚇 Metro: Tiananmen East

www.chnmuseum.cn

assembly of wide-eyed Chinese.

A motley assortment of historical buildings, garish, Soviet-style monuments, and huge museums flank the square. To the north is Tiananmen and its huge portrait of Chairman Mao Zedong. In the center of the square stands the **Monument to the People's Heroes** (Renmin Yingxiong Jinianbei). Erected in 1958, the monument is dedicated to the memory of the martyrs who gave their lives for the communist revolution.

To the south is the **Mao Zedong Mausoleum** (Mao Zhuxi Jinian Tang), where the waxen-faced Great Helmsman lies in state. The hall was completed in 1977, one year after Mao's death. Today long lines of people still file through to pay their respects to the former chairman, who lies on a slab of black granite from Taishan, one of the five sacred Taoist

mountains. Each night, his crystal coffin is returned to its refrigerated resting place beneath the hall. Many rumors about the state of Mao's body still circulate. Mao's personal physician, Dr. Li Zhisui, offers gory details on the bungled embalming in his book, *The Private Life of Chairman Mao*. (Visitors to the mausoleum must store bags and cameras at special booths on the building's east side.)

South of the mausoleum stand socialist realist statues that depict scenes of China's revolutionary past. They are a mixture of angry students, fierce workers, and determined peasants. A tangible reminder of China's past, the statues offer an interesting contrast with today's free-market capitalism.

The venerable **Zhengyang Gate** (or Qianmen) and the **Arrow Tower** (Jian Lou), in the south, are two of the few remaining gates of Beijing's original early 15th-century wall. The two gates, which were once connected to each other via a semicircular enceinte wall, underwent a major renovation in 2006.

The west side of the square is dominated by the **Great Hall of the People** (Renmin Dahui Tang), where China's rubber-stamping parliament meets on a regular basis. You can enter the building when the annual session of the National People's Congress (NPC) is not in session *(usually March)*.

Opposite is the cavernous **National Museum of China** (Guojia Bowuguan), which reopened in 2011 after a four-year overhaul and expansion (see also sidebar p. 71). ■

Drum & Bell Towers

Sounding out the hours to regulate the functions of daily life and official ceremonies, drum and bell towers have been an integral part of urban life throughout modern Chinese history.

According to the old Chinese system, the night was divided into five *gengs,* each representing two hours. After the watch had been "set" at 7 p.m. with 13 drum beats, each subsequent geng was marked by one drum beat. Civil and military officials organized their lives around these signals. At the sounding of the third watch (1 a.m.), officials attending the morning court audience climbed out of their beds, and at the fourth (3 a.m.), they gathered outside the Meridian Gate (Wu Men) of the Forbidden City. At the fifth watch (5 a.m.), they marched into the Imperial Palace and knelt on the Sea of Flagstones in front of the Hall of Supreme Harmony to wait for orders from the emperor. Only one of the original drums survives. Today 24 new drums are beaten every half hour, from 9 a.m. to 11:30 a.m. and from 1:30 p.m. to 5 p.m.

Just across the square to the north stands the 108-foot-tall (33 m) Bell Tower. The original tower burned down and was rebuilt in stone by Qianlong in 1747; a stele from the Qianlong period stands at the entrance to mark the occasion. The massive bronze bell—which is audible more than 12 miles (20 km) away—was rung every evening at 7 p.m. until 1924, when Puyi, the last emperor, left the Forbidden City. When you exit the Bell Tower, walk to the rear yard where you'll find a collection of turn-of-the-20th-century steles. They are damaged, but some still bear the carved name of Qianlong. Others are covered in red paint, indicating that they may have been the victims of rampaging Red Guards.

The towers provide wonderful vistas of the *hutongs* and courtyard houses below. But be warned, the climb up is steep. After, stop by the **Drum & Bell Café** (*41 Zhonglouwan Hutong, tel 010/8403-3600*) for a well-earned drink or snack on the terrace with its views of the Drum and Bell Towers. ■

Drum Tower
- 🅰 63 B5
- ✉ 3 Zhonglouwan Linzi (N end of Di'anmen Dajie)
- ☎ 010/8403-6706
- 💲 $
- 🚇 Metro: Gulou Dajie

Bell Tower
- 🅰 63 B5
- ✉ 9 Zhonglouwan Linzi (N end of Di'anmen Dajie)
- ☎ 010/8403-6706
- 💲 $
- 🚇 Metro: Gulou Dajie

EXPERIENCE: Culture in the Temple

For a taste of Beijing's hidden historic treasure, explore **The Temple** *(www .temple-restaurant.com and www .thetemplehotel.com)*, where you'll find a year-round program of choral, orchestral, and Chinese folk performances, as well as literary events in one of Beijing's most evocative settings. Northeast of the Forbidden City, follow the Shatan Bejie *hutong* lane and you'll reach a 600-year-old walled compound housing a Tibetan Buddhist temple, stone courtyards, and a 1950s TV factory converted into a fine-dining European restaurant. The former monk's quarters plus a converted modern building now house a boutique hotel. Set on a stone plinth in the center of the courtyard is **Zhizhusi**, the main hall of worship, featuring carved wooden beams, upturned eaves, Mao-era revolutionary slogans, and great acoustics.

Walk Among the *Hutongs*

This walk will take you through some of the rapidly fading *hutongs* of Beijing. You'll also have a chance to experience some of the old traditions of the city, passing by shops selling traditional goods and snacks and the occasional itinerant peddlers carrying the tools of their trade on their bicycles. Fortunately, many of the streets along this walk have their names written in Pinyin, which should keep you on track.

Start at the **China National Museum of Fine Arts** *(1 Wusi Dajie, $)*. Turn left after exiting the museum onto Meishuguan Dongjie then turn immediately left into the courtyard and you will come to a *siheyuan*, a large courtyard house said to have been a gift from the Empress Dowager Cixi to her niece. Like many in Beijing, this house has been added to by the families who moved in during the Cultural Revolution. Two wood carvings of a lotus flower—a symbol of purity and happiness—hang from the door. The two lions on either side of the door, as well as the four lintels *(mendang)*, indicate that this house once belonged to a high official. If the door is open, you'll notice two large stone screen holders inside, each covered with intricate drawings; unfortunately the screens are long gone.

Leaving the gate turn to your left, walk a short distance, and make a left at the corner of Meishuguan Dongjie. Cross the street where it veers to your left and continue north down the smaller street on your right. **Dafosi Dongjie ➊** is lined with food shops. No. 24-2 sells snacks like *youtiao*, a Chinese-style cruller, and *huoshao*, a round roll with a filling made of sesame paste and brown sugar. The shop next door sells handmade noodles. At the next corner, you'll come to a shop that sells all kinds of nuts, plus sunflower and watermelon seeds.

The street bears left at the next corner. Walk past the big red gate with the Chinese roof. The **second house** has two large square stones on either side of the door for mounting horses, a relic of the days when horses were still quite common in this part of the city. If the door is open, you might notice the small screen

NOT TO BE MISSED:

Dong Mianhua Hutong
• Nan Luogu Xiang

wall, or *yingbi*, just inside. Turn your back to the door and you'll see a similar screen *(zhaobi)* across the street. The Chinese once believed the screens could prevent evil from entering the house.

Shijin Huayuan & Gangcha Hutongs

Retrace your steps back to Dafosi Dongjie. Turn left into the narrow hutong, then bear right on to **Shijin Huayuan Hutong ➋**. Just follow the winding street—there's only one way to go. At the first building on your right is a semicircular millstone used to grind corn.

Turn left on to **Gangcha Hutong.** Take the first right. The first house on the left has four lintels, another symbol of high rank. At **No. 1** on this street you'll see a pigeon coop on the roof and 13 electric meters at the entrance, which indicates that there are 13 families living in this compound that was built for one. Unfortunately, the beautiful *mendun* (doorstone) are usually hidden behind a pile of trash and bicycles.

At the next corner, turn left onto **Nanjianzi Xiang ➌**, or South Scissors Street. Notice the new courtyard house on your right. At **No. 78** *(also on right)*, you'll see the *pushou*, or son of the dragon, door handles, with huge rings in their mouths, which are good for protecting the home. **No. 72** is a Republican-era structure with a European look. The wooden window over the door is decorated with peaches and a bat.

At some point during the walk, you may hear the loud whistling made by pigeons, with bamboo whistles tied to their tails, that have just been released from a nearby pigeon coop.

Wang Zhima Hutong

After you pass **No. 33** (with a round red door and brass door rings), turn right down **Wang Zhima Hutong ❹**. This street has small courtyard houses. The roof tiles on **No. 59** have been decorated with the symbol for double happiness, as well as the characters *xinxiang shicheng*, meaning "whatever you wish will come true." **No. 56**

has two small mendun, and the door, like most courtyard houses, has a brass plate to protect it. The shape of the plate and the order of the nails resemble an auspicious motif. **No. 49** has one of the few doors that is painted green, and the mendun are carved with gourds with a lion sitting on top. The beam over **No. 39** has magpies, which symbolizes double happiness coming to your doorstep (*shuangxi linmen*).

No. 28 has two nicely carved horse-mounting stones—one carved with a reverse swastika and a bat, a symbol for long life. The second

🅰	See also area map p. 63
➤	China National Museum of Fine Arts
🕓	2 hours
↔	4 miles (6.4 km)
➤	Nan Luogu Xiang

A group of men pass the time playing a game of *xiangqi,* or Chinese chess.

has an ancient coin motif, indicating the owner was a merchant. The second door of this complex is the **Huadu Hotel.** On two sides of the doors are stone carvings of baskets and grapes. In addition, there are two large red lanterns. Finally, notice the rare communist-looking stars on the lintel at **No. 15.**

Dongsi Batiao

At the end of the street, you'll come to Dongsi Bei Dajie. Cross it and plunge into **Dongsi Batiao ⑤,** the lane opposite. **No. 70** has two cylindrical millstones beside the door, which means that this must have been a grinding shop. A local old women says that

the house belonged to a *lao dizhu,* or old landlord. "It used to be quite nice," she says.

Enter the small yard that leads to **No. 111** and you'll see two storage places to your right —one for cabbage, one for coal. Enter the next door and turn right. The windows are Republican era with wooden shutters. Walk to the end and enter the covered walkway for a peek at the colorful Western-style floor tiles. There's a stone carving over the door, and the mendun is carved with a bat and coin, both symbolizing the wish to achieve prosperity.

Retrace your steps back to Dongsi Batiao and turn left. Notice the roof tiles on **No. 109,** which have the infinity knot on them and mendun designed with Buddhist symbols. There's a swastika over the door and a plaque decorated with chrysanthemums.

A sign at **No. 89** indicates that it's a Muslim eatery with bean-curd custard, flat breads, lamb, and intestines with sesame sauce specialties. The stone squares flanking the door at **No. 71,** a historically protected house, feature nicely carved lions, their heads stolen long ago.

With two stone lions guarding **No. 67,** it's clear that this was once the home of an official. The lintels have four beams, each with a Chinese character for a popular flower or plant: plum, orchid, bamboo, and chrysanthemum. **No. 61** has two large stones for mounting horses and good mendun.

At **No. 43** you'll see a wooden door unlike many of the doors remaining in China. The characters are carved in the standard style, which indicates that the writing probably predates liberation in 1949, before the party officially switched to simplified characters.

Menlou Hutong

When you reach the end of Dongsi Batiao, turn left on Chaoyangmen Bei Xiaojie. Cross the intersection and walk down to Dongsishitiao *(marked by a big street sign)*. The large, gray, modern complex on your right is the former site of the Haiyuncang Imperial Granary. Walk to **Menlou Hutong** ❻, the third alley on your left—marked by a red sign—and turn left. The big gray building on your right is identified as the site of the old pawnshop. There used to be a guard tower on the corner here.

The redbrick building on your left is an example of 1950s urban-socialist housing— there is no central heating (coal briquettes are burned for heat and cooking) and the bathrooms on each floor are shared. At the corner of **No. 55,** you will see another millstone planted on the corner to protect the building.

At the intersection, the name of the street changes to **Xinsi Hutong** ❼. Formerly a nunnery, **No. 35** on the right is home to

INSIDER TIP:

Riding a rented bike is the best way to survey the cozy back-street world of the *hutongs*. Pedicab drivers will speed you through—it's best to take the hutongs at your own pace.

—DAMIEN HARPER
National Geographic author

several families today. Bear left here, and then turn right onto **Dongsi Bei Dajie.**

Fuxue Hutong & Dong Mianhua Hutong

Cross Dongsi Bei Dajie and walk about 55 yards (50 m) to **Fuxue Hutong** ❽. There's not much to see at first, but you'll discover several geomancy, or feng shui, masters. Several neighboring shops have hung mirrors to repel any evil emanating from the feng shui shops. On the right is the **Wen Tianxiang Temple,** built in the Ming dynasty. **No. 65** is a school.

Cross Jiaodaokou Nan Dajie and enter **Dong Mianhua Hutong** ❾, or East Cotton. At **No. 15** notice the plaque that marks the home as a protected site. Walk inside the gate and continue to the carved brick archway. The former residence of a Qing-dynasty general, named Feng Shan, this archway combines Chinese and Western architectural styles with carved flowers, animals, and other auspicious symbols.

After exiting the hutong, turn right and continue walking west. This street houses part of the **Beijing Central Academy of Drama,** so the streets are filled with students. A few blocks ahead is **Nan Luogu Xiang** (see p. 82), the end of your walk and a wonderful place to stop for a drink or a meal. Afterward explore the boutiques or head up and down the neighboring hutongs, which are rich in history and architectural detail.

Confucius Temple & the Imperial Academy

With the Great Sage once again revered around China (see pp. 80–81), this once dusty and neglected temple—which stands north and west of the Lama Temple (see p. 79)—was first built in 1306 and underwent a much needed renovation in 2007.

Confucius Temple & the Imperial Academy

 63 C5

 13–15 Guozijian Jie

☎ 010/8402-7224

💲 $

🚇 Metro: Yonghegong

Enter the temple through the **Gate of the First Teacher** (Xianshi Men). In the first courtyard, you'll find 198 stone steles carved with the names and towns of 51,624 successful candidates in the civil service examination (see sidebar below) during the Yuan, Ming, and Qing dynasties.

Continue north to the **Gate of Perfection** (Dacheng Men), to the left of which is the well-named **Pool of Water for Inkstones** (Yanshui Hu). It was said that anyone who drank water from this well would pass the imperial exam with flying colors.

The annual sacrifice to Confucius was made in the **Hall of Perfection** (Dacheng Dian), the temple's main structure. The spirit tablets of Confucius were placed on the altar during the rituals, with those of his disciples to the side.

On the west side of the temple is the site of the former **Guozi Xue,** a school set up in 1306 to educate the Mongol sons of Yuan rulers. Ming rulers turned it into an institution of higher education, today known as the **Imperial Academy** (Guozi Jian).

In the second courtyard you'll find a **drum** and **bell tower** on each side. In the center is an impressive glaze-tiled pai-lou, or commemorative arch, with a line from the *Analects* by Confucius. In front of the arch is **Biyong,** a hall built in 1784 where the emperor would give a speech each spring. Walk around the **River of Crescents** (Pan Chi), which has four marble bridges breaking the pool into four arcs. ∎

Examination Hell

Passing the imperial civil service exam was an essential step up the career ladder. Candidates traveled to Beijing from the provinces every three years to take the exam, which tested their ability to remember huge portions of the Confucian classics.

For three days and two nights they labored in solitary confinement in tiny cells, their only comforts a board for a seat and another that served as a small table. Once the cell doors were shut and sealed by the Imperial Commissioners, they could not be opened again until the exam was over. To further prevent cheating, vigilant overseers patrolled the corridors between the cells. Nevertheless, evidence suggests many of the men cheated in one way or another.

The system of imperial exams came to an end after 1900, when the Empress Dowager Cixi reformed the system entirely, substituting modern education for the Confucian classics.

Lama Temple

The Lama Temple (Yonghe Gong) was originally a mansion built in 1694 for Prince Yong, better known to the world by the name Yongzheng. After Yongzheng ascended the throne in 1723, some of the buildings in the large complex were converted into a Lama temple, and the roof tiles were changed to yellow, a royal color. Yongzheng died in 1735, and his son, Qianlong, made the complex a lamasery, inviting hundreds of lamas from Mongolia to stay permanently.

A long path runs north and south along the center of the entrance to the temple. The first building you come to is the **Hall of Heavenly Kings** (Tianwang Dian). Today, the ebullient Future Buddha, in his guise as the Laughing Buddha and accompanied by the Four Heavenly Kings on either side, greets all. Behind him is trusty Weituo, the defender of the faith, holding his scepter, to ward off evil spirits.

In the next courtyard, the **Yonghe Palace** (Yonghe Dian), with a startlingly beautiful ceiling, houses statues of the 18 luohan, or arhats (see p. 117), and three golden, robed Buddhas. In front of the three Buddhas are the eight magic weapons of Tibetan Buddhism: the umbrella, infinity knot, conch shell, lotus, vase, fish, canopy, and wheel of the law. The **Hall of Eternal Divine Protection** (Yongyou Dian) was once the home of Prince Yong.

On the altar of the Qing-dynasty **Hall of the Wheel of the Law** (Falun Dian) stands a statue of Tsong Khapa, the founder of the Yellow Hat sect of Lamaism. The lamas who live here visit five times a day to take part in religious activities. The roof is an interesting mixture of Chinese and

A yard in the Lama Temple fills with the swirling smoke of burning incense.

Tibetan architectural styles; piles of Tibetan scriptures printed from woodblocks lie against the walls.

The **Wanfu Pavilion** (Wanfu Ge), or Pavilion of Ten Thousand Happinesses, is built around a statue of the Maitreya Buddha. Carved from a single block of sandalwood, the statue stands 86 feet (26 m) high, with one-third of its body below ground.

In the northwestern part of the temple is a display of Qing-dynasty articles from Tibet and an exhibition on Tibetan Buddhism. The collection includes dharma wheels, scepter-like *dorjes*, bells, effigies of Buddha, and a multiarmed statue of Guanyin, goddess of mercy. ∎

Lama Temple

🅰 63 C5

✉ 12 Yonghegong Dajie

☎ 010/6404-4499

💲 $

🚇 Metro: Yonghegong

Confucius: The Comeback Kid

Once banned, works by Confucius—who is the country's most influential and inspiring philosopher—are again being studied and celebrated throughout China.

Inside a classroom on the campus of Tsinghua University, Tang Wenming, an associate professor of philosophy, is having an animated discussion with ten students about the differences between the Greek and Confucian concepts of virtue. He pauses to take a drink of water, jumps into the differences between Taoism and Confucianism, and then continues on to other classical Chinese concepts: the I Ching, yin and yang.

Mr. Tang's course, "The Ethics of Qin Confucianism," is just one of many manifestations of the Confucian fever that is currently sweeping across China. Scholars and students are dusting off classics and the general public is snapping up books and attending university lectures on this formerly taboo topic.

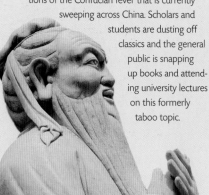

Attack Against Confucianism

For more than 2,500 years, China was guided by Confucian thought, which advocates a state guided by highly ethical scholar-bureaucrats and a society ruled by morality with a strong emphasis on hierarchical relationships. But by the end of the 19th century, the Chinese state, powerless to fight off foreign encroachment and growing public dissatisfaction, was teetering on the brink of collapse.

Leading intellectuals pointed an accusing finger at Kong Fuzi (551–479 B.C.), better known outside China as Confucius. During the May Fourth Movement of 1919, intellectuals frustrated by China's failures shouted "Down with the Confucian store!" and called for science and democracy to replace the Great Sage.

Confucius suffered harsher attacks when the communists came to power in 1949. During the Cultural Revolution, Confucian temples throughout China were damaged by rampaging Red Guards, and Confucian scholars were frightened—and often beaten—into silence.

Revitalization

Now, almost a century after Confucianism first came under attack as an obstacle to development, it is being heralded as a solution to the many political, economic, and ethical problems China faces.

In addition to impressive economic gains over the past 30 years, China has experienced a growing gap between rich and poor and a rise in corruption, crime, and divorce. Academics say few people still believe in communism, or even in the party's overt dogma, but nothing has risen yet to take their place, leaving an

The once reviled philosopher Confucius is now basking in newfound popularity.

ideological vacuum. Nevertheless, many Chinese find Confucianism an appealing alternative to both free-market economics and hard-line communism.

Confucian scholars are now basking in a newfound popularity that none could have imagined just a decade ago. Books and DVDs on Confucianism are selling well, and numerous universities around the country offer courses on Confucianism or have set up Confucian institutes. Academic conferences on the philosophy have become regular events, so that even the most dedicated Confucianists find it difficult to keep up with the pace of events.

Even children are caught up in Confucian fever. On a Saturday morning at Beijing's Confucius Temple, a five-year-old girl recites from the Confucian classic, *Discipline of Students*. Her mother confesses that she's not even sure her child, who has not yet learned to read, understands her lines, but she insists, "My daughter has become much more polite since she started attending classes here."

INSIDER TIP:

Confucius gave timeless advice for the geo-savvy traveler: "Wherever you go, go with all your heart."

—JUSTIN KAVANAGH
National Geographic International Editions editor

China's national fascination with the topic was made evident in the fall of 2006 when Yu Dan, a 41-year-old media professor at Beijing Normal University, appeared on "Lecture Room," a popular television program. For seven nights, millions of people around the country watched Professor Yu as she put the *Analects* of Confucius into simple words. A book based on the lectures sold three million copies over the next four months.

Jiang Qing, a retired humanities professor who is now a guest lecturer at Shenzhen

A man reads an inscription carved on a stone slab in the Confucius Temple.

University and a conservative Confucianist, applauds Professor Yu's effort to simplify Confucianism. "Chinese who once felt Confucianism had no value have now found that it is very valuable," he says. "That's incredible."

Mr. Jiang is probably the most extreme example of the love affair with Confucianism. In many of his articles he argues that only a Confucian revival can save China. *Political Confucianism*, a 462-page work, calls for a legislature made up of elected officials, the successful candidates of a rigorous examination based on Confucian texts, and elites charged with ensuring cultural continuity. The latter would be proven descendants of Confucius.

Mr. Jiang says further that he'd like to see required college courses on Marxism replaced by courses on Confucianism. "Confucian principles teach one how to be an upright person and the right way to do things," he says. "No matter what you do, you need to know this."

Confucianism survived the attacks of the influential May Fourth generation and more than three decades of harsh persecution by the communists. The 2,500-year tradition permeates Chinese society and culture in ways that many may not even realize. No matter what form this revival takes, it's not likely that Confucianism will disappear anytime soon.

More Places to Visit in Dongcheng District

Ancient Observatory

Construction on the Ancient Observatory (Guanxiang Tai)—which was built on the remains of the old city wall—began in 1437. Dedicated to astronomy, astrology, and seafaring navigation, it was operated by Muslims and later Jesuits. The observatory museum is dedicated to Chinese astronomy.
🅰 63 C2 ✉ Jianguomenwai Dajie 💲 $
🚇 Metro: Jianguomen

Ditan Park

Built in 1530, the **Altar of the Earth** (Ditan Gongyuan) was the second most important imperial altar after the Temple of Heaven (see pp. 98–101), which stands at the opposite end of the city's north–south axis. The altar consists of two square terraces of marble (symbols of the earth). South of the altar, the **House of the Imperial Gods** holds the spirit tablets for the earth, mountains, seas, and rivers. 🅰 63 C6 ✉ Andingmenwai Dajie 💲 $; extra fee for altar & Huangqi Shi (House of the Imperial Gods) 🚇 Metro: Yonghe Gong/Andingmen

Lao She Memorial Hall

Lao She, one of China's most talented writers, was the author of *Rickshaw Boy (Luotuo Xiangzi),* a 1936 novel that tells the tragicomic tale of a rickshaw puller's life, and *Teahouse,* a bittersweet play from 1957. The living room and adjoining bedrooms of this traditional courtyard house remain much as they appeared when Lao She lived here in the 1960s. Two other rooms house his personal effects and books.
🅰 63 B3 ✉ 19 Fengfu Hutong, just off Dengshikou Xijie ☎ 010/6514-2612 💲 $
🚇 Bus: 103, 104, or 108 to Dengshikou

Nan Luogu Xiang

In recent years this narrow street, which dates back some 700 years, has taken on new life with a string of artsy restaurants, coffee shops, bars, and boutiques. Check out **Wenyu Nailao**

(No. 49, tel 010/6405 7621) for delicious Chinese custard; **Plastered 8** (No. 61), a shop offering T-shirts with amusing Beijing motifs; and the **Pottery Workshop** (No. 23).
🅰 63 B4–B5 ✉ Between Di'anmen Dong Dajie & Gulou Dong Dajie

Imperial Granary at Nanxingcang

The beautiful old structures at Nanxincang were among more than 300 imperial granaries. Their floors were paved with thick bricks and covered with wooden boards resting on brick shoulders to insulate the grain from moisture. The elevated opening in the roof was enclosed with woven bamboo strips to prevent birds from entering. The 5-foot-thick (1.5 m) walls stabilized the temperature and prevented mold from forming. Today this historic site is home to a theater, art galleries, shops, a teahouse, bars, and restaurants.
🅰 63 D4 ✉ SW of Dongsi Shitiao Qiao, 1 block W of the 2nd Ring Road
🚇 Metro: Dongsi Shitiao

Poly Art Museum

This very impressive museum, located in the New Poly Plaza, a beautiful glass office tower, is divided into two galleries: one for the display of early Chinese bronzes, and the other for Buddhist scriptures carved in stone.
🅰 63 C2 ✉ 9 New Poly Plaza Tower, 1 Chaoyangmen Bei Dajie ☎ 010/6500-8117
💲 $$ 🚇 Metro: Dongsi Shitiao

Zhihua Temple

This complex, an excellent example of Buddhist architecture in the Ming dynasty, has three impressive courtyards. Rulai Hall, in the rear, houses a 29.5-foot-high (9 m) copper seated Maitreya Buddha of the Future. More than 9,000 small Buddhas fill niches in the wall. 🅰 63 D3
✉ 5 Lumicang Hutong ☎ 010/6525-3670
💲 $ 🚇 Metro: Jianguomen

An eclectic hodgepodge of old *hutongs*, idyllic lakes, and quaint old homes dating back to imperial days

Xicheng District

Introduction & Map   84–85

Beihai Park   86–87

Bicycle Tour Around the Forbidden City   88–89

Rear Lakes   90

Mei Lanfang Museum   91

Feature: *Hutongs*   92–93

More Places to Visit in Xicheng District   94

Hotels & Restaurants   298–299

Prayers written on small wooden plaques hang from trees in Beihai Park.

Xicheng District

Xicheng, or the West District, is a romantic lake area that includes Beihai Park (the former romping ground of the Manchu royal family), temples, and a series of lakes ringed by willow trees and *hutong*-lined courtyards. Located between the university area to the northwest and the Forbidden City to the southeast, this area provides a quiet respite from the hustle and bustle of the city center.

Residents do their morning exercises alongside the lake in Beihai Park.

NOT TO BE MISSED:

Strolling and stretching in Beihai Park 86–87

A cycling tour of the Forbidden City 88–89

Visiting the ghost of Madame Soong Qing-ling at her former Jishuitan residence 90

The courtyard mansion of the Mei Lanfang Museum 91

Seeking out the soul of Old Beijing among its myriad *hutongs* 92–93

The age-old Temple of Moon 94

Six connected lakes pierce the eastern edge of Xicheng District. Farthest north are the three Rear Lakes: Xi Hai, Hou Hai, and Qian Hai. In the middle is popular Bei Hai, located just north and west of the Forbidden City. Zhong Hai and Nan Hai are situated to the south, with the walled Communist Party headquarters known as Zhongnanhai standing between them.

All of the rulers who made Beijing their home used the lakes and the beautiful grounds around them as their imperial playground. Rulers of the Jin dynasty built Hortensia Isle, the hill in the middle of Bei Hai. Later the 13th-century Mongol rulers of the Yuan dynasty created an imperial garden here, while the areas around Bei Hai, Zhong Hai, and Nan Hai were the pleasure gardens of the imperial court during the Ming and Qing dynasties.

The Republic of China, which was established in 1911 after the fall of the Qing dynasty, had its presidential office on the shores of Nan Hai until 1925, when the capital was moved to Nanjing. In 1949, after much debate, the party took up residence in Zhongnanhai, making this the center of politics in China. Party officials contemplated a move to the Forbidden City but opted for Xicheng District, fearing that the old imperial city reeked too much of feudalism.

A number of notable figures in Chinese history called Xicheng home, including Princes Gong and Chun, Song Qing-ling (the wife of Sun Yat-sen), and opera star Mei Lanfang. A bike ride provides an excellent opportunity to explore their former residences. ■

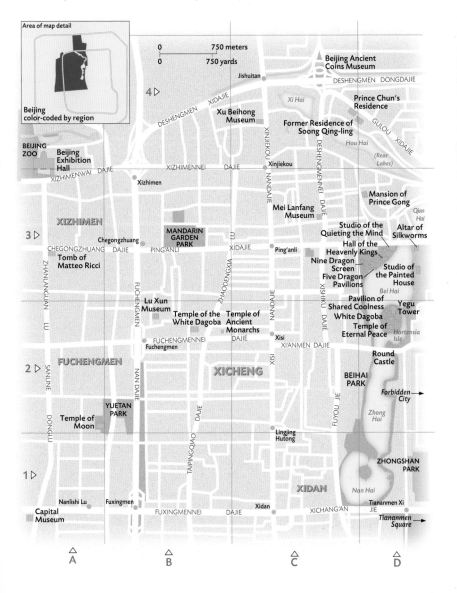

Area of map detail

Beijing color-coded by region

0   750 meters
0   750 yards

Beijing Ancient Coins Museum

Jishuitan

DESHENGMEN DONGDAJIE

4▷

Xi Hai

Prince Chun's Residence

DESHENGMEN XIDAJIE

Xu Beihong Museum

Former Residence of Soong Qing-ling

GULOU XIDAJIE

XINJIEKOU NANDAJIE

DESHENGMENNEI DAJIE

Hou Hai

(Rear Lakes)

BEIJING ZOO

Beijing Exhibition Hall

XIZHIMENWAI DAJIE

XIZHIMENNEI   DAJIE

Xinjiekou

Xizhimen

Mansion of Prince Gong

Qian Hai

Mei Lanfang Museum

XIZHIMEN

3▷

Chegongzhuang

MANDARIN GARDEN PARK

Studio of the Quieting the Mind

Altar of Silkworms

ZHANLANGUAN LU

CHEGONGZHUANG   DAJIE

PING'ANLI

XIDAJIE

Ping'anli

Hall of the Heavenly Kings

Tomb of Matteo Ricci

FUCHENGMEN

ZHAODENGXIA LU

Nine Dragon Screen

Five Dragon Pavilions

Studio of the Painted House

NANDAJIE

XISHIKU DAJIE

Bei Hai

Lu Xun Museum

Pavilion of Shared Coolness

Yegu Tower

Temple of the White Dagoba

Temple of Ancient Monarchs

White Dagoba

FUCHENGMENNEI   DAJIE

Xisi

Temple of Eternal Peace

Hortensia Isle

Fuchengmen

XI'ANMEN DAJIE

2▷

FUCHENGMEN

NAN DAJIE

XICHENG

ISIX

Round Castle

SANLIHE

BEIHAI PARK

Forbidden City

DONGLU

YUETAN PARK

DAJIE

FUYOU JIE

Zhong Hai

Temple of Moon

TAIPINGQIAO

Lingjing Hutong

ZHONGSHAN PARK

1▷

XIDAN

Nan Hai

Nanlishi Lu   Fuxingmen

Xidan

Tiananmen Xi JIE

Capital Museum

FUXINGMENNEI   DAJIE

XICHANG'AN

Tiananmen Square

△   △   △   △
A   B   C   D

Beihai Park

Located to the northwest of the Forbidden City, Beihai Park (Beihai Gongyuan) is a pleasant place to relish the atmosphere of Beijing. The park's many historic and cultural sites—not to mention its idyllic setting—draw families, the faithful, and tourists, all eager to relax, have fun, or find a little peace.

The White Dagoba looms above the trees of Hortensia Isle.

Beihai Park
- 🅰 85 D1–D2
- ✉ 1 Wenjin Jie
- ☎ 010/6403-3225
- 💲 $
- 🚍 Bus: 101, 103, 109, 812, 814, or 846 to Beihai

Round Castle

Begin your visit at the Round Castle (Tuancheng), just inside the South Gate. The castle's main feature is the **Hall of Received Brilliance** (Chengguang Dian), which now houses a large jade Buddha. The Jade Wine Pot, which sits in a glass-enclosed pavilion in front of the hall, is said to date back to the days of Kublai Khan.

Hortensia Isle

After leaving the Round Castle, walk north across the white marble bridge—with archways known as pailous at each end—to Hortensia Isle. Climb the hill to the **Temple of Eternal Peace** (Yong'an Si), a Lamaist temple built by Shunzhi, the first emperor of the Qing dynasty. After this, you will come to the **Hall of the Wheel of the Law** (Falun Dian).

Continue up to the **Hall of Universal Peace** (Pu'an Dian) and the **Hall of True Enlightenment** (Zhengjue Dian). Climb the staircase on either side, which will bring you to the base of an observation tower. The building to the left is the **Hall of Joyful Hearts** (Yuexin Dian), where Qing-dynasty emperors held meetings with senior officials. The **White Dagoba,** which crowns this hill and offers great views of Beijing, is a Tibetan structure that was built in 1651 to mark the visit of the first Dalai Lama to Beijing. It was completely restored after the Tangshan earthquake in 1976.

Behind the dagoba, paths head down the hill. Walk east at the bottom of the hill (with the lake on your left) until you come to a tower called the **Pavilion of Shared Coolness** (Fenliang Ge). This is the beginning of a two-story veranda that winds along the island's north shore. Soon you will reach the **Fangshan Restaurant,** with its huge red door attended by young women dressed in colorful Chinese outfits. Originally opened in 1926, the restaurant, which specializes in imperial cuisine, is moderately expensive but a nice place to stop for a meal.

North End of the Lake

From this area you can take a boat for the short ride across the lake to the **Five Dragon Pavilions** (Wulong Ting) on the north side. Otherwise, head east and pass through the **Tower Leaning Toward the Blue Sky** (Yiqing Lou). Walk across the bridge, then turn left and walk north, with the lake to your left, until you reach the **Haopu Water Pavilions** (Haopu Jian), which were built in 1757, and one of the many inner gardens inside the park. This small garden has roofed corridors and a nice pond.

Return to the main lakeside road and continue heading north. The next building on your right—opposite the teahouse–is the **Studio of the Painted House,** where the emperor once presided over archery contests.

Continue walking until you reach the bridge that will take you to the park's North Gate. Cross the bridge and bear east, left, until you reach the **Studio of Quieting the Mind** (Jingxin Zhai), a garden built in 1758.

Turn right after you exit and walk southwest along the lake's shore until you come to the **Hall of the Heavenly Kings** (Tianwang Dian), a Ming-dynasty workshop. To the northeast is the **Nine Dragon Screen** (Jiulong Bi), one of three such walls in China.

Farther south along the western shore is the **Five Dragon Pavilions** (Wulong Ting), a summer retreat for empresses and high-ranking concubines during the Qing dynasty. Just past

INSIDER TIP:

To visit the Rear Lakes [see p. 90] from Beihai Park, exit through the park's North Gate.

—PAUL MOONEY
National Geographic author

the pavilion is a small **botanical garden.** In the northwest corner of the garden is a pagoda with 16 stone portraits of arhats that were carved during the Qing dynasty.

The final structure is a large square pagoda called **Little Western Heaven** (Xiao Xi Tian), a shrine built in honor of Guanyin Bodhisattva, the mercy Buddha, in 1770. The pagoda is circled by a moat, with four guard towers and four pai-lous. ■

Bicycle Tour Around the Forbidden City

Flat as a Peking duck pancake, Beijing's wide avenues and vast distances are awash with a sea of cyclists. Bicycles have their own broad lanes on many streets, where cyclists jockey for position and lobby for control at junctions. It looks terrifying, but this is one of the best ways to bring this huge city to heel. Go with the flow.

Heading North

Set out on Xichang'an Jie, cycling west between the **Forbidden City** and **Tiananmen Square.** Turn right (north) on Nanchang Jie, the tree-lined road that runs north just to the west of the Forbidden City. Just before the imperial stomping ground of **Beihai Park ❶** (see pp. 86–87), turn left on Wenjin Jie and continue to Xishiku Dajie. Then turn right.

Head toward the Gothic-style **Northern Cathedral ❷** (Bei Tang), Beijing's largest Catholic church. Erected in the 17th century and moved to its present location in 1887, the church was badly damaged in the 1900 Boxer Rebellion and eventually shut down in 1958, after Beijing broke relations with the Vatican. Like most of Beijing's other Christian churches, however, the Northern Cathedral has been renovated. The church reopened in 1985, when the government declared it a cultural relic. With its impressive new stained-glass windows, the church is once again crowded with worshipers on Sunday mornings.

Exit the church and turn right at the next intersection, then turn left. Head north up to Di'anmen Xidajie and then turn right. At the second traffic light, turn left and continue north along Qianhai Xijie to the **former residence of Guo Moruo ❸** (18 Qianhai Xijie, tel 010/6612-5392, closed Mon., $), one of China's most famous contemporary poets, who lived in this courtyard house between 1963 and his death in 1978.

Continue north and turn left at the corner. Follow the gray walls on your right, bearing

NOT TO BE MISSED:

Beihai Park • Mansion of Prince Gong • Residence of Song Qing-ling

right at the end of the block onto Liuyin Jie, where you'll come to the marvelous **Mansion of Prince Gong ❹** (Gong Wang Fu), home of the last Qing emperor's father. The extensive mansion consists of a series of elegant courtyards and gardens.

Backtrack to the crossroads. Turn left (east), along Qianhai Xijie to Houhai Nanyan, passing the entrance to Lotus Lane (Hehua Shichang) on your right, a great place to enjoy a meal or drink beside the lake.

Along the Lake

Leave Lotus Lane at the same point where you entered, and continue along Qian Hai Beiyan to the arched **Silver Ingot Bridge ❺** (Yinding Qiao), just to the north. Cross the bridge and follow the road that runs along the lake on your left.

When you reach the large opening on the right-hand side of Houhai Beiyan, turn and follow the road to **Guanghua Temple ❻** (31 Year Hutong, Houhai), which was constructed during the Yuan dynasty. In the main hall, a large golden Maitreya Buddha, or Milefo in Chinese, is watched over by guards.

Returning to the Wall Ruins

Retrace your steps back to the road along the lake, and go north until you reach the

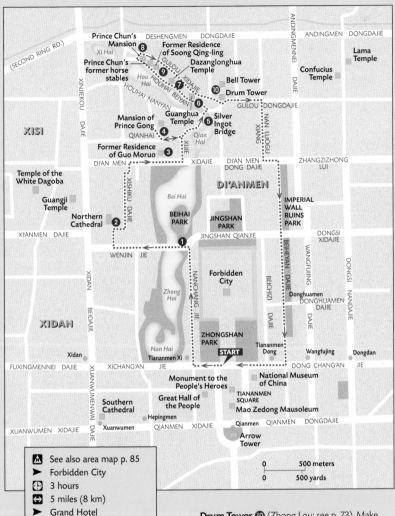

See also area map p. 85

Forbidden City

3 hours

5 miles (8 km)

Grand Hotel

0   500 meters

0   500 yards

Dazanglonghua Temple 7 *(23 Houhai Beiyan),* now a nursery school. Continue on to **Prince Chun's Mansion** 8 (Chun Qinwangfu; *44 Houhai Beiyang*). From here, proceed to the sprawling **former residence of Soong Qing-ling** 9 (see sidebar p. 90).

Exit the complex and head south. Turn left at the first alley, and follow it until you reach a T-intersection. Turn left onto Gulou Xidajie, then turn right and ride to the **Bell Tower** and

Drum Tower 10 (Zhong Lou; see p. 73). Make the steep climb to the top of the towers for an interesting view of the *hutongs* below.

Cycle south to Gulou Dong Dajie, and then head east to **Nan Luogu Xiang** (see p. 82). Turn right on Nan Luogu Xiang and then left on Di'an Men Dong Dajie. The **Imperial Wall Ruins Park** begins at the first intersection. Follow this tree-shaded street south to Dong-hua Men, where you can examine the original foundation of the old city wall. Turn right at Dong Chang'an Jie to reach your starting point.

Rear Lakes

The Rear Lakes is actually a single, crescent-shaped lake divided into three sections: Xi Hai to the north and west, Hou Hai in the center, and Qian Hai to the south and east. This busy, sometimes noisy area is nevertheless a great place for a quick taste of Old Beijing.

Rear Lakes

 85 C1, D1–D4

✉ Ping'an Da Dao

$ $

🚌 Bus: 111, 107, or 108 to Beihai Houmen (rear gate of Beihai Park)

In the 12th century, Jin-dynasty leaders adopted this area as their imperial playgrounds, and the lake—first formed here during the Wei dynasty (ca 250 B.C.)—was incorporated within the new city wall under the Mongols. Gradually Manchus built elaborate homes facing the lakes and in the narrow surrounding hutongs.

In recent years, much of the property facing the once idyllic lakes has been turned into a bustling bar area crowded with cars and rickshaws. Nevertheless, the Rear Lakes is a popular place to pick up traditional treats like candied hawthorn berries and roasted sweet potatoes, as well as other old favorites, such as tripe and sour bean juice.

You can still visit many of the area's historic mansions, such as the **Mansion of Prince Gong** (see p. 88) and the **former residence of Soong Qing-ling** (see sidebar below). You can also visit the **Mei Lanfang Museum** (see p. 91), as well as the **home of Prince Chun** (see p. 89).

For a leisurely hour-long walk, start on the west side of Qian Hai, and go north to the **Silver Ingot Bridge** (Yinding Qiao). Turn right on **Yandai Xiejie,** which has a lot of small boutiques. Return to the bridge and proceed north along Hou Hai with the water on your left. When you reach the lake's northern end, turn left and continue south to the other side of the bridge. Walk along Qian Hai until you reach an archway on your left. This is the pleasant **Lotus Market** (Hehua Shichang).

Soong Qing-ling

Madame Soong Qing-ling was the wife of Sun Yat-sen, the father of the Republic of China. Sun died in 1926, but Soong, who was some 30 years younger, lived more than five decades longer. Her **former residence** (map 85 C4–D4, 46 Houhai Beiyan, tel 010/6404-4205, $, metro: Jishuitan) stands on the northeast shore of Hou Hai, the largest section of the Rear Lakes. She spent her last years in this spacious and well-manicured garden compound, enjoying special status until her death in 1981. Walk around the beautiful grounds and look at Madame Soong's personal possessions and black-and-white photos.

Xu Beihong Museum

Known as the father of modern Chinese art, Xu Beihong (1895–1953) is best known for his realistic portrayal of galloping horses. Located to the west of Xi Hai, the Xu Beihong Museum (map 85 C4, 53 Xinjiekou Bei Dajie, tel 010/6225-2042, closed Mon., $, metro: Jishuitan, bus: 22, 38, 47, 409, 626, or 726 to Xinjiekou Huokou) has seven exhibition halls displaying works from throughout his career. ■

Mei Lanfang Museum

The fame of legendary Beijing opera performaer Mei Lanfang (1891–1961) stretched as far as Europe and the United States. In Beijing opera, all female roles are played by men, and Mei excelled in the role of the *huadan*, a spirited young woman. He visited the United States in 1930, performing in front of enthusiastic audiences and receiving glowing reviews. He made an even bigger splash in Europe, where he made a deep impression on dramatist Bertolt Brecht.

Bust of Beijing opera star Mei Lanfang

Mei's home, an excellent example of the courtyard style of architecture, is alone worth the visit. At the end of the 19th century, it was part of a much larger mansion that belonged to an imperial prince. The house had become quite run-down over the years, but it was renovated for Mei and fitted with Chinese and Western furniture and fixtures.

During the Cultural Revolution in 1966, Red Guards plastered the outer walls with posters attacking the actor's "bourgeois life." His family abandoned the house, which remained closed until 1986 when it was reopened as a museum.

By boosting the status of actors, Mei made a major contribution to Chinese theater. More important, he went against contemporary practice and invited women to perform. The museum features wonderful black-and-white photos from Mei's many performances. An interesting poster hanging in one of the back rooms features pictures of his hand in dozens of traditional Beijing opera poses. ∎

Mei Lanfang Museum

🅰 85 C3
✉ 9 Huguosi Jie
☎ 010/8322-3598
🕐 Closed Mon.
💲 $
🚇 Metro: Changqiao; Bus: 13, 22, 42, 55, 107, or 111

Hutongs

There is probably nothing more representative of old Beijing than its charming—but ever fading—*hutongs* lined with courtyard houses. "To a certain extent, the hutongs and lanes are the soul of Beijing," wrote Liang Bingkun, a well-known Beijing writer, in a book on hutongs.

Young girls play jump rope in an alley.

No one knows how many of these alleyways there are, but according to an old Beijing saying, "There are as many as the number of hairs on an ox," or more than one can count. The Beijing urban planning committee says there were 3,000 hutongs when the Communist Party came to power in 1949, but that only 1,559 still existed in 2003, and hundreds more have disappeared since.

The word hutong is said to come from the Mongolian *hong tong*, which means "water well." And they date back more than seven centuries to the Yuan dynasty (1271–1368), when Kublai Khan built his capital, Dadu, where modern-day Beijing stands.

During imperial days, the names of the hutongs were only passed on orally. It was not until the fall of the Qing dynasty that street signs were hung up on the walls. Many of these names come from the trades that once gathered on these streets. Thus, we have Cotton Hutong, Rice Hutong, Scissors Hutong, Tea Leaf Hutong, and Great Li's Hat Hutong.

Architectural Notes

The smallest hutong in the city stretches just 1.3 feet (0.4 m) wide at its narrow end, which means only one bicycle can head down it at one time. The shortest hutong is no more than 82 feet (25 m) in length, the longest 1.8 miles (3 km).

Architectural details still visible today reveal a great deal about the former inhabitants of these houses. In imperial days, there was a

INSIDER TIP:

To find a small township of *hutongs*, navigate the historic grid southeast of the Bell and Drum Towers [see map p. 89].

—DAMIEN HARPER
National Geographic author

strict hierarchy that dictated style and design. Places with elaborate Chinese gates were the residences of imperial officials or prosperous businessmen; the commoners had basic square-topped gates, known as "eagle will not alight" gates.

There are two to four lintels, usually decorated with auspicious Chinese characters, above each doorway. Common families would have two lintels, wealthy ones four. A typical phrase on the lintels includes the characters *ru yi*, or as you wish. Others say "revolution." Wealthy homes also had decorative door clasps, cymbal-shaped door knockers, and protective brass wrappings often in the shape of a pomegranate—popular because of its many seeds, a wish for many offspring.

When walking through a hutong, note the beautiful carved *mendun*—doorstone. The purpose of which is to provide a brace for the door axle. These stones tell us about the status of the early residents. The bigger the doorstone, the more important the person inside.

The round doorstones represent drums and indicate that the owner has some sort of government tie; rectangular ones graced the homes of scholar-officials, usually found in houses built in the last century. The tops of the stones seat small lions, while the front, right, and left sides are usually carved with flowers and auspicious things, such as magpies, plum blossoms, and gourds.

Normally facing south, the houses are made up of one or more quadrangles, depending on the family's wealth. Five courtyards were the limit because of the streets on the house's

two sides. The exception, of course, was for members of the royal family. Ronald Knapp, an expert on traditional Chinese architecture, notes that the quadrangle complexes "echo on a small scale the plan of the imperial palaces."

The open central courtyard accounts for some 40 percent of the total area, making it bigger than all the combined structures. Narrow verandas provide a covered space to walk around the complex. The surrounding walls and gates offer seclusion, so sitting in a courtyard house, even in a bustling area, allows one to feel miles away.

A pair of traditional brass door knockers

One good way to explore the insides of these houses is by visiting one of the restored homes, which have been transformed into museums. The house of opera legend Mei Lanfang (see p. 91) is an excellent example open to the public.

Over the years, Beijing's old hutongs and their courtyard houses have inspired hundreds of the city's artists and writers. Well-known authors such as Lu Xun, Lao She, and Mao Dun all lived in Beijing courtyard houses. "Without the hutongs, modern Chinese literature in China would only have been half as significant as it is," opines one writer. The same can be said of Chinese art, as famous painters such as Qi Baishi and Xu Beihong also thrived in the old city's beautiful courtyard houses.

More Places to Visit in Xicheng District

Beijing Ancient Coins Museum

Located within the Desheng Gate, the Beijing Ancient Coins Museum (Gudai Qianbi Zhanlan'guan) comprises just two small halls, but they have on display more than a thousand examples of ancient coins and paper money from the past 2,500 years. ⓐ 85 C4 ✉ 9 Deshengmen Dong ☎ 010/6201-8073 🕐 Closed Mon. 💲 $ 🚇 Metro: Deshengmen

Capital Museum

The imposing Capital Museum (Shoudu Bowu-guan) focuses on the history and culture of Beijing. The **second floor** display includes imperial robes, military outfits, ancient horse fittings, and religious items. The **third floor** focuses on urban construction in the ancient capital, while the **fourth floor** has exhibits on Beijing opera and a display about traditional weddings, hutongs, and courtyard architecture. www.capitalmuseum.org.cn ⓐ 85 A1 ✉ 16 Fuxingmennei Dajie ☎ 010/6339-3339 💲 $ 🚇 Metro: Nan Lishi Lu; Bus: Muxidi

Lu Xun Museum

The Lu Xun Museum (Beijing Luxun Bowu-guan) commemorates Lu Xun (1881–1936), one of China's outstanding modern writers, whose short stories include "The Diary of a Madman" (1918) and "The True Story of Ah Q" (1921–1922). The state-of-the-art museum stands next to Lu Xun's former residence. www.luxunmuseum.com.ca ⓐ 85 B2 ✉ 19 Gongmenkou Ertiao, Fuchengmennei Dajie, beside Baita Si ☎ 010/6616-4169 or 010/6616-4080 🕐 Closed Mon. 💲 $ 🚇 Metro: Fuchengmen

Temple of Ancient Monarchs

The little-known Temple of Ancient Monarchs (Lidai Diwang Miao) was built some 470 years ago by Ming-dynasty emperors to worship their ancestors, but the ceremonies came to an end with the fall of the Qing dynasty. Ask at the ticket window for the printed guide. ⓐ 85 B2 ✉ 131 Fuchengmennei Dajie ☎ 010/6612-0186 💲 $ 🚌 Bus: 101, 103, 109, 812, 814, 846 to Baita Si

Temple of the White Dagoba

When construction was completed in 1279, the 150-foot-high (48 m) Yuan-dynasty Temple of the White Dagoba (Baita Si) was considered one of the highlights of the Mongols' new capital. The four remaining halls date to the Qing dynasty. ⓐ 85 B2 ✉ 171 Fuchengmennei Dajie ☎ 010/6616-6099 💲 $ 🚇 Metro: Fuchengmen

Tomb of Matteo Ricci

Matteo Ricci was a Jesuit priest who came to China in the late Ming dynasty. Constructed of square bricks and surrounded by a brick wall, his 17th-century tomb is entered through an iron latticework gate. The gate to the burial place is locked and entrance gained only by prior arrangement. ⓐ 85 A3 ✉ 6 Chegong-zhuang Dajie (inside Beijing Communist Party School) ☎ 010/6800-7279 (Foreign Affairs Office of the Beijing Communist Party School) 🕐 By appt. 💲 $ 🚇 Metro: Chegongzhuang

---

Temple of Moon

Built in 1530, the Temple of Moon (Yuetan Gongyuan; map 85 A2, 6 Yuetan Beijie, tel 010/6802-0940, $, metro: Nan Lishi Lu) was the site of imperial sacrifices to the moon. Enter at the north gate. Just past the bell tower is a section of the **Ming-dynasty wall,** now enclosed in protective glass. From the **East Gate of the Altar,** a prominent three-tiered gate with cloud designs, walk south and turn right to reach the **Sacrificial Slaying Pavilion.** Keep heading south to explore the park's newer section.

Offering a slice of the past, with theaters, acrobatic halls, and shops and restaurants that continue to flourish after more than a century

Chongwen District

Introduction & Map   96–97

Temple of Heaven   98–101

Feature: Legation Quarter   102–103

Experience: Walking in the Steps of History   103

Legation Quarter Walking Tour   104–105

More Places to Visit in Chongwen District   106

Hotels & Restaurants   299

Colorful painted umbrellas for sale at a Beijing stall

Chongwen District

One of the four districts that originally composed the old city, Chongwen District has a completely different feel from other parts of Beijing, which traditionally have been more residential or historically significant. Still rich in local color and bursting with energy, it also contains some intriguing sights—most notably, the breathtaking Temple of Heaven.

The lively Qianmen Dajie draws crowds day and night.

NOT TO BE MISSED:

Shopping in the faux-historic quarter around Qianmen Dajie 97

Contemplating the cosmic harmonies of the Temple of Heaven 98–101

A walk through Beijing's cosmopolitan past in the Legation Quarter 104–105

The fabulous Beijing Mumingtang Ancient Porcelain Museum 106

Modern art at the Red Gate Gallery in Dongbianmen Watchtower 106

Qianmen Dajie, the street running directly south of Tiananmen Square, is located just outside Qianmen, or the Front Gate. It has been a bustling commercial area for 500 years. Before the communists took control of the city and curtailed capitalist practices in 1949, the area was packed with street peddlers, small stores, and some of the city's most famous *laozihao*, or old brand-name shops, some dating back more than a hundred years. According to legend, some emperors would sneak out of the Forbidden City disguised as merchants to enjoy a meal or a night in one of the many "song houses" in this small, colorful neighborhood.

Today, the warren of narrow streets around Qianmen that compose Chongwen District is packed with tourists and locals, cars and bikes, rickshaws and carts, all fighting for every inch of free space. The area is overloaded with peddlers hawking their goods and restaurants spilling out onto the sidewalk. Enter any *hutong* and you'll find yourself immediately rubbing elbows—and a bit more—with everyone else.

In this nearly forgotten little district you'll discover one of the city's most splendid structures, the fabled Temple of Heaven, once the holiest shrines in China. The Ming Dynasty City Wall Ruins Park holds a reconstructed section of the city's original inner wall, dating from 1419; now landscaped, it's a popular refuge for city dwellers. Here, too, is the Legation Quarter, the 19th-century foreign enclave where remnants of European-style architecture still survive.

In the run up to the 2008 Olympics, Qianmen Dajie and its adjacent alleyways underwent a large-scale renovation that saw many old buildings—even entire streets— disappear. The old China brand stores were rehoused in rebuilt faux-historic buildings, next to contemporary main-street brands and coffee chains. There's even a 1920s-style tram running up and down the street for shoppers too lazy to walk. Chinese shoppers and tourist flock here in the thousands. ■

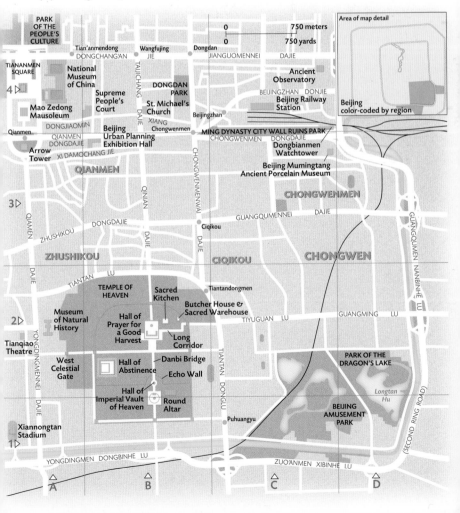

Temple of Heaven

The Temple of Heaven (Tian Tan) is one of China's finest examples of religious architecture. Construction began in 1406 and took 14 years to complete. Emperor Qianlong later carried out an extensive renovation of the complex, which has three main buildings, where ritual ceremonies took place, and a host of other Taoist structures associated with sacred rites.

A worker's daily ritual at the Temple of Heaven

Temple of Heaven

🔼 97 B1–B2

✉ Yongdingmen Dongjie (south gate)

☎ 010/6702-8866

💲 $ (extra fee for Yuanqiu & Qinian Dian)

🚌 Bus: 2 or 35 to Tiantan Ximen; 36, 53, 120, or 122 to Tiantan Nanmen

www.tiantanpark .com

Each year during the winter solstice, Ming- and Qing-dynasty emperors visited the Temple of Heaven in their capacity as the Son of Heaven in order to offer their prayers, make sacrifices for a good harvest, and present the annual ceremonial report to heaven of the events in the past year.

For three days before the rituals began, the emperor would not drink wine, or eat meat or pungent vegetables, such as garlic and scallions. Instead, he ate simple vegetable dishes. He also abstained from sex.

The day before the ceremony, the emperor departed the Forbidden City via the Wu Men, carried in a yellow palanquin (litter) that was borne by 16 men. He was accompanied by ceremonial elephants, his master of ceremonies, a cavalry escort packing bows and arrows, dancers, musicians, and eunuchs on horseback decked out in gorgeous robes and carrying paraphernalia for the various rites. Following all these were the imperial standard-bearers—in all, more than 200 people composed the procession.

The procession, which stretched for several miles, continued south all the way to the west gate of the temple complex, where the emperor made his grand entrance. After he arrived, he would take a ritual bath then spend the night fasting in the Hall of Abstinence.

The winter solstice ceremony was last held by a Manchu in 1910, during the regency of Puyi (see sidebar p. 32), the last emperor, when he was just four years old. In 1914, would-be emperor Yuan Shikai, president of the new republic, performed the sacrifice for the last time. In 1918 the public was admitted.

Round Altar

The Round Altar (Yuanqiu Tan or Yuanqiu), also known as the Circular Mound, was added to the temple complex in 1530. It's an open altar erected on three round marble terraces, surrounded by two sets of walls. The outer square wall represents Earth, while the inner circular wall represents heaven.

It was at this altar that, on the solstice, the emperor would present his annual ceremonial report to heaven on the events of the past year. In addition to this report, he would offer animal sacrifices to implore of heaven a good harvest in the upcoming year. The most important sacrifice was an unblemished ox, which was ritually burned in the small oven decorated with green tiles that's located in front of the altar; it would then be "delivered" to heaven via smoke.

Hall of the Imperial Vault of Heaven

Just to the north of the Round Altar is the Hall of the Imperial Vault of Heaven (Huangqiong Yu), which is encircled by the traditional symbol of heaven: a round wall. The structure, which sits on a marble platform, is capped with blue tiles and was once home to the spirit tablets of Shangdi, which were used in the ritual ceremony associated with the Round Altar.

The circular brick wall surrounding the imperial vault is known as the **Echo Wall** (Huiyin Bi) or the Whispering Wall, since its design allows two people standing at opposite points on the wall to hear each other speaking softly. A second phenomenon is the **"echo stones,"** the first three rectangular stones at the foot of the staircase leading up to the imperial vault. If you stand on the first stone at the foot of the incline and clap your hands once, you'll hear one echo. Clap once on the second stone, and you'll hear two echoes. A single clap from the third stone will be answered with three echoes.

> ## Visiting the Temple
>
> The temple complex lies in the midst of a great park popular with Beijing residents. The temple's design emphasizes the basic tenets of imperial religious belief, with repeating symbols of heaven and earth: circles and squares, for example, and colors such as blue and yellow. Even the shape of the park follows this principle: The northern end is semicircular, for heaven, and the southern end is square, for earth. You can enter the park through any of several gates. If you enter through the south gate and proceed north to the triple gate, you'll be in front of the Round Altar. From here you can proceed to the Hall of the Imperial Vault of Heaven, Hall of Abstinence, Divine Music Bureau, Hall of Prayer for a Good Harvest, and Long Corridor.

Exit the Hall of the Imperial Vault of Heaven at the south gate where you entered. Turn right and look for the path heading east. You'll soon come to a triple gate. Turn right here and walk to the Hall of Abstinence.

Hall of Abstinence

Destroyed by fire in 1807 and immediately rebuilt, the Hall of Abstinence (Zhai Gong) was where the emperor met his ministers and fasted for three days before the sacred rites were held. It is surrounded by a moat once guarded by eunuchs. The main hall is also known as the Beamless Hall because no beams support the roof.

The sleeping quarters behind the main hall contain two imperial bedrooms. The emperor slept in the southern chamber during the summer and in the northern one on the night before the winter solstice rituals. The northern room had a *kang,* a brick bed heated by wood burning underneath.

Exit the Hall of Abstinence, and turn back south to the main path. Turn right and walk to the Divine Music Bureau.

INSIDER TIP:

Arrive at the park early in the morning, when the grounds are full of people singing, practicing *tai ji quan,* dancing, playing badminton, and more.

—MARY STEPHANOS
National Geographic contributor

Divine Music Bureau

The Divine Music Bureau (Shenyue Shu), which has been rebuilt, was the site of a Taoist temple during the Ming dynasty. When the Temple of Heaven was first built, it included a hall dedicated to Guan Di, the patron saint of Manchu emperors. The structure was enlarged and later turned into a music hall, where musicians and dancers were trained before

they took part in imperial rituals. The complex now houses exhibits on ancient Chinese ritual music, dance, and instruments.

Return to the outside path and turn left. Walk north until you reach the **West Celestial Gate** (Xi Tianmen). Turn right at the gate and proceed down a path, shaded by scholar trees, to the **Danbi Bridge** (Danbi Qiao), a raised causeway. Turn left after the bridge and proceed to the most impressive structure in the Temple of Heaven complex—the Hall of Prayer for a Good Harvest.

Hall of Prayer for a Good Harvest

Perhaps the most celebrated building in Beijing, the hall was first built in 1420 during the reign of Yongle, whose geomancers determined this as the point where heaven and earth meet. The hall was the focus of prayers for fruitful harvests.

It was rebuilt in 1545 into a triple-eaved structure that glistened with blue, yellow, and green glazed tiles. This chromatic scheme symbolized, in turn, heaven, earth, and the mortal world. Qing emperor Qianlong replaced the tiles with the present azure roofing to symbolize sky.

The beautiful conical roof symbolizes the extent of heaven. The 120-foot-high (36.5 m) vault was skillfully slotted together without nails. The four inner pillars represent the seasons, and two sets of 12 columns denote the months and the division of the 24-hour day into two-hour units.

Exit through the hall's east gate and walk to the Long Corridor.

Long Corridor

The Long Corridor (Chang Lang) is a covered walkway that takes you past the **Sacred Kitchen, Butcher House** (Zaisheng Ting), and **Sacred Warehouse** (Shenku), where the products for sacrifice were kept and prepared before the rituals. The 72 bays of the Long Corridor, which linked these buildings, were built to keep the weather from damaging the offerings. At midnight on the day of the sacrifice, they were carried from the Long Corridor to the altar.

You can exit the park at the east gate, which is just past the Long Corridor, or return to the south gate where you started. ■

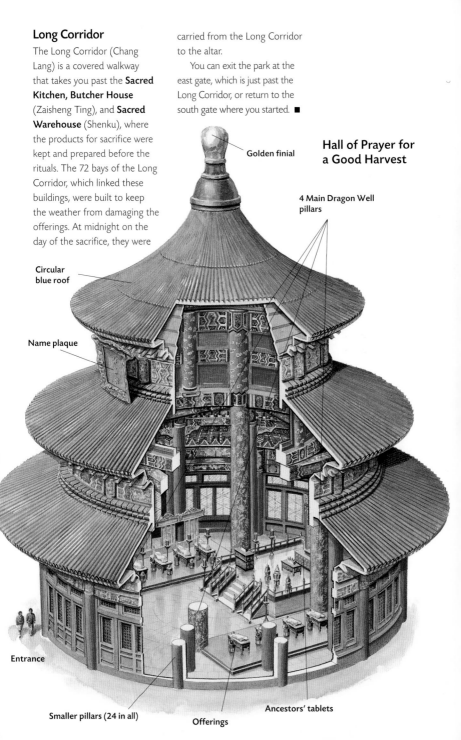

Hall of Prayer for a Good Harvest

Golden finial

4 Main Dragon Well pillars

Circular blue roof

Name plaque

Entrance

Smaller pillars (24 in all)

Offerings

Ancestors' tablets

Legation Quarter

Bordering Dongjiaomin Xiang, east of Tiananmen Square, Beijing's Legation Quarter is where a number of foreign powers set up consulates and businesses in the late 19th century. They built lavish, Western-style churches, banks, embassies, and a post office that, alas, suffered severe devastation during the Boxer Rebellion of 1900. Nevertheless, a visit evokes a sense of bygone times.

The site of the former Yokohama Species Bank in the old Legation Quarter

History

Dongjiaomin Xiang, literally "eastern alley where the people mingle," has long been a foreign ghetto. The street is thus named because it was here that Manchus hosted envoys from states such as Mongolia, Korea, Vietnam, Burma, and Tibet, who came to pay their obeisance to China's emperors. During the Yuan dynasty, the street was known as Dongjiangmi Xiang, or Eastern Alley of Glutinous Rice, because

boats sailing north on the Grand Canal, carrying rice and other goods, supplied a neighborhood market here. When the Grand Canal fell into disuse, the street's name was changed to its present one.

The Russians were the first to open an embassy here, in 1727, although some sources say the Russian presence goes back more than a century earlier. It was more than a hundred years later before England and France gained a foothold on the street, only after their soldiers

The former U.S. Embassy now houses the Maison Boulud restaurant of celebrity chef Daniel Boulud *(tel 010/6559-9200, www.danielnyc.com/maison boulud_chinese_en.html).*

—GARY BOWERMAN
National Geographic contributor

trashed the Old Summer Palace during the Opium War (1856–1860). The right of other countries to establish a mission here was one of the terms of the infamous 1858 Treaty of Tianjin. The court had apparently tried to dupe the foreigners into moving out by the Old Summer Palace, a ruse to keep them outside the city. They refused. Over the years, a number of foreign banks and other businesses set up in the foreign enclave. Every architect who built here tried to re-create a piece of his own country, which explains the clashing architectural styles.

During the Boxer Rebellion of 1900 (see pp. 33, 36), the Legation Quarter was under attack by the Boxers (the Group of Righteous Harmony) for nearly two months until the Eight Nation Alliance lifted the siege.

The end came less than two months later when an 18,000-man joint military force, made up of American, British, French, German, Italian, Japanese, and Russian troops, entered Beijing. The resulting 1901 Peace Protocol paved the way for more foreign governments to open consulates and businesses here.

The Legation Quarter continued to serve as an embassy area after liberation and during the 1950s, when many foreign companies followed the defeated Nationalist government to Taiwan. Some of the embassies that stayed behind—mainly from Eastern bloc countries— moved northeast of here in the late 1950s.

What to See

Among the structures that survived are the twin-spired **St. Michael's Church** at the corner of Taijichang Dajie and Dongjiao-min Xiang; the buildings of the **Belgian Embassy** across from the church; and a former **French Post Office** at 19 Dongjiao-min Xiang. You can also see the **arched gate** of the entrance to the former Japanese Legation on Zhengyi Lu near the British Legation, which is now part of State Security buildings. The **Huafeng Hotel,** south on Zhengyi Lu, occupies the former site of the Grand Hotel des Wagons-Lits, dating from 1905. The walk described on pages 104–105 provides an intimate tour of the old quarter.

EXPERIENCE: Walking in the Steps of History

The area around the Legation Quarter and ancient Tartar Wall is imbued with mystery, intrigue, and folklore. The **Dongbianmen Watchtower** was known as the Fox Tower, because historically it overlooked a derelict and dangerous area beyond the city wall that was believed to be haunted by ill-willed fox spirits. Retrace the history of the fascinating district of old Beijing that bordered the city wall—known as the Badlands, because of its reputation for vice, crime, and squalor—by following the walking map and self-guided audio tour on the website of Paul French's book *Midnight in Peking* (www.midnightinpeking.com). This dramatic tale of the unsolved 1930s murder of a young Englishwoman in the Legation Quarter details a period in time when Beijing was living under Japanese invasion. The walk begins at the scene of the crime, the Fox Tower, and winds through both ancient *hutongs* and the more genteel Legation Quarter.

Legation Quarter Walking Tour

The Legation Quarter on Dongjiaomin Xiang is today a pale shadow of its former self. This street features a surprising amount of historic European architecture, but it is going fast—and in many instances you have to peek over walls or through cracks to see what has survived. Most interesting are the old French Catholic church, St. Michael's, the Yokohama Species Bank, and the former National City Bank of New York.

The old French Post Office, now a Sichuan restaurant, on Dongjiaomin Xiang

Begin your walk on Dongjiaomin Xiang, most easily reached by entering the lobby of the Novotel Xinqiao Hotel and exiting through the back door. At the intersection with Taijichang Dajie, you'll come to one of the more prominent landmarks in the neighborhood, **St. Michael's Catholic Church ❶**. Built by French Vincentian priests in 1902, the Gothic church, with nice stained-glass windows and beautiful ceilings, is packed on Sundays—the only time the gate is unlocked for visitors.

The red building opposite the church is the former **Belgian Embassy ❷**. After liberation in 1949, it became the Burmese Embassy; today it is part of the Ruijin Hotel.

On the north side of the street is No. 15, the location of the former **French Legation ❸**, which was destroyed during the Boxer Rebellion. This was once the property of a Manchu

NOT TO BE MISSED:

St. Michael's Catholic Church
• **Yokohama Species Bank**
• **Beijing Police Museum**

prince fallen on hard times. The old **French Post Office** is now a restaurant.

Located at No. 28, **Hongdu Tailors ❹** is a Beijing *laozihao* (traditional shop) that served top Communist Party officials. Nearby once stood Keirulf's, the first shop serving foreigners in Beijing. The Chinese were adamantly opposed to the shop opening here as foreign trade was strictly forbidden in the city. But foreign ministers argued that they needed the biscuits, condensed milk, cotton, and horse saddles that

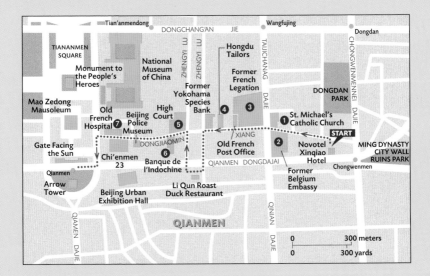

the shop offered. Ironically, it was the Chinese who became its most loyal customers.

The grand looking building at the northeast corner of Zhengyi Lu was formerly the **Yokohama Species Bank.** It's now a Chinese bank, so feel free to have a look inside.

There's a pleasant patch of greenery running down the center of Zhengyi Lu, which was built in 1925 when the old rice-bearing canal was filled in. Walk down to Qianmen Dong Dajie and cross the street. Here you can plunge through the alleyways to **Li Qun Roast Duck Restaurant,** located in an old courtyard house. Stacks of fruitwood piled outside are ready for roasting. Or take a rickshaw to the Underground City (see p. 106) nearby.

Return to Dongjiaomin Xiang and continue walking west. In the middle of the next block on your right is the gleaming new headquarters of China's **High Court ⑤**, the former site of the Russian legation. One original gate remains.

On the opposite side is the old **Banque de l'Indochine ⑥**, which was first occupied by Americans. A bit farther down the street is a building with thick Roman columns that was first the Russia Asiatic Bank and later the National City Bank of New York, marked by the fading letters "NCB" at the top of the building.

> 🅰 See also area map p. 97
> ▶ Novotel Xinqiao Hotel
> 🕐 90 minutes
> ↔ 1.5 miles (2.4 km)
> ▶ Tiananmen Square

Today it has been converted into the **Beijing Police Museum** (36 Dongjiaomin Xiang, tel 010/8522-5018, $).

Still farther down the street is the old **French Hospital ⑦** and opposite this is Chienmen 23, an estate of restored heritage buildings, including the century-old **American Legation**, that have been converted into upscale restaurants, including Maison Boulud, Ristorante Sadler, and Shanghai -based Lost Heaven, plus a boutique by Patek Philippe.

Directly across Qianmen Dongdajie is the **Beijing Urban Planning Exhibition Hall** (see p. 106) with interactive exhibits showing the capital's ongoing metropolitan makeover. It also houses a repertory theater, art gallery, café, and an outdoor concert space.

From here you can walk down the short flight of steps that leads to **Tiananmen Square** (see pp. 70–72), where you can visit the old **Arrow Tower** (Jian Lou) and the **Zhengyang Gate.**

The urban planning museum offers a bird's-eye view of Beijing's layout.

More Places to Visit in Chongwen District

Beijing Mumingtang Ancient Porcelain Museum

If you like pottery, be sure to visit the Beijing Mumingtang Ancient Porcelain Museum (Beijing Mumingtang Guci Biaoben Bowuguan), which boasts a collection of more than 50,000 pieces of porcelain. Spanning the 7th through the 20th centuries, the museums exhibits number more than a thousand.
🅰 97 C3 ✉ 1 Huashi Beili Dongqu
☎ 010/6718-7266 💲 $ 🚇 Bus: 43, 44, or 800 to Dongbianmen; Bus: 12, 610, or 723 to Baiqiao Dajie

Beijing Urban Planning Exhibition Hall

The Urban Planning Exhibition Hall (Beijing Chengshi Guihua Zhanlanguan) examines the history and future of planning in Beijing. A balcony overlooks a scale model of the city, equivalent to viewing the city at 20,000 feet, and there is an interesting section on the city's comprehensive construction overhaul ahead of hosting the 2008 Olympic games. The hall also shows 3-D films about urban planning. *www.bjghzl.com.cn*
🅰 97 B3 ✉ 20 Qianmen Dong Dajie
☎ 010/6701-7074 💲 $ 🚇 Metro: Qianmen

Dongbianmen Watchtower

The last remaining watchtower in the city,

the imposing Dongbianmen Watchtower today hosts the **Red Gate Gallery,** which exhibits the work of contemporary Chinese artists. The second and third floors of the tower, which was formerly the Fox Tower, are devoted to the history of the Chongwen District, with some interesting historic photos and artifacts on display.
🅰 97 C4 ✉ 9 Chongwenmen Dongdajie
☎ 010/6527-0574 💲 $ 🚇 Metro: Jianguomen, then walk south; Metro: Chongwenmen, then walk east; or Bus 44 to Dongbianmen

Ming Dynasty City Wall Ruins Park

A reconstructed section of Beijing's old inner-city wall, Ming Dynasty City Wall Ruins Park (Ming Chengqiang Yizhi Gongyuan) is a nicely landscaped area with paths.
🅰 97 C4 ✉ Chongwenmen Dongdajie

Museum of Natural History

Originally founded in 1951, shortly after the Communist revolution, the Museum of Natural History (Ziran Bowuguan) presents the evolution and development of man over the last 300 million years. Kids in particular will be engaged by the Gallery of Ancient Reptiles, including a skeleton of the first known dinosaur uncovered in China. *www.bmnh.org.cn*
🅰 97 A2 ✉ 126 Tianqiao Nan Dajie ☎ 010/6702-7702 💲 $ 🚇 Bus: 2, 6, 15, 17, 20, 25,35, 36, 45, 53, 110, or 120 to Tianqiao

Beijing's oldest district, whose colorful culture remains alive in the many old shops, temples, and churches that still grace its streets

Xuanwu District

Introduction & Map   108–109

Liulichang   110–111

Experience: Temple Fair
   Tradition   111

Qianmen Dajie & Dashilan
   Walk   112–113

Source of Law Temple   114

Ox Street Mosque   115

Feature: Gods & Goddesses   116–117

White Cloud Temple   118–119

More Places to Visit in Xuanwu
   District   120

Hotels & Restaurants   299–300

The dragon and the snake are two of the 12 animals in the Chinese zodiac.

Xuanwu District

The Xuanwu District (Xuanwu Qu) is considered the birthplace of Beijing. For some 3,000 years Chinese from around the country have come here to make their fortunes. In turn they have helped the city prosper and created history.

At the Source of Law Temple, a golden Buddha stares out from his perch at a passing monk.

During the Qing dynasty, the government decreed that Han Chinese and Manchus must live in separate districts. Located just outside the imperial inner city, Xuanwu was the home of the common classes, aristocrats, merchants, and scholars. Provincial guildhalls set up around the district catered to wealthy merchants visiting from all over China and to scholars who came to take the imperial civil service exam.

NOT TO BE MISSED:

Browsing in the *laozihao*, Beijing's old brand-name shops 108

Buying art supplies in Liulichang, Beijing's old art street 110–111

Welcoming the Chinese New Year at the Liulichang Temple Fair 111

Walking through Dashilan 112–113

The Buddha, in statuesque splendor, at the Source of Law Temple 114

Exploring the Muslim Quarter 115

The White Cloud Temple 118–119

The variou s people living here all contributed to commerce in the district, and prosperity led to the establishment of ever more shops, many of which are still in business today. The Dashilan area, with a history going back 570 years, is home to many *laozihao*, or old brand-name shops. The street names that remain today in Xuanwu District are a testimony to the area's once bustling commercialism: Caishikou, or "vegetable market"; Meishijie, or "coal market"; Guozixiang, or "fruit market"; and Zhubaoshi, or "jewelry market."

Xuanwu District is also famous as the birthplace of Beijing opera and provided stages for hundreds of opera stars—including the legendary Tan Xinpei, Yang Xiaolou, Mei Lanfang, and Ma Lianliang—who lived in the area's narrow lanes. As a result, out of the city's alleyways grew an entire industry of producing costumes, musical instruments, and props used in opera productions across the city.

The district had an extensive face-lift in preparation for the 2008 Olympics, which unfortunately erased many old buildings and streets. The area still has much to offer,

however. The busy Dashilan area, for example, has its laozihao and old theaters. Liulichang, long the gathering place of the literati, still sells the "Four Treasures of the Studio" (ink, brushes, paper, and inkstones). Beijing's Muslim faithful crowd the bustling Ox Street Mosque, while Dashilan is also peppered with colorful ancient Buddhist and Taoist temples–such as the White Cloud Temple–and Ming-dynasty Catholic churches that are once again crowded on Sunday mornings. ■

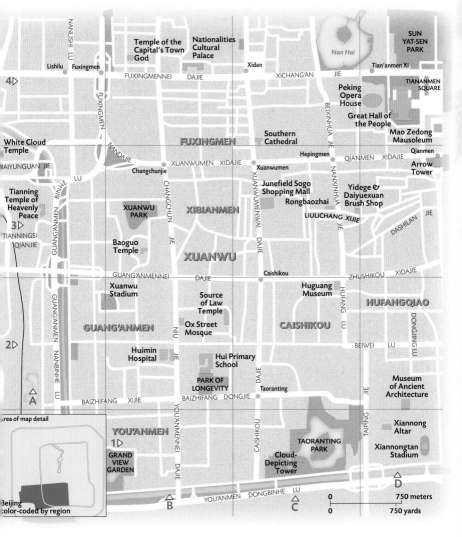

Liulichang

Liulichang, Beijing's old art street, is where the literati, painters, and calligraphers of the Ming and Qing dynasties gathered to shop for rice paper, calligraphy brushes, inkstones, art, antiques, and other items. It is possible that they even met to compose a few lines of poetry over a pot of tea.

A man examines a calligraphy brush along Liulichang.

Liulichang

 109 C3

✉ Liulichang Xijie & Liulichang Dongjie

 Metro: Hepingmen, then Bus: 7, 14, or 15 to Liulichang

History

The name Liulichang translates as "glazed tile factory." This lively and beautiful old street was originally famous for its kilns, in which Chinese craftsmen began making glazed tiles in the 13th century, during the Yuan dynasty. About a century later, when the emperors of the Ming dynasty began to build their imperial palaces in Beijing, the tile factory in Liulichang was expanded and became one of five factories under the direction of the Board of Works. Most of the glazed pieces that were used in the Ming-dynasty halls and palaces that were built on the order of Emperor

Yongle were made here. Clay and other raw materials needed by the tile factory were brought to the area via the canals nearby.

During the Qing dynasty, Liulichang became a residential neighborhood for officials who worked for the Manchus. Provincial and prefectural guesthouses provided lodging for visiting business people and for candidates taking the imperial exams, who would spend hours wandering the shops and selling the tools of the intellectual trade. It is said that, by the late 17th and early 18th centuries, Liulichang had become a bustling cultural center and that the "homes and buildings lined up like fish scales."

EXPERIENCE: Temple Fair Tradition

Despite the cold, Chinese Lunar New Year is best celebrated on the streets. Wrap up warm and join locals at a colorful temple fair, which are held outside temples in neighborhoods across Beijing during the weeklong New Year holiday. These *miao hui* fairs date from the Ming dynasty when farmers dedicated sacrifices to the village gods for Spring Festival in the hope of a propitious new year ahead. The **Liulichang Temple Fair**, which spreads across the *hutong* streets around Nanxinhua Jie, is one of the city's most photogenic and family-friendly celebrations. Watch calligraphers paint ancient poems on the cobbled streets, enjoy street performances and local folk songs, and devour winter treats sold by street vendors, such as roasted sweet potatoes, hot chestnuts, candied hawberries, and sweet crepes. Other temple fair locations include **Chaoyang Park** and the **White Cloud Temple**. For organized temple fair tours see **China Culture Center Tours** *(tel 10/6432-9341, www.chinaculturecenter .org/tours)* and **Beijing Urban Adventures** *(tel 139/1176-4908, www.beijingurban adventures.com/events)*.

Visiting Liulichang

Once home to antiquarians, the goods sold on any street were known by the street's name, such as Jade Street, Embroidery Street, and Lantern Street. It was common for merchants and artisans who were members of the same guild to live in the same area.

Today this area continues to sell many of the items it was famous for a century ago, and it remains a fun place to explore, despite having been turned into what looks like a touristy and unrealistic set for an old Chinese movie. **Cuiwenge** *(58–60 Liulichang Dongjie)* carves traditional Chinese seals, or chops. At **Yidege** *(67 Liulichang Dongjie)* you can buy old-fashioned India ink sticks, which the company has been making for calligraphers and painters since 1865. Yidege ink is made of high-pigment carbon black using traditional methods. The sticks are rubbed in water on an inkstone until the required consistency is reached.

Selling inkstones and thick calligraphy brushes for close to a century, the **Daiyuexuan Brush Shop** *(73 Liulichang Dongjie)* produces several types of writing brushes, including *yang hao* (goat hair) and *ang hao* (wolf hair). **Xinghai Yuehaixuan Musical Instruments** *(97 Liulichang Dongjie)* is the place to buy traditional musical instruments.

Cross Xinhua to West Liulichang Xijie and stop by **Rongbaozhai** *(19 Liulichang Xijie),* which still sells the "Four Treasures of the Studio": ink, brushes, paper, and inkstones. The shop also sells scrolls and woodblock prints. It is said that the master painter Qi Baishi could not distinguish a Rongbaozhai wood-block from his original. ∎

INSIDER TIP:

Liulichang is the place to come for souvenirs, ersatz imperial porcelain, and momentos.

—DAMIEN HARPER
National Geographic author

Qianmen Dajie & Dashilan Walk

The Dashilan area of Xuanwu was the home of many Qing-era *laozihao*, or old brand-name shops. "Ruifuxiang and Tongrentang should be preserved for ten thousand years," wrote Mao Zedong in the ultimate testament to their popularity. This walk will take you past—and into—many of these time-honored shops, and up to Liulichang.

The walk begins on **Zhubaoshi Jie,** a narrow street with small shops. Head down the street until you arrive at a narrow alleyway on your right—**Qianshi Hutong ❶,** or Money Alley, said to be the narrowest *hutong* in the city. During the Qing dynasty and early years of the Republic, this was the official financial market and mint for Beijing, as well as the place where private banks determined the exchange rate between silver and copper cash. The last building here **(No. 7)** houses the vault. It's said that the alleyway was deliberately narrow to deter bandits. Nevertheless, soldiers and bandits did rob the place during an uprising in 1912.

Retrace your steps to Zhubaoshi Jie and continue past the Republican-era buildings on your right and onto Qianmen Dajie pedestrianized

NOT TO BE MISSED:

Money Alley • Ruifuxiang Silk Store
•Tongrentang • Neiliansheng

street. Around 300 feet (90 m) along this street, turn right onto Dashilan Dajie.

The first old shop you will run across is **Liubiju** *(No. 3)* on the left-hand side, a century-old foodstore with a huge counter selling Chinese pickles and sauces from huge porcelain pots. Next door is **Ruifuxiang Silk Store ❷** *(No. 5),* which began selling bolts of cloth to the royal nobility, high-ranking officials, actors, and wealthy families in 1893. The first national flag unfurled by Mao Zedong at the founding of the People's Republic of China in 1949 was made from silk that came from this shop. The tailors can turn out suits for men and *qipaos* for women.

Established in 1908, the **Zhang Yiyuan Tea Store** *(No. 22)* sells hundreds of different types of tea. China's most famous traditional Chinese medicine company is **Tongrentang ❸** *(No. 24).* The large and colorful building, is easy to pick out especially because of the thick herbal smell emanating from the front door. Enter the shop and you'll see deer antlers, shark fins, royal jelly *(fengwang jiang),* dried lizards, sea horses, and black ants. *Lingzhi,* a type of grass soaked in wine or cooked in soup with red dates, wolfberry, and pork, will supposedly cure a variety of ailments—diabetes, high blood pressure, cancer, allergies, and more. Such cures don't come cheap, however.

Founded during the Qing dynasty, **Neiliansheng ❹** *(No. 34),* has been making shoes since 1853. Popular for their bright black satin and the 32 layers of cloth used to make their soles, the

Displayed for customers, a variety of Chinese teas sits in porcelain bowls.

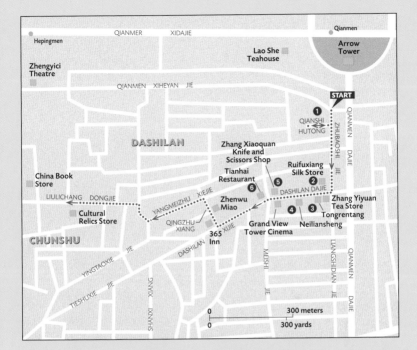

See also area map p. 109

▶ Zhubaoshi Jie

⏱ 90 minutes

↔ 1.5 miles (2.4 km)

▶ Liulichang

court shoes of Neiliansheng soon became a mark of high status. But don't come here if you need your new shoes in a hurry—it takes three months to have a pair of shoes custom made.

On your left, at No. 36, the **Grand View Tower Cinema** (Danguanlou Yingyuan), China's oldest cinema, first began showing films in 1905 and still shows movies. The Chinese Film Gallery lobby displays an old projector as well as a series of black-and-white photos of old movie stars and the history of Chinese cinema. The café in the rear serves coffee and tea.

The **Zhang Xiaoquan Knife and Scissors Shop** ❺ (No. 37), which stands opposite, stocks cutting utensils in all shapes and sizes. The record-setting King Scissors model is 3.8 feet (115 cm) long and weighs 125 pounds (57 kg), while the smallest pair of scissors is only 1.2 inches (3 cm) long. Special scissors can be bought for cracking pine nuts, sunflower seeds, and melon seeds. The shop also carries very long knives for slicing watermelons, the official fruit of Beijing.

Cross Meishi Jie and proceed down Guanyin Si Jie, which is also known as Dashilan Xijie. On the corner stands the **Tianhai Restaurant** ❻ (No. 37), which sells traditional snacks.

Popular with backpackers, **Helen's Restaurant & Bar at the 365 Inn** (Anyi Zhijia; No. 55), is a good place to stop for refreshments and tourist information. The small hutong that runs along its east side is called Qingzhu Xiang, or Green Bamboo Lane. **Zhenwu Miao** (No. 4), a former Taoist temple along this lane, has been turned into a house. At the end of the street, turn left on Yangmeizhu Xiejie, a traditional hutong. Go straight until you come to **Liulichang** (see pp. 110–111), a good place to browse for books, paper, and artwork.

Source of Law Temple

Built in 645, the Source of Law Temple (Fayuan Si) was originally dedicated to soldiers killed in battle. It was transformed into a Buddhist temple during the Qing dynasty. While many temples in Beijing are more akin to museums, this is a functioning place of worship and crowded with people. It's also the site of the Chinese Buddhist Academy.

A procession of monks and visitors, with hands folded, pay homage at the Source of Law Temple.

Source of Law Temple

- 📍 109 B2
- ✉ 7 Fayuan Si Qianjie
- ☎ 010/6353-4171
- 💲 $
- 🚇 Metro: Caishikon

In the first courtyard you'll see the typical drum and bell towers. The first hall, the **Hall of Heavenly Kings** (Tianwang Dian), has a statue of Milefo, or the Laughing Buddha, inside. At the rear is a statue of Wei Tuo, Buddhism's protector, squatting slightly as if ready for battle.

Six large steles, their tops hugged by dragons, stand in the second courtyard. The main hall here is the **Daxiong Baodian,** which has a statue of Sakyamuni.

The third courtyard has a large incense burner sitting on an elaborately carved stone base that depicts the mythological beast known as a qilin. The **Minzhong Ge** has a gold statue of Sakyamuni holding a lotus cup in his hand.

Located in the sixth and final courtyard, the **Fa Tang** has a magnificent sleeping Buddha made of sandalwood and covered in a golden robe. Small Buddha statues have been placed in notches in the wall by patrons of the temple.

The temple has a wonderful collection of stone and wood sculptures dating from the Liao and Tang dynasties. There's one particularly interesting statue of Guanyin, the goddess of mercy, holding a small child in her hand. Women anxious to get pregnant come to the temple to pray to Guanyin. (At the time of writing, the temple was under construction and the statues scattered in different halls.) ■

Ox Street Mosque

In the late seventh century, camel and horse caravans traveling across the Central Asia steppe brought Muslim merchants and soldiers from the west. Today there is little left of Beijing's once exotic Muslim Quarter, home to the city's Islamic community for more than a thousand years. Few Muslim shops still line the streets, and they are now dwarfed by tall apartment complexes. The streets, however, are packed with bearded men in white skull caps and women in head scarves, and the ancient Ox Street Mosque is crowded with the faithful at prayer time.

The largest of Beijing's mosques, the Ox Street Mosque (Niujie Qingzhen Si or Libai Si) is a living reminder of this neighborhood's once exotic atmosphere. It was built in the Chinese style in 996, though its present layout dates from the Qing dynasty, when it was enlarged and restored.

Just inside the mosque complex is the **Tower for Observing the Moon** (Wangyue Lou). This hexagonal observation tower was once used to make astronomical calculations and to observe the movements of the moon. Behind the tower is the **prayer hall,** which faces west toward Mecca and can accommodate up to a thousand worshipers. Only Muslim men are allowed to enter the hall, but a new

hall nearby provides a separate place for women to worship.

Facing the prayer hall is the **minaret,** from which the call to prayer summons the faithful each day. It is flanked by two small towers with steles inside said to commemorate the founding of the mosque and its restoration on two occasions, once in 1442 and again in 1692.

Except during certain celebrations, the mosque's front gate is locked, so you must enter through the side gate. Visitors must dress modestly; the ticket office will provide baggy clothes for those whose outfits are deemed unacceptable to enter. The mosque is crowded at 1 p.m. on Fridays, when hundreds of faithful come here to pray. ■

Ox Street Mosque

- 🅰 109 B2
- ✉ 18 Niujie
- ☎ 010/6353-2564
- 💲 $
- 🚇 Metro: Caishikon (walking distance)

Muslim Quarter

The Ox Street Mosque is located in Beijing's Muslim Quarter, which is currently home to about 200,000 Chinese Muslims known as the Hui. Hui men are recognizable for the white caps they wear. This historic quarter is small, spreading about 1 square mile (2.6 sq km) around the mosque, with few visitors.

While here, be sure to try one of the area's authentic Muslim restaurants. Typical dishes include lamb coated with sesame, a long-standing favorite, and

shuan yangrou, rinsed mutton cooked in a brass hot pot heated with charcoal. Warm and hearty, shuan yangrou is especially popular during cold Beijing winters. The Hui also excel in making many types of tasty bing (baked bread) as well as snacks like deep-fried dough glazed with honey.

Visitors can easily identify Hui eating establishments by their green-and-white signs. The signs are adorned with flowing Arabic script and the Chinese characters qingzhen, or halal.

Gods & Goddesses

China has two main religions, Buddhism and Taoism, each with a host of deities ruling over the sacred domain.

Weituo, the guardian of Buddhism, covers the back of the Laughing Buddha.

Buddhist Gods & Goddesses

Historical Buddha (Sakyamuni) The founder of Buddhism, the Present Buddha was born Siddhartha Gautama, Prince of Sakyans. At age 35 he attained supreme enlightenment and became the Buddha. For the rest of his life, he was known as Sakyamuni, which means "capability and kindness."

The main hall of every Buddhist temple holds a trinity of golden Buddhas. Often shown reclining, the Historical Buddha sits in the middle with the Past Buddha on his left and the Future Buddha on his right.

Past Buddha (Randengfo) The Past Buddha gave Siddhartha the name Sakyamuni. He is also typically represented reclining.

Future Buddha (Milefo or Maitreya) The Future Buddha is a bodhisattva (see p. 117) who will eventually manifest himself on Earth. Sometimes portrayed with a small group of children, this jovial, golden fellow (also known as the Laughing Buddha) will greet you at the entrance to any Buddhist temple.

Bodhisattva The term refers to the Historical Buddha and to those who are capable of becoming Buddhas; in other words, they have attained a pre-Buddha stage of enlightenment. The most prominent bodhisattvas in China are the goddess Guanyin and the Future Buddha, both of whom typify the essentially compassionate mission of the bodhisattva.

Guanyin (goddess of mercy) Guanyin, whose name literally means "hearing the sounds of the world," is one of the most popular bodhisattvas in China. Of the Four Great Bodhisattvas, she is the most compassionate and merciful and always heeds cries for help. Buddhists believe that she can alleviate suffering, so many petition her for money, good luck, and children. In temples, her statue is often located at the rear of the main temple, facing north.

Wenshu (Manjusri) Wenshu is the chief of the Four Great Bodhisattvas. He is also the one with the greatest wisdom. Considered the ninth ancestor of the Historical Buddha, he is especially venerated by pilgrims visiting the Wu Tai Shan in Shansi Province. He is usually depicted riding on a lion.

Puxian (Visvabhadra) Puxian is guardian of the *dhyana*, fundamental Buddhist law. He is always depicted riding on a white elephant. Often he appears to the right of the Historical Buddha, with Wenshu to the left.

Dizangwang (Ksitigarbha) Dizangwang, or Earth Womb, is more popular in the Far East than he ever was in India, where he originated. He is usually depicted standing up, holding a pilgrim's staff in his right hand and a pearl in his left.

Luohan (arhats) The luohan are perfect humans who have been freed from the cycle of rebirth but who remain on earth in order to preach Buddhist doctrines. There are usually 18 of them, and they are often depicted worshiping Guanyin or ranked in two lines

of nine alongside temple walls. Occasionally they appear as a gilded group of 500, as in the Temple of the Azure Clouds (Biyun Si; see p. 141). They remain in this world until the coming of the next Buddha.

Weituo The defender of the Buddhist faith can be found standing with a staff behind the Future Buddha at the entrance to a temple.

Four Heavenly Kings Large and ferocious, the Four Heavenly Kings are dressed in armor and carry musical instruments. They are usually represented in pairs on either side of the Future Buddha and Weituo.

INSIDER TIP:

Your visit will be richer if you get to know the local pantheon and to recognize some of the more popular celestial beings.

—LARRY PORGES
National Geographic Travel Books editor

Taoist Gods

Laozi Born in the seventh century B.C., Laozi was the founder of philosophical Taoism. He is always shown in Taoist temples, and he is often depicted riding an ox and holding his classic book, the *Daodejing* (*Classic of the Way of Power*).

Jade Emperor (Yu Huang Dadi) Frequently represented with a black beard and seated on a dragon throne, the Jade Emperor is the supreme god of Taoism. Together with Laozi and the Yellow Emperor, he is part of the San Qing, or Three Pure Ones.

God of War (Guandi) This god, typically red-faced, adorned with a black beard, and clad in armor, is also the god of literature and represents both civil and military aspects.

Taoist door gods Taoist temples have similar defenses against evil spirits as those found in Buddhist temples. The Green Dragon and the White Tiger are Taoist door gods.

White Cloud Temple

Considered the center of Taoism when it was first built in 739, this sacred complex, with its myriad small and large halls dedicated to various Taoist gods, is one of Beijing's most colorful temples. When you arrive, you will probably be pursued by people selling incense sticks and other Taoist items. You might even be approached by a Taoist master or two offering to tell your fortune. The Chinese Taoist College and the Chinese Taoist Association are also found here.

The scent of burning incense sticks pervades the courtyard at the White Cloud Temple.

The Bai Yun Quan (White Cloud Temple) complex is laid out on three parallel axes, with the main structures located on the central axis. Brief English descriptions in front of each structure provide basic information. In order to enter the temple, you must pass under a three-tiered gate guarded by lions. In the first courtyard there are two *huabiao,* marble ornamental pillars normally placed in front of imperial buildings.

After you pass through an inner gate with three rounded doors—the stone frame covered with carvings of cranes—you'll come to the small **Wofeng Bridge,** under which hang two large coins, each with two small bells in their holes. On the coins is written, "When the bell rings it is the omen of happiness." It has become a custom during the spring festival season to try and make the bells ring by throwing coins through the holes.

The main hall is the **Shrine Hall for the Tutelary God** (Lingguan Dian). In the hall, which was erected in 1443 and rebuilt in 1662, sacrifices are made to Wang Guangling,

INSIDER TIP:

If you have time, visit the smaller halls to the left of the fifth courtyard. Especially noteworthy is the Temple of the God of Thunder, with bronze statues of the Four Heavenly Kings.

—PAUL MOONEY
National Geographic author

the god responsible for maintaining kindness and eliminating evil. His wooden statue has three eyes and a horsehair beard.

In the third courtyard stands the **Jade Emperor Hall** (Yuhuang Dian). The building was erected in 1438 and rebuilt in 1662 and again in 1778, and it features a statue of the Jade Emperor sitting on his throne, shoulders draped in a gold cloth. Inside the hall on the left, the **God of Wealth Hall** (Caishen Dian), are three gold statues, all with horse-hair beards growing from their wooden chins. On the right is the **Temple of Three Emperors** (Sanguan Dian), which is dedicated

to the god of heaven (who brings good luck and reduces suffering), the god of Earth (who pardons blame and releases grievances), and the god of water (who eliminates all diseases, bad luck, and disasters).

Built in 1456, the **Lao Lu Temple** in the fourth courtyard is one of the oldest halls. The hall on the left is the **God of Medicine Temple** (Yaowang Dian), dedicated to Sun Simiao who is said to have been able to cure diseases and raise the dead. On the right is the **Temple of the God of Releasing Sufferers** (Jiuku Dian).

In the fifth courtyard, the **Temple of Founder Qiu** (Qiu Zu Dian) dates back to 1228. The hall is dedicated to a Yuan-dynasty monk said to be buried there. The interior walls are filled with elaborate scenes from the Book of Qiu.

The sixth and final courtyard along the main axis is the **Temple of Four Emperors** (Siyu Dian), where the clay statues date back to the Qing dynasty.

Walk north to the garden, cut across to the west side of the temple, and walk back down south on the opposite side looking at the various temples. In one yard you'll see representations of the Chinese zodiac and Chinese folktales. ∎

White Cloud Temple

🅰 109 A3
✉ Baiyunguan Jie, Binhe Lu
☎ 010/6346-3531
💲 $
🚇 Metro: Nanlishi Lu, plus 15-min. walk or taxi; or Metro: Changchunjie, then Bus 9 to Baiyun Qiaoxi

Chinese Lions

Pairs of Chinese lions, playful looking creatures with a curly mane, sharp talons, and open mouths, are found sitting guard outside all buildings of note, temples of worship, and—increasingly less frequently—the entrance to ancient river bridges. Made of stone, most lion pairs were painted, although time and weather conditions have often eroded the coloring. It is easy to distinguish which lion is male and which is female—the male holds a ball (said to represent the globe) under one paw, while the female holds a lion cub under a paw (the Chinese believed that lionesses could secrete milk through their paws).

More Places to Visit in Xuanwu District

Posters and artwork for sale at the bustling Baoguo Temple Saturday market

Baoguo Temple

The 1466 Buddhist Baoguo Temple (Baoguo Si) was converted into a smelting factory after liberation in 1949. Today it's a flea market (see p. 320), selling Cultural Revolution kitsch, old coins and stamps, jade, and books. 🅰 109 B3 ✉ 1 Baoguo Si, Guang'anmennei Dajie ☎ 010/6317-3169 🚇 Metro: Xuanwumen, then Bus 109 to Guang'anmen

Museum of Ancient Architecture

This is the site of the Xiannong Tan, or Altar of Agriculture, where Qing-dynasty emperors held lunar equinox ceremonies. The halls are as impressive as the famous architecture that runs along the old capital's north–south axis. The Museum of Ancient Architecture (Gudai Jianzhu Bowuguan) displays architectural models of all eras, from ancient thatched huts to the magnificent structures of the Qing dynasty. The displays feature English captions. This is a great place to visit before heading out to see Beijing's architectural wonders. 🅰 109 D2 ✉ 21 Dongjing Lu ☎ 010/6317-2150 or 010/6301-7620 💲 $ 🚇 Bus: 803 to Nanwei Lu, near north gate of Xiannong Tan

Southern Cathedral

Known as the Church of the Immaculate Conception of the Blessed Virgin Mary, the Southern Cathedral (Nantang) was built during the Ming dynasty, making it Beijing's oldest Catholic church. First constructed by Italian Jesuit Matteo Ricci in 1605, it was initially large enough to accommodate only a hundred or so Chinese converts at its services. It was rebuilt in the 17th century and again in 1904 after the Boxer Rebellion. 🅰 109 C4 ✉ 141 Qianmen Xi Dajie ☎ 010/6602-6538 🚇 Metro: Xuanwumen

Tianning Temple of Heavenly Peace

The first Tianning Temple of Heavenly Peace (Tianning Si) was originally built during the Northern Wei dynasty (386–543), while the pagoda was added a millennium later. The pagoda is recognized as the oldest structure in Beijing. Three layers of carved lotus petals decoratively support its first story. Above this are 13 levels of eaves. 🅰 109 A3 ✉ 3A Tianningsi Qianjie, Guang'anmenwai Dajie ☎ 010/6343-2507 🚇 Metro: Nanlishi Lu, then Bus 42–46

The face of new China and the place where you'll find lots to do, from quiet walks in tree-shaded parks to shopping and dancing

Chaoyang District

Introduction & Map   122–123

Ritan Park   124

Dongyue Temple   125

Experience: Dashanzi
   (798) Art District   126

Beijing Olympic Park   127

More Places to Visit in Chaoyang
   District   128

Experience: China's Ocean Life   128

Hotels & Restaurants   300–302

A lotus in Beijing's ancient Ritan Park

Chaoyang District

Fast becoming a hub of international business, sprawling Chaoyang District is in the midst of a construction renaissance, as glass towers, high-class international hotels, new malls, and commercial complexes are going up seemingly overnight. Working-class homes are giving way to sleek new high-rise malls and apartment buildings for Beijing's growing middle class. Here, too, is the Olympic Park built for the 2008 Summer Olympics.

Hip boutiques, bars, and restaurants make The Village at Sanlitun the hub of the Chaoyang District.

NOT TO BE MISSED:

The architectural wonder of Rem Koolhaas's "Glass Pants" CCTV headquarters **122**

Morning exercise rituals in Ritan Park **124**

The fearful hell depicted in Dongyue Temple's sculptures **125**

Cool Chinese culture in Beijing's 798 Art District **126**

Lapping the incomparable "Bird's Nest" National Stadium **127**

Diving deep into China's marine life at the Blue Zoo **128**

The Village at Sanlitun **128**

In the district's eastern urban section, between the Third and Fourth Ring Roads, the Beijing Central Business District area is soaring to new heights—literally. Among the skyscrapers in this show of business might is Rem Koolhaas's CCTV headquarters, nicknamed the "Glass Pants," which is a continuous square-shaped loop rising 755 feet (234 m). Here, too, is the 41-floor Beijing TV Center and the 81-floor China World Trade Center Summit Towers, currently Beijing's tallest building, with an observation deck on the top floor.

China's past and present meet in the large parks of Chaoyang District. In the morning, gaggles of people enjoy both the traditional and the new pastimes of China, moving gracefully with ancient Chinese architecture serving as a backdrop. Ritan Park is among the favorites, dating from 1530 and once part of a network of imperial altars used to worship the natural world. Here the emperor made sacrificial offerings to the sun god. All traces of the altar are gone, but the park remains a tranquil spot for a pleasant stroll.

Continuing on the theme of old and new, Dongyue Temple, founded in 1319, is a popular Taoist temple just north of the park, while, the cavernous Workers' Stadium, fronted by

ideology-rich socialist-realist statues sits amid the trendy café buzz of Gongti Bei Lu. Farther afield, Dashanzi (798) Art District houses a thriving artist community located within 50-year-old factory buildings; it's often compared to New York's SoHo or Greenwich Village.

Amid all the bustle, The Village at Sanlitun is Beijing's see-and-be-seen center for shopping, dining, and nightlife. ∎

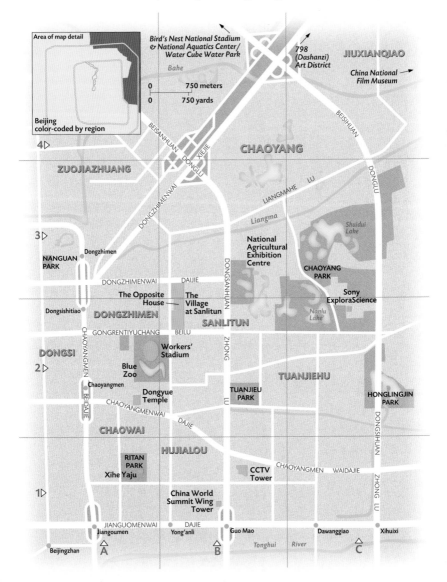

Ritan Park

Ritan Park (Ritan Gongyuan), also known as Temple of the Sun Park, was built in 1530, making it one of the city's oldest recreational areas. Today this former sacred site is the central location for the meeting between old and new China.

Look for life beneath the lotus plants in a Ritan Park pond

Ritan Park
- 123 A1
- 6 Ritan Bei Lu
- 010/8561-6301
- Metro: Jianguo-menwai; Bus: Ritan Lu

Enter the park through its north gate and pass under a looming pai-lou, or archway. Sprinkled throughout the park are little stone monuments and historical sites, such as the place where the emperor would change his robes and the hall where musical instruments and sacrificial objects were stored. Pockets of peaceful green solitude are ideal for a picnic or for quiet contemplation on one of the benches.

Among the park's many restaurants is **Xihe Yaju,** in the northeast corner, which serves Cantonese and Sichuanese fare in an outdoor setting. **Xiao Wangfu**'s dishes out home-style cooking near the north gate, with a nice rooftop dining area.

Kids love the small playground, two rock-climbing walls (one easy, the other a bit more daunting), mini-golf course, bumper cars, and, of course, the chance to fish for chubby goldfish. ■

Ancient *Tai Ji Quan*

Health and serenity are the aims of *tai ji quan*, the slow-motion routine that scores of people practice in Ritan Park, indeed, in parks around the world. Sometimes called a moving meditation, it's a traditional form of martial arts in which more than a hundred possible movements and positions are performed in a slow, graceful manner. You can stick to a few, or push your body through the whole range.

Dongyue Temple

Dongyue Temple (Dongyue Miao), one of Beijing's most colorful Taoist temples, is dedicated to the Supreme Celestial Emperor of Taishan Mountain—the Eastern Peak Equal to Heaven—the guardian of the offices of hell who oversees the good and evil that people do.

Built between 1314 and 1320, Dongyue Temple—which is still an active place of worship—was once one of the largest Taoist temples in the city. Destroyed by fire, it was rebuilt during the Ming dynasty. Although the current complex dates from the Qing dynasty, it still retains its earlier style.

Like many Chinese temples, its **gateway** is guarded by two sacred custodians, General Heng and General Ha, two deities wearing fierce facial expressions.

On the left (west) side is a large **abacus,** a reminder that everyone's good and bad behavior will be calculated some day. The small cubicles running along the sides of the first courtyard house the Taoist deities that hand out penalties.

In the main courtyard stands the **Hall of Taishan** (one of China's five sacred mountains), showcasing statues of the Supreme Celestial Emperor of Taishan and his senior attendants. A corner of this hall is occupied by the god of writing, to whom all those keen to excel in literature bring offerings of brushes and ink slabs.

The complex also has hundreds of frightening life-size sculptures of those who suffer in the 18 layers of hell or serve in the 72 departments. "When you go in the Dongyue Miao," warns one ancient inscription, "you encounter the gates of the seventy-two offices and are immediately fearful." Each of the vestibules display different officials—many of them extremely grotesque—handing out punishments.

The minor shrines here are filled with deities that control diseases, because as author Juliet Bredon pointed out in the early 1900s, gods exist governing "every part of the body from the hair to the toe nails."

INSIDER TIP:

Don't miss the Museum of Beijing Folk Custom, located in the back of the Dongyue Temple complex. The captions are in Chinese, but the interesting items on display speak for themselves.

—PAUL MOONEY
National Geographic author

Despite its darker aspects, Dongyue Temple is a wonderful place to visit during festival season, especially Chinese New Year, when you can sample one of Beijing's traditional temple fairs. At that time, the old complex pulses with stilt walkers—heavily made-up young children—and a number of people selling traditional folk crafts and snacks. ∎

Dongyue Temple

- ⓐ 123 A2
- ✉ 141 Chaoyangmenwai Dajie
- ☎ 010/6551-0151
- $ $
- Ⓜ Metro: Chaoyangmen; Bus: 101, 109, 112, 750, 846, 858, or 855 to Shenlu Jie

Dashanzi (798) Art District

More popularly known as the 798 Factory, the Dashanzi Art District (Dashanzi Yishu Qu) is located in an old factory complex now converted into galleries, restaurants, and nightlife spots. Whether or not you love art, this is a great place to see some of the cooler aspects of Chinese culture. New contemporary art exhibitions are held regularly—from oil paintings and installation art to ceramics and sculpture. It's best to go to Dashanzi late on a weekend afternoon, when you can browse the galleries until it gets dark, and then have dinner at one of the hip restaurants or coffee shops.

The **Dashanzi Art District** *(map 123 C4, 4 Jiuxianqiao L. tel 010/5978-9180, www.798space.com, closed Mon., best reached by taxi, bus: Dashanzi Lukou Nan)* consists of a complex of Bauhaus-style factories, built in 1953 under the auspices of the East

Germans. On some of the walls it's still possible to see fading political slogans from the Cultural Revolution. When business declined in the 1980s, the factories began pulling out, and by the late 1990s, many of the buildings were vacant.

This proved perfect timing for a group of daring independent artists, who had recently ruffled the feathers of the cultural czars. The artists were kicked out of their commune at the Old Summer Palace, where they had been based for some ten years. Around 2000, some of Beijing's best artists began to flock to Dashanzi, attracted by the large spaces, cheap rents, and ample natural light pouring through the huge ceiling windows. The artists were soon followed by hip coffee shops and Western and Chinese restaurants.

The Dashanzi Art District now has the best English-language art bookstore in Beijing: **Timezone 8** *(24-AZ Meishuguan Dongjie, tel 010/6400-4427).*

Taxis are not usually allowed inside, so you'll have to get out at the main gate. Start from the end of the main road. All galleries welcome visitors, and some may have maps available. Among the best **galleries** to explore are Beijing Commune, Faurschou Gallery, 798 Photo Gallery, Beijing Tokyo Art Projects, The Pace Gallery, Chinese Contemporary, Contrasts Gallery, Galleria Continua, Ullens Center for Contemporary Art, Star Gallery, and White Space.

The annual Dashanzi (798) International Art Festival is held in the district every September.

A socialist-themed sculpture stands in the Dashanzi Art District.

Beijing Olympic Park

The 2008 Olympics were a source of immense pride for China's 1.4 billion people. The visually extravagant opening ceremony symbolized the desire of a new superpower economy to impress the watching world. Beijing made no disguise of its plan to host the "best games ever."

The Olympic legacy is twin-edged. On the streets, people rarely discuss the games, but the constructive impact is everywhere. Myriad new roads, subways, hotels, malls, and office towers bear testament to the multibillion dollars invested to transform Beijing into a city of world standing.

INSIDER TIP:

The "Bird's Nest" architecture changes perspective as you walk around the outside. The effect is especially impressive on a sunny day.

—GARY BOWERMAN
National Geographic contributor

At the head of the north–south axis on which the ancient capital was constructed sits the greatest monument to Beijing's Olympic adventure. Accessible by metro, the Beijing Olympic Park features two contemporary Chinese architectural treasures, the "Bird's Nest" and the "Water Cube."

The jewel in the crown is the **"Bird's Nest" National Stadium,** which hosted the spectacular 2008 Olympics opening and closing ceremonies, and all athletics events. This space-age looking stadium is made of bands of great steel intertwined like twigs in a bird's nest—which is a favored local delicacy. The stadium was designed by Swiss architectural firm Herzog and de Meuron, with input from Chinese artist Ai Weiwei.

Since the Olympics, it has become one of Beijing's most visited tourism attractions. Most days you will find camera-toting tour groups lining up for photographs in front of a structure that is now enshrined in modern Chinese folklore.

Equally impressive is the **"Water Cube" National Aquatics Center.** Wrapped in a translucent skinlike bubble wrap, the $125 dollar design utilizes the newest plastic materials for an eye-catching sensory effect, especially when illuminated at night. The facility, which seated 11,000 spectators for the Olympic swimming, diving, and water polo events, was designed by PTW Architects of Australia. In 2010, the main section of the center was reopened to the public as a themed water park featuring water slides, a wave pool, and water rides for kids. ∎

"Bird's Nest" National Stadium

- 123 B4
- 1 National Stadium South Road
- 010/8437-3011
- Olympic Green
- $$

www.bopac.gov.cn
www.n-s.cn/en

National Aquatics Center / "Water Cube" Water Park

- 123 B4
- Olympic Park, No. 11 Tianchen Donglu,
- Olympic Green
- 10 a.m.–9 p.m.
- $$$$

More Places to Visit in Chaoyang District

Chaoyang Park

This huge and pleasant park—Chaoyang Gongyuan—does not have the imperial history of the city's other parks, but it has plenty to offer in terms of recreation. About one-fourth of the park is water, so there are opportunities for boating (primarily paddle-boats). There's also a nice swimming pool, as well as beach volleyball grounds, tennis courts, a gymnasium, and a small amusement park. You can rent a slow-going electromobile (*$ for 30 min.*) to get around this sprawling park. Numerous stands serve food, or walk around to the west gate, where you'll find a street with popular Western and Chinese eateries. 🅰 123 C2–C3 ✉ 1 Chaoyang Gongyuan Nan-lu 🅂 $ 🅿 Bus: 117, 302, 406, 419, 608, 703, 705, or 710 to Chaoyang Gongyuan Qiaoxi

INSIDER TIP:

The Bookworm bookshop and cafe [Building 4, Nan Sanlitun Road, tel 010/6586-9507, www.beijingbookworm.com] is a great place to kick back with a good book and a cup of Chinese tea.

—GARY BOWERMAN
National Geographic contributor

China National Film Museum

The China National Film Museum (Zhong-guo Dianying Bowuguan) is located in a hip, ultramodern building in the far outskirts of northeastern Chaoyang District, near Beijing's Caochangdi Art District. The building, shaped like a black box, has screening rooms, a four-story circular walkway, and Beijing's first IMAX. The development of the Chinese film industry exhibition is welcome but the exhibit does not mention several of the international block-busters that government censors did not approve for domestic viewers. The presenta-

EXPERIENCE:
China's Ocean Life

If you or your family want to immerse yourselves in the exotic marine life off the coast of China, you won't even have to leave the mainland. Some 5,000 ocean creatures—from dangerous sharks and piranhas to marvelous rays—swim just beneath the surface of the **Blue Zoo** (Fuguo Haidi Shijie; *map 123 A2, 141 Gongti Nanlu, tel 010/6591-3397, www.bluezoo.com.cn, $$$, bus: 101, 109, 112, 750, 846, 848, or 855 to Shenlu Jie, or 43, 110, 118, 120, 403, or 813 to Chao-yang Yiyuan*), a magnificent aquarium beneath the surface of a dried-up, man-made lake in the Workers' Stadium. Visit at feeding time (*10 a.m. & 2:30 p.m.*), when brightly dressed divers jump in to feed the sea creatures by hand and check their health. PADI scuba lessons are given here in the early morning hours (*SinoScuba, tel 86/1369 3028 913*).

tion is top-notch, with brief English translations for each section. *www. cnfm.org.cn* 🅰 123 C4 ✉ 9 Nanying Lu ☎ 010/8435-5959 🕐 Closed Mon. 🅂 $ 🅿 Best reached by taxi; Bus: 402, 418, 909, or 973 to Nangao

The Village at Sanlitun

This eye-catching development, cast in multicolored glass, is Beijing's hippest destination for shopping, dining, and entertainment. The city's glitziest boutiques are interwoven with a fine selection of rest-aurants, an art gallery, and the Upper House Boutique Hotel. The adjacent Nali Patio fea-tures several trendy bars and lounges, where affluent young Beijingers spend their money when darkness falls. *www.sanlitunvillage.com* 🅰 123 B2–B3 ✉ 6A Gongti Bei Lu ☎ 010/6417-6110 🅿 Metro: Tuanjiehu

Almost an hour northwest of the city center and home to intellectuals, important temples, palaces, and gardens

Haidian District

Introduction & Map   130–131

Big Bell Temple   132

Experience: An Imperial
   River Ride   132

Old Summer Palace   133

A Walk Around Peking
   University   134–135

Summer Palace   136–137

Feature: Dancing in the
   Streets   138–139

Experience: Cycling Around
   & Beyond Beijing   138

Military Museum of the Chinese
   People's Revolution   140

Fragrant Hills Park   141

More Places to Visit in
   Haidian District   142

Hotels & Restaurants   302–303

A painting from the Long Corridor
at the Summer Palace

Haidian District

Haidian District (Haidian Qu) is home to some of China's best universities, including Peking University and Tsinghua University. Both universities date back more than a century and count the country's most prominent figures among their graduates. This busy area is also home to China's version of Silicon Valley, plus prime tourism attractions including the Summer Palace, Big Bell Temple, and the intriguing Military Museum of the Chinese People's Revolution.

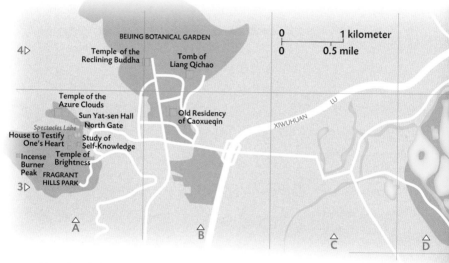

Name-brand electronics can be significantly more expensive in China, but if you're looking for high-tech gadgets, then Zhongguancun is the perfect place. Known as the Silicon Valley of China, this area has row after row of electronics shops. The huge five-story Hailong Electronic City is the place to go for no-frills computers, MP3 players, and many other components. But buyer beware—the quality is often uneven.

Haidian District is not all work and no play, however. Just like any university area, the district is packed with student bars, cafés, and restaurants. Wudaokou has a bustling night scene reminiscent of college towns all over the world. You can stop for dinner at one of the many international restaurants—Korean, Mexican, Japanese, Italian, American—

NOT TO BE MISSED:

An imperial Beijing river ride   132

Walking through historic Peking University   134–135

The sumptuous expanses of Beijing's Summer Palace   136–137

Dancing in the streets   138–139

Millennia of military history at the Military Museum of the Chinese People's Revolution   140

A paradise of plants at the Beijing Botanical Garden   141

Exploring the heavens above at the Beijing Planetarium   142

and then go out for a night on the town.

A good deal of old Beijing is also still alive here in Haidian, including the Summer Palace —the emperor's hot-weather retreat. Other historic sites in this area provide some surprises as well as a number of Beijing's oldest temples and parks: the rustic Dajue Temple, dating from the Liao dynasty; the Biyun Temple, built during the Yuan dynasty; the Jietai

Ordination Temple; and the Big Bell Temple.

Haidian also has dozens of gardens designed by Ming- and Qing-dynasty emperors, including the Summer Palace, the popular Old Summer Palace (Yuanmingyuan), and the Fragrant Hills. ■

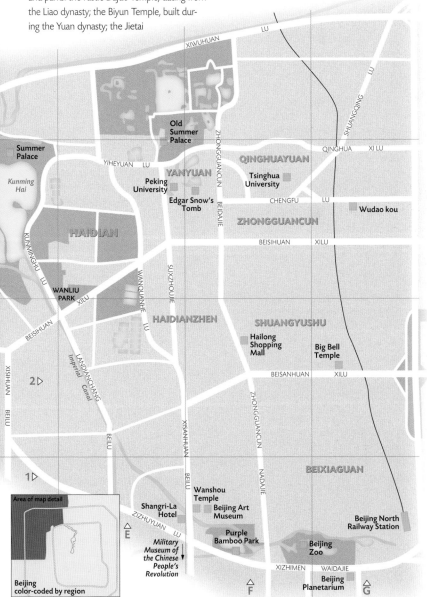

Big Bell Temple

Built in 1733, Big Bell Temple (Dazhong Si) was originally called Juesheng Temple, or the Temple of Awakening to a Sense of a Former Existence. In 1734 a huge bell was installed, and the name was changed. Since then, the temple has amassed 700 bells, some dating back to ancient times.

Big Bell Temple
- 131 G2
- 31 Beisanhuan Xilu
- 010/6255-0843
- $
- Light Rail: Dazhong Si; Bus: 361, 367, 718, 727, or 730 to Dazhong Si

During the Qing dynasty, a ceremony was held in the temple every year to pray for rain. Several emperors came, and large numbers of farmers also participated, donning willow wreaths (as the willow is associated with water). They prayed to the Dragon King, who controls the rain. According to one Manchu observer, for ten days each year men and women flocked here "in groups like clouds" to witness the ceremony.

Like most temples, the Big Bell Temple, which is also known as the Great Bell Temple, is set on a north–south axis. The **first hall** introduces visitors to the history of the temple. A stele here bears an edict written by Yongzheng, who ordered the temple built. More exhibitions of Chinese bells are on display through the other halls.

The **second hall** has a collection of bells from the Warring States period, while Buddhist and Taoist bells are featured in the **third hall**. The **fourth hall** displays Ming- and Qing-dynasty bells, including fine examples of the large and elaborate bells that graced Buddhist and Taoist temples. Many of these are decorated with traditional Chinese motifs, such as dragons and clouds.

The giant **Yongle Bell** is located in the last hall. It's believed to have been cast in the Ming dynasty, during the reign of Yongle, which would make it more than 550 years old. More than 23 feet (7 m) tall, the bell is inscribed with an entire sacred verse.

The temple features an exhibit on the casting of bells, including the production of molds and the melting of bronze, as well as exhibits of bells from other countries around the world. ∎

EXPERIENCE:
An Imperial River Ride

After visiting the Big Bell Temple, why not travel to the **Summer Palace** (see p. 136) the way the emperor did—via the **Changhe Canal**? Your ride begins at the **Beijing Zoo** (see p. 142), 2.5 miles (4 km) south of the Temple. You will cruise by the **Five Pagoda Temple**, the **Wanshou Temple**, and **Purple Bamboo Park**, a shallow area where you must transfer to a smaller boat. As you float along, you'll pass beneath willow trees and many moon-shaped bridges. Enjoy also the many historic sights that overlook the river. The ticket for the ride includes entrance to the zoo. The dock is located at the north end, behind the Elephant Hall. The ride takes one hour, punctuated by a Chinese-speaking tour guide. You can buy a ticket for the Summer Palace on the boat, which will take you in through the south gate. Contact **Yunhe Travel Agency** (behind Beijing Zoo, 137 Xizhimenwai Dajie, tel 010/8836-3576, closed Nov.–March, $$, bus: 7, 15, 19, 27, 45, 102, 103, 105, 111, 332, 334, 347, 380, 812, 808, or T4 to Dongwu Yuan).

Old Summer Palace

A walk around the enchanting Old Summer Palace (Yuanmingyuan) is the perfect antidote to the mayhem of the metropolis. Move away from the grinding snarl of Beijing's traffic by walking leisurely along the palace's shaded paths, meandering past ponds thick with lilies.

The stone ruins at the Old Summer Palace

The Old Summer Palace is a lovely complex of three gardens, constructed during the reigns of Emperors Kangxi, Yongzheng, and Qianlong–who were father, son, and grandson. The original palace, designed by Jesuit priests serving the imperial court, had more than 200 buildings and a circumference of 4.5 miles (7 km).

The park was looted in 1860 by Anglo-French troops and again in 1900 by Western soldiers, who filled their knapsacks with treasures that still pass through Western auction houses. Today the Old Summer Palace is a collection of fallen stone columns, marble pillars, and plinths scat-tered about the **Eternal Spring Garden.** Some argue that the park should be rebuilt, others prefer that it remain in ruins, a bitter historical reminder of the evils of foreign imperialism. ∎

INSIDER TIP:

Several sculpted animal heads, ransacked by Western troops from the palace, can now be viewed at the Poly Art Museum [see p. 82].

—JUSTIN KAVANAGH
National Geographic International Editions editor

Old Summer Palace

🅰 131 E3–E4
✉ 28 Qinghua Xilu
☎ 010/6262-8501
💲 $
🚍 Bus: 331, 365, 375, 717, 801, 810, or 973 to Yuanmingyuan Nanmen

A Walk Around Peking University

Founded in 1898, Peking University (PKU) has a large green area, many trees, winding paths, traditional architecture, and beautiful places like Weiming Lake and Boya Tower.

On the way to classes on the campus of Peking University

Enter the university via the bright red **West Gate** ❶, a traditional Chinese gate guarded by two lions. The gate was first built in 1926; it was repaired in 1998 to celebrate the hundredth anniversary of the university.

Just inside the gate you'll come to a stone bridge that crosses a pond. Walk straight ahead on the main path, which is flanked by two *huabiao* ❷, or decorative pillars. Believed to have been made in 1742, they once stood in the Summer Palace.

Straight ahead is the **Administration Building** ❸, built in 1926 and guarded by two *qilin* (mythical hooved Chinese creatures). These came from the Old Summer Palace. The Chinese unicorn and vermilion steps in front of the building are also relics from the destruction of the Old Summer Palace.

Turn left and walk straight ahead. Turn left at the first corner to stop and visit the **Arthur**

NOT TO BE MISSED:

Arthur Sackler Museum of Art and Archaeology • The tomb of Edgar Snow, chronicler of Chairman Mao

Sackler Museum of Art and Archaeology ❹ *(tel 010/6275-1667, $)*. Its worthwhile collection of artifacts from all over China covers 280,000 years: from the Paleolithic era to the Qing dynasty in the 20th century.

Retrace your steps and take the path to the left just before the Administration Building. On your right you'll see **Weiming Lake** ❺, where hawkers sell a variety of PKU souvenirs, from pens and notebooks to T-shirts, all emblazoned with the university logo. Walk along the south side of the lake, where, in the lake, you'll see the **Stone Fish with Curled Tail** ⑥ (Fan Wei Shi Yu). A relic from Changchun Garden in the Summer Palace, the stone fish was sold to Zaitao, younger brother of Emperor Guangxu. In 1930, students of Yanjing University, the former name of PKU, bought the fish and donated it to the school—it's remained in the lake ever since.

Continue straight along the south path that cuts away from the lake until you reach the **Bronze Statue of Cai Yuanpei** ⑦, the president of PKU from 1916 to 1927. On the left is **Qianlong's Poem Tablet** ⑧, on which is carved a poem describing a happy day of archery spent at the Changchun Garden in the Summer Palace.

Head up the small hill, then descend back to the lakeside and continue walking north. Facing the lake stands **Ciji Si** ⑨, or Flower God Temple. The nicely carved decorations above the door are worth a look.

Edgar Snow's Tomb ⑩ stands on the opposite side of the path. An American journalist, Snow (1905–1972) lived in China during the 1920s and 1930s and taught journalism at the university. In 1934, he made the treacherous journey—through nationalist lines—to Yan'an, the communist base in the northwest, to interview Chairman Mao, as recounted in his 1937 book, *Red Star Over China*. Snow was the first Westerner to tell Mao's story, and the interview propelled Mao onto the international scene.

In front of you is **Boya Tower** ⑪. Made of brick, the tower was built over a well dug on the north side of the lake in 1924.

Turn left and continue around the eastern end of the lake then move west, past the willow trees that hang over the lake. Cross the small bridge on your left, then bear left until you reach what looks like the base of a **stone boat.** This is a perfect place to stop and enjoy the wonderful view of the pagoda reflected in the water. Ahead on the right, just past a stone arched bridge, you'll see **four stone screens** ⑫, each with poetic descriptions of scenic spots in the Old Summer Palace, their original home. Continue around to the other side of the island and return to the main path.

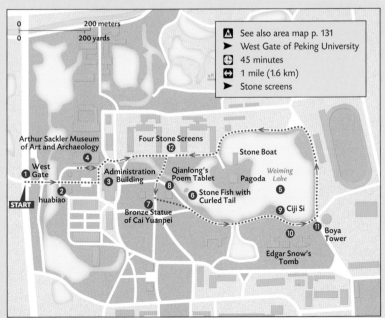

0 —————— 200 meters
0 —————— 200 yards

🖼 See also area map p. 131
► West Gate of Peking University
🕐 45 minutes
↔ 1 mile (1.6 km)
► Stone screens

Arthur Sackler Museum of Art and Archaeology ④

Four Stone Screens ⑫

Stone Boat

West Gate ①

Administration Building ③

Qianlong's Poem Tablet ⑧

Pagoda

Weiming Lake

⑤

START huabiao ②

Stone Fish with Curled Tail ⑥

Bronze Statue of Cai Yuanpei ⑦

Ciji Si ⑨

⑩ ⑪ Boya Tower

Edgar Snow's Tomb

Summer Palace

Built as a retreat from the intense summer heat, the Summer Palace (Yihe Yuan) is a sprawling imperial complex set in a large park around vast Kunming Lake. The first emperor of the Jin dynasty (1115–1234) built the Gold Mountain Palace on Longevity Hill; succeeding dynasties added new structures and landscaping. Expect to spend at least half a day exploring.

Summer Palace
- 131 D3
- Xinjian Gongmen Lu
- 010/6288-1144
- $ (extra fees for sites inside park)
- Bus: 332, 333, 346, 362, 374, or 375

www.summerpalace -china.com

Main Palace Complex

Opposite the **East Palace Gate** stands the **Hall of Benevolence and Longevity** (Renshou Dian), where Emperor Guangxu and the Empress Dowager Cixi administered state affairs. On your right is the **Garden of Harmonious Virtue** (Dehe Yuan), which has what was reputed to be one of China's best Beijing opera halls. Turn right at the small well, and follow the path to the **Violet Vapors from the East** (Ziqi Donglai Chengguan),

a martial-like tower. Pass through the opening, and continue on to the peaceful **Garden of Harmonious Interests** (Xiequ Yuan).

Longevity Hill

The most important sites are on Longevity Hill. Walk along the narrow path with Back Lake on your left until you reach a bridge, then cross the water. When you reach a T-intersection, turn left and walk until you reach a path on the right that leads to the **Glazed Tile Pagoda** (Duobao Ta).

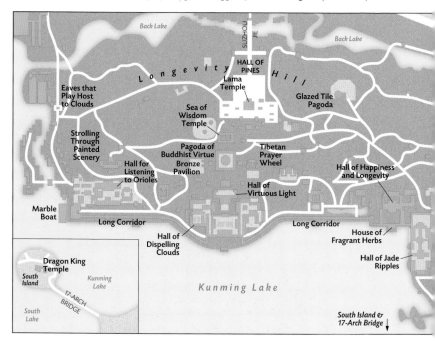

From the pagoda, turn left and head west on the main path along the shore to the **Hall of Pines** (Song Tang), a large square where you'll find Chinese dancing, flying kites, and playing other games. Go south through the square and climb up to the **Lama Temple** (Sida Buzhou or Xiangyan Zongyin Zhige). At the top, take the path to the **Sea of Wisdom Temple** (Zhihui Hai), with wonderful views of **Kunming Lake.**

Move west along the path until you reach a pavilion called **Strolling Through Painted Scenery** (Huazhong You), then head northwest. Turn left and descend the hill, passing through a fortlike gate known as **Eaves that Play Host to Clouds** (Suyun Yan). Head south. The bridge on your right is a good vantage point for viewing the infamous **Marble Boat** (Qingyan Fang or Shi Fang), of which only the hull is marble. Cixi was long alleged to have built the "boat," but it was actually Qianlong who built it.

Long Corridor

Continue south along the path until you reach the brightly painted Long Corridor (Chang Lang). Follow the corridor east past a number of traditional structures, including the **Hall for Listening to Orioles** (Tingli Guan) and the **Hall of Dispelling Clouds** (Paiyun Dian). Set back on the hill, the imposing **Pagoda of Buddhist Virtue** (Foxiang Ge) is flanked by the **Bronze Pavilion** (Baoyun Ge or Tongting) and the **Tibetan Prayer Wheel** (Zhuanlun Zang).

At the end of the Long Corridor, follow the path past the **House of Fragrant Herbs** (Yiyun Guan). Turn south to visit the **Hall of Jade Ripples** (Yulan Tang), where the Empress Dowager held her nephew Guangxu under house arrest for his involvement in the 100 Days Reform Movement.

South Island

Follow the contour of Kunming Lake to the graceful **17-arch Bridge** (Shiqi Kong Qiao). Cross the bridge to South Island (Nanhu Dao). Here you'll find the **Dragon King Temple** (Longwang Miao), where the Empress Dowager came to pray for rain. Inside you can catch a glimpse of the Dragon King. From here, walk back to the East Palace Gate. ■

0   150 meters
0   150 yards

YIHEYUAN   LU

Longevity Hall

Garden of Harmonious Interests

KUNMINGHU LU

Pavilion of Great Happiness

Violet Vapors from the East

Garden of Harmonious Virtue

East Palace Gate

Hall of Benevolence and Longevity

Dancing in the Streets

Cruise just about any area of Beijing in the evening, and you are likely to find yourself within earshot of the cacophonous clash of drums and gongs punctuating the early evening darkness. If you follow the beat of the music, you will soon come upon a circle of dancers, accompanied by musicians. You have stumbled upon Beijing's most popular fad—the revival of the popular *yangge* folk dance.

A typical Han folk dance, yangge is very popular in China's northern area, having originated among rural peasants. Translated, the term means "the song sung while transplanting rice." The People's Liberation Army, which learned it from peasants in the 1940s, brought the traditional dance to Beijing in 1949.

The dancers, mostly retired women (and some men) in their 50s and 60s, appear to have discovered the fountain of youth. Boldly made-up and dressed in brightly colored traditional costumes, these smiling senior citizens look more like high-school girls than grannies as they sway their hips and wave ornate fans and handkerchiefs.

To the uninitiated observer, yangge looks a bit monotonous. Dancers make circle after circle, seemingly performing the same steps over and over again. Not so, says Granny Pang, the leader of the Shougang Yangge Troupe. Pang, who is in her 60s, says the steps change at the start of each new circle and that more than 30 different routines can be performed.

After spending the day in their apartments, cooking and looking after their grandchildren, many of Beijing's senior citizens take pleasure in getting out for some exercise and a chance to mingle with their neighbors as soon as the evening meal is over.

"I watch my grandson all day long, do the shopping for groceries, and then cook dinner," says Granny Pang, whose family encourages her to take part in the dancing. "After dinner, my husband shoos me out of the house, and I head for the park to dance with my friends."

Song Mei-ying, Pang's number two in the Shougang Yangge Troupe, chips in. "We worked hard for so many years and now we are retired with little to do," she says. "Yangge dancing gives us a chance to get together with friends. It's a good form of exercise for old people, and it's fun."

Yangge advocates point out that participation is inexpensive and the style very easy to learn, encumbered by none of the complicated steps found in ballroom dancing, which is also popular

---

EXPERIENCE: Cycling Around & Beyond Beijing

Perhaps the ultimate way to see Beijing is by the time-honored transport used by millions of Chinese every day—on a pair of wheels. A savvy cyclist will chose a route preferably well off the main roads, zigzagging your way through the narrow *hutongs* that crisscross old Beijing. You can take your time, stopping whenever the mood, or the view, hits you.

By far the best plan is to rent a bike from your hotel; alternatively, there are numerous small rental shops in tourist areas such as Dazhalan Xijie, where you can hire a bike at a reasonable rate.

If you're fit, a mountain bike is a great way to experience the hilly and often dramatic landscapes around Beijing. With a little pedal-power, a bike is a cheap way to escape far from the crowded streets of China's capital and into the municipality's vast rural hinterlands. For a range of individual and group tours, contact **Wan Lin Bicycle Tours** (*tel* 186/0112-6254, *www.wanlinbicycletours.com*, $$$$$).

Practicing in the cold for Beijing's New Year's celebration

in parks each morning all over the country. The yangge craze is also boosted by growing feelings of nostalgia in the capital city. As China continues down the road toward reform, say academics, it is natural that some people take solace in the more familiar, traditional customs of the past, when life moved at a slower pace.

While, in the past, ceremonies marking the opening of new business ventures would not have been complete without a performance by the local high-school band or lion dance team, more and more companies—including foreign ones—are inviting yangge groups to perform at their openings.

City officials, concerned that the revelry of older residents may keep the younger ones awake at night, are trying to work out a compromise to accommodate this popular form of recreation for senior citizens. Under consideration is the suggestion that tape players be used, with the volume turned a few decibels lower than the original instruments—a suggestion that so far has not been met with much enthusiasm.

Regardless of where the music comes from, the yangge renaissance is putting a spring back into the step of Beijing's old folks and delighting spectators of all ages.

Military Museum of the Chinese People's Revolution

Presenting 5,000 years of Chinese military history, the collection housed at the Military Museum of the Chinese People's Revolution (Zhongguo Renmin Geming Junshi Bowuguan) includes everything from ancient weaponry to the tools of modern warfare. It also boasts a bit of nostalgia: Zhou Enlai's airplane, Mao's limo (a gift from Stalin), and U.S. tanks captured during the Korean War.

Military Museum of the Chinese People's Revolution

🗺 131 E1

✉ 9 Fuxing Lu

☎ 010/6686-6244

💲 $

🚇 Metro: Military Museum (Junshi Bowuguan); Bus: 1, 4, 21, or 337 to Junshi Bowuguan

www.jb.mil.cn

The building is vintage Soviet-era architecture, its center adorned with a large red star and the Chinese characters *ba yi,* which refer to August 1, the founding date of the People's Liberation Army. A huge red star decorates the museum's interior ceiling dome.

Step inside the main hall, where a larger-than-life-size **statue of Mao** greets you inside the cavernous hall. The **first floor** of the museum displays military uniforms and weapons used in the 1927 Autumn Harvest Uprising. The **second floor** focuses on the War of Resistance against Japan and the "war for liberation," while the **third floor** explores modern warfare, as well as the Opium Wars of the mid-1800s.

The topic of ancient warfare dominates the **fourth floor.** The objects on display include a model of a war chariot, Ming-dynasty weapons, and lacquer shields from the Warring States period.

Other interesting items in the museum's collection include a variety of American, Japanese, and Soviet tanks, several fighter planes, and Chinese missiles. ■

MiG jet fighters and tanks face off at Beijing's Military Museum.

Fragrant Hills Park

Less than an hour's drive from the center of the city, Fragrant Hills Park (Xiangshan Gongyuan) served as an imperial retreat for centuries. Today it is a pleasantly laid-out park with numerous pools, pavilions, and temples, as well as row upon row of apricot, pear, and peach trees. The best time to visit is in late autumn, when the leaves of the smoke tree turn a fiery red.

Temple of the Azure Clouds

The Temple of the Azure Clouds (Biyun Si), just to the right after you enter, features a number of wonderful halls, as well as six courtyards rising in succession up the mountain slope.

Visit the **Gate Hall** and the **Hall of Milefo** (Milefo Dian or Tianwang Dian), and then cross a small stone bridge to the **Hall of Lokapalas** (Daxiong Baodian), with a statue of Sakyamuni sitting in a lotus blossom inside.

Next is the Ming-dynasty **Hall of Bodhisattvas,** which houses statues of five bodhisattvas. Behind here is **Sun Yat-sen Hall,** which displays some of the former leader's personal effects.

Turn left to reach the **Hall of Arhats** (Luohan Tang). Built in 1748, the hall holds 508 unique, life-size statues of luohan. Behind, a flight of stairs leads up to a large triple archway. The steles mark the 1748 construction of the **Vajrasma Pagoda,** on the next level. There are nice panoramic views from the top.

More Sights

From the park entrance, you can also visit **Spectacles Lake** (Yanjing Hu). A bridge that divides the lake in two gives it the look of a pair of eyeglasses.

Walk Through Paradise

Located just to the north and east of Fragrant Hills Park, the **Beijing Botanical Garden** (Beijing Zhiwuyuan; map p. 130 A4–B4, Wofosi Lu, Xiangshan, tel 010/6259-1283, $, bus: 318, 331, or 360 to Zhiwuyuan/ Wofo Si) houses China's largest plant collection. Along with a state-of-the-art greenhouse and a variety of different gardens, this is a pleasant place to stroll, especially in spring, when the peach and pear trees burst with pretty blooms. An added feature is the striking **Temple of the Reclining Buddha** ($), boasting an enormous 14th-century bronze statue.

To the west of the lake awaits **House to Testify One's Heart** (Jianxin Zhai), which features a semicircular pond and a pavilion. A rounded wall and promenade surround the entire complex.

Built in 1780, the **Temple of Brightness** (Zhao Miao) was a Tibetan-style lamasery. On its east side stands a white marble triple memorial archway with green tiles; a pagoda with yellow and green glazed tiles stands beside it.

With an elevation of 1,827 feet (557 m), **Incense Burner Peak** (Xianglu Peak) is the park's highest peak and offers great vistas of the surrounding area, including the Summer Palace. If you're not up to the climb, take the chairlift to the top from the North Gate. ■

Fragrant Hills Park

🅰 130 A3
✉ 40 Maimai Jie, Xiangshan
☎ 010/6259-1155
💲 $
🚍 Bus: 90, 318, 360, 714, 733, 737, or 833

More Places to Visit in Haidian District

A panda carefully negotiates its way down a log at the Beijing Zoo.

Beijing Art Museum

The museum has a permanent collection of ancient calligraphy, imperial weavings, bronzes, jade, pottery, porcelain, furniture, coins, paintings, ceramics, ivory, and embroidery. 131 F1 Xi Sanhuan Beilu (S of China Grand Theater, No. 16) 010/6842-3380 Bus: 300, 323, 374, or 830 to Wanshou Si

Beijing Planetarium

Using the latest in high-tech equipment, the Beijing Planetarium (Beijing Tianwen Guan) has three theaters, two observatories, and a solar exhibition hall. Take a 45-minute star trek via the Planetarium's SGI Digital Universe Theatre and view galaxies, constellations, nebulae, planets, and spacecraft. Or enjoy the 3-D space-shuttle simulator. *www.bjp.org.nc* 131 G1 138 Xizhimenwai Dajie 010/5158-3311 Closed Mon.–Tues. $ (extra fee for shows & special exhibits) Bus: 7, 15, 65, 102, 103, 107, 111, or 334 to Dongwuyuan

Beijing Zoo

In 1906, the imperial court opened an experimental farm and zoo called the Garden of Ten Thousand Animals; two years later it opened to the public. The Beijing Zoo (Beijing Dongwu Yuan) features a number of special halls, including the **Giant Panda House, Bird Garden,** and **Aquarium.** 131 F1 137 Xizhimenwai Dajie 010/6831-4411 $ (extra fee to visit Giant Panda House) Bus: 7, 15, 19, 27, 45, 102, 103, 105, 111, 332, 334, 808, 812, or T4 to Dongwuyuan

Purple Bamboo Park

Purple Bamboo Park (Zizhuyuan Gongyuan) comprises three lakes built during the Yuan dynasty to control water flow to Beijing's moats. Book a boat ride to the Summer Palace (see pp. 136–137), or rent a small boat and sail the park's vast canals. The park offers a painting and pottery workshop for children. 131 F1 35 Zhongguancun Nan Dajie 010/6842-5851 Metro: Baishi Qiao (East Gate); Metro: Zizhu Qiao (West Gate)

The Great Wall of China, on everyone's must-see list, but also temples, tombs, museums, and beach resorts

Excursions North to the Great Wall

Introduction & Map   144–145

The Great Wall   146–149

Experience: Venturing Beyond the Wall   149

Feature: The Disappearing Wall   150–151

Commune by the Great Wall   152

Ming Tombs   153

Shanhaiguan & Beidaihe   154

Chengde Imperial Mountain Resort   155–156

Hotels & Restaurants   303–304

Guarding the Spirit Way, Ming Tombs northwest of Beijing

Excursions North to the Great Wall

The northern areas of greater Beijing offer a wide variety of opportunities to climb the Great Wall, from the renovated—and crowded—sections, such as Badaling and Mutianyu, to isolated areas, where you can walk, and sometimes claw and crawl, your way over the crumbling structure.

A guard tower overlooks the mountain ridges in Jinshanling.

While the Great Wall is the most significant attraction for most tourists traveling north of Beijing, there are several other places near the wall worth a visit. Many visitors to the Great Wall at Badaling—northwest of Beijing—combine their excursion with a stop at the Ming-dynasty imperial tomb complex, Shisanling, in Changping District. The principles of feng shui guided the design of the entire complex, from site selection to landscaping to tomb architecture. The site was designated a World Heritage site in 1987.

Like today's tourists, China's emperors frequently ventured north of Beijing and stopped at the temples nestled in the hills of this rural and sparsely populated area. From the 18th century, many emperors escaped the summer heat at the Chengde Imperial Mountain Resort, a complex of pavilions and temples set on a sheltered river plain ringed by mountains.

In the past, countless threats laid in the mountainous region north of Beijing, making defensive fortifications like the Great Wall essential. Located where the Great Wall meets the sea, the former garrison town of Shanhaiguan is a short train or bus trip east from Beijing. The museum in this pleasant town is dedicated to the history of the wall. Nearby the popular beach resort of Beidaihe on the Hebei Coast offers a retreat from the dry and dusty Beijing summer.

In June 2012, the Chinese government opened two new parts of the Great Wall to ease problems of overcrowding at the main Badaling and Mutianyu sections. Two renovated sections of the wall will also be opened to the public at Huanghua Cheng and Hefangkou, although no date had been given at the time of publication ■

NOT TO BE MISSED:

Trekking along the Great Wall from Jinshanling to Simatai   149

A night spent beneath the stars on the Great Wall at Jinshanling   149

Meditation in luxury within the Commune by the Great Wall   152

Sunrise on the wall at Old Dragon's Head in Shanhaiguan   154

The accursed history of Chengde Imperial Mountain Resort   155–156

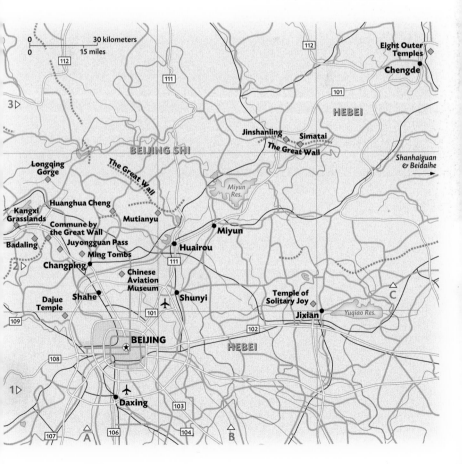

The Great Wall

Colossal endeavor, brave folly, futile contrivance, or splendid achievement, the Great Wall (Changcheng) inspires awe no matter how you look at it. Straddling northern China from the Yellow Sea in the east to its crumbling finale beyond Jiayuguan in the Gobi, its entirety measures nearly 4,000 miles (6,430 km) long. Several sections outside Beijing have been restored, but wilder parts like Jinshanling, Simatai, and Huanghua Cheng are worth the jaunt.

A lone walker explores an unrestored section of the Great Wall at Jinshanling.

History

The Great Wall was built to prevent hostile nomadic groups from the north–like the Huns, Khitans, Jurchens, Mongols, and Manchus– from invading. Not so much one wall as an articulation of ramparts, most of the Great Wall's sections were built independently of the others during different dynasties.

The earliest parts date back to the seventh century B.C., when many ducal states began buildings walls along their boundaries. The wall did not take on its gargantuan character until the third century B.C., when China became a united nation. Emperor Qin Shihuang (r. 221–210 B.C.), of terra-cotta warrior fame, ordered Gen. Meng Tian to incorporate existing walls into his own defense network, threading together the ramparts, erecting watchtowers, and constructing beacons to alert the capital (near present-day Xi'an) of attack. His creation became the first Ten Thousand Li Great Wall.

The wall advanced during the Han dynasty, whose emperors

extended Qin Shihuang's efforts into the Gobi desert. Little was done to lengthen the wall during the flourishing Tang and Song dynasties, but the Jin and Ming dynasties heralded a spate of enthusiastic construction—most of the wall we see today dates from the Ming dynasty. In some areas, two walls built in two different dynasties can be seen running side by side over the hills and mountains.

Construction & Height

Construction methods varied through the centuries. In general, the wall's foundation consisted of multiple layers of tamped earth, often mixed with sticks, pebbles, or reeds. The Ming encased exterior sections in brick that was fired locally. Many of the kilns can still be found in the valleys around Beijing.

The Great Wall's average height is 32 feet (10 m), with an average width of 16 feet (5 m)—wide enough for ten soldiers or five horses to stand abreast. Natural features such as mountain ridges, river gorges, and narrow passes were incorporated into the design. Watchtowers, signal towers, and moats are regularly spaced. Three overlapping layers protected key strategic areas.

Despite the care taken to erect an impenetrable structure, the wall failed spectacularly, most notably with the incursions of nomadic groups from the north that established the dynasties of the Jin (Jurchen) in the 12th century, the Yuan (Mongol) in the 13th century, and the Qing (Manchu) in the 17th century.

The Ming dynasty fell to a peasant rebellion in 1644, but the new regime was short-lived. Gen. Wu Sangui, who commanded the forces guarding the Great Wall in Shanhaiguan, decided to throw his lot in with the nomadic Manchus from the north and opened the gates. Manchu forces poured into China. The early Manchu rulers debated the need for such border defenses and apparently decided not to put any more effort or money into them. Eventually they were too occupied with the onslaught of Western forces and European Catholic missionaries coming from the coast to spend time maintaining the wall.

Ultimately, the wall was superseded by technology and circumvented by forces moving into China from other directions, such as the Japanese and the Western powers that mustered along the coastline.

Debunking the Space Myth

Despite common belief, astronauts cannot see the wall from space. American astronaut William Pogue, who reported that he had seen it from Skylab, discovered he was actually looking at the Grand Canal near Beijing.

Though much preservation work needs to be done, the Great Wall became a UNESCO World Heritage site in 1987. The sections you can realistically visit have been rebuilt and cosmetically touched up for the benefit of visitors; this gives a false impression of the condition of the

Badaling

- 145 A2
- 010/6912-1737
- $$
- Bus: 919 from Deshengmen; or Tour Bus 1 from Qianmen (Beijing Sightseeing Bus Center, west of Tiananmen Square, mornings.; tel 010/8353-1111)

Mutianyu

- 145 A2–B2
- Mutianyu Town
- 010/6162-6505
- $$
- Taxi is the best. Bus: 916 or 936 from Dongzhimen Station to Huairou International Conference Center, then minibus; or Tour Bus 6 from Xuanwumen on weekends & national holidays

wall (in large measure derelict). The fortresslike segments viewable around Beijing quickly peter out. But that doesn't make a visit here any less impressive.

Badaling

Most day-trippers from Beijing visit the Great Wall at Badaling, 43 miles (70 km) northwest of the capital city. A hallmark of Ming-dynasty construction, the wall here undulates dramatically peak to peak, punctuated occasionally by watchtowers and gates. Some parts of the wall here can be extremely steep, so wear good shoes. To the west, this stretch eventually dissolves into ruins.

Most times of the year, Badaling is besieged by tourists and commercialization, so don't expect a romantic sojourn with just you and the wall. If you visit in midwinter, however, you will be rewarded with relative peace and quiet and a wonderfully frosted landscape. In addition, you won't be surrounded by a crowd of T-shirt sellers. Just be sure to wrap up—it gets bitter cold.

Entrance to the **Great Wall Museum,** which covers the wall's long history, is included in the ticket for the wall. Also be sure to check out the **International Friendship Forest.** This landscaped path is not well known or marked, so it's usually empty. At the top of the small hill leading from the parking lot toward the steps to the wall, look for the opening to the walkway on the left, just where the souvenir stands begin. Follow the path to a deserted guard tower and nice views of the wall from below.

Mutianyu

Located about 56 miles (90 km) from Beijing, Mutianyu is one of the wall's most overdeveloped and crowded sections. Nevertheless, once you climb the wall and escape the crowds, it offers picture-postcard views of the Great Wall and the countryside.

INSIDER TIP:

Just 37 miles (60 km) northwest of Beijing, Juyongguan Pass is a popular addition to a Badaling visit. Be sure to stop at the Yuan-dynasty Cloud Platform in the middle of the pass.

—MARY STEPHANOS
National Geographic contributor

Originally built in the sixth century, this portion of the wall was given renewed attention after the fall of the Yuan dynasty in 1368, when the new Ming government bolstered security along the northern border. This section—just a mile long (1.6 km)—was repaired and expanded twice during this period, first in the 14th century and then in 1570, when the structure grew to its current size. Take the cable car to the top of the wall, then slide back down on the toboggan track.

A good respite option is the Schoolhouse *(12 Mutianyu Village, 010/6162-6506, www .theschoolhousemutianyu.com),* which also organizes guided wall hikes.

Jinshanling & Simatai

Located about 60 miles (100 km) from Beijing, Jinshanling is one of the few sections of the wall that allow visitors to spend the night. You can sleep in a tent or under the stars in the warmer months, but beware: Mice rule this part of the Great Wall after dark.

One of the most secluded and historically authentic parts of the Great Wall can be found at Simatai, which has been only partially restored. The powerful landscape makes for a marvelous backdrop while hiking along the crumbling remains. Be careful, however: The wall can be dangerously steep in parts and occasionally comes to an abrupt halt over a dangerous drop.

The four-hour walk between Jinshanling and Simatai is very popular. As you leave one site and head for the other—you can go in either direction—the condition of the wall worsens, and the vendors thin out. This is not an easy walk, and in some spots you'll cross narrow remnants of the wall or climb around areas that have been heavily damaged. Don't attempt the walk unless you're in relatively good physical shape and wearing proper hiking shoes.

Jinshanling and Simatai are best reached by taxi. If you plan to walk between the sites, have the driver wait for you at your destination. Or organize your visit through the Peking Downtown Backpackers Hostel (Dongtang Kezhang; 85 Nanluogu Xiang, tel 010/8400 2429, $$$$$). Trips leave every other day at 7 a.m.

Huanghua Cheng

Located about 40 miles (65 km) north of downtown Beijing, Huanghua Cheng is less developed than other sections of the wall, and in some places is heavily damaged. The entire segment, nearly 7 miles long (11 km), joins with the Mutianyu section of the Great Wall in the east and Juyongguan Pass and Badaling in the west. Despite its challenges for hikers—no stone steps and a single pathway—this section is increasingly popular. Huanghua Cheng and Mutianyu are both slated for future upgrades. ∎

Jinshanling & Simatai

- 🅐 145 B3
- ✉ Miyun District
- ☎ 010/8402-4628 & 010/6903-5025
- 💲 $$
- 🚌 Jinshanling: Bus from Dongzhimen bus station to Chengde then taxi
  Simatai: Bus 980 from Dongzhimen to Miyun, then bus to Simatai

Huanghua Cheng

- 🅐 145 A2
- ✉ NW of Huangrou District
- 💲 No gate, but local farmers will sometimes try to charge visitors who wish to climb on the wall.
- 🚌 Bus: 916 from Dongzhimen to Huairou, then switch to the minibus, or hire a taxi.

EXPERIENCE: Venturing Beyond the Wall

Experience a bit of Mongolia on the **Kangxi Grasslands** (map 145 A2, Yangqing County, tel 010/6913-1601, $, bus: 919 from Deshengmen) the largest grassland in the Beijing area. Located just west of the wall at Badaling, this vast plain peppered with yurt villages was once a favorite hunting spot of Qing-dynasty emperors. **Bike Beijing** (tel 133/8140-0738, www.bikebeijing.com/cycling_holidays/kangxi_grassland, $$$$$) runs 2-day tours from the Ming Tombs to the Grasslands. You can also take a horse or camel ride, or spend a few nights in a yurt hotel. The wildlife on the plain is most striking May through September.

Longqing Gorge (Longqing Xia; map 145 A2, Yanqing County; tel 010/6353-2564, closed Nov.–Dec., $$, bus: 919 from Deshengmen to Yanqing Station, then bus 920 or taxi) is just 50 miles (80 km) from Beijing. Take the escalator 1,150 feet (350 m) to the reservoir at the top of the biggest dam in northern China, where you can catch a boat for a 30-minute cruise through the gorge.

The Disappearing Wall

According to a survey conducted in 2006 by the Great Wall Society of China, only 20 percent of the Great Wall is in "reasonable" condition, and another 30 percent lies in ruins. The rest has already disappeared.

Workers repair a broken section of the Great Wall at Jinshanling.

Throughout the 20th and 21st centuries alone the wall has suffered decades of government neglect and intentional destruction. During the 1950s Mao Zedong exhorted the Chinese people to "allow the past to serve the present" (*"Gu wei zhong yong"*). He had farmers demolish parts of the wall and use the bricks to build houses and pigpens. When capitalism began making inroads in the 1980s, many officials believed the tourist industry would save the wall. But today tourism may be its biggest threat.

Poorly executed restoration efforts have left some sections near Beijing looking like a Hollywood set. Entrepreneurs have set up cable cars, souvenir stalls, fast-food restaurants, amusement facilities, villas, and crowded parking lots—all within a stone's throw of the wall.

In Gansu Province, a portion of the wall was rented to farmers, who "restored" it by sealing the section with cement and installing a gate so they could charge admission. A short distance away, tourists have pulled grass from rammed-earth walls—among the wall's oldest and most endangered segments. And Christmas lights have been nailed to the 14th-century towers guarding the gate at Jiayuguan.

The Great Wall Revisited

For his 2007 book, *The Great Wall Revisited,* expert William Lindesay gathered hundreds of photos of the wall taken at the turn of the 20th century. He then set out to rephotograph 150 of the locations, some of which he found had already disappeared. The result was a sobering reminder of how much the wall suffered in just a single century. Lindesay, who is founder of the Friends of the Great Wall conservation group, has continually lobbied Beijing officials to urge better protection of unprotected and overvisited sections of the wall.

In 2002, when the New York–based World Monuments Fund put the Great Wall on its list

A hiker picks her way across a broken section of the disappearing wall.

of the World's 100 Most Endangered Sites, Chinese government officials finally sat up and took notice of their national treasure.

In 2003, Beijing announced its first regulations to protect the wall near the capital. In December 2006, the government announced a new national law: It is now illegal to remove bricks or stones, carve into the wall, or build a house against it. The law also states that "all citizens, legal entities, and organizations" have the responsibility to protect the wall and report illegal activity to government agencies.

Global brands have held fashion shows and banquets on the wall, and a music festival even took place beside the wall at Badaling in 2011.

Still the wall's biggest problem today may be the lack of understanding among some Chinese, especially in poor areas outside Beijing. Parts of the wall have been covered in Chinese graffiti, and farmers continue to cart bricks away.

According to Dong Yaohui, of the Great Wall Society of China, "Trying to get the significance of the wall across to a people worried about their survival is not easy."

Commune by the Great Wall

One of the more interesting architectural projects in the Beijing area is Soho China's Commune by the Great Wall (Changcheng Jiaoxia De Gongshe). The project, which was the brainchild of Zhang Xin and Pan Shiyi, is part commercial enterprise, part artistic endeavor. The hotel won a prize at the 2002 Venice Biennial, when it was unveiled to great acclaim. Zhang says it was designed in part to fill China's gap in architectural awareness.

Cantilever House offers a grand view of the countryside.

Commune by the Great Wall

- 145 A2
- Great Wall Exit 53, at Shuiguan 96, Jingzang Highway, Badaling
- 010/8118-1888
- By appointment
- $$
- Bus: 919 from Deshengmen, then take taxi

www.commune
.com.cn

Staff at the hotel wear bright red stars on their hats and uniforms, but there's nothing communist about this fashionable enclave, which features 12 luxury villas and more than 45 guest rooms designed by Asia's most talented young architects. In 2009, extra chalets plus replicated versions of the original 12 villas were also opened, expanding the size of the resort to a capacity of 201 rooms.

The most impressive of the villas is the **Bamboo Wall,** designed by Japanese architect Kengo Kuma. The structure's interior and exterior walls, and some floors, are made of bamboo, while the elegant but sparsely decorated rooms create a Japanese aesthetic. One of the most interesting parts of the house is the meditation space. The dining room door opens onto a granite bridge that spans a shallow moat within the house, leading to a bamboo cage comprised of sliding doors. The view of the Great Wall from inside the cage is magnificent.

The **Split House,** designed by Yung Ho Chang, is split down the middle to create various angles and spaces. A stream meanders up to the front door then flows beneath the glass walkway into the vestibule. This wood-framed house was built in the Chinese tradition; the earthen walls keep the house warm in winter and cool in summer.

Designed by Hong Kong architect Gary Change, the **Suitcase House** is just as its name suggests. Pneumatic panels on the floor open up to reveal hidden bedrooms as well as a submerged kitchen and bathroom. There are hidden work and storage spaces throughout the house, and even a hidden sauna and shower. Wall panels slide back and forth to provide privacy.

The villas are available as accommodations, but visitors are welcome to admire their exteriors any time and to look inside when they are vacant. The somewhat pricey restaurant serves classic Beijing, Sichuan, and Cantonese dishes and offers great views of the surrounding countryside. ∎

Ming Tombs

Thirteen of the 16 Ming-dynasty emperors are buried in the Ming Tombs (Ming Shisanling), which are located in a valley about 30 miles (48 km) northwest of Beijing. Three tombs in the valley are open to the public: Changling, Dingling, and Zhaoling.

Spirit Way

After an emperor died, his body was placed in a coffin and carried to his tomb along an impressive pathway called the Spirit Way (Shen Dao or Ling Dao). The body was accompanied by 24 carved stone statues: six pairs of animals—lions, *xiechi* (a mythical beast), camels, elephants, unicorns, and horses—and three pairs of humans—scholars, administrators, and soldiers.

INSIDER TIP:

Take note of the protective arc that the Jundu Mountains form around the site of the Ming Tombs. This restful valley was chosen according to feng shui principles.

—ALISON WRIGHT
National Geographic photographer

In order to reach the tombs, you must also walk along the Spirit Way, which begins beneath a stone portico with five carved archways and continues through the **Great Red Gate** (Da Hongmen Do Gongmen). The gate's central archway was reserved solely for the coffins of deceased emperors. Next is the **Stele Pavilion** (Bei Ting), which holds a large stele eulogizing the Ming-dynasty emperors. The Spirit Way comes to an end at the **Dragon and Phoenix Gate** (Lingxing Men and Longfeng Men), which the dead emperor passed on his way to the tomb.

After crossing the arched bridge, you can visit the tombs, which are scattered throughout the valley.

The Tombs

Changling is the first tomb ahead. Considered the most important in the valley, it is the tomb of Emperor Yongle, who died in 1424. Although the tomb itself has not been excavated, you can visit the imposing Hall of Sacrifice, which is supported by 32 huge pillars, each of which was carved from a single tree and transported from Yunnan Province.

Dingling, the tomb of Emperor Wanli (r. 1573–1620) and his two concubines, was excavated in 1958. The excavation team found a number of underground vaults and around 300 garments and many pieces of jewelry, curios, and porcelain packed in 26 lacquer chests, all of which are now displayed in two exhibition halls outside.

Zhaoling is the tomb of the Ming-dynasty emperor Longqing (r. 1567–1572).

The remainder of the tombs are awaiting excavation. ∎

Ming Tombs

- 🅰 145 A2
- ✉ Shisanling Changping County
- ☎ 010/6076-1888
- 💲 $$, plus $$ to visit Sacred Way & each of the tombs
- 🚌 Bus: 1–5 (before 9 a.m.) or 345, then transfer to 314

Shanhaiguan & Beidaihe

A 3.5-hour train ride from Beijing, Shanhaiguan offers history and spectacular views of the Great Wall. Combine your visit with a stop at the seaside resort of Beidaihe.

Shanhaiguan
 145 C2
✉ Qinhuangdao City, Shanhaiguan District
💲 $$

Beidaihe
145 C2
🚆 Trains: Several per day from Beijing

Shanhaiguan

Shanhaiguan, which means the "pass between the mountains and the sea," is a fortress town located where the Great Wall dips down from the mountains in the west and plunges east into the sea. Built in 1381 by Ming-dynasty general Xu Da to keep marauders out of the northeast, this square fortress now draws visitors from all over China.

The fortress at Shanhaiguan played a key role in Chinese history, but not exactly what General Xu intended, for at the end of the Ming dynasty, it failed to prevent the Manchus from entering.

The east gate in Shanhaiguan's city wall, called the **First Pass Under Heaven** (Tianxia Diyi Guan), also passes through the Great Wall. The adjacent **Great Wall Museum** has exhibits of armor, weapons, and photographs related to the history of the wall as well as a scale model of the entire area.

A nice place to view the sunrise, **Old Dragon's Head** (Lao Longtou)—the easternmost portion of the wall built during the Ming dynasty—has been nicely restored. The old **Navy Barracks** along the shore have also been rebuilt. The Qing-dynasty **Temple of the Sea God** (Haishen Miao), on the other side of the beach, is a good place to view the wall.

Jiao Shan is a very steep section of the Great Wall just 2.5 miles (4 km) outside the city. From its apex you'll have wonderful views of the city and Old Dragon's Head plunging into the sea. For those who can't climb, there is a chairlift that makes the ascent.

Beidaihe

Foreigners living in the Beijing legations and the Tianjin concession areas established the popular beach resort of Beidaihe during the 19th century as a respite from city life. After the diplomats, businessmen, and missionaries left, the Communist Party stepped in quickly to fill the gap. Chairman Mao, renowned for his love of swimming, came here for a dip in the ocean, and the top party leadership held secretive meetings here each August, until they were finally discontinued in 2003. Many senior officials own beach villas in this small oceanfront town.

Beidaihe, one of few worthwhile beaches along China's coast, sits along the Hebei Coast just an hour away from Shanhaiguan. The sand and water here are not much to talk about, nonetheless this resort remains a pleasant and quick getaway from the hustle and bustle of downtown Beijing. Come here to escape life's cares, soak up some sun, swim, walk along the beach, and eat plenty of seafood. ■

Chengde Imperial Mountain Resort

Located 159 miles (225 km) northeast of Beijing, Chengde Imperial Mountain Resort is a sprawling 18th-century complex of palaces, pavilions, temples, and monasteries (the latter two known together as the Eight Outer Temples). Although a number of the buildings are in ruins, much survives, offering visitors an impressive architectural museum.

A man burns an offering at the Putuo Zongcheng Temple in Chengde.

Originally a 6-mile (10 km) wall enclosed the resort, whose chief entrance is called **Lizheng Men;** another entrance—**Dehui Men**—pierces the wall to the east. The **Main Palace** (Zheng Gong), with its nine courtyards (nine being the number of heaven) set amid pines and rocks, houses a museum of imperial memorabilia.

The plain that stretches to the north of the main park was the site of imperial hunting parties and archery competitions, and the lake to the east (divided into Ideal Lake and Clear Lake) is studded with temples and pavilions. The **Hall of**

Mist and Rain (Yanyu Lou) sits on a small island.

On the lake's eastern shore is **Gold Mountain** (Jinshan), a small hill topped by the **Pavilion of God** (Shangdi Ge), an elegant hexagonal pagoda and temple built for Emperor Kangxi. Also on the lake are the **Water's Heart Pavilions** (Shuixin Xie), which were erected for Qianlong as one of his 36 spots of beauty on the grounds of the resort.

Nearby is the **Temple of Eternal Blessing** (Yongyou Si), and on **Canglang Island** (Canglang Yu) you will find a copy of one of Suzhou's famous gardens.

Chengde
- 145 C3

Temple of Universal Tranquility
- ✉ Just off Puning Si Lu
- ☎ 031/4205-8209
- 💲 $$
- 🚌 Bus: 6 or 118

Puyou Temple
- ✉ Beside Puning Si
- ☎ 031/4216-0935
- 💲 $
- 🚌 Bus: 6 or 118

Putuo Zongcheng Temple
- ⊠ Shizi Gou Lu
- ☎ 031/4216-3072
- 💲 $$
- 🚌 Bus: 118

Temple of Sumeru Happiness and Longevity
- ⊠ Shizi Gou Lu
- ☎ 031/4216-2972
- 💲 $
- 🚌 Bus: 118

Temple of Universal Happiness
- ⊠ Just off Hedong Lu
- ☎ 031/4205-7557
- 💲 $
- 🚌 Bus: 10

Temple of Appeasing the Distant
- ⊠ To the north of Pule Si
- ☎ 031/4205-7809
- 💲 $
- 🚌 Bus: 10

Eight Outer Temples

From the front of the imperial garden, catch a bus to the Eight Outer Temples (Wai Ba Miao), which lie a couple miles to the north and northeast. Of the original 12 temples, 8 remain, built mainly between 1750 and 1780 during the reign of Qianlong. You may find that some temples are closed or partially off-limits for preservation.

Tibetan motifs dominate the peaceful **Temple of Universal Tranquility** (Puning Si), built in 1755 and styled after a Tibetan monastery. This is still a working temple. Inside, the magnificent 75-foot-tall (23 m) statue of Guanyin, the goddess of mercy, is said to be the largest statue of the goddess in the world.

To the east stands the **Puyou Temple** (Puyou Si), which once had a collection of 500 luohan statues, many of which were destroyed during the war with Japan in the 1930s and 1940s.

Located in the hills to the north of the imperial complex, **Putuo Zongcheng Temple** (Putuo Zongcheng Zhi Miao) is the largest of the eight temples. It was built in 1771 by the very religious Emperor Qianlong to mark his 60th birthday and with the hope that the Dalai Lama would visit Chengde (he didn't). The dagoba-topped temple is known as the mini-Potala, a reference to Potala Palace in Lhasa.

To the east is the magnificent **Temple of Sumeru Happiness and Longevity** (Xumi Fushou Zhi Miao). High outer walls surround the temple, whose huge roof is covered with dragons.

Just to the south is the **Temple of Universal Happiness** (Pule Si), which resembles Beijing's Hall of Prayer for a Good Harvest at the Temple of Heaven (see p. 100). The temple, which has a circular, two-tiered roof, was built in 1776 to entertain envoys.

The **Temple of Appeasing the Distant** (Anyuan Miao), with its unusual black-tiled roof, was built to assuage Mongol tribes. The huge, quadrilateral temple is decorated with decayed Buddhist frescoes.

Other temples in the complex include the Chinese-style **Temple of Extensive Benevolence** (Puren Si), said to be the oldest of the temples, and the **Shuxiang Temple** (Shuxiang Si), located northwest of the complex. Neither is open to the public. ∎

Centuries of Superstition

Chengde Imperial Mountain Resort is known in Chinese as Bishu Shanzhuang, literally "mountain villa for escaping the heat." Established during the reign of Emperor Kangzi (r. 1662–1722), the resort was much expanded during the reign of Kangxi's grandson, Qianlong (r. 1736–1795). Work continued during the reign of Emperor Jiaqing (r. 1796–1820), but his death from a fire at the resort (ignited, according to rumor, by a bolt of lightning) tarnished Chengde's reputation, which was further blackened after the death of Emperor Xianfeng in 1861 under suspicious circumstances. Even the last emperor, Puyi, refused to visit the resort.

Temples, museums, ancient architectural sites, and the former foreign concession city of Tianjin

Excursions South

Introduction & Map   158–159

Qing Tombs   160–161

Tianjin   162–163

Marco Polo Bridge   164

Zhoukoudian Peking Man
   Site & Shidu   165

Feature: Chinese Temples   166–167

Experience: Sampling Buddhist
   Vegetarian Cuisine   167

Fahai Temple   168

Badachu   169

Temple of the Ordination
   Terrace   170

Tanzhe Temple   171

Cuandixia   172–173

Experience: Hiking the Hills
   Around Beijing 173

Hotels & Restaurants   304–305

Burning incense at Tanzhe Temple

Excursions South

If you have a bit of extra time during your visit to Beijing, you can significantly deepen your experience in China by taking advantage of any one of the numerous historical and cultural attractions located within a couple of hours' drive of the country's old imperial capital.

The imperial tombs offer fascinating insight into the lives of China's former emperors. Many of them are set in Hebei Province, such as the fine Eastern Qing Tombs, 78 miles (125 km) northeast of Beijing, and the Western Qing Tombs, 68 miles (110 km) to the southwest. To learn about someone even older, visit the caves of Zhoukoudian, the home of Peking Man, who roamed this neighborhood 30 miles (48 km) southwest of Beijing some half a million years ago.

Because Beijing was an ancient center of Buddhism, the mountain areas ringing the city are rich in rustic old temples, many dating back more than 500 years. Completed in the 15th century, Fahai Temple, to the west, impresses with its gorgeous interior frescoes.

In the fast-changing city of Tianjin, just half an hour by train southeast, walk around the old European neighborhoods and peek into a Qing-dynasty mosque.

For a nice escape from the city, explore Cuandixia, a village where farmers still live in centuries-old courtyard houses. Or visit the scenic area of Shidu, about 30 miles (50 km) south of Beijing, which provides many opportunities for enjoying the outdoors. ■

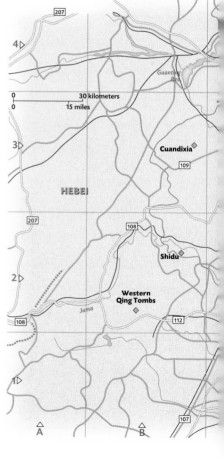

NOT TO BE MISSED:

The imperial Qing Tombs of Hebei Province 160–161

Tianjin's bustling markets 162–163

A stroll across the Marco Polo Bridge 164

The mystery of Peking Man 165

Exploring Chinese temples 166–167

The fabulous frescoes of Mahavira Hall in Fahai Temple 168

Hiking between the eight great sites of Badachu 169

Cuandixia: the Qing dynasty village that time forgot 172–173

One of the oldest temples in the Western Hills, dating from the Jin dynasty (265–420), the Buddhist Tanzhe Temple features a series of arched roofs.

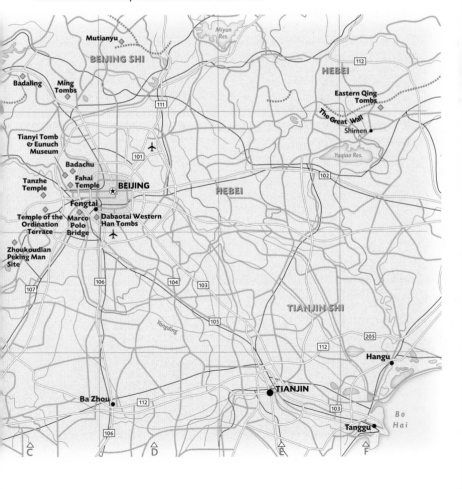

Qing Tombs

Unlike Ming-dynasty emperors, the rulers of the Qing dynasty had two burial sites: the Eastern and Western Qing Tombs. The idea probably began with Emperor Yongzheng (r. 1723–1735), who some historians now believe usurped the throne from his brother. Wary of being buried alongside those he had betrayed, Yongzheng ordered that a second Qing-dynasty tomb be built. Later, Emperor Qianlong decreed that burials should alternate between the two sites.

The Tomb of the Empress Dowager Cixi cost 2.27 million tales of silver to build.

Eastern Qing Tombs

🅰 159 F4

✉ Malan Yu, Zunhua County, Hebei Province

☎ 031/5694-9851 or 031/5694-5471

💲 $$$

🚍 Bus: from Sihui Long Distance Bus Terminal (just S of Sihui Subway Station, Beijing) toward Zunhua. Get off at Shimen, then taxi.

Eastern Qing Tombs

Five emperors, 15 empresses, 3 princes, 2 princesses, and 136 concubines are interred at the Eastern Qing Tombs (Qing Dongling), located 78 miles (125 km) east of Beijing. All 15 tombs are open to the public. The tombs of Emperor Qianlong and the Empress Dowager Cixi are the best ones to visit.

Yuling: Yuling—the underground tomb of Emperor Qianlong—is the finest of the Eastern Qing Tombs. Its interior walls, high arched ceilings, and huge marble doors are decorated with beautiful carved images of the Buddha, the Four Heavenly Kings, and bodhisattvas, as well as passages from Buddhist scriptures in both Sanskrit and Tibetan. The emperor is buried here along with his empresses and consorts.

Ding Dong Ling: The tomb of the Empress Dowager Cixi has many reminders of the Forbidden City. The carved ramp leading to her sacrificial hall depicts the phoenix (representing the empress) above the dragon (the emperor), reflecting her final years in the court when she ruled from behind the proverbial screen. **Longen Hall,** located just before her burial chamber, features elaborate wooden carvings of gold-painted bats and dragons. Cixi's tomb is located next to the tomb of her co-regent, Ci'an.

Western Qing Tombs

The Western Qing Tombs (Qing Xiling), located 87 (140 km) miles west of Beijing, are the final resting place for four emperors—Yongzheng, Jiaqing, Daoguang, and Guangxu—who are buried here with 9 empresses, 76 princes, and 57 imperial concubines.

Tailing: Tailing is the tomb of Emperor Yongzheng and the largest in the complex. It has a 2-mile-long (3 km) **Spirit Way,** attended by 40 flanking ministers, generals, and animals, all in stone. The tomb's gateways and buildings were used during the various Buddhist rituals and sacrifices held in memory of the emperor.

Muling: The tomb that Emperor Daoguang (r. 1821–1850) built for himself is small and relatively modest compared to Tailing. It also has neither a Spirit Way nor a stele pavilion. Shortly after taking the throne, Daoguang began planning his burial in the Eastern Qing Tombs, according to the alternation plan. One year after it was finished, however, the underground chamber flooded, and the superstitious Daoguang turned to the Western Qing Tombs to select a new and more auspicious site.

Convinced that the flooding was caused by several dragons losing their homes, he included many pleasing dragon images in his second tomb. He is buried along with three empresses.

Chongling: The tomb of Emperor Guangxu (r. 1875–1908) was not yet finished when the Qing dynasty collapsed in 1911, and it would not be complete for another four years. Guangxu was the nephew of Cixi, who held him under house arrest in the Summer Palace during his final years because of the emperor's support for the reform movement. He died mysteriously, and it's widely believed that the

INSIDER TIP:

If you plan to venture farther south from Beijing, use *ctrip.com* or *elong.net* to book internal flights and hotels in China. The website and phone service [400/619-9999] are in English.

—JENNIFER ALLARD
National Geographic contributor

Empress Dowager had him poisoned. His tomb has wonderful stone doors carved with bodhisattvas. Keeping him company in an adjoining tomb is Zhenfei, the Pearl Concubine, who is probably best known for allegedly being forced down a well in the Forbidden City after upsetting the Empress Dowager. ∎

Western Qing Tombs

- 158 B2
- Yixian County, Hebei Province
- 031/2471-0012
- $$$
- Bus: from Lizeqiao Long Distance Bus Terminal, Beijing, to Yixian County, then taxi

Tianjin

At first glance, Tianjin might appear as an uninviting industrial city. A closer look at the center of town, however, reveals a patchwork of European, Russian, and Japanese architecture in this former foreign concession city and is easily reached in 30 minutes by high-speed train.

European-style buildings line the banks of the Hai River.

Tianjin

🅰 159 E1

Visitor Information

☎ 010/5186-7999

🚆 Frequent daily trains from the Beijing South Railway Station

Notre Dame des Victoires Catholic Cathedral

✉ 292 Shizilin Dajie

☎ 022/2635-1172

🕐 Inside closed for renovation

🚍 Bus: Shizilinqiao

Ancient Culture Street

✉ Dongbei Jiao, Nankai District

☎ 022/2735-8682

🚍 Bus: Dongbeijiao

Tianjin lies just 60 miles (97 km) southeast of Beijing and has a long history as an urban and trading center. Established as a walled garrison in 1404, it became the economic heart of northern China by the early Qing dynasty. The 1858 Treaty of Tianjin—ending the Second Opium War—opened the city to British and French concessions and construction by other Western nations along the Hai River. Foreign troops shelled and occupied the city during the Boxer Rebellion (see pp. 33, 36), destroying its old walls. Following that Westerners turned Tianjin into a hub for trade and industry. In the late 1970s, it became one of the first cities

opened to foreign investment, and today it is the biggest shipping port in northern China.

Visiting the Town

Starting on the north side, the **Notre Dame des Victoires Catholic Cathedral** (Shengmu Desheng Tang or Wanghailou Jiaotang), Tianjin's earliest cathedral, was first built in 1869. It was destroyed during the Boxer Rebellion and again in 1976 by the brutal Tangshan earthquake. The cathedral was rebuilt in 1983.

Head southwest of the church to search for souvenirs and elusive historic relics in the **Ancient Culture Street** (Gu Wenhua Jie). Meant to re-create the structures that once stood on this old street, the buildings here have carved balconies, red-and-green painted shops, and curling tile roofs. The stalls offer a colorful array of items, including documents from the Cultural Revolution, kites, and clay figurines (a local handicraft).

Peeking out through the bric-a-brac for sale on Ancient Culture Street is the wonderful little **Tianhou Temple** (Tianhou Gong). Dedicated to Tianhou, the goddess of the sea, the temple, built in 1326, has undergone numerous renovations. The restored frescoes show scenes from the life of Tainhou (Haishen Niangniang or Mazu). Also on display are models of Ming- and Qing-dynasty ships from the coastal provinces of Fujian and Zhejiang (where Tianhou is most actively worshiped).

One block west of Ancient Culture Street stands the **Confucius Temple** (Wen Miao), a monument to the Great Sage.

A statue of Confucius sits on the altar, surrounded by ancient musical instruments. The temple, built in 1436, has been restored many times. The temple was reopened in 2010 after three years of comprehensive renovations.

European Legacy

The Romanesque **Xikai Cathedral** (Xikai Jiaotang) was built in 1916 in the shape of a crucifix. Originally managed by missionary priests, the cathedral is a copy of Notre Dame de la Garde in Marseille, France. The area south of the Hai River was home to the former European and Japanese concessions. **Central Park** was located in the old French concession (Jiefang Lu), where French chateaux line the streets.

Farther down Huayuan Lu, the British concession reveals grand Edwardian establishments. The recently renovated **Astor Hotel** *(33 Tai'erzhuang Lu, tel 022/2331-1688)* on the riverbank is worth a look. Like many of the fine buildings around it, this exemplifies the European influence of the early 20th century. Nearby on Jiefang Bei Lu were the offices of British commercial houses. Across the river lay the Russian concession.

The **Shenyandao Antiques Market** *(Shenyang Dao)* is open every Thursday from 4 a.m. and has a wide variety of real and factory-fresh antiques. As usual, unless you're an expert, steer away from the antiquities.

On the Yongle river bridge is the city's newest attraction, the Tianjan Eye Ferris Wheel, which stands 395 feet (120m) high and looks spectacular when neon-lit at night. ■

Confucius Temple

✉ 1 Dongmenli, Nankai District

☎ 022/2727-2812

🚇 Metro: Xibeijiao or Xinanjiao

Xikai Cathedral

✉ 9 Xining Dao, Heping District

☎ 022/2835-8812

The Grand Mosque

The **Grand Mosque** (Tianjin Qingzhen Dasi; *Qingzhen Xiang Zhenbu Jie, Hongqiao District, tel 022/2727-1056, metro: Xibeijiao*), which adds a bit of exotic variety to Tianjin's cityscape, is believed to have been built in 1644, right at the start of the Qing dynasty. This impressive structure, which has been renovated and expanded over the centuries, is an excellent example of Chinese Muslim architecture, a style that emerged during the Ming dynasty. The mosque is still an active place of worship for the city's Muslims; while guests are allowed to roam the complex, certain halls of worship are off-limits to visitors.

Marco Polo Bridge

The Marco Polo Bridge (Lugou Qiao), located in the Fengtai District 10 miles (16 km) southwest of Beijing, is so named because of its mention in the Italian explorer's famous travelogue. The bridge, wrote Marco Polo, "is a very fine stone bridge, so fine indeed, that it has very few equals in the world." Erected in 1189, the elaborate structure is Beijing's oldest marble bridge.

Marco Polo Bridge
- 159 C3
- 77 Wanping Chengnan Jie Lugou Qiao
- $ ($ extra to visit tower)
- Metro: Qianmen, Beijing, then bus 301 to Kangzhan Diaosu Yuan; or Wukesong, then bus 624

Museum of the War of Resistance Against Japan
- 101 Chengnei Lu, Fengtai District
- 010/8389-2355
- Tues.–Sun. 9 a.m.–4 p.m.

The Marco Polo Bridge stretches 873 feet (266 m) over the dry ground that was once the Yongding River. Its original thick stone slabs have survived on its center surface. More than 500 carved **stone lions** run across the balustrade and **imperial steles** stand at both ends. The bridge, with its 11 **arches,** can best be seen from the riverside. The bridge is most famous as the site of the Marco Polo Bridge Incident of 1937, when Japanese troops in the area exchanged gunfire with Chinese soldiers. The Japanese used this skirmish as a pretext for their occupation of China. On one end of the bridge, within the walls of **Wanping Fortress,** you'll find the full history in the **Museum of the War of Resistance Against Japan** (Zhongguo Renmin Kangri Zhanzheng Jinianguan). ∎

INSIDER TIP:

For (free) multimedia exhibits on the 1937 bridge incident, step off the bridge and into the adjacent Museum of the War of Resistance Against Japan.

—KENNY LING
National Geographic contributor

Pedestrians have worn smooth the bridge's stones over centuries of use.

Zhoukoudian Peking Man Site & Shidu

The Zhoukoudian Peking Man Site (Zhoukoudian Yizhi Bowuguan) will fascinate not only archaeologists and anthropologists but also anyone interested in the lives of ancient humans. Located about 30 miles (48 km) southwest of Beijing, the site was once home to Peking Man, or *Homo erectus pekinensis,* who roamed the area half a million years ago.

In 1929, a Chinese archaeologist discovered a number of skulls belonging to Peking Man and his neighbors. These early humans could stand upright, hunt, make fire, and use simple stone tools. The find has been called one of the most important paleontological discoveries of the 20th century. Unfortunately, the bones mysteriously disappeared soon after they were discovered (see sidebar right).

The trails at Zhoukoudian Peking Man Site will lead you through several areas of excavation and past the caves where this primitive man lived. The small **museum** displays related artifacts, including flint tools, bone needles, and animal parts. Although this is a UNESCO World Heritage site, it has not been well taken care of, and there is little information available in English.

Shidu

Located about 68 miles (110 km) southwest of Beijing, Shidu *(map 158 B2, Shidu Fangshan District, tel 010/6134-9009, $$, train: 6095 from Beijing West Railway Station to Shidu Station or bus: 917 from Tianqiao)* sits on the winding Juma River near the Zhoukoudian Peking Man Site.

The Disappearance of Peking Man

At the height of the war with Japan, archaeologists—worried that Peking Man fossils might fall into Japanese hands—put the 5 skulls, 147 teeth, and a number of other bones into two large wooden boxes and turned them over to the U.S. Marine Corps for safekeeping. The remains were housed in the American-run Peking Union Medical Hospital, which oversaw the Cenozoic Research Lab. The plan to transport the fossils to the United States was interrupted when the Japanese bombed Pearl Harbor on December 7, 1941. Sometime shortly after, the fossils disappeared. Since then, the fate of Peking Man has been the subject of much speculation. In 2005, the Chinese government announced a new investigation. It seems that the beguiling mystery of Peking Man continues.

Easy paths in the area wander past karst formations, or you can tour the place on horseback. You may also find it worthwhile to soak up local culture in the small villages. If you wish, you can rent a room in a private home.

For the adventurous traveler, Shidu is famous for its outdoor activities—especially its bungee-jumping facilities. This is also an excellent place for those interested in rock climbing. ∎

Zhoukoudian Peking Man Site

🗺 159 C2

✉ 1 Zhoukoudian Dajie

☎ 010/6930-1272

$ $

🚌 Bus: 917 from Tianqiao Bus Station, Beijing, to Fangshan, then taxi

Chinese Temples

Three recognized and interlinked faiths belong to traditional China: Confucianism, Taoism, and Buddhism. Of these, the first two are purely indigenous, while Buddhism traveled to China from India at least two millennia ago via the Silk Road. Although most Chinese temples are readily identifiable as predominantly Confucian, Taoist, or Buddhist, symbols and deities from all three interrelated faiths often appear in a single temple.

The Temple of the Azure Clouds, located in Fragrant Hills Park, in Beijing's Haidian District

Confucian

Confucian temples, or *wenmiao,* are essentially dedicated to tradition, education, and filial piety. They commonly house stone steles mounted on the backs of stone tortoises recording the names of literary graduates, honoring the tradition of learning, which "hangs like perfume through the ages." Most contain a statue of the Great Sage, Kong Fuzi (Confucius, 551–479 B.C.), as well as images of his disciples, especially the Confucian philosopher Meng Zi (Mencius, 372–289 B.C.). There are relatively

few Confucius temples, the most important being in the master's hometown of Qufu, in Beijing, appropriately called the Confucious Temple (see p. 78).

Taoist

Taoist temples, or *guan,* are dedicated to the teachings of Laozi (sixth century B.C.), founder of the faith and author of the *Daodejing (Classic of the Way of Power).* Besides images of Laozi, Taoist guan generally contain images of the Eight Immortals, the Jade Emperor, and often the goddess charged with protecting seafarers, Tianhou (aka Mazu). Taoism teaches practicing harmony with Tao, the Way, and is often described as naturist. Taoist monks, or *taoshi*, wind their long hair up in knots and wear jackets and trousers. Dongyue Temple (see p. 125) and White Cloud Temple (see pp. 118–119) are among the most celebrated Taoist temples in Beijing.

Buddhist

Buddhist temples, or *simiao* (those dedicated to Zen Buddhism are called *chansi*), are distinguished by images of a laughing and jovial Buddha and by statues of Sakyamuni, also called Gautama (the Historical Buddha), Maitreya (the Future Buddha), and Amitabha (the infinite Buddha). Also enduringly popular is the goddess of mercy, Guanyin, who was somehow transformed into a female deity in her passage across the Himalaya, from her Indian male form Avalokitisevara. In addition, the east and west walls of the main hall of many Buddhist temples typically depict the 18 luohan (arhats). The temples are guarded by the Four Heavenly Kings, filled with incense smoke, and inhabited by shaven-headed, robe-wearing Buddhist monks. The most famous in the Beijing area include the Lama Temple (see p. 79) and Tanzhe Temple (see p. 171).

Religious Minglings

All *sanjiao* temples—Confucian, Taoist, or

Boaters glide past the Pavilion of Buddhist Incense on Longevity Hill, at Beijing's Summer Palace.

Buddhist—are arranged according to divine cosmological principles, and more especially to feng shui, the science of geomancy. Accordingly, temple axes run north–south, with doors and entranceways facing the auspicious south. Evil spirits can only travel in straight lines or across dry land, so walls blocking gateways, ponds, and reflective mirrors fend them off. Auspicious beasts like lions and dragons decorate the temples and intertwine across pillars and eaves.

EXPERIENCE: Sampling Buddhist Vegetarian Cuisine

Eating Chinese vegetarian food is a little different to a meat-free diet back home. Buddhists believe that animals and humans can be reincarnated in different forms, so many do not eat animal meat. Chinese Buddhist chefs found a way around this by using gluten, tofu, and mushroom proteins to fashion dishes that look, smell, and taste like

Chinese meat dishes while remaining wholly vegetarian.

Vegetarian China (*www.vegetarian -china.info*) is a useful website for visitors wanting to sample—and be able to pronounce—Chinese vegetarian dishes. It also features a comprehensive listing of Buddhist temple restaurants to try in Beijing and Shanghai.

Fahai Temple

Worthwhile Fahai Temple (Fahai Si) is located at the foot of Cuiwei Hill, about 12 miles (19 km) west of Beijing. The temple's detailed and colorful Buddhist murals are considered to be the finest examples of mural art remaining in China today.

A portion of the centuries-old mural that adorns the walls of the Fahai Temple

Fahai Temple
- 159 C3
- 28 Moshikou, Shijingshan District
- 010/8871-6743
- Metro: Line 1 from Beijing to Pingguo Yuan, then taxi; or bus 331 to temple

The temple was completed in about 1443 by Li Tong, a eunuch in the court of Emperor Zhengtong (r. 1435–1449 and 1457–1464), with funds he collected from various officials, Buddhist leaders, and lay people. The design of the temple is laid out on three levels.

The best works of art found here are the wonderful Ming-dynasty frescoes painted on the inner walls of the **Mahavira Hall** (Daxiong Baodian), which stands on the north side of the rear courtyard. This is the only original structure still standing; the others have all been replaced. The paintings were created at the time of the temple's construction. Two master palace artists and 13 artisans spent four years completing the work.

The artists' names are carved on a stone tablet outside.

Considered to be very important works in the history of Chinese art, the amazingly detailed frescoes depict the bodhisattvas Guanyin, Puxian, and Wenshu. The latter two are considered to be the finest paintings in the temple. Take note also of the six-tusked elephant on the back wall. Each of the tusks represents a quality that is believed to lead to enlightenment.

During the frenzied days of the Cultural Revolution, rampaging Red Guards destroyed the statues that originally stood in the temple. Reproductions of the statues were erected in the temple in 1996. ■

Badachu

Badachu, or "eight great sites," refers to the eight monasteries, nunneries, and temples nestled in woods at the foot of the Western Hills, about 12 miles (19 km) northwest of Beijing. Most of these religious complexes were built during the late Sui (581–618) and early Tang (618–907) dynasties and later renovated. The landscape makes for wonderful hiking between the sites.

Built in 1504, the Ming-dynasty **Temple of Eternal Peace** (Chang'an Si) is located outside the main gate of Badachu at the foot of Cuiwei Hill. About a mile (1.6 km) up the hill you'll find the Tang-dynasty **Temple of Divine Light** (Lingguang Si). The only one of the eight that still has monks as residents, this temple is the most worthwhile to visit in Badachu. A statue of Sakyamuni sits in the main hall.

Built in 1956, the **Pagoda of the Buddha's Tooth** (Foya Sheli Ta) sits on a huge pedestal. The relic tooth is preserved in a small gold pagoda. A short walk away is the **Three Hill Nunnery** (Sanshan An), built in 1151 and named for its location between Cuiwei Hill, Pingpo Hill, and Lushi Hill.

Walk up from the convent to reach the **Temple of Great Mercy** (Dabei Si), built sometime before 1033. The courtyard in front of **Daxiong Hall** has a rare species of bamboo that stays green all winter. To the northwest is the **Temple of the Dragon King** (Longwang Tang), also known as Dragon Spring Nunnery (Longquan An).

The largest temple in Badachu, the Tang-dynasty **Temple of the Fragrant World** (Xiangjie Si) was the summer getaway for China's emperors. It also has many historic relics, paintings and calligraphy.

Take the steep steps up to the **Mahayana Gate,** the temple's entrance. The **Scripture Repository** has statues of Randengfo, Sakyamuni, and Maitreya–the Past, Historical, and Future Buddhas. In the entrance hall of the **Imperial Palace** (Xing Gong) to the east is the **Study for Distant Viewing,** which offers nice vistas.

INSIDER TIP:

Watch out for the five elements of feng shui (metal, water, wood, fire, and earth) in the design of the temples you visit in China.

—ALISON WRIGHT
National Geographic photographer

Continue up the steep path to the 18th-century **Cave of the Precious Pearl** (Baozhu Dong). The hall behind the memorial archway is the **Temple of Precious Pearls,** the highest of the eight temples. On a clear day, you can see the city of Beijing.

The large bell in **Zhengguo Temple** was cast during the Ming dynasty. Two steles mark the entrance. Built in either the Tang or Sui dynasty, the temple is said to be the oldest in the complex. ∎

Badachu

- 🗺 159 C3
- ✉ Badachu Lu, Shijingshan District
- ☎ 010/8896-4661
- 💲 $
- 🚌 Bus: 972 from Pingguo Yuan Metro Station; 347 from Xinjiekou; or 389 from Yuquan Lu Metro Station

Temple of the Ordination Terrace

The Temple of the Ordination Terrace (Jietai Si) lies in the Western Hills, about 21 miles (35 km) southwest of Beijing. There has been a temple on this mountain for 1,350 years. However, it was not until the Liao dynasty (916–1125) that a monk built an altar to be used in the ordination ceremony of Buddhist novices; monks have been coming here to take their vows ever since.

Temple of the Ordination Terrace

 159 C3

 Ma'an Shan (Saddle Hill), Mentougou District, Western Hills

 010/6980-6611

$ $$

Bus: 931 from Pingguo Yuan Metro Station, Beijing

Chinese temples normally face south, but this temple was built according to Liao custom, facing east. Most of the structures that exist at the site today, however, date from the Ming and Qing dynasties, and many of the current buildings are the result of Emperor Qianlong's largesse.

Statues of General Ha and General Heng watch over the **Hall of the Front Gate.** Pass the traditional drum and bell towers in the first courtyard, where four steles rest on the backs of impressive stone tortoises.

The **Hall of Heavenly Kings** (Tianwang Dian) has a Maitreya Buddha, also known as the Bag Buddha because of the large cloth bag that he carries with him. The fierce-looking Four Heavenly Kings, with Weituo, the guardian of Buddhism, protect Maitreya.

Take the stairs up to the terrace. Note the **stone column** that dates from 1075. Said to be the oldest and best preserved around Beijing, the eight-sided column is beautifully inscribed with Buddhist scriptures and *zhou*, Chinese for "magic spell" or "charm."

Opposite lies the elaborate Ming-dynasty **Dragon Carved Niche** (Diaolong Fokan), elaborately decorated with slithering dragons. Next to this hall, another **stone column** from the Yuan dynasty (1369) records the life of Yuequan, a former abbot of the Jietai Temple. At the end of this section of the complex, the **Temple of the God of Wealth** (Caishen Shengdian) has a small shop selling Buddhist statues.

To the north of the Dragon Carved Niche awaits the **Hall of Ordination Altar** (Jietai Dian), also known as Xuanfo Chang. Four carved steles stand in its courtyard, along with a golden statue of Sakyamuni. The three tiers of the **Ordination Altar**—one of China's tallest—are carved with 113 figures of the ordination god. ■

Temple Trees

As you stroll the courtyard of the Temple of the Ordination Terrace, take note of the old trees. These ancient trees, scattered throughout the complex, are renowned, the subject of song and poetry. **Sleeping Dragon Pine** (Wolong Song), a pine tree with scale-shaped bark resembling a sleeping dragon, is said to be more than a thousand years old. **Nine Dragon Pine** is so named because of its nine large branches or trunks. The pines add to the allure of the temple, whose grounds are also covered with beautiful cypress and ginkgo trees.

Tanzhe Temple

According to an old saying, "first there was Tanzhe, then came Youzhou" (one of Beijing's ancient names), hinting that Tanzhe Temple (Tanzhe Si) predates the imperial capital. Built during the Jin dynasty (265–420), probably in 400, the temple–with its tree-covered grounds–may not really be older than Beijing, but it is one of the oldest temples in the Western Hills. Located about 18 miles (30 km) west of Beijing, it still attracts Buddhist monks from around China.

Tanzhe Temple is divided into four sections, with the main attractions—the memorial archway, Hall of Heavenly Kings, Mahavira Hall, Pilu Pavilion, Dizang Hall, and Guanyin Hall—all situated along the central north–south axis.

Among the statues of six Buddhas in the **Hall of Heavenly Kings** (Tianwang Dian), the Maitreya Buddha, better known as the Laughing Buddha because he is always smiling, sits in the seat of honor. As usual, he is flanked by the Four Heavenly Kings. The second building is **Mahavira Hall** (Daxiongbao Dian), or the Great Hall of the Powerful Treasure, which is devoted to Sakyamuni.

The Yuan-dynasty **Pilu Pavilion** (Pilu Ge) occupies the temple's highest point and provides an expansive view of the surrounding countryside. To its right stands **Yanshou Pagoda** (Great Longevity Pagoda), built by a prince during the Ming dynasty.

On the right-hand wall of **Dizang Hall** (Dizang Dian), grotesque depictions of the 18 levels of hell recall Dante's *Inferno*. Follow the path behind the hall to **Guanyin Hall** (Guanyin Dian), the last hall in the complex.

Another popular attraction are the so-called **footprints of**

Tanzhe Temple nestles in the Western Hills.

Princess Miaoyan, the daughter of Kublai Khan, who became a nun here during the Yuan dynasty. The temple's abbots lived in the **Hall of Patriarchs** (Zushi Dian), to the west.

Continue moving west, heading down one flight of stairs and up another, to reach **Guanyin Cave,** a quiet, tree-shaded courtyard. To exit the complex, retrace your steps back east and take the first row of steps down.

Tanzhe Temple is also famous for its old and beautiful trees, including sal trees as well as some very old and attractive ginkgo and magnolia trees.

There is a small hotel outside the main gate and several vegetarian restaurants in the area.

Tanzhe Temple
- 🅰 159 C3
- ✉ At foot of Tanzhe Shan, Mentougou District, Western Hills
- ☎ 010/6086-2505
- 💲 $$
- 🚌 Bus: 931 from Pingguo Yuan Metro Station

Cuandixia

Situated in the far west of Beijing municipality, Cuandixia, which literally means "under the earthen cooking pot," is the village that time forgot. According to local legend, this small, out-of-the-way town dates back more than 600 years to the Ming dynasty (1368–1644). It was then that a man and a woman, fleeing floods in Shanxi Province, found their way to this haven, which has seen little change in the past few hundred years—a living fossil of the Qing dynasty.

Life in the village of Cuandixia has changed little since it was first established some 600 years ago.

Cuandixia

- ⌧ 158 B3
- ☎ 010/6981-9333 (village office)
- 🛇 $
- 🚇 Metro: Pingguo Yuan Subway Station, Beijing, then bus 929 to Cuandixia, leaving at 7.30 a.m. and 12.40 p.m. daily (taking two hours)

There are now just around 20 households left here, a sharp decline from the 108 families at the end of the Qing dynasty. Locals attribute the village's preservation—and its impoverished economy—to poor local transportation and emigration over the past century.

Situated in a valley, the small village of Cuandixia is surrounded by four rocky hills and divided into two sections by a curved stone wall.

The houses were constructed in accordance with strict norms, which included arched gates, tiled roofs, and even hitching posts for horses. Though worn by time, the wooden parts of the houses are intact, and you can still see intricate carved bats (symbolizing fortune), magpies (happiness), peonies (splendor), and peaches (longevity).

Vertical couplets hang from the front door of one house, whose walls are covered with fading murals—dating back to the Qing dynasty—that depict stories from the past. In another courtyard house, rabbit and squirrel skins hang from the walls. There are also several wooden boxes filled with honeycombs, as well as the sound of bees busy at work. A press used to extract the honey stands beside the front door. Grass grows out of the roof tiles, and the torn paper covering the windows blows in the wind.

In the past, the huge stone wheel in the village shed was used to grind corn kernels into corn gruel; such grinding stones are common in rural areas outside Beijing. The villagers don't use it anymore, however, preferring to buy their ground products from local shops.

EXPERIENCE:
Hiking the Hills Around Beijing

The city of Beijing is remorselessly flat, but the environs of the municipality are hilly and even mountainous, with hiking trails winding into gullies, ravines, lakes, and remnants of the Great Wall that beckon lovers of the great outdoors.

For fun and energetic treks into the West Mountains and the Cuandixia area, contact **Beijing Hikers** (tel 010/6432-2786, www.beijinghikers.com, $$$$). They offer regular weekend hikes, some midweek hikes, as well as overnight trips. Reservations are a must, and prices include transportation, guides, and snacks. Hikers meet at the Starbucks in the Metropark Lido Hotel (6 Jiangtai Lu, Chaoyang) in the east of Beijing. Beijing Hikers can also arrange tours for small groups, as long as you give five days' notice; they also conduct tours to other parts of China. Kids are welcome.

INSIDER TIP:

Stop into one of Cuandixia's rustic inns for a home-cooked lunch of corn bread, mutton, and wild vegetables picked from nearby mountains.

—DAMIEN HARPER
National Geographic author

Especially interesting are the painted slogans from the Cultural Revolution that remain on the walls of some of the houses. "Long Live Chairman Mao," says one, paint peeling from the wall. "Arm Our Minds with Mao Zedong Thought!" proclaims another. And finally, "Mao Zedong Thought is the Red Sun in Our Hearts."

A winding stone path leads to a small, lonely looking temple situated on a hill; this site is a great vantage point for taking in the entire prospect of the village. The temple is very rundown, but there are some faded murals on the walls, and a stone tablet dating back to the reign of Kangxi lists the names of villagers who donated money for the construction of the temple.

There is little in the way of tourist comforts in Cuandixia, but any of the small "inns" in the village offer a rough and ready insight into the realities of small-town life in rural China. ∎

shanghai

The Bund to People's Square 177–200 ■ **Nanshi: The Old Town** 201–212 ■ **Fuxing Road to Huaihai Road** 213–226 ■ **Pudong** 227–236 ■ **North Shanghai** 237–248 ■ **West Shanghai** 249–258 ■ **Excursions From Shanghai** 259–280

The vibrant, bustling heart of downtown Shanghai, home to the Peoples's Park and the city's elegant International Settlement

The Bund to People's Square

Introduction & Map   178–179

The Bund   180–181

Experience: Sipping Cocktails at the Long Bar   181

Walk the Bund   182–184

Nanjing East Road & Around   185–187

Feature: Shanghai's "Yellow Creek"   188–189

Huangpu   190–191

People's Square Area   192–195

Shanghai Museum   196–199

Experience: Following the Art Deco Trail   197

More Places to Visit From the Bund to People's Square   200

Hotels & Restaurants   305–307

Pages 174–175: The Pudong District's fast-changing skyline is an index of Shanghai's amazing recent growth.
Above: Stone lions guard the entrance to the Shanghai Museum.
Opposite: Nanjing Road pagoda

The Bund to People's Square

The geographic center of Shanghai, this area encompasses the city's grandest buildings, as well as its busiest shopping thoroughfare. Not to be missed is People's Square (Renmin Guangchang). Packed with art deco buildings, sky-high hotels, a theater, opera hall, and the city's best museum, the oval-shaped "square" forms the cultural heart of Shanghai.

When Shanghai emerged from the Sino-British First Opium War of 1842 as a major international port, the triumphant British decreed that the undistinguished riverfront area on the west bank of the Huangpu River just south of Suzhou Creek—the best real estate available to them at the time—would front the new British settlement.

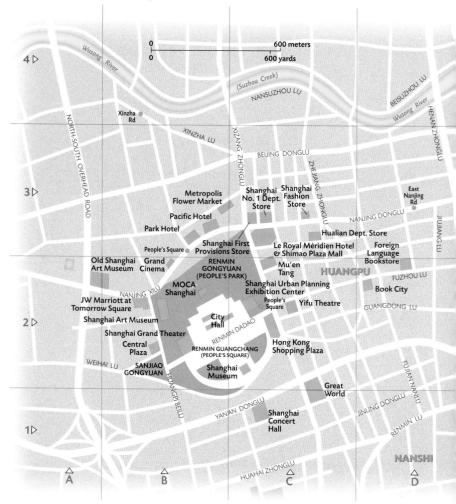

The British named the waterfront road the Bund, derived from the Hindi word meaning "embankment." Although the communist take-over largely purged the Bund (Waitan) of its shocking social and racial inequalities, it likewise sapped the avenue's commercial prosperity and joie de vivre. Since Shanghai reopened to foreign commerce in the 1990s, however, the Bund has staged an astonishing comeback and is now a prestigious address for luxury hotels, restaurants, and cocktail lounges.

Threading west from the Bund, Nanjing Road (Nanjing Donglu) is a bustling pedestrian thoroughfare that extends to People's Square and beyond into Jingan District.

Like Nanjing Road, the extraordinarily prosperous People's Square area is ringed by fine art deco and civic buildings. Underneath is Shanghai's busiest subway station, which connects the cities three main lines. It is also home to the best museums and theater in Shanghai. Here dignified civic buildings dating from the early 20th century huddle in the shadow of futuristic towers of steel and glass that have soared into the sky during the last 15 years.

Beyond the People's Square area to the immediate west lies the small recreational area of Triangle Park (Sanjiao Gongyuan). Quiet and less crowded, the park attracts older city denizens who congregate here to chat, read newspapers, play chess or mahjong, exercise, or admire one another's caged pet birds. It's a pleasantly laid-back conclusion to any exploration of busy downtown Shanghai. ■

Area of map detail

Shanghai
color-coded by region

WAIBAIDU BRIDGE

Rockbund
Art Museum

SICHUAN ZHONGLU

The Peninsula
Shanghai

JIANGXI ZHONGLU

BEIJING
DONGLU

ZHONGSHAN DONG 1-LU

Monument to the
People's Heroes

Bund History
Museum

HUANGPU
PARK

Peace
Hotel

BUND SIGHTSEEING
TUNNEL

Bank of
East Asia

Chen Yi
Monument

PUDONG

Guangdong
Development Bank

Hong Miao
(Red Temple)

Customs House

BINJIANG AVE

Metropole
Hotel

The
Bund

Hamilton
House

JIANGXI
HONGLU

People's
Court

Waldorf Astoria
Shanghai on
the Bund

YANTAN DONG LU
TUNNEL

Westin
Bund
Center

Shanghai Museum
of Natural History

Puxi-Pudong
Ferry Pier

Huangpu
River

Yon'gan
Market

St. Joseph's
Church

ZHONGSHAN DONG 2-LU

E   F

NOT TO BE MISSED:

Cocktails at Shanghai's iconic Long Bar 181

Walking through the historic streets of the Bund 182–184

Cruising the Huangpu River, the city's commercial lifeline 188–189

The Uighur enclave of Little Xinjiang 191

Visiting People's Square 192–195

The Shanghai Museum of Contemporary Art 193

Following Shanghai's art deco trail 197

The Bund

The Bund, known colloquially as Waitan, comprises a string of grand mansions that developed along the Huangpu River in the aftermath of the 1842 Treaty of Nanjing, one of many treaties forced upon China by the West (and later Japan). Its provisions initially threw open five ports—Fuzhou, Guangzhou, Ningbo, Xiamen, and Shanghai—to foreign trade, residence, and consulates and ceded Hong Kong Island to Great Britain until 1997.

A smattering of Shanghai's increasingly prosperous citizens enjoy a stroll along the Bund.

The Bund

 179 E2–E4 &
184

After the Treaty

Within months of the treaty's signing, British merchants and seamen, together with their South Asian associates—soldiers, servants, and camp followers—began pouring into the most important of the five treaty ports: Shanghai. They landed at the Bund and established a toe-hold south and west of Suzhou Creek. The British Consulate was later built at the convergence of the Huangpu River and Suzhou Creek at the Bund's north end.

The British settlement in Shanghai more than doubled in size from 1843 to 1848, spurring other Western nations covetous of the rich China trade to follow suit. Both the United States and France used similar unequal treaties to wrest concessions of their own elsewhere in Shanghai.

Yet the Bund remained paramount, an emblem of Shanghai's trade driven ascendancy. Ships carrying silk, ceramics, and tea plied the Pacific to America, then returned with their holds full of opium. The British controlled most of the narcotics trade, and while Britons and other Western-ers profited, China and the people of Shanghai decidedly did not.

The China trade soon outgrew its drug-soaked roots. Financial houses, though founded largely on opium wealth, were eager to move into more legitimate spheres: banking, insurance, shipping, and real estate. They needed local bases in China. In Shanghai, the preferred location was the Bund, which became known in the 1930s as the "Wall Street of Asia."

In 1863 the British Concession merged voluntarily with the American Concession on the northern side of Suzhou Creek, and the International Settlement was born. By the early 20th century, the banks and trading houses dotting the Bund represented many nations, including Great Britain, the United States, Russia, Germany, Japan, Holland, and Belgium. The French kept to their own exclusive preserve.

The citadels of commerce set up by British banking giants slowly transformed the Bund into a financial hub. Against all odds, these stone-and-marble edifices have survived years of communist austerity to reclaim their former splendor. The Bund waterfront itself was relandscaped ahead of the 2010 World Expo.

massively impressive Pudong International Airport, whence travelers are whisked into Pudong on the Maglev railway.

The Bund's storied grandeur is easy to appreciate. Magic infuses an early morning stroll along this fabled section of the Huangpu

EXPERIENCE:
Sipping Cocktails at the Long Bar

If you've ever dreamed of a life of 1920s elegance, one way to live the dream is by taking drinks at Shanghai's famous Long Bar (The Long Bar at the Waldorf Astoria Shanghai on the Bund, 2 The Bund, tel 21/6322-9988, www.waldorfastoriashanghai .com). Experience what was once an elite treat—exclusively reserved for wealthy taipans and gentleman members of the Shanghai Club. In 2010, this legendary bar was restored to its past glory in its original location—amid the Sicilian marble columns and patina marble floors of the Waldorf-Astoria Shanghai on the Bund hotel. So dress up and sip champagne or a gin and tonic. Puff on a Cuban cigar in the style of the patrons of yesteryear while propping up the 110-foot (34m) bar counter—a replica of the original. Soak up the ambience of the sepia-tinted photos of the old Long Bar, live evening jazz, and the marbled Oyster Bar. Same again please, barman.

Visiting the Bund

Foreign visitors to Shanghai once approached the city by water, disembarking at Wusong (where the Yangtze meets the Huangpu) or sailing up along the Huangpu to the Bund. Nowadays the visitor's first impressions are no less vivid, but they are forged by the new and

River, especially when ships' sirens sound eerily in the mist. The evenings can be equally enchanting, as hundreds gather on the west side of the Huangpu, to watch the sinking sun light Pudong's great skyscrapers and other futuristic structures of Pudong. As darkness falls, the lights on both sides of the river illuminate the city. ∎

Walk the Bund

With the Huangpu River on one side and a string of historic buildings on the other, the Bund is a great place for a gentle north-to-south walk. There's some greenery at the northern end in Huangpu Park (Huangpu Gongyuan), and streetside stalls sell tempting snacks such as roast chestnuts—the ideal restorative on a cold winter day.

Start to the north, by Suzhou Creek and the **Waibaidu Bridge** ❶. This venerable structure, once made of wood but replaced by a steel span in 1907, sits so low above Suzhou Creek it's a wonder how even the low flat-bottomed sampans once managed to sail beneath it.

Heading south, on the left you'll come across **Huangpu Park.** Just beyond, where Suzhou Creek meets the Huangpu River, stands the massive **Monument to the People's Heroes.** The park is also home to the **Bund History Museum** ❷ (*Waitan Lishi Jinianguan, closed Sat.–Sun.*). Opposite, on the west side of the road (where you'll find most of the action), stands the **former British Consulate.** It dates from 1873, making it the oldest surviving building on the Bund; next door is the Peninsula Shanghai, the first new

NOT TO BE MISSED:

Jardine Matheson Building • Customs House • Shanghai Pudong Development Bank

buidling on the Bund in more than 60 years.

The long stretch of fine neoclassical buildings running south along the west side of the Bund is best admired from the promenade along the Huangpu River. At No. 29 is the old building of the evocatively named **French Banque de l'Indochine** (now the Everbright Bank), and

Bank of Communication

Customs House

Hong Kong & Shanghai Bank

at No. 28 you'll find the former **Glen Line Steamship Building**. Next, at No. 27, is the former **Jardine Matheson Building ❸**, today the Corinthian column-fronted House of Roosevelt wine club, restaurant, and lounge.

No. 26 once housed the Danish Consulate and the Italian Chamber of Commerce, but it is now the **Agricultural Bank of China.** The upswept eaves and repeated geometric motifs of No. 23 **(Bank of China Building)** distinguish the address as the only Chinese-influenced building of any significance on the Bund.

Opposite the **Peace Hotel** (see sidebar right) and the eastern end of Nanjing East Road, close by the embankment, stands a large **statue of Marshal Chen Yi ❹** (1901–1972), commander of the communist New Fourth Army and later the mayor of Shanghai.

South of Nanjing Road at No. 18 rises the **Chun Jiang Building,** now known as Bund 18. Formerly the Chartered Bank of India, Australia, and China, the structure today hosts various high-end boutiques and restaurants. On the seventh floor, the Bar Rouge lounge and terrace offers inspiring views of Pudong.

Just next door, No. 17 once housed the *North China Daily News,* the English-language newspaper that closed its doors in 1951.

Peace Hotel

Built by flamboyant entrepreneur Sir Victor Sassoon, this graceful art deco building with a green copper tower was originally designed as a private home called Sassoon House. During construction, Sassoon decided to convert it into the Cathay Hotel, which opened in 1929 and set a new benchmark for luxury hotels in China. After the formation of the PRC, the Cathay was twinned with the Palace Hotel in 1956, and jointly renamed the Peace Hotel. Thereafter, standards of service and upkeep deteriorated markedly, and it closed in 2007 for much needed renovations. In late 2010, the Cathay of yore reopened as the Fairmont Peace Hotel.

A lengthy tenancy by an austere communist bureaucracy ensued, but today the building houses the American International Assurance Company—another sign of Shanghai's

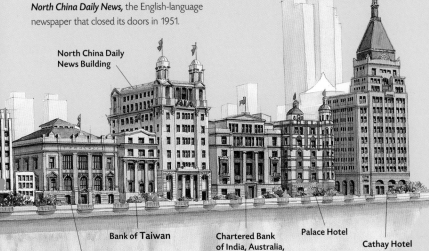

North China Daily News Building

Bank of Taiwan

Russo-Asiatic Bank

Chartered Bank of India, Australia, & China

Palace Hotel

Cathay Hotel

The Bund & Its Early Tenants

headlong reversion to capitalism.

At No. 16, the former Bank of Taiwan is now the **China Merchants Bank** ⑤, while No. 15 (the former Russo-Asiatic Bank) today houses the **Shanghai Gold Exchange.** Once the Bank of Communications, No. 14 these days is the **Bank of Shanghai.** At No. 13 note the neoclassical **Customs House,** built in 1925 and dominated by a clock tower.

At No. 12, you'll find the Bund's most celebrated building: the imposing **Shanghai Pudong Development Bank** ⑥, formerly the Hong Kong and Shanghai Bank Building. More than any other icon, the paired bronze lions guarding the main entrance have come to symbolize the Bund. Inside admire the mosaic

floor and ceiling panels, depicting the bank's eight global finace centers. Near the south end of the Bund, beyond Guangdong Lu, the former **Shanghai Club** is now the Waldorf Astoria Shanghai on the Bund Hotel, featuring the re-created Long Bar (see sidebar p. 181). This preserve once catered to rich British business-men. Cross back to the embankment and enter the **Gutzlaff Signal Tower** ⑦ for spectacular views of Pudong.

> ◪ See also area map pp. 178–179
> ▶ Waibaidu Bridge
> ⊕ 1.5 hours
> ⬌ 1 mile (1.6 km)
> ▶ Gutzlaff Signal Tower

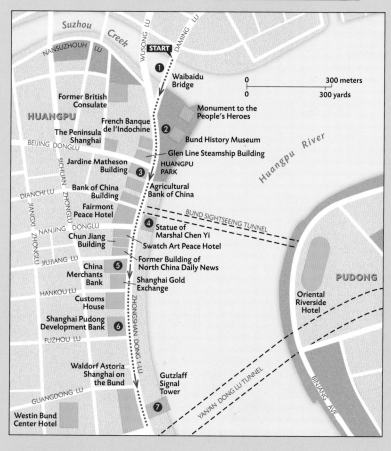

Nanjing East Road & Around

Heading west of the Bund is Nanjing East Road (Nanjing Donglu), China's most celebrated shopping street. Almost all the shoppers are locals: some intent on buying, others bound to see the sights, still others just keen to be seen. Once congested with vehicular traffic, a large part of Nanjing East Road has been reinvented as a pedestrianized walkway. This street connects to People's Square (Renmin Guangchang), and continues thereafter as Nanjing West Road (Nanjing Xilu).

The famous Nanjing East Road at night

Nanjing East Road seems to be busy from early morning to late into the neon-illuminated night. As with the nearby Bund, the best way to find your way about is on foot or via tourist tram. There's an apparently endless array of glitzy malls and three large department stores, as well as rows of billboards advertising the latest luxury goods. The busiest section, brimful of street artists and trendy shoppers, stretches from the Bund to Henan Central Road (Henan Zhonglu) to People's Square.

The pedestrianized walking street starts with two large malls on either side, Henderson Metropolitan (featuring the Apple Store) on the north side, and Hongyi Plaza directly opposite. Heading west from here, you'll find ample opportunities (in the form of concrete benches and other perches) to sit and watch the lifeblood of Nanjing East Road flow by, or to stop and snack on everything from Shanghai dumplings to roast chestnuts. The architecture, a somewhat less grand echo of that on the Bund, combines Shanghai in its 1930s heyday with glassy 21st-century constructs celebrating

Nanjing East Road
🅰 178–179 C3–E3

consumerism and free enterprise. This is one of the city's parade grounds of prosperity. Affluent Shanghainese come here to strut their stuff, and street beggars are seldom seen, although hawkers peddling everything from counterfeit watches to prostitutes work the area, especially at night.

The Big Three

At the junction with Zhejiang Central Road (Zhejiang Zhonglu) is the first of the city's original big four department stores, the **Hualian Department Store** (635 Nanjing Donglu). The Hualian was renovated over the past decade in a bid to recapture Shanghai's European ambience. It was opened in 1918 (under its original name, Wing On) by Guo Lesheng, a Chinese millionaire who had made his fortune in Australia. Guo established something of a pattern for Shanghai department stores by retailing everyday items, such

as food, cigarettes, and cosmetics, on the easily accessible first floor; cloth, clothing, and woolen articles on the second floor; clocks, watches, jewelry, and similar accessories on the third floor; and furniture on the fourth. A street saxophone player performs here most late afternoons and draws large crowds.

Almost directly opposite the Hualian, on the north side of the street, is the **Shanghai Fashion Store** (479 Nanjing Donglu; there is no system in China of odd/even numbers for opposite sides of the street). This was formerly the Sincere, the second of the big four department stores; it was established by Ma Yingbiao, a rich, Australian-based supporter of Sun Yat-sen. Although the Sincere opened a year before the Hualian, Ma quickly adopted the latter's layout and design. Like the Hualian, the Shanghai Fashion Store has been renovated to

What's in a Number?

The Chinese have traditionally regarded certain numbers as lucky and others—such as No. 4—as unlucky. This belief—frowned on under hard-line communism, but staging a comeback today—hinges on the tonal nature of the Chinese language, which decrees that one-syllable Chinese words have wildly different meanings depending on the tone with which they are pronounced.

Lucky numbers include 2 or èr, because good things generally come in twos (double happiness and so on). The number 6 is also lucky because liù or "six" sounds very similar to liú, or "flowing easily." Whereas 666 is considered unlucky or even Satanic

in some Western cultures, in China it is highly auspicious. The number 8, too, is considered lucky because it is pronounced bā, which sounds similar to fā, meaning wealth or prosperity. Finally, 9 is also con-sidered fortuitous, as its pronunciation, jiŭ, sounds like jiŭ or "longlasting." On the other hand, the number 4 is definitely bad news. Its Mandarin pronunciation, sì, sounds similar to the word sǐ or "death." For this reason, many streets—the Bund included—skip house No. 4. Likewise, many hotel and apartment blocks lack a fourth floor. The superstition has even gone high-tech: Nokia phones have no exchanges beginning with a 4.

re-create its pre-communist aura.

Farther west, almost at People's Park (Renmin Gongyuan) and on the north of Nanjing, stands the third of the big four, **Shanghai No. 1 Department Store** *(800 Nanjing Donglu).* This opened in 1936. Striving to best its competitors, the Sun (its original name) was the city's first department store to introduce elevators. Putative customers mobbed the store just to ride its astonishing new contraptions.

INSIDER TIP:

Grab a copy of *That's Shanghai* or *Time Out* at any expat bar or restaurant: Both offer complete bar, restaurant, and club listings.

—KENNY LING
National Geographic contributor

One of the city's other formative department stores, the Shanghai First Provisions Store, which opened for business as the Sun Sun in 1925, used to reside directly opposite, but was demolished to make way for the gargantuan Shimao Plaza Mall and Le Royal Méridien Hotel, which now dominates the landscape.

Nanjing East Road becomes Nanjing West Road (Nanjing Xilu) just west of the Shanghai No. 1 Department Store, where it passes north of People's Park and continues to the trendy "West End." Here you'll find a cluster of many of the city's most deluxe brand boutiques.

Viewed in its totality, Nanjing East Road is fascinating, even if shopping is not your bag. Exploring the area is a tutorial of the economic and societal changes that continue to take place all over China at an exponential rate, and— most notably—Shanghai's enduring penchant for shopping.

Beyond Nanjing East Road

To continue browsing turn south (left) at Tibet Central Road (Xizang Zhonglu) at the western end of Nanjing East Road. In about 80 yards (75 m) you will reach the **Mu'en Tang** (Moore Memorial Church; *316 Xizang Zhonglu*), named after the American benefactor who funded its construction in the 1920s. The church became a school after the revolution, but it reopened in 1979 and is once again a house of worship today.

To the south (and closely paralleling Nanjing East Road) runs Fuzhou Road. This street lies in the heart of Huangpu District, noted more for its history than its shops, but head here if you are looking for books. Two of the biggest and best bookshops in the city, both stocking English-language selections, are the more modern **Book City** *(465 Fuzhou Lu)* and the **Foreign Language Bookstore** *(390 Fuzhou Lu).* Both are exceedingly tolerant of browsers. It's not uncommon to see dozens of people sitting or lying quietly around the stores, reading whatever takes their fancy for hours at a time. ∎

Shanghai's "Yellow Creek"

The Huangpu River is and always has been Shanghai's commercial lifeline. Neither the largest nor the longest river in the world—British spy James Davidson-Houston dubbed it Shanghai's Yellow Creek—the Huangpu is nonetheless both commercially significant and historically fascinating.

Freight ships and tugboats ply the Huangpu River in front of Shanghai's 21st-century skyline.

Although Huangpu means "yellow-shored river," the name may in fact derive from the perennially yellow color of its waters. Just over 70 miles (114 km) long, the river rises in Lake Dianshan, west of Shanghai. It flows southeast and then north through the heart of the city to join the mighty Yangtze at Wusong. After flowing through Shanghai's outlying districts of Qingpu, Songjiang, and Minhang, the waterway courses through the city proper via the Baoshan District, then melds with its more powerful sibling near Changxing Island.

A statistical snapshot would show the Huangpu to average 1,312 feet (400 m) wide and 29.5 feet (9 m) deep; it would further reveal that the river supplies Shanghai with 70 percent of its drinking water. So crucial is the Huangpu River as a source of city water that in 1996 a project was completed to divert part of the Yangtze's flow to the upper Huangpu.

Past & Present

Although the Huangpu is now treasured for slaking Shanghai's thirst, historically it was prized as a lifeline to the sea. Even if ninth-century Shanghai was nothing more than a small settlement under the jurisdiction of Songjiang County in Suzhou Prefecture, shipping was already starting to call there because of its appeal as a harbor, safe from the flooding Yangtze and the stormy South China Sea. Not until after the start of the Qing period in 1644, however, did Shanghai become a major seaport for two neighboring provinces, Jiangsu and Zhejiang.

As a safe haven not far from the Yangtze's mouth, Shanghai had attracted Western commercial attention by the 18th century, even though the Qing authorities still strictly banned trade at this time. The Huangpu River had made Shanghai, and in the 19th century it provided a path to its undoing—and its eventual rebirth. During the First Opium War in 1842, British naval forces sailed up the Yellow Creek to occupy first Wusong and then Shanghai.

The British made the Bund the center of their commercial operations for the Yangtze Valley, ensuring Shanghai's future prosperity—as well as its colonial subservience as a treaty port. In 1937, the Huangpu betrayed the city once again, permitting the Imperial Japanese Navy to steam upriver and occupy the city. The invaders would not be repulsed until 1945.

Since the communist victory of 1949, the Huangpu has served not as an avenue of attack but an artery of trade, allowing for an influx of imports—and, especially since about 1990, for an exodus of the goods that Shanghai and its hinterland now export to the rest of the world. The river also divides the city into two sectors: Puxi, west of the river, and the newer, larger

INSIDER TIP:

Why not hop on a Huangpu River cruise? Take a 1-hour cruise from the wharf south of the Bund, or take a 40-minute trip from the Pearl Dock in Lujiazui [see pp. 234–235; 501 Zhongshan East Road, tel 021/6374-4461, $$–$$$ for 3.5-hour trip with dinner, $ for 1-hour trip].

—DAMIEN HARPER
National Geographic author

district of Pudong to the east. Bridging this riverine gap has inspired a series of engineering feats: the Dalian, Yan'an, Fuxing, and Dapu road tunnels as well as the Yangpu, Nanpu, and Lupu bridges are all fine examples of the application of Chinese mind and muscle power.

Today the Huangpu River appears well and truly tamed, though the vicissitudes of nature could easily refute that impression. In 2005, engineers dug a road tunnel under the mouth of the river, allowing a new beltway to pass beneath the yellow waters of the Huangpu and circumscribe the metropolis.

Inside Yuanmingyuan

Walk along Yuanmingyuan Road, a stone's throw from the Huangpu River and one block behind the north end of the Bund, on any weekend and you notice a very Shanghainese phenomenon. Couples pose for pre-wedding photos in white gowns and suits against a backdrop of renovated 1920s warehouses and heritage buildings. The paved street has been revamped as part of the Rockbund urban renewal project. The first project completed was the David Chipperfield–designed **Rockbund Art Museum** (www.rockbundartmuseum.org), a conversion of the 1932 Royal Asiatic Society headquarters. Also here is a branch of Italian eatery **8½ Otto e Mezzo Bombana** (Yuanmingyuan Road, Huangpu, tel 021/6087-2890, www.ottoemezzobombana.com), which excelled in Hong Kong before expanding to Shanghai. More restaurants and museums are slated to open in late 2012 and 2013.

Huangpu

One of Shanghai's smallest but most historic districts, Huangpu extends west from the lower Bund and south from Nanjing East Road to the massive elevated highway of Yan'an East Road (Yan'an Donglu). To the west it is bounded by People's Park. In 2000, Huangpu was conjoined with Nanshi (see pp. 201–212) to create New Huangpu, an enlarged district of 4.5 square miles (12 sq km) and the most densely populated urban area in the world.

Dinosaur skeletons on display at the Natural History Museum

Huangpu
🗺 178–179

Guangdong Development Bank
✉ 261 Sichuan Middle Road

Metropole Hotel
✉ 180 Jiangxi Middle Road

People's Court
✉ 209 Fuzhou Road

Westin Bund Center
✉ 222 Yan'an East Road

Huangpu's main thoroughfares—Nanjing East Road and Yan'an East Road—run roughly east–west, sandwiching a maze of smaller streets that are worth a detour for a morning's exploration. Just west of the Bund is the **Guangdong Development Bank,** designed in the 1930s.

As you continue west, the next cross street is Jiangxi Middle Road (Jiangxi Zhonglu). Were it not for the distinctly Shanghai street life, one might be in New York City. At the intersection of Jiangxi and Jiujiang Road is an 1866 Gothic church, known locally as **Hong**

Miao (Red Temple), now a government building. To the south Jiangxi Middle Road is lined with distinguished colonial buildings, including the 14-story art deco **Metropole Hotel** and the neighboring art deco **Hamilton House** apartment building, which dominate the junction of Fuzhou Road and Jiangxi Middle Road. Completing the Gotham mimicry is the redbrick Georgian-style **People's Court,** erected in 1924.

In contrast, to the south stands the bright **Westin Bund Center.** This 50-story tower, topped by an elaborate crown designed to resemble the petals of a flower, houses the Westin Shanghai Hotel and the **Museum of Public Art,** featuring more than 2,000 Chinese and Western masterpieces.

At night the center's crown flashes an eye-catching laser beam across the city, incidentally illuminating the **Shanghai Museum of Natural History.** This Victorian-style museum is housed in the neoclassical former Cotton Exchange (1923).

From either the Bund Center or the museum, it's easy to spot the Gothic spire of **St. Joseph's Church** (Ruose Tang).

Fuzhou Road

One of the architectural highlights of this old street, which has long been famed for its printing and calligraphy stores, is the former **American Club.** Sadly now shuttered, this fine building at 209 Fuzhou Road was designed by the famous Slovakian architect Ladislav Hudec in 1923 and was the hub of the U.S. business and after-work social life in the late 1920s and 1930s.

To the west, the buildings lose distinction and the streets grow more crowded. One exception is **Yifu Theatre** (Yifu Wutai), featuring performances of Beijing opera (*jingxi*) every evening at 7:15 p.m.

In prerevolutionary times, much of the area around Fuzhou Road was a flourishing red-light district called Huileli ("lingering happiness"). But by 1949, when the People's Liberation Army entered the city, the number of brothels had withered to a mere ten.

Today there are no brothels, but you can read about those decadent days in the area's bookshops, which, despite all the other changes, have managed to survive and thrive, a testament to the enduring love of the written word among the citizens of one of the most mercurial cities on Earth. ■

Shanghai Museum of Natural History (Shanghai Ziran Bowuguan)
- ✉ 260 Yan'an East Road
- 🕐 Closed Mon.
- 💲 $

St. Joseph's Church
- ✉ 36 Sichuan South Road

Yifu Theatre
- ✉ 701 Fuzhou Road
- ☎ 6351-4668

Little Xinjiang

In 1949, when the People's Liberation Army (PLA) swept into Xinjiang Province in far western China, only about 5 percent of the area's population was ethnic Han Chinese; the remainder was predominantly Uighur Muslim. Today, due to forced migration and resettlement, the situation has changed drastically, and Han Chinese are now thought to be the majority population.

Yet the traffic hasn't been one way only. Since the communist victory, thousands of Turkic-speaking Muslim Uighurs have ventured east to seek their fortunes in Shanghai. Many settled in western Huangpu, in an area around Zhejiang and Guangdong roads. Today there is a palpably Uighur feel to this area, which has become known as Little Xinjiang. Central Asian Turkic features are everywhere in evidence, as is music redolent of the Middle East, delicious naan breads and curries, and *laghman* noodles. Pervading it all is the aroma of mutton kebabs and mutton stew.

Regrettably, land prices are transforming the area, forcing the Uighur restaurants and foodstalls to move or go upmarket. Savor the culture—and the cuisine—while you still can!

People's Square Area

As Nanjing East Road is the commercial center of Shanghai, People's Park (Renmin Gongyuan) and the adjacent People's Square (Renmin Guangchang) are the city's cultural and recreational heart. The recreational aspect has existed since the heady days of old Shanghai, when the entire area was a racecourse and public park. The racecourse disappeared soon after the communist takeover in 1949, dismissed as an avatar of capitalist corruption and frivolity.

Highways and skyscrapers make today's People's Square a futuristic fantasia of asphalt, steel, and glass.

People's Park
🗺 178 B2–C2

To be fair to the communists, the Shanghai Racecourse Club was turned into a cultural center—the Shanghai Museum—in 1952. Other cultural attractions were established in this area in the years that followed.

A notable hiatus in this flowering was the Great Proletarian Cultural Revolution (1966–1976), when the quartet of political hard-liners known as the Gang of Four made Shanghai their headquarters and hundreds of thousands of Red Guards swarmed the area to herald continuing world revolution.

Vestiges of the old racecourse

are still apparent today. The oval-shaped outline of the People's Park area shows where the former track ran, while the neoclassical clock tower that now houses the Shanghai Art Museum was once the Shanghai Jockey Club.

Pace yourself: It takes some time to hit all the highlights arrayed around People's Park. The Shanghai Museum, for example, merits at least a full day to explore. But with its spotlessly maintained gardens and stunning architecture, the entire area lends itself to recreation and relaxation as well. So take time off between visits to cultural attractions to relax in the park, meeting local people or just lying on the grass and admiring the surrounding buildings.

People's Park

The People's Square area is split in two by a broad boulevard, People's Avenue (Renmin Dadao). To the north is People's Park, to the south is People's Square, and beneath lies the city's main subway interchange and an extensive shopping center with food halls. To the east, Tibet Central Road (Xizang Zhonglu) separates the entire complex from Nanjing East Road and the more built-up area of Huangpu. And smack dab in the middle of it all stands the imposing bulk of **City Hall** (Shanghai Renmin Zhengfu). Although the structure forcefully projects Shanghai's

---

INSIDER TIP:

For a fabulous overview of the racecourse shape of People's Square, go to the 38th floor lobby of the Tomorrow Square building [see p. 195].

—LARRY PORGES
National Geographic Travel Books editor

---

emerging power and prestige, it is not a tourist attraction; instead it's an administrative center and, as such, is closed to the public. The stand-out feature of the People's Park is the **Shanghai Museum**

of Contemporary Art (MOCA). Housed in an avant-garde glasshouse, this inventive art museum exhibits painting, photography, industrial, and installation art from across Asia and around the world.

Two significant structures stand at either end of People's Avenue, effectively flanking City Hall. To the east is the **Shanghai Urban Planning Exhibition Center.** A futuristic, five-story structure, this institution tells the story of Shanghai from its genesis as a sparsely populated fishing village in the 1600s through its turbulent colonial and revolutionary periods to the pre-2010 World Expo makeover that changed the city's appearance and infrastructure—and even into the future. The building—part museum, part planning center, part advertisement for Shanghai's successful development—was designed by Xing Tonghe, author of the imposing structure to the south, the **Shanghai Museum** (see pp. 196–199).

West of City Hall is the massive and more impressive **Shanghai Grand Theater.** Designed by French architect Jean-Marie Charpentier and completed in 1998, the ten-story, 1,800-seat theater complements the Planning Center to the east. Yet the two buildings are also dissimilar. In contrast to the Planning Center's flat, square roof, Charpentier's theater features an upswept, futuristically Chinese roof. The theater is currently home to both the Shanghai Ballet and the Shanghai Broadcast Symphony Orchestra. The theater stages

---

Shanghai Museum of Contemporary Art

- ✉ 231 Nanjing West Road (Nanjing Xilu)
- ☎ 6327-9900
- 💲 $

www.mocashanghai.org

Shanghai Urban Planning Exhibition Center (Chengshi Guihua Zhenshiguan)

- ✉ 100 Renmin Avenue
- ☎ 6327-2077
- 💲 $

www.supec.org

Shanghai Grand Theater (Shanghai Dajuyuan)

- ✉ 300 People's Square (Renmin Da Dao)
- 💲 Admission to performances by ticket; $ for guided tours

China Art Museum

⚐ 235

✉ The China
Pavillion at the
2010 World
Expo Site

💲 $$

regular performances of classical music, opera, and ballet. The latter range from *Swan Lake* and the *Nutcracker Suite* to Madame Mao's favorite revolutionary ballet, *Red Detachment of Women*. (The growing demand for such kitschily evocative reminders of China's recent past is a testament to the city's heady progress.)

Going Underground

It is fitting that the geographical center of Shanghai—officially measured as the middle art deco column on the facade of the Park Hotel—should overlook the city's underground metro hub. Most visitors will pass through People's Square station at some point, although rush hours in the morning and evening are best avoided—as the platform crush can be eye-watering.

Redeveloped ahead of the 2010 World Expo, Shanghai's busiest transport terminal connects the city's two original—and still most used—subway lines; the north–south 1 (color-coded red), and the east–west line 2 (green), plus one of the city's longest routes, the looping line 8 (blue).

North of the theater, at 325 Nanjing West Road, you'll find an elegant builidng with a clock tower, built in 1933. This was the former Jockey Club, and, up to October 2012 it housed the Shanghai Art Museum. On moving to its new home in the China Pavilion at the World Expo Site, the museum was renamed the **China Art Museum.** It's worth the trek to the new location to see impressive galleries that include changing exhibits of contemporary art, a permanent installation of modern art, and exhibits from

the Shanghai School of Painting.

At the old Jockey Club, renovations in 1999 removed most of the former colonial fittings, but the initials "SRC" (Shanghai Racing Club) remain inviolate over the entrance—as do the art deco chandeliers, the decorative iron horses' heads on the banisters, and the 1933 clock tower itself.

Outside the Park

A short stroll north of the art museum and across Nanjing Road West leads to a number of attractions, presented here in the sequence you will encounter them from east to west. The **Metropolis Flower Market** (Dadu Shixianhua Shichang), opened in 2000, sells cut flowers and houseplants grown locally or imported from international floral meccas such as Thailand and the Netherlands. Although it's open from 7 a.m. to 6:30 p.m., the flower market is best visited in the morning when the flowers are fresh.

Next, topped by its distinctive clock tower at 108 Nanjing West Road, rises the eight-story **Pacific Hotel** (Jinmen Dajiudian). Upon its construction in 1924 as the Union Insurance Building, this massive edifice was the tallest building in Shanghai. A decade later it was surpassed by Ladislau Hudec's 24-story brownstone masterpiece, the art deco **Park Hotel** (Guoji Fandian; *170 Nanjing West Road*). Both structures have since been overshadowed by skyscrapers that might feel at home in midtown Manhattan.

Continue west along Nanjing West Road and you'll find the

Grand Cinema (Daguangming Dianyingyuan; *No. 216*). This is yet another Ladislau Hudec creation; it dates from 1928 and was originally called the Cinema of the Far East. Renovated and refurbished in 2008, it features a rooftop café and the Grand Cinema History archive (entrance at No. 248), with fascinating images and artifacts from the building's history.

You can't miss the massive, modernistic, and (some would say) menacing bulk of **Tomorrow Square** (Mingtian Guangchang; *399 Nanjing West Road*); it fairly dominates the western side of People's Square. Soaring 934 feet (285 m) high—yet only the fourth tallest building in Shanghai—it houses the J.W. Marriott Hotel. Depending on your view of life (literal or figurative?), Tomorrow Square resembles a futuristic

Note the clock tower of the 325 Nanjing West Road, formerly the Jockey Club. The colonials called it Big Bertie, to distinguish it from Big Ching on the Bund and Big Ben back home in London.

—DAMIEN HARPER
National Geographic author

fountain pen or a nightmarishly huge dental instrument.

Across the square, on the corner of Tibet Road and Nanjing Road, is the equally gargantuan **Shimao Plaza Tower,** notable for its eerie double antennas extruding from the roof. ■

At the China Art Museum, Chinese artists offer visitors modern perspectives on light and space.

Shanghai Museum

Partly for the intrinsic elegance of its design but mainly for its stupendous contents and state-of-the-art displays, the Shanghai Museum (Shanghai Bowuguan) south of People's Avenue (Renmin Dadao) is the single most impressive modern building in People's Square. The site is a treasure trove of Chinese art, culture, and history. It holds more than 120,000 artifacts, representing almost five millennia of continuous civilization.

Serenity suffuses this painted and gilded wooden Bodhisattva from the Song dynasty (960–1279).

Shanghai Museum (Shanghai Bowuguan)

🅰 178 C2
✉ 201 People's Avenue
☎ 6372-5300
💲 $

www.shanghai museum.net

Shanghai architect Xing Tonghe designed the building to represent a *da ke ding,* an ancient, three-legged bronze cooking vessel. The museum also incorporates the sacred geometry of Yuanqiu, the circular altar at the Temple of Heaven in Beijing (see pp. 98–101). Its square base, representing the earth, is surmounted by a circular superstructure, representing heaven. The particularly elegant plaza fronting the museum features a circular pool and elaborate fountains, which—like so much

of the People's Square area—are illuminated at night.

First Floor

The most celebrated display in the museum is the **Gallery of Chinese Ancient Bronze,** where you can see more than 400 bronzes—some dating back more than four millennia to the Late Xia dynasty in the 21st century B.C. Marvelous examples of early vessels, weapons, instruments, and burial objects abound; often these are elaborately decorated with people, animals, and pastoral scenes, including perhaps the earliest representations of housing in China. Chinese bronze-casting technology reached its apex in the late Shang and early Western Zhou periods (ca 1700–771 B.C.), when artifacts were adorned with complex patterns, animals, or religious motifs. Of special note are the impressively preserved racks of musical bells.

Also on this floor is the **Gallery of Chinese Ancient Sculpture,** where you'll find Buddhist artifacts recovered from ancient cities along the Silk Road in Tibet, Mongolia, and Chinese Central Asia (now Xinjiang). There are Confucian steles—some borne on the backs of turtles—imperial decrees, and records of

EXPERIENCE: Following the Art Deco Trail

The Shanghai Museum seems a rarity in the city's architecture—a modern building that isn't a skytower. But look closer and you'll find that the real architecture treasures are woven in between the glass and concrete monoliths. Art deco was Shanghai's signature design style during the prewar boom era of the 1920s and 1930s. The city boasts one of the world's best urban portfolios of art deco buildings. Eye-catching banks, hotels and private homes built in art deco style dot the city. To experience Shanghai through the eyes of an expert, you can take a guided tour of the city's art deco heritage with resident historian and heritage architecture expert Patrick Cranley. Founder of the **Historic Shanghai** (*www.facebook .com/historic.shanghai*), a not-for-profit heritage conservation group, Cranley was closely involved in Shanghai's successful bid to host the 2015 World Congress on art deco—and narrates private tours to both lesser known art deco gems and more famous buildings like the **Park Hotel** on People's Square and the **Bank of China** on the Bund. Two seminal books by historian Tess Johnston and photographer Deke Erh, called *Shanghai Art Deco* and *Art Deco Shanghai and Miami Beach* (*www.tessinshanghai.com*), are available to buy at the **Old China Hand Reading Room** (*27 Shaoxing Road, Luwan, tel 021/6473-2526, www.han-yuan.com*).

battle triumphs. The eras covered extend from the Warring States period (475–221 B.C.) to the Ming dynasty (1368–1644). The museum shop is also on this floor.

Second Floor

Dominating this floor is the **Gallery of Chinese Ancient Ceramics,** which is arranged from Neolithic times to the late Qing dynasty (1644–1911). Artifacts range from early proto-celadon to the painstakingly finished polychrome-glazed ware of the Tang dynasty (618–907). You'll learn about the famous ceramic kilns of Jingdezhen in northeastern Jiangsi, China's center of porcelain production from 1279 to 1911. The world-famous Jingdezhen cobalt blue-and-white porcelain, which reached its zenith in the Ming and Qing periods, is especially well represented.

Third Floor

There are three galleries on this floor, including the superbly lit **Gallery of Chinese Paintings.** Here each exhibit illuminates automatically as you approach, only to fade into darkness as you move on. It's not a tourist gimmick but a state-of-the-art technique designed to keep the antique displays from fading. Many of the paintings are landscapes, though exquisite portraits await here as well. More than 120 masterpieces are on display; they date from the early T'ang period onward.

Also on this floor is the **Gallery of Chinese Calligraphy,** similarly protected by the technique of momentary-illumination. On parchments and manuscripts dating as far back as the Tang period, you'll see examples of seal script (*zhuanshu*), official script (*lishu*), running script (*xingshu*), grass script (*caoshu*), and regular

NOTE: The museum allows flash photography except where it might damage artifacts, such as in the painting and calligraphy halls. If you plan to use a tripod, you'll need to request a permit in advance from the counter.

script (kaishu). Even with the ability to read modern standard Chinese characters, most people are hard-pressed to decipher much of this calligraphy—notably the fast-flowing, imaginative caoshu. Nonetheless, you needn't be a scholar of classical antiquities to appreciate the extraordinary elegance and sophistication with which cursive Chinese has evolved over the centuries.

Finally on this floor is the **Gallery of Chinese Seals,** displaying fine examples of Chinese seals (yin) through the ages, from Western Zhou to Qing times (ca 700 B.C.–A.D. 1911). The Shanghai Museum has more than 10,000 seals in its collection, but space constraints limit the actual gallery displays to approximately 500 pieces at any given time.

INSIDER TIP:

Unless you speak fluent Chinese, you'll want to rent an audio guide at the Shanghai Museum. This is available in eight languages and requires a deposit (or passport).

—ANDREW FORBES
National Geographic author

Fourth Floor

Four galleries occupy this, the topmost museum floor open to the public. The first is the **Gallery of Chinese Ancient Jade,** a stone that has long held pride of place in Chinese civilization. Most of the jade pieces here originated in the Khotan region of distant Xinjiang, or in the Myitkyina region of Myanmar. This gallery exhibits the apotheosis of jade carving, achieved by Chinese craftsmen from Zhou to Qing times.

The **Gallery of Chinese Ming and Qing Furniture** may appear more familiar to Western visitors. The exhibits re-create rooms fully furnished in contemporaneous styles, all artfully arranged to synthesize the sensation that, as the museum brochure puts it, "you will feel like [you are] walking in a traditional Chinese house with a garden behind grilled windows."

The **Gallery of Chinese Coins** marshals more than 7,000 specimens to trace the development of currency in China. Dedicated numismatists will likely find this one of the museum's more exciting exhibits.

Finally, the **Gallery of Chinese Minority Arts** valiantly attempts to do justice to China's *shaoshu minzu,* or national minorities. It devotes 7,500 square feet (700 sq m) to the quotidian cultural touchstones of the non-Han peoples of the Chinese People's Republic: costumes, textiles, embroidery, metalware, sculpture, and pottery.

Given the country's ethnic diversity, however—no fewer than 55 ethnic groups are officially recognized—only the larger (Uighur, Mongol, Tibetan, Manchu) or more distinctive groups (Hani, Bai) garner much recognition. ∎

Shanghai Museum

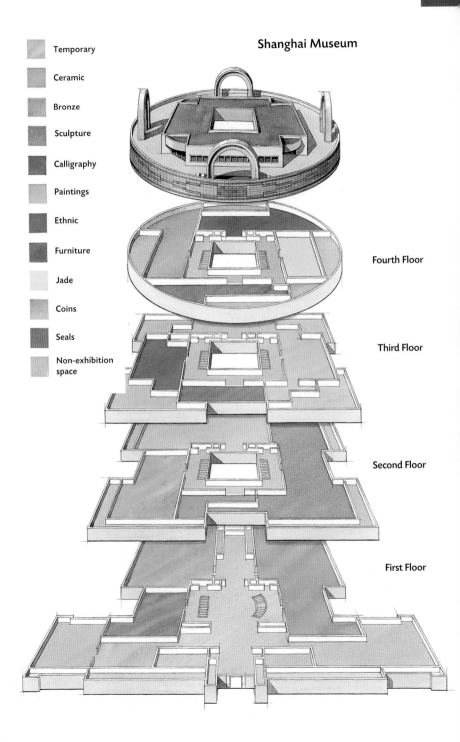

Temporary

Ceramic

Bronze

Sculpture

Calligraphy

Paintings

Ethnic

Furniture

Jade

Coins

Seals

Non-exhibition space

Fourth Floor

Third Floor

Second Floor

First Floor

More Places to Visit From the Bund to People's Square

Central Plaza

One of Shanghai's most prestigious office buildings, Central Plaza (Zhongqu Guang-chang) towers above the western end of People's Park. With two massive round buttresses embracing either side of the main facade, this 1998 monolith is easy to spot. Its many restaurants and bars offer expansive views of People's Park and San Jiao Park. 178 B2 227 Huangpi Beilu (Huangpi Road North) 3212-0931 Metro: People's Square

Great World

Once a brothel, Great World (Da Shijie) today offers such wholesome entertainments as acrobatics, video games, Beijing opera, and a Guinness Book of Records Exhibition Hall. 178 C1–C2 1 Xizang Nanlu (Tibet Road South) 6326-3760 9:30 a.m.–6:30 p.m. $–$$$$$ for individual venues Metro: People's Square

San Jiao Park

San Jiao Park (Sanjiao Gongyuan), at the west end of People's Park, holds out a very simple attraction: serenity. As in China

generally, older people or retirees are exempt from the small admission charge. This is one reason why so many elderly folk, especially men, flock here to compare their beloved songbirds, reminisce, or read the papers. 178 B2 Near People's Square $

Shanghai Concert Hall

Constructed in classical style in 1930, the Shanghai Concert Hall (Shanghai Yinyue Ting) was deemed so rich in cultural value that city authorities spared it from demolition when the nearby Yan'an Donglu area was redeveloped in the 1990s. In an engineering coup, the concert hall was lifted intact and moved 74 yards (67 m) south to its present location. The relocation did not degrade the hall's epic acoustics, whose world-renowned fidelity has attracted per-formers such as Isaac Stern, Yo-Yo Ma, the Philadelphia Chamber Orchestra, and the Hong Kong Philharmonic. www.concerthall.org 178 C1 523 Yan'an East Road 6386-2836 9:00 a.m.–7:30 p.m. (box office) $–$$$$ for performances Metro: People's Square

Blood Alley

It's been swept away in the tide of modern redevelopment, but branching off the street that led from the waterfront to the French Concession during the colonial era was a narrow lane the Europeans nicknamed Blood Alley. The place epitomized the decadence of 1930s Shanghai. It was a vortex of teeming vice, whorehouses, and low bars patronized by sailors seeking high times.

Ralph Shaw, a Briton living in Shanghai at the time, noted that Blood Alley swarmed with women on the prowl for "tall U.S. Navy men, seamen from the Liverpool tramps, and French Grena-diers." These easy marks, he added, made willing prey; they "had ears only for the girls clinging to them in the half light of dance-floor alcoves."

The city has spent a long time living down this legacy. Today it would be a challenge to find an equally rough-and-tumble place "entirely dedicated to wine, women, song, and all-night lechery."

A haven of traditional narrow lanes and busy markets, and home to the classical Yuyuan Gardens and the temples of three ancient faiths

Nanshi: The Old Town

Introduction & Map   202–203

Fangbang Middle Road &
    Around   204

Yu Yuan Bazaar & Teahouse   205

Walk Shanghai's Old Town   206–207

Yuyuan Gardens   208

Nanshi Temples   209

Feature: Shikumen Architecture—
    Twilight of a Tradition   210–211

Experience: Voyage in a Vintage
    Sidecar   211

More Places to Visit Around
    Nanshi   212

Horticulture meets architecture meets nature at the peaceful Yuyuan Gardens.

Nanshi: The Old Town

Nanshi stands in stark contrast to the former colonial area around Huangpu and to booming, ultramodern Pudong. The chief areas of interest are the main street, the carefully restored Fangbang Middle Road; the traditional Yuyuan Gardens and neighboring Yu Yuan Bazaar; Dongtai Lu Antiques Market; and the variety of Taoist, Confucian, and Buddhist temples.

A flower vendor peddles her wares in Nanshi.

Nanshi is changing fast, and—if you ask most inhabitants—it is changing for the better. Though sometimes likened to a Ming- or Qing-dynasty theme park, Nanshi has become clean, safe, and prosperous. What's more, despite the area's skyrocketing real estate, it is increasingly likely to retain the more appealing aspects of its past character. Locals are beginning to calculate the area's value not only in tourist dollars but also its cultural, historical, and social significance for Shanghainese in the 21st century.

The name Nanshi means "southern town," but in Shanghai it is synonymous with Old Town. No longer a walled settlement, Nanshi is still delimited by an approximately circular highway that follows the line of the old city walls—Renmin Road to the north and Zhong-hua Road to the south.

The first city wall was erected under the Ming dynasty in 1553. By then the former

Songjiang County fishing village had become a large enough and rich enough port to warrant fortification against the Japanese pirates, or *wako*, who had been ravaging the Chinese coast since about 1350. The city walls shielded Shanghai admirably for the next 289 years, but they did little to deflect the imperious British, who only needed one June day in 1842 to surmount them. The onset of Western imperialism marked the gradual eclipse of Nanshi, forcing the center of Shanghai to move inexorably northeast, to the Bund.

Western newcomers largely left Nanshi to its own devices. Their artillery did, however, keep the Taiping armies from storming the Old Town in August 1860. The intervention preserved the 3-mile-long (4.8 km), 27-foot-high (8 m) walls until they were torn down as part

NOT TO BE MISSED:

Exploring the Fangbang Road   204

The medicinal magic of Yu Yuan Bazaar & Teahouse   205

Strolling slowly through Shanghai's Old Town   206–207

The Suzhou-style formal beauty of Yuyuan Gardens   208

China's "three teachings," as seen in Nanshi's temples   209

The fading glory of Shikumen architecture   210–211

Endless varieties of cloth at South Bund Fabric Market   212

of a modernization campaign in 1913–1914.

Accounts of the time indicate that foreigners saw Nanshi as dirty, dangerous, and impenetrably alien—a refuge for anti-Qing revolutionaries and common bandits alike. What a difference a few decades make! Today the customary way to enter Nanshi from Shanghai proper is via Henan Road South (Henan Nanlu), which crosses Renmin Road where the old North Gate once stood. Beyond, in the heart of the Old Town, redeveloped Fangbang Middle Road (Fangbang Zhonglu), once just a polluted canal, is now a thriving business center that offers souvenirs, delicious local foods, and imperial and revolutionary nostalgia. For a time-warp tingle, stand beneath the upturned eaves of a traditional two-story shop house on Fangbang Middle Road and cast your eyes up and to the east, where the steel-and-glass towers of Pudong glitter in the near distance.

East and north along Fangbang Middle Road are the restored (largely re-created) bazaars around traditional Yuyuan Gardens.

Depending on your tolerance for teeming masses, you can also visit the famous Huxinting Teahouse, set in the middle of a small man-made lake. ■

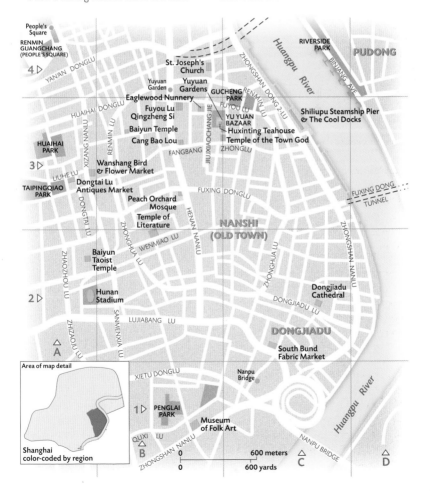

Fangbang Middle Road & Around

Going east from Henan South Road (Henan Nanlu), Fangbang Middle Road (Fangbang Zhonglu) traverses the Old Town, accessing its popular gardens, bazaars, restaurants, and temples.

Embroidered bags and reproductions of 1930s posters are part of the swag to be had on Fangbang.

Fangbang Middle Road
203 B3–C3

Westernmost Fangbang Middle Road runs east as far as a narrow cross street called Jiujiaochang Road. Entered through a newly built traditional Chinese gateway, this western segment has been restyled Lao Jie, or Old Street. It's chockablock with souvenirs and reproduction antiques, most of acceptable quality. The robust commerce has turned Fangbang Middle Road into an accessible traffic-free walking zone.

Start here if you are looking for any of these iconic curios: reproduction Qing opium paraphernalia or Jingdezhen blue-and-white ceramic pots; pictures of idealized 1930s Shanghai calendar girls; Chairman Mao books and lapel pins; or propaganda posters from the Great Proletarian Cultural Revolution. The atmosphere is relaxed, and it's fun to watch China's financially empowered populace rediscover so many stages of their past history in a single place.

For a break from the ancient-modern commercial theme, the **Old Shanghai Teahouse** (*385 Fangbang Middle Road*) serves a range of Chinese teas. Situated on the second floor of an old shop house, it displays a museum-style collection of authentic 1920s and 1930s Shanghai memorabilia. ∎

Yu Yuan Bazaar & Teahouse

Crowds fill the re-created, Ming-dynasty–style, low-rise shopping area called Yu Yuan Bazaar (Yu Yuan Shangcheng). Named for the celebrated Yuyuan Gardens next door, this conglomeration of shops, stores, and an indoor mall sells a wide range of traditional Chinese arts and crafts—everything from traditional medicines and chopsticks to fans and silks, umbrellas and walking sticks, rattan and bamboo furniture, ceramics and pottery (including Yixing teapots).

Head for **Mid-Lake Pavilion Teahouse** (Huxinting Chashi), which stands in the middle of a small artificial lake neatly situated between Yu Yuan Bazaar and the neighboring classical walled gardens. This structure has been here for more than four centuries but was converted to a teahouse relatively recently, in 1855. Once part of the original Ming-dynasty gardens, the teahouse is now a separate enterprise in its own right. To reach it, you must cross the lake on the **Bridge of Nine Turnings** (Jiu Qu Qiao), a stone causeway of rectangular zigzags. The serpentine approach is designed not to dissuade human visitors but to confound evil spirits and malicious ghosts, who, of course, travel only in straight lines.

The teahouse is generally crowded with customers, drawn there by its elegant classical lines, with upswept eaves and traditional geometric designs. The teahouse stands not on an island but on stone pillars set in the lake. Well-fed golden carp sweep hither and thither, thrashing the surface as people toss in handfuls of locally sold fish food.

It's not the cheapest place in Shanghai to enjoy a cup of tea, but it is the city's most celebrated. Queen Elizabeth II, Jimmy Carter, and Bill Clinton have all taken tea here, so perhaps the premium is worth it.

From the second floor, there's a great view across the willows and ponds of the exquisite Yuyuan Gardens next door (see p. 208). The tea itself is accompanied by complimentary snacks (xiaochi), and traditional music is performed live on the upper floor Friday through Sunday after 6:30 p.m., and every Monday from 2 to 5 p.m. ∎

Yu Yuan Bazaar
- 203 B3

Huxinting Teahouse
- 203 B3
- 257 Yu Yuan Road
- 8:30 a.m.– 10 p.m.

Yixing Teapots

One of the best buys in this area is a Yixing teapot. The city of Yixing, 120 miles (192 km) northwest of Shanghai, has been celebrated for its deposits of a purple clay, called zishayao, since the days of the Song dynasty (960–1279). Zishayao teapots are renowned throughout China for their ability to absorb and retain the flavor of whatever tea is brewed in them. Indeed, legend has it, a well-used Yixing teapot can produce a delicious cup of tea even when no leaves are added!

Yixing teapots are unglazed; they should therefore be rough both inside and out. In times past, they were carried about for individual use, hence their small size. Don't forget to pair them with a set of Yixing teacups and a box.

Walk Shanghai's Old Town

This circuit of north–central Nanshi rewards the walker. The heart of the Old Town has been restored and rebuilt to an extent that leaves little genuinely old about it, yet the district still feels surprisingly authentic. It also happens to offer some of the best—and most reasonably priced—eating places in town.

Chefs prepare *xiao long bao* dumplings at Nanxiang Steamed Dumpling restaurant in Yu Yuan Bazaar.

Start the walk (as you will finish it) at **Yu Yuan Bazaar** ❶ (see p. 205). Even if your Chinese language skills are nonexistent, the bazaar is easy to reach; every taxi driver will assume you wish to go there. Alternatively hop onto the subway (line No. 9) and alight at Yuyuan Gardens Station. Head west along Fangbang Middle Road, stopping to inspect the panoply of goods on sale in the shops and stalls along **Lao Jie** (Old Street). The restored Ming architecture is only about as old as People's Square, but forget authenticity for now; Lao Jie is as genuine as downtown Nanshi gets.

At the western entrance to Lao Jie, near bustling **Cang Bao Lou** ❷ market, turn right along Henan South Road (Henan Nanlu) and head north about 150 yards (135 m) to the intersection with Dajing Road and Zihua Road. Turn left (west) along Dajing Road, passing through an area once

NOT TO BE MISSED:

Lao Jie • Baiyun Temple
• Wen Miao

notorious for its opium dens, and continue for about 320 yards (290 m) to **Baiyun Temple** ❸ (Baiyun Guan; see p. 209), Shanghai's finest Taoist temple.

After visiting Baiyun, keep walking west a short distance to reach busy Renmin Road. At this point you are standing roughly atop the site of the Old Town's West Gate (Lao Ximen), though not a trace remains. Just north stands the sole true surviving remnant of the Old Town wall, **Dajing Tower** (Dajing Ge; *269 Dajing Road, $, 9 a.m.–4 p.m.*). Dating from 1815, this small pavilion contains early photographs of Nanshi and a model of the

Old Town in its former incarnation. (The descriptions are in Chinese only.)

Turn south down **Renmin Road,** noting on the left the stone archways, or *shikumen,* that lead into narrow *longtang* alleys plus the modern new apartment blocks. Renmin Road soon becomes Zhonghua Road, and above the red-tiled roofs of the surviving shikumen housing there rises into view the gray-tiled roof and ornamental dragons' heads of **Wen Miao** ❹ (*$, 9 a.m.– 4:30 p.m.*), the city's venerable Confucius Temple. Enter the temple via the back entrance along Menghua Street (Menghua Jie).

From the temple, continue east along Wen Miao Lu as far as the junction with Henan South Road, then turn left (or north)

past No. 52, the **Peach Orchard Mosque** ❺, or Xiaotaoyuan Qingzhen Si. Anyone can enter if it's not prayer time. You'll know from the muezzin's Arabic call to prayer and from the orderly ranks of Hui Muslim men prostrating themselves westward, toward Mecca.

Continue north along Henan South Road until you reach the now familiar junction with Fangbang Middle Road. Turn right and retrace your steps along Lao Jie, stopping for some delicious *xiao long bao.* These pork dumplings are a local specialty, and they can be seen (and, long before that, smelled) cooking in the doorways of a number of small Nanshi restaurants. Most notable among these is Shanghai Lao Fandian (Old Shanghai Restaurant) at 242 Fuyou Road.

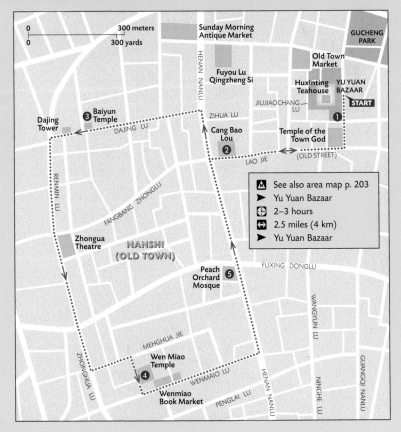

	0		300 meters	
	0		300 yards	

Sunday Morning Antique Market

GUCHENG PARK

Old Town Market

HENAN NANLU

Fuyou Lu Qingzheng Si

Huxinting Teahouse

YU YUAN BAZAAR

JIUJIAOCHANG LU

START ❶

Dajing Tower

❸ Baiyun Temple

DAJING LU

ZIHUA LU

Cang Bao Lou ❷

Temple of the Town God

LAO JIE

(OLD STREET)

🗺 See also area map p. 203
▶ Yu Yuan Bazaar
🕐 2–3 hours
↔ 2.5 miles (4 km)
▶ Yu Yuan Bazaar

RENMIN LU

FANGBANG ZHONGLU

Zhonghua Theatre

NANSHI (OLD TOWN)

Peach Orchard Mosque ❺

FUXING DONGLU

WANGYUN LU

GUANGQI NANLU

MEHGHUA JIE

ZHONGHUA LU

Wen Miao Temple ❹

WENMIAO LU

HENAN NANLU

NINGHE LU

Wenmiao Book Market

PENGLAI LU

Yuyuan Gardens

East of the Huxinting Teahouse, and abutting Yu Yuan Bazaar but not part of it, are the Yuyuan Gardens, a sterling specimen of a traditional Suzhou garden.

Hopeful visitors to Yuyuan Gardens toss wishes wrapped in red cloth into a famous wishing tree.

**Yuyuan Gardens
(Yu Yuan)**
🅰 203 B4
✉ 218 Anren Road
🕐 8 a.m.–4:30 p.m.
💲 $

Established in 1559, the Yuyuan Gardens took two decades to create. Restored between 1956 and 1961, the gardens are today once again at their best.

Traditional and formal like most Suzhou-style gardens, the Yuyuan Gardens create the illusion of size but are in fact quite small—and, on weekends and public holidays, crowded. Spread over 5 acres (2 ha) and surrounded by a wall topped by an undulating dragon, they feature six main scenic areas and 30 pavilions, all linked by fanciful bridges and causeways.

The classical intent was to re-create a world in microcosm, with mountains and ridges, lakes, forests, and caves. These gardens had a more practical aim, too: to create an idyllic retreat, where the founder, Pan Yunduan, and his family could relax apparently far from, but in reality close to, the travails of local government.

The **Grand Rockery** (Dajia-shan)—a 40-foot-high (12 m) stone "mountain range"—is intended to resemble southern China's limestone peaks. The **Exquisite Jade Rock** (Yulinglong) is said to have been acquired by the Pan family when the boat carrying it to the Imperial Court in Beijing sank nearby. Also worth inspection is the **Ten Thousand Flower Tower** (Wanhua Lou). From 1853 to 1855, the **Heralding Spring Hall** (Dianchun Tang) was reputedly used as a headquarters by the revolutionary Small Swords Society, which sought to overthrow the Qing-dynasty emperor. ∎

Nanshi Temples

As the oldest and most traditional quarter of Shanghai, Nanshi has it fair share of temples. Within the bounds of the former Old Town, China's three main religious traditions—Buddhism, Taoism, and Confucianism—are amply represented.

In northwest Nanshi, **Baiyun Temple** is headquarters to the Shanghai Taoist Association. Taoist monk Xi Zicheng left Beijing's White Cloud Temple (Baiyun Guan), the spiritual center of Taoism in China, and made his way to Nanshi's Ancestor of Thunder Temple (Leizu Guan) in 1882. Six years later he transferred 8,000 Taoist scriptures from the temple in Beijing to Shanghai; to honor the event, Leizu was renamed Baiyun. Centered on three halls, the temple is dedicated to seven Taoist deities, the most important being the Jade Emperor (Yuhuang Dadi). Red Guards ravaged the temple during the Cultural Revolution, but it has since been beautifully restored.

The heart of Buddhism in Nanshi is located farther east, near the Yu Yuan Bazaar, at the **Eaglewood Nunnery** (Chenxiangge An; 29 Chenxiangge Lu, $). This small, ocher temple houses several impressive images of the Buddha, 348 smaller figurines representing his disciples, and a community of 40 nuns clad in dark brown robes.

Taoism and Buddhism dovetail in the nearby **Temple of the Town God** (Chenghuang Miao), devoted to Han-dynasty Gen. Huo Guang and Qin Yubo, the patron deity of Shanghai. Established during the reign of Emperor Yongle

(1403–1425), this venerable building was turned into a factory during the Cultural Revolution. It, too, has since been restored.

Confucianism, the third of China's enduring san jiao (three teachings), is represented at the **Temple of Literature** (Wen Miao) in southwest Old Town. Girt by a bright yellow wall, the temple remains relatively quiet and free of visitors; Confucianism hasn't enjoyed the same rebirth experienced by Buddhism and Taoism in the last three decades. Visits do spike each July, however, the month for annual college-entrance exams, when anxious parents and students gather here to importune Master Kong (Confucius) for academic success. ■

Baiyun Temple (Baiyun Guan)
- 203 B3 & 207
- 239 Dajing Road
- $

Temple of the Town God
- 203 B3–C3
- 249 Fangbang Middle Road
- 8:30 a.m.–5 p.m.
- $

Temple of Literature
- 203 B2
- 215 Wenmiao Road
- 9 a.m.–4:30 p.m.
- $

Shanghai's Hui Minority

Of China's 55 officially recognized national minorities, no fewer than 10 are Muslim, but only one sect, the Hui, speak Chinese. According to recent counts, there are approximately 10 million Hui scattered throughout every province in China.

Shanghai's Hui Muslims form a small minority with a strong sense of identity. They are chiefly distinguished by their dress (prayer caps and beards for men, but the women do not wear veils); by their places of worship (the mosques known as Qingzhen Si, or "pure truth temples"); and by their seemingly ubiquitous and undeniably popular qingzhen (halal) restaurants.

Shikumen Architecture—
Twilight of a Tradition

Not long ago, traditional Shanghai architecture was distinguished by a style known locally as *shikumen,* or stone gate tenement housing. Once as unique to Shanghai as *hutong* lanes and courtyards were to Beijing, such housing is threatened today. Indeed, it may soon disappear altogether, except in such restored, upmarket areas such as Taikang Road.

Residents gather in a *longtang,* or narrow alley, to gossip and play cards.

Shikumen owes its development to the city's unusual and close association with Westerners through the foreign concessions. Essentially a blend of Chinese and Western styles, shikumen housing is aligned along straight, narrow alleyways called *longtang,* with each alley accessed via a stylized stone gateway in the form of an arch. First introduced to the city in the 1860s, houses of this type held as much as 80 percent of the population by the 1930s. Today that percentage is far lower—and, as land values skyrocket and an increasingly affluent population demands more comfortable, more convenient, and, above all, more modern accommodations, it continues to fall lower still.

In traditional Chinese domestic architectural design, a central courtyard (the Beijing hutong is the exemplar) offered families an inner sanctum in which to relax, tend small gardens of herbs or flowers, and perhaps keep caged songbirds. Shikumen housing can be seen as a compromise between that model and the space constraints of cheek-by-jowl 19th-century Shanghai. The tiny, almost vestigial courtyards of shikumen houses permit some fresh air to enter the building and allow a few potted plants to grow.

During the early 20th century, regrettably, the population of the city swelled still further, making even this style of low-rise, densely packed housing no longer feasible. Shikumen houses were divided and then subdivided, until the only way out was up. (Some Chinese would argue that the shikumen style was done in by the Shanghainese love of change for change's sake, and it's undeniable that new styles and ideas are embraced here with an ardor unmatched in the rest of the country.) Whatever the precise forces, the introduction of free-market economics in the 1990s was the writing on the wall: The days of shikumen living were drawing to an end.

Few Shanghainese live in shikumen today. The narrow longtang alleys have largely disappeared, giving way to high-rise tower apartments for most people. The seriously

INSIDER TIP:

Start your search for *shikumen* **at Taikang Road Art Centre** *[Lane 210 Taikang Road]*. **The** *lilong* **lanes off Nanjing Road (opposite Nanhui Road) are also worth exploring.**

—KENNY LING
National Geographic contributor

affluent have moved out to mock-Tudor housing estates and high-rise apartments in the suburbs. A few traditional shikumen blocks survive, notably at Taikang Road beside Suzha Creek and along Huahai Road, but the value of these restored or completely rebuilt buildings is astronomical. Many now serve as clubs, restaurants, or shopping complexes for the city's nouveau riche.

It's all very cyclical. In Shanghai (as in Beijing), buildings once deemed archaic and fit for demolition are newly chic—and suddenly worthy of preservation. This dynamic will keep the last authentic shikumen houses alive. It may even spur modern architects to incorporate elements of this uniquely Shanghai style into contemporary designs.

EXPERIENCE: Voyage in a Vintage Sidecar

How about seeing Shanghai's buildings at real street level? Perhaps the city's most inventive tour operator is **Shanghai Sideways** (*www.shanghaisideways.com*), which guides passengers around Shanghai in a vintage Changjiang motorbike and sidecar—originally built for the Chinese army.

Personalized day and night tours are offered, and the commentary as you zoom through the streets is knowledgeable and well researched. The motorbike guides are also open to questions—as

long as you can shout loud enough above the traffic buzz. Of course, the sidecar is open to the elements, so be prepared and wrap up warm. Winter tours have the added benefits of free mulled wine in addition to heated seats and heated blankets in the sidecars. For two-wheeled trips around the Shanghai backstreets, **Bike Shanghai** (*www.bikeshanghai.com*) offers full- and half-day tours, plus more adventurous cycling rides in countryside locations. They also offer bike rentals for more leisurely cyclists.

More Places to Visit Around Nanshi

Dongjiadu Cathedral

Dongjiadu Cathedral (Dongjiadu Tianzhutang) is one of the few buildings of architectural merit southeast of Nanshi, an area of government-built high-rises. Nevertheless, if you're in the vicinity, this twin-spired Catholic cathedral is worth a visit. Built in an appealing Baroque style in 1853, it features four arched clay roofs and eight Spanish pillars. The cathedral is open for worship, with Sunday Mass held at 7:30 a.m. 🗺 203 C2 ✉ 185 Dongjiadu Road ☎ 6378-7214 🚍 Bus: 65, 305

Dongtai Road Antiques Market

This antiques emporium near Renmin Road and the former Old Town walls comprises more than one hundred stalls and numerous two-story shop houses. Stashed away among the usual Mao memorabilia and 1930s calendars, look for the tiny and elaborately embroidered shoes once made for women with bound feet. You'll also find Tibetan tanka wall hangings. 🗺 203 A3 ✉ Dongtai Road & Liuhe Road 🚇 Metro: South Xizang Road

Nanpu Bridge

The first bridge to traverse the Huangpu River in central Shanghai and one of the city's iconic structures, the 12,870-foot-long (3,920 m) Nanpu Bridge (Nanpu Daqiao) links Puxi's central Huangpu District on the west bank with Pudong to the east. An impressive piece of engineering by any standards, it is accessed from both Zhongshan South Road and Lujiabang Road on the west bank via a gigantic spiral interchange.

The six-lane highway suspended from the twin towers rises 150 feet (46 m) above the swirling waters of the Huangpu, allowing ships to pass beneath. An elevator whisks visitors to a viewing platform high ($) on the west tower, offering unparalleled views of the city and the waters below. 🗺 203 C1 🚇 Metro: Nanpu Bridge

---

Museum of Folk Art

One of Shanghai's quirkier museums, the **Museum of Folk Art** (Minjian Shoucangpin Chenlieguan; *1551 Zhongshan South Road, tel 6313-5582, $, metro: Nanpu Bridge*) is off the beaten track, but it merits a visit if you're in the area. The displays are eclectic to say the least, and the links to folk art can test the skills of even the most inventive rationalizer. Embroidered golden lotus shoes for women's tiny bound feet can be thought of as folk art, but butterflies and 1930s cigarette labels? Still, the exhibits are well presented, and the building itself—a former community hall, built in 1909 by merchants from Fujian Province—is traditional.

The elaborate roof rests on upturned eaves and carved ceiling joists. Rafters are colorfully painted, while the stage is adorned by many detailed carvings.

South Bund Fabric Market

Formerly known as Dongjiadu Shichang and located at the intersection of Dongjiadu Road and Zhongshan South Road, the South Bund Fabric Market (Nanwaitan Mianliao Shichang) moved a short distance to its new indoor location on Lujiabang Road in 2006.

The three-story air-conditioned enterprise remains Shanghai's best-known textiles market. It covers more than 100,000 square feet (9,300 sq m) and offers a huge assortment of every sort of uncut fabric, from cotton to silk and cashmere. There are finished goods as well—tablecloths, towels, bed linen, and curtains—and a profusion of tailors' shops that sew items to order at warp speed. Allow 24 hours for a suit, a *qipao* or *cheongsam* dress, or similar items and expect to pay surprisingly reasonable prices. 🗺 203 C2 ✉ 399 Lujiabang Road 🚇 Metro: Nanpu Bridge

The heart of the former French Concession, with fine restaurants and the landmark Xintiandi shopping area

Fuxing Road to Huaihai Road

Introduction & Map   214–215

Fuxing Park & Surrounds   216–219

Walk Around Xintiandi   220–221

Xujiahui   222

Longhua & Around   223

Feature: The Original Power
    Couple   224–225

More Places to Visit From Fuxing to
    Huaihai   226

Experience: Learning Mandarin or
    Shanghainese   226

Hotels & Restaurants   307–309

Gold Buddhist statue in Longhua Temple

Fuxing Road to Huaihai Road

The thoroughly modernized area immediately west of the Old Town, extending from Fuxing Park to central Huaihai Road, is more or less adjacent to the former French Concession and continues to display vestiges of its former French ambience. It is, without question, Shanghai's chic district par excellence—especially after nightfall, when the city's young and upwardly mobile come out to play.

In the early 20th century, Shanghai's French Concession was synonymous with just about every character trait for which the city had become both celebrated and notorious. Shanghai's great and good, its wicked and feared—all seem to have lived or gathered here at one time or another.

In the former category were such visionaries and revolutionaries as Sun Yat-sen (1866–1925), known to some as the father of modern China; his wife, Soong Qing-ling (1893–1981); and Zhou Enlai (1898–1976), first president of the People's Republic of China and an early pillar of the Chinese Communist Party (CCP). In the latter category were notorious mobsters

NOT TO BE MISSED:

All the fun of Fuxing Park   216–218

Sinan Mansions: Shanghai's party central   219

Walking around Xintiandi   220–221

A visit to Longhua, Shanghai's largest Buddhist temple   223

The 367 steps to the top of Lupu Bridge   223

The politics of the past at the Propaganda Poster Art Center   226

Learning Mandarin or Shanghainese   226

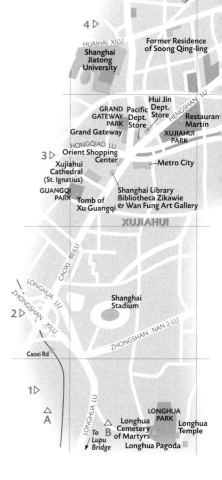

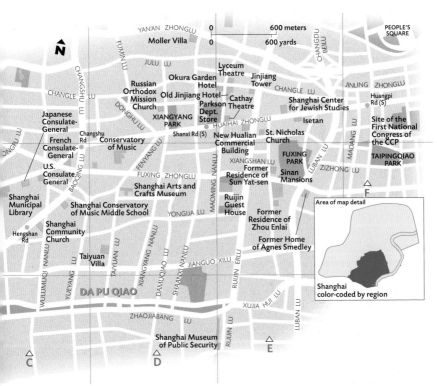

Shanghai
color-coded by region

Huang Jinrong (1868–1953) and "Big Ears" Du Yuesheng (1888–1951).

The Fuxing-Huaihai area is linked to other pivotal players on China's modern political stage as well. These include Nationalist Kuomintang (KMT) leader Chiang Kai-shek (1887–1975), a figure execrated on the communist mainland but honored in nearby Taiwan, and Communist leader Mao Zedong (1893–1976), now deemed a monster by many—but not by the CCP, whose revisionist line rates Mao as "70 percent good and 30 percent bad."

The Fuxing-Huaihai area was likewise the incubator of many Shanghai's artists, writers, and painters. At the same time, the district embraced pimps, prostitutes, and masters of flimflam, to say nothing of venal police. In other words, if one had the money—"a return ticket," in the wry parlance of writer Graham

Greene—the French Concession was an exciting and vibrant place to be. And the good news is that it still is, though far safer and more prosperous than in the bad old days of imperialism.

The central axis of the area is Huaihai Road, which runs southwest from Renmin Road and the northwestern part of Nanshi all the way to Hongqiao Road. Along the way, Huaihai Road passes the historic district around Fuxing Park; the restyled shikumen-chic shopping district of Xintiandi; the burgeoning nightlife area of Sinan Mansions, and hip Yongfu Road bar district. Beyond its intersection with Changshu Road, Huaihai Middle Road (Huaihai Zhonglu) continues past the Soong Qing-ling residence to Jiaotong University, while Hengshan Road runs southwest to Xujiahui and southern Shanghai, continuing along Caoxi South Road to Longhua Temple and Pagoda, the largest Buddhist monastery in the city. ∎

Fuxing Park & Surrounds

The French established Fuxing Park (Fuxing Gongyuan) in 1909 as a tree-lined retreat from the city's busy—and often malodorous—areas. That use prevails today, as locals of all ages and from all walks of life flock to the park. Young lovers woo on benches. Men play games of checkers and chess. And clusters of fitness enthusiasts engage in tai chi, jogging, and even ballroom dancing.

Shanghainese flock to parks such as Fuxing on Sunday mornings to perfect various dance moves.

**Fuxing Park
(Fuxing
Gongyuan)**
⚠ 215 E4
🕒 6 a.m.–6 p.m.

**St. Nicholas
Church**
⚠ 215 E5
✉ 16 Gaolan Road

In recent years Fuxing Park has become a popular venue for music concerts and laser light shows. The founding fathers of communism might frown upon such extravaganzas, but their presence still pervades the park in the form of two massive statues, one of Karl Marx and the other of Friedrich Engels.

As the epicenter of Shanghai's most elegant and affluent district, Fuxing Park is surrounded by numerous points of interest, all

within easy walking distance. Symbolizing the thawing trend in this unabashedly capitalist enclave, **St. Nicholas Church,** which once served the city's sizable White Russian population (see sidebar p. 217), has been converted into an expensive restaurant. Built in 1932, the church boasts an unmistakably Russian Orthodox style.

Around the Park

To the east of Fuxing Park, on the eastern side of the Xintiandi

INSIDER TIP:

Just north of Fuxing Park visit the Shanghai Science Hall [47 Nan Chang Rd.], a heritage building that originally housed the French Club (le Cercle Francais Sportif) circa 1904.

—KENNY LING
National Geographic contributor

shopping and dining district, stands the **Site of the First National Congress of the Chinese Communist Party.** Within the grounds of this rebuilt *shikumen* building, the Chinese Communist Party (CCP) was formally established on July 23, 1921. Now something of a CCP shrine, the building houses pictures and documents from the early days of their struggle.

Less well known, but still worth at least a glance from the southeast corner of the park, is the **Former Home of Agnes Smedley.** In 1929, Smedley

(1892–1950) moved to Shanghai to cover the Chinese Civil War as a reporter. In this capacity she traveled with both the Eighth Route Army and the New Fourth Army, becoming a passionate supporter of the CCP in the process. Smedley went on to author six books that chronicled the rise of Chinese communism, including the classic *Battle Hymn of China.*

Just north is the **Sinan Mansions** dining and nightlife district (see sidebar p. 219). Occupying a cluster of restyled 1930s mansions and a handful of new buildings, the area is a mid-market competitor to Xintiandi.

To the west of Fuxing Park, a short distance south of St. Nicholas Church, stands the **Former Residence of Sun Yat-sen.** The father of modern China lived here with his wife, Soong Qing-ling (see sidebar p. 90) from 1918 until his death in 1925. The furniture, decorations, and library are all as Sun Yat-sen left them.

Yet another building of historic and symbolic significance to the CCP may be found a short distance south of Fuxing Park: the **Former Residence of Zhou Enlai.** Mao

Site of the First National Congress of the Chinese Communist Party (Zhonggong Yidahuizhi Jinianguan)

🅰 215 F4
✉ 76 Xingye Road
💲 $

Former Home of Agnes Smedley

🅰 215 E4
✉ 185 Fuxing Middle Road

Former Residence of Sun Yat-sen (Sun Zhongshan Guju)

🅰 215 E4
✉ 7 Xiangshan Road
🕐 9 a.m.–4:30 p.m.
💲 $

Former Residence of Zhou Enlai (Zhou Enlai Gongguan)

🅰 215 E4
✉ 173 Sinan Road
🕐 9 a.m.–4 p.m.
💲 $

White Russians

Following the Bolshevik victory in the Russian Civil War (1918–1922), tens of thousands of defeated anti-communists, known as White Russians to distinguish them from the Bolshevik Reds, fled their homeland. A large number of these refugees sought safety in Shanghai's foreign concessions.

By 1932, about 25,000 White Russians lived in Shanghai. Some used the city as a

stepping-stone to the United States. Others managed to make a good living locally. The penurious majority, however, served as laborers, bodyguards, gangsters, entertainers, and prostitutes. Huaihai Lu became the center of Russian life in old Shanghai. Today—with China open to free enterprise and the Soviet Union no longer extant—Shanghai's Russian population is staging a comeback.

Conservatory of Music (Yinyue Xueyuan)
🅰 215 C4
✉ 20 Fenyang Road
☎ 6431-2000

Shanghai Arts & Crafts Museum (Shanghai Gongyi Meishu Bowuguan)
🅰 215 D4
✉ 79 Fenyang Road
☎ 6437-3454
💲 $

Taiyuan Villa (Taiyuan Bieshu)
🅰 215 D4
✉ 160 Taiyuan Road

Shanghai Center for Jewish Studies (Shanghai Youtai Yanjiu Zhongxin)
🅰 215 E5
✉ 7 Lane 622 Huaihai Middle Road (Huaihai Zhonglu)
☎ 6/384-4022

Zedong's charmingly sophisticated—and, when necessary, utterly ruthless—deputy, Zhou Enlai (1898–1976) lived here in 1946–1947 as head of the Shanghai branch of the CCP. Zhou's simple office has been preserved.

Just a short distance west of the Former Residence of Zhou Enlai stands the **Ruijin Guesthouse** (Ruijin Bingguan; *118 Ruijin No. 2 Road*), built in 1928. Today this extensively refurbished complex houses one of Shanghai's more exclusive lodgings.

Farther Afield

Slightly farther afield, but still in the Fuxing area, Fenyang Road branches southwest from Fuxing Road, past the **Conservatory of Music,** which holds classical music concerts each Sunday at 7 p.m., to the **Shanghai Arts & Crafts Museum,** which also comprises a research institute for arts and crafts.

Just southwest of the museum, at the junction of Fenyang Road

and Yueyang Road, stands a small **bust of Russian poet Alexander Pushkin** (1799–1837). Although the memorial was damaged during the Cultural Revolution, it has since been restored. Today it pays quiet homage to the White Russian association with Shanghai, as well as to the city's multicultural tradition.

Southeast of the Pushkin Monument stands the elaborate **Taiyuan Villa,** built in the 1920s by a French aristocrat. In 1945, Gen. George C. Marshall, the U.S. Army Chief of Staff, used the mansion as his headquarters in an unsuccessful bid to arrange an 11th-hour truce between the KMT and the CCP in the Chinese Civil War. After the latter's ultimate victory in 1949, the house was taken over by Mao Zedong's fourth wife, the redoubtable Jiang Qing. Today the villa is an upscale guesthouse.

Huaihai Middle Road

North of Fuxing Park, bustling tree-lined Huaihai Middle Road (Huaihai Zhonglu), which bisects the former French Concession, has emerged as the most fashionable shopping street in Shanghai, with giant department stores and malls selling everything from designer goods to children's toys.

On the north side of Huaihai Middle Road, as you make your way east, the giant **Parkson Department Store** and the **Cathay Theatre** (Guotao Dianyingyuan; *870 Huaihai Middle Road, tel 5404-2095*) mark the junction with noisy, vibrant Shaanxi South Road (Shaanxi Nanlu).

Also on the north side you'll find the **Shanghai Center for**

Photos of early Communist Party members are displayed at the Site of the First National Congress of the CCP Building.

Shanghai's New Party District

In 2002, Xintiandi set a new trend for redeveloping historic neighborhoods into dining and entertainment zones aimed at an affluent young set plus visiting tourists. Similar schemes across Shanghai have since had varying success, but the best planned and delivered is Sinan Mansions in the former French Concession. Spanning a large block of reclaimed and rebuilt 1930s villas at the junction of Sinan and Fuxing Roads, it has become a fashionable nightlife area. Among the eclectic highlights are **Chicha** (chichashanghai.com), which combines a Pisco Sour lounge with an upstairs dining room serving modern Peruvian cuisine; **Boxing Cat Brewery** (www.boxingcatbrewery.com), a brewpub that cooks up hearty Cal-Tex cuisine; and the **Fat Olive** (www.thefatolive.com), a modern meze lounge and wine bar.

Jewish Studies. Tucked away at the end of a short alley, it contains a library and information center. It also organizes tours of "Jewish Shanghai" (see pp. 242–243).

Changle Road & Beyond

A short walk along Changle Road northwest of the Center for Jewish Studies looms **Jinjiang Tower** (Xin Jinjiang Dajiudian; *161 Changle Road*), offering wonderful views across the former French Concession from its observation room on the 42nd floor.

Continuing west and around the corner brings you to the **Old Jinjiang Hotel,** an art deco complex built in 1928. The hotel is best known as the place where Zhou Enlai and Richard Nixon signed the celebrated (and unexpected) 1972 Shanghai Agreement. The pact normalized Sino-American diplomatic relations for the first time since 1949.

Opposite the hotel is the **Okura Garden Hotel.** Built in 1926 as the Cercle Sortif Francais, the hotel features the art deco style that was all the rage in colonial Shanghai, especially the

French Concession. It has been restored with marble columns, stairways, and a grand ballroom.

Just across Changle Road from the Old Jinjiang Hotel sits the venerable art deco **Lyceum Theatre,** built in 1931. The renowned British ballerina Margot Fonteyn (1919–1991) danced here as a young girl (her father worked for the British Tobacco Company in Shanghai), but modern-day productions focus on traditional Chinese performing arts, and children's theater.

A quick jaunt west on Changle Road and then north along Shaanxi South Road (Shaanxi Nanlu) delivers you to yet another product of the extravagant French Concession architecture of the early 20th century. The **Moller House** built in the 1930s, is distinctly Gothic in style (the peaked towers are a dead giveaway). Having weathered the period of orthodox communist austerity before 1990—when it functioned for a time as the unlikely headquarters of the Shanghai Communist Youth League—the miniature château has since been redeveloped as a history-themed boutique hotel, the Hengshan Moller Villa. ∎

Old Jinjiang Hotel (Lao Jinjiang Fandian)
- 🅰 215 E5
- ✉ 59 Maoming South Road (Maoming Nanlu)
- ☎ 3218-9888

Okura Garden Hotel (Huayuan Fandian)
- 🅰 215 E5
- ✉ 58 Maoming South Road (Maoming Nanlu)
- ☎ 6415-1111

Lyceum Theatre (Lanxin Daxiyuan)
- 🅰 215 E5
- ✉ 57 Maoming South Road (Maoming Nanlu)
- ☎ 6256-4738
- 🕐 Box office 9 a.m.–7 p.m.

Moller House (Male Bieshu)
- 🅰 215 D5
- ✉ 30 Shaanxi South Road (Shaanxi Nanlu)
- ☎ 6247-8881

Walk Around Xintiandi

The Xintiandi complex occupies just two blocks. It is bordered to the north by Taicang Road, to the south by Zizhong Road, to the east by Huangpi Road South (Huangpi Nanlu), and to the west by Madang Road. A walk around the district will open your eyes to the style and prosperity of Shanghai in the 21st century. Even the name of the complex is aspirational: Xintiandi means "new heaven and earth."

The Xintiandi district offers visitors a small haven of cultural and dining delights.

Xintiandi is easy to reach. It's a 15-minute walk south from People's Square, or you can take the metro to either **Huangpi Road Station** or **Xintiandi Station** ❶. From the station walk south on Huangpi to the Xintiandi complex, a creation of the New China, which opened in 2001.

Turn right on Taicang Road and enter Xintiandi from the north; look for the Starbucks marking the narrow *longtang* alley leading south and two glitzy new hotels, the Langham Xintiandi and Andaz Shanghai, which rise above the low-rise landscape. Centered on a largely rebuilt area of *shikumen* housing (see pp. 210–211), the complex is distinguished by rows of trendy bars and restaurants (alfresco dining is very much in vogue here). Walk south past

NOT TO BE MISSED:

Shikumen Open House Museum
• Museum of the First National Congress of the CCP • Taipingqiao Park

two narrow, covered side alleys; these lead to a parallel longtang to the east, likewise lined with attractive restaurants.

Located in Xintiandi North Block on the left, the **Shikumen Open House Museum** ❷ (Wulixiang Shikumen Minju Chenlieguan; *tel 3307-0337, 10 a.m.–10 p.m., $*) is a well-presented museum devoted to the architecture and lifestyle of the area before its recent gentrification. It depicts a century and a half of life in traditional shikumen housing through artifacts and photographs. This shikumen built in the 1920s houses seven exhibition rooms.

Continue your stroll south to Xingya Lu and turn east to the **Site of the First National Congress of the Chinese Communist Party ③** (see p. 217), a museum located in a typical shikumen house.

Next door the tiny **Xintiandi Postal Museum ④** showcases Chinese postal history and has an intriguing display of new postal technology.

Most of the South Block is given over to sheer indulgence. Here you will find everything from stylish restaurant dining to fast-food outlets imported from the West.

Exit the South Block via the narrow alley leading east to **Taipingqiao Park ⑤** (Taipingqiao Gongyuan), which is located just across Huangpi South Road (Huangpi Nanlu). This leisure area and 11-acre (4.5 ha) artificial lake (Shanghai's largest) is a place to relax—and maybe to recover from any bouts of overindulgence at one of Xintiandi's numerous bars and restaurants. The park features fountains and two islets, Magnolia and Unison, on the lake.

At the south end of Xintiandi, just across from Zizhong Road, is **Xintiandi Style ⑥**, a four-story shopping mall. The upper floors feature flash brands and fine dining, while the lower levels feature up-and-coming local designers such as Jenny Ji (La Vie), Uma Wang, and ZucZug.

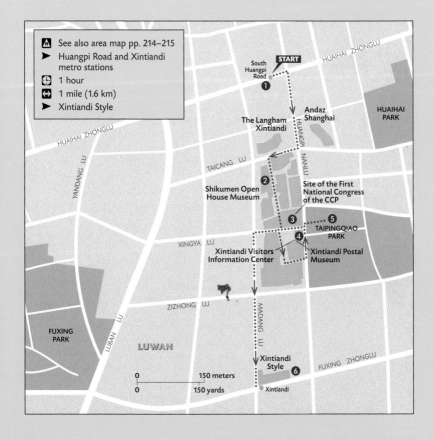

Xujiahui

About 550 yards (500 m) before the start of the consular district on Huaihai Middle Road, (Huaihai Zhonglu) near Changshu Road metro station, Baoqing Road briefly heads due south, then does a dogleg southwest to become Hengshan Road. This stretch is the gateway to Xujiahui and southern Shanghai.

Xujiahui
🗺 214–215 A3–C4

Shanghai Community Church (Guoji Libai Tang)
🗺 215 C4
✉ 53 Hengshan Road
☎ 6437-6576

Restaurant Martín (Xiao Hong Lou)
🗺 214 B3
✉ Villa Rouge, 811 Hengshan Road
☎ 6431-6639

The **Shanghai Conservatory of Music Middle School** (Shanghai Yinyue Xueyuan Zhongxueo; *9 Dongping Road*) sits amid extensive gardens. The vineclad, redbrick building was bought for Meiling Song upon her 1927 marriage to Nationalist leader Chiang Kai-shek. The couple, who lived in Nanjing, used the house whenever they visited, so it is now known as the Former Residence of Chiang Kai-shek. Though the building has been restored, it retains its grand fireplaces, sweeping stairways, and wide windows.

A short distance south along Henghshan Road stands the city's largest Christian place of worship, the 1925 **Shanghai Community Church,** built of red brick with an elaborate timberwork roof.

Around Xujiahui Park

Hengshan Lu continues southwest until it meets well-maintained Xujiahui Park (Xujiahui Gongyuan). Mid-park, just east off Hengshan Road, stands the former **Villa Rouge,** a nicely restored redbrick villa dating from 1921. For years this was the EMI studio, recording home to stellar musicians and singers. Today it's an upscale eatery, **Restaurant Martín,** a creation of Martín Berasategiu, the acclaimed Spanish chef.

Opposite the park, on the west side of Hengshan Road, stands the **Headquarters of the Shanghai Communist Party** (Zhonguo Gongchandang Shanghai Shiwei Yuanhui). Its brooding presence lasts only as long as it takes to walk beyond the southwest corner of Xujiahui Park, where department stores and shopping malls cluster in a glittering celebration of consumerism. They include the Hui Jin Department Store, the huge Pacific Department Store (which has the widest selection), the Grand Gateway, Metro City, Pacific Digital Plaza 2, and Orient Shopping Center. ∎

Missionary Legacies

Long before the new capitalism there were old-school Jesuit missionaries, of whose work some fascinating memorials survive. Most significant is the remarkable **Shanghai Library Bibliotheca Zikawei** (*80 Caoxi South Road, tel 6487-4072, tours Sat. 2 p.m.–4 p.m.*). Opened in 1847, the library houses more than half a million tomes, plus the Shanghai Archives' incredible collection of old newspapers, dating back to the late 19th century. You'll find another vivid evocation of Xujiahui's rich Jesuit past at St. Ignatius Cathedral. Today this redbrick edifice with twin gray spires is often called **Xujiahui Cathedral** (Tianzhu Jiaotang; *158 Puxi Road*).

Longhua & Around

South of Guangqi Park (Guangqi Gongyuan), Xujiahui blends gradually into Longhua District, home to Longhua, Shanghai's largest temple. The area is easily accessed from Huaihai Road and Xujiahui by the broad, north–south Caoxi South Road (Caoxi Nanlu) and Metro Line 3, which runs beside it. This district merits a visit for its appealing gardens and parks. The main draw remains glittering Longhua Temple and the intriguing Longhua Cemetery of Martyrs.

Longhua Park

Longhua Road lies south of Xujiahui and beyond the elevated Zhongshan South Road 2 (Inner Ring Road). **Longhua Temple**—the name means "lustrous dragon"—is Shanghai's largest Buddhist temple. It has five main halls, including the **Great Treasure Hall,** flanked by traditional bell and drum towers. The images of the Laughing Buddha, the Maitreya Buddha, and the Sakyamuni Buddha are especially worth seeking out here. Representations of arhat saints (those who have attained enlightenment) fill the **Thousand Luohan Hall.** Here you will also find a 7-ton (6,350 kg) bell, which is struck on Chinese New Year to dispel sins and promote good fortune.

Outside the front entrance stands the impressive, 140-foot-high (44 m) yellow octagonal **Longhua Pagoda.** Though clearly restored, Shanghai's tallest pagoda is said to date from 977.

Nearby **Longhua Cemetery of Martyrs** commemorates the victims of the 1927 White Terror, when mobsters and Chiang Kai-shek's Kuomintang (KMT) colluded to murder hundreds of communists and striking workers. The park features a fascinating

Father and son savor a quiet stroll through Longhua Park.

display of large socialist-realist stone sculptures with propagandist imagery of peasants, workers, and students, all fighting to protect the communist revolution.

To the South

Farther southeast still, massive **Lupu Bridge**—the world's longest arched bridge—appears to vault the Huangpu River. In order to allow freighters to pass under it, this 1,804-foot-long (550 m) span, opened in 2003, rises a dizzying 330 feet (100 m) above the surface of the river below. Bird's-eye views of the busy Huangpu River and both sides of Shanghai await those with the stamina to climb the 367 steps to the arch's apex. ■

Longhua Temple & Pagoda (Longhua Si & Longhua Ta)
🗺 214 B1
✉ 2853 Longhua Road
☎ 6456-6085
🕐 7 a.m.–5 p.m.
💲 $

Longhua Cemetery of Martyrs (Longhua Lieshi Lingyuan)
🗺 214 B1
☎ 6468-5995
🕐 9 a.m.–4 p.m.

Lupu Bridge (Lupu Daqiao Qiao)
🗺 214 B1
✉ 909 Luban Road
🕐 10 a.m.–4 p.m.
💲 $$

The Original Power Couple

The founding fathers of Chinese Communism—Chairman Mao Zedong (1893–1976) and Premier Zhou Enlai (1898–1976)—are both associated with Shanghai. In the minds of city dwellers, however, their respective legacies could not be more distinct.

Zhou Enlai (second from left) and Mao Zedong (center) sport nearly identical jackets—and gestures—in this 1950s photo.

Mao was born into a relatively prosperous peasant family in Shaoshan Village, Hunan Province. He graduated from the First Provincial Normal School of Hunan in 1918 and headed for Beijing, where he got caught up in the revolutionary May Fourth Movement of 1919. In 1921, Mao traveled to Shanghai to attend the first session of the Congress of the Communist Party (CCP) of China; within two years, he would sit on the CCP's Central Committee. He stayed in Shanghai for some

time but eventually returned to Hunan, where he honed his concept of a peasant-based revolutionary war.

Zhou Enlai was born to a relatively poor mandarin family in Huaian, Jiangsu Province. Because his family prized education, he was sent to the prestigious Nankai School in Tianjin. He then attended university in Tokyo but abruptly returned to China to take part in the May Fourth Movement. A year later found Zhou studying in Paris, where in 1922 he joined a cell of the CCP. Zhou came back to China in 1924, this time to Shanghai, where he helped organize the city's 1926 general strike.

Politically savvy from an early age, Zhou Enlai neatly sidestepped the White Terror waged against the CCP and its allies by Du Yuesheng's fearsome Green Gang on behalf of Chiang Kai-shek. Zhou next resurfaced in the Jiangxi Soviet area, where he forged what would become a lifetime alliance with Mao Zedong. Together Mao and Zhou survived the Long March, then organized and led the anti-Japanese resistance from the CCP base at Yan'an. They subsequently confronted—and conquered—Chiang Kai-shek and his Kuomintang forces in the Chinese Civil War.

During their years in power—notably the desperate years of the Great Leap Forward and the disastrous years of the Cultural Revolution—Zhou acted as a moderating influence on the impulsive Mao. Too bad his sway wasn't family-wide: Mao's irrational and vindictive fourth wife, Qiang Qing, made Shanghai her power base in the early 1970s, then led the notorious Gang of Four in causing more than half a million Chinese deaths and devastating the nation's economy. Both men died within a few months of each other in 1976—Zhou of cancer in January, Mao of Lou Gehrig's disease in September.

Whereas Mao is remembered for his unpredictable irascibility, Zhou is revered for his suave urbanity. Indeed, though now officially deemed "70 percent good and 30 percent bad," Mao remains a difficult figure for many Chinese to evaluate. Respected for unifying the country and ousting its foreign invaders, Mao cannot escape the fact that his social policies yielded almost universally catastrophic results. Zhou, by contrast—though sometimes equally ruthless—remains genuinely loved and respected by most Chinese. At the foot of his statue near Fuxing Park, fresh flowers continue to materialize daily.

Socialist Realism

After the Bolsheviks seized power in Russia in 1917, revolutionary art tended to be radical. It emphasized such idealized notions as the withering away of the state and the law. Following the death of Vladimir Lenin in 1924, however, his brutally pragmatic successor, Josef Stalin, decreed a more conservative approach. Art was to be traditional in form, aimed at the masses, laudatory of the party, and generally optimistic. As a result, by 1939 Soviet cultural life was firmly cast in a constricting mold that ultimately dictated its own collapse.

In the dust yellow hills of distant Yan'an, meanwhile, the Chinese communists were developing policies on literature and art designed to promote their cause in the bitter two-way struggle against the Japanese and the KMT. The resultant party line was spelled out in May 1942 with the publication of Mao Zedong's *Talks at the Yenan Forum on Art and Literature*. Mao's view: Revolutionary art was intended specifically for "the people"—that is, for workers, peasants, and soldiers. Above all else, literature and art should exalt "the Proletariat, the Communist Party, and Socialism." As a consequence, when the People's Republic of China was established in 1949, socialist realism (as this school of politicized aesthetics has come to be known) cast an artistic straitjacket over a vast region stretching from the Adriatic to the South China Sea, constricting the cultural life of nearly half of humankind.

Since the easing of party control over art in the 1990s, socialist realism is out of official vogue—but increasingly embraced by a populace in nostalgic search of the bad old days.

More Places to Visit From Fuxing to Huaihai

Propaganda Poster Art Center

Though somewhat off the beaten track to the north and west of central Huaihai, the **Propaganda Poster Art Center** (Xuanchuanhua Nianhua Yishu Zhongxin) rewards politically or nostalgically minded visitors with its remarkable collection of socialist realist posters from China's recent revolutionary past. Maps of old Shanghai and other memorabilia are also on display. A separate section of the center sells reproduction posters and postcards lauding bumper harvests, eternal opposition to U.S. imperialism, boundless admiration of popular struggles in Africa and Latin America, and undying resistance to Soviet socialist imperialism. They make poignant souvenirs of a time that was certainly more strident than our own.
🅐 214 C5 ✉ 868 Huashan Road
☎ 6211-1845 💲 $ 🚇 Metro: Changshu Road

Shanghai Museum of Public Security

If you happen to be traveling with teenage boys, bring them here. Tucked away on Ruijin South Road in an otherwise uninteresting part of Dapuqiao east of Xujiahui, the **Shanghai Museum of Public Security** (Shanghai Gong An Bowuguan) constitutes that true rarity: a subversive museum visit. Spread over four floors in an unprepossessing concrete building, the displays catalog not just "public security" but multiple aspects of crime in Shanghai, both in the colonial period and since.

Exhibits feature contemporaneous photographs and weapons, as well as such fascinating ephemera as mobster Huang Jingrong's cigarette-case gun, a brace of pistols once owned by Sun Yat-sen, racks of Al Capone–style tommy guns, weaponry used by the Green Gang in the vicious White Terror of 1927, opium-smoking pipes and equipment, and the business cards of high-class sing-song girls and prostitutes. As a souvenir you can purchase a rather sinister-looking high-caliber brass bullet; upon inspection, it turns out to be a cigarette lighter. 🅐 215 D3 ✉ 518 Ruijin South Road ☎ 6472-0256 💲 $ 🚇 Taxi or Bus: 72, 786, or 932 💲 $

EXPERIENCE: Learning Mandarin or Shanghainese

Even with a rudimentary grasp of Mandarin, it's pretty easy to discern that Shanghai locals speak a very different language. Debate rages about whether Shanghainese is a regional Chinese dialect, or—as the locals believe—entirely its own language. Either way, it sounds very different to Mandarin (Putonghua). Ask any northern Chinese, and they too will tell you how difficult Shanghainese is to understand and learn.

So which is best to learn? If your travels are to take you beyond Shanghai, the short answer is Mandarin. In truth, Shanghai locals speak and understand Mandarin too; it's just that they prefer their local patois. Online Mandarin learning can be an effective starting point for developing a basic grasp of the language, and **Chinese Pod** (www.chinesepod.com) offers a range of downloadable role-plays, home-study activities, and Skype-based personal tuition. The Chinese Pod app is available for Apple iOS and Android devices for learning on the move.

If your Chinese character reading is relatively advanced, **Dict.cn** is a very useful online database of Shanghainese phrases. If you don't read Chinese, **Think Shanghainese** (www.thinkshanghainese .com) translates scores of everyday words and phrases into the local tongue.

A 21st-century shrine to international finance and commerce rising on the east bank of the Huangpu River

Pudong

Introduction & Map   228–229

Century Avenue & Around   230–231

Century Park 232

Experience: Ride the
  Shanghai Ferry   232

The Three Megatowers   233

Cruise the Huangpu River   234–235

More Places to Visit in
  Pudong   236

Hotels & Restaurants   309–311

The Oriental Pearl TV Tower, icon of new Pudong

Pudong

Pudong (east of the Huangpu River) is a startlingly futuristic cityscape that leaves most visitors searching for superlatives. Before 1990, when Shanghai's modern development took off in the wake of China's economic reforms, little lay east of the Huangpu but rice paddies, market gardens, and rows of run-down warehouses. The years since then have witnessed a staggering transformation, as Pudong has blossomed into a thrumming urban landscape.

Pudong's skyscrapers dazzle the eye with height and light.

NOT TO BE MISSED:

Shanghai's "Wall Street" 228

A drive along the futuristic
Century Avenue 230–231

Exploring the Shanghai Science and
Technology Museum 232

The welcome green relief of the
Pudong waterfront 232

Soaring to the top of one of
Pudong's megatowers 233

Cruising on the Huangpu
River 234

Speeding at 270 miles per hour
(435 kph) on the Shanghai Maglev
Train 236

Pudong is the new face of Shanghai. Already it has grown to be 1.5 times larger than the old city west of the Huangpu River. It's a modern monument to commerce and capitalism—impressive, yes, but at the same time rather soulless. So whereas it is reasonable to feel drawn to Pudong for its futuristic architecture and amazing views, don't waste your time searching for the Old World charm of the Bund or the former French Concession.

Pudong's most impressive skyscrapers cluster on the east bank of the Huangpu River, directly facing the Bund. This area, sometimes referred to as Shanghai's Wall Street, is easy to reach from the Bund via the Bund Sightseeing Tunnel or by ferry; the latter offers fine views of both shores of the river. (Shanghai Metro Lines 2 and 4 also provide swift access.) Beyond

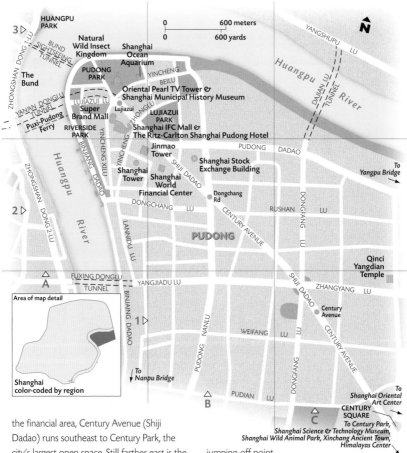

the financial area, Century Avenue (Shiji Dadao) runs southeast to Century Park, the city's largest open space. Still farther east is the impressive Pudong International Airport (which opened in 1999), the mouth of the Yangtze River, and beyond it the East China Sea. The airport was brought even closer with the 2003 opening of the Shanghai Maglev (magnetically levitated) Train, the fastest train in the world, which has come to symbolize the aspirations and achievements of Shanghai in general and Pudong in particular.

So what's there to see here beyond the mammoth architecture? Pudong offers a handful of intriguingly eclectic museums as well as several out-of-town attractions, such as Shanghai Wild Animal Park and Xinchang Ancient Town. Best of all, perhaps, it is also the jumping-off point for cruises on the Huangpu River, either just around the city and docks or farther downriver to the great Yangtze River and Chongming Island.

One of the most rewarding excursions here is a simple stroll along the riverside. The avenue—Binjiang Dadao—runs south from the Bund Sightseeing Tunnel through Riverside Park to the ferry pier by Dongchang Road.

Otherwise, Pudong does not enjoy a reputation as a pedestrian-friendly place. Distances are considerable, attractions are spread out, and the boulevards, though wide, can get surprisingly winding. Fortunately, a phalanx of taxis are on hand to ferry visitors about. ∎

Century Avenue & Around

Designed to add grandeur to Pudong, Century Avenue (Shiji Dadao) constitutes one of the city's most attractive and pleasant drives. This huge 21st-century boulevard leads southeast from Pudong Park and Lujiazui financial district all the way to Century Park (see p. 232).

It's an ocean up there: Inside the underwater tunnel at Shanghai Ocean Aquarium.

**Pudong Park
(Pudong
Gongyuan)**

🅜 229 A3

💲 $

**Oriental Pearl TV
Tower (Dongfang
Mingzhu
Guangbao
Dianshi Ta)**

🅜 229 A3

✉ 2 Lane 504
Lujiazui Road

☎ 5879-1888

💲 $$–$$$
(Shanghai
Municipal
History
Museum: $$)

Rising above the southern part of **Pudong Park,** just a stone's throw from the eastern exit of the Bund Sightseeing Tunnel, is one of Shanghai's most iconic landmarks: there is no missing the **Oriental Pearl TV Tower,** the 1,535-foot (468 m) tower that dominates the eastern shore of the Huangpu. Although the majority of Shanghai residents seem justifiably proud of it, it is not the loveliest structure in Pudong. Nevertheless, it offers an undeniably impressive view from inside looking out and is startling itself when illuminated at night.

Erected in 1995, the tower is

open to the public and has three observation levels. The highest, the Space Module, is at 1,148 feet (350 m); the Sightseeing Floor can be visited at 863 feet (263 m); and for those more comfortable closer to terra firma, Space City is at 295 feet (90 m). There's also a revolving restaurant at 876 feet (267 m). All offer great views across the Huangpu to The Bund.

Beneath the tower is the excellent **Shanghai Municipal History Museum** (Shanghai Chengshi Lishi Fazhan Chenlieguan). The well-designed exhibits shepherd the visitor through the history of Shanghai from the Opium War of 1842 to the present, showcasing all aspects of life from trade and transport to opium dens and crime. A number of exhibits take the form of audiovisual dioramas. Keep your eyes peeled for a stone that once marked the boundary of the International Settlement, and one of the bronze lions that once guarded the entrance of the Hong Kong and Shanghai Bank Building on the Bund.

On the east side of Pudong Park, the **Shanghai Ocean Aquarium** is a see-worthy sight. It features a 509-foot-long (155 m) underwater tunnel that allows the visitor 270-degree views of sharks, turtles, and other marine creatures. Additional galleries furnish details and samples of 15,000 fish from all over the world, with a special emphasis on species indigenous to the nearby Yangtze River.

At the northwest corner of Pudong Park, the **Natural Wild Insect Kingdom** features snakes, lizards, and other reptiles, plus a host of bugs from around the world—everything from gorgeous butterflies and moths to distinctly less appealing creatures such as scorpions and centipedes. It's a good place to take children, and those under 2.6 feet tall (0.8 m) are admitted free of charge.

The area around Lujiazui metro station has been redesigned to feature an elevated circular walkway keeping pedestrians out of the way of the manic traffic below. Across Century Avenue on the corner of Yincheng Road is the entrance to **Shanghai IFC**—a sibling building to Hong Kong's second tallest buidling. In addition to hosting the sky-high Ritz-Carlton Shanghai, Pudong Hotel, it is home to Pudong's glitziest mall, with an Apple Store, flash boutique brands and excellent restaurants and cafés.

Across the street is the entrance to the **Bund Sightseeing Tunnel,** which offers an unnervingly psychedelic journey, by glass capsule from the Huangpu River to the Bund. ∎

Shanghai Ocean Aquarium (Shanghai Haiyang Shuizuguan)

- 🅰 229 A3
- ✉ 158 Yincheng South Road
- ☎ 5877-9988
- 💲 $$$

Natural Wild Insect Kingdom (Da Ziran Yesheng Kunchong Guan)

- 🅰 229 A3
- ✉ 1 Fenghe Road
- ☎ 5840-5921
- 💲 $$

World Expo Legacy

In 2010, the World Expo, a six-month-long global showcase that takes place every five years, was hosted by Shanghai. The Chinese government prepared for this vital international event by transforming Shanghai's infrastructure. Both of Shanghai's international airports were enlarged, several new roads, metro lines, and rail routes were built, and many international hoteliers opened swanky new properties. In addition, the Bund was relandscaped, and all road and metro signage was made bilingual, written in Chinese characters and English. The Expo itself, which garnered a record-breaking 73 million visitors, was hosted at a purpose-built 5.28-square-mile (13.6 sq km) site straddling the Pudong and Puxi banks of the Huangpu River. Much of it was torn down afterward, but the Expo Site's handful of permanent attractions includes the bright red **China Pavilion**, and the oyster shell-shaped Expo Performance Centre, now rebranded as the **Mercedes-Benz Arena**. In 2012, the Shanghai Art Museum became the **China Art Museum** and moved from the old Jockey Club to its new home in the China Pavilion.

Century Park

All great cities need a great park, and 1 mile (1.6 km) southeast of Jinmao Tower is Century Park, Pudong's version of London's Hyde Park and Central Park in New York. On weekends and holidays, local families are drawn in large numbers to its expanses of grass and man-made lakes and ponds, plus the very popular Shanghai Science and Technology Museum.

Century Park

- ▲ 229 C1 & 235
- ✉ 1001 Jinxiu Road
- ☎ 5833-5621
- 💲 $
- Ⓜ Metro: Century Park (Shiji Gongyuan)

Shanghai Science and Technology Museum

- ▲ 229 C1 & 235
- ✉ 2000 Century Ave.
- ☎ 6862-2000
- 🕐 Closed Mon.
- Ⓜ Metro: Shanghai Science and Technology Museum
- 💲 $$

Century Park (Shiji Gongyuan) is the largest park in Pudong, and indeed all of Shanghai. On weekends and public holidays its vast terrain attracts families and young couples who escape the woes of urban living to picnic, cycle, roller blade, and go boating on the lake.

Known as the "green lungs of Pudong," the park offers an appealing respite from the frenetic pace of Shanghai life, although the reminders of weekday working are readily evident by standing in the park and looking up toward the the soaring commercial towers that ring its bucolic landscape.

Overlooking Century Park is the enormous **Shanghai Science and Technology Museum** (Shanghai Kexue Keji Bowuguan). Opened in 2001, this impressively modern museum has special appeal for children and teenagers thanks to its interactive exhibits and multimedia installations set across 14 themed exhibition halls.

Among the museum's highlights are the Earth Exploration center, World of Robots exhibition, Space Navigation Hall, and an IMAX cinema. ∎

EXPERIENCE: Ride the Shanghai Ferry

The **Huangpu River Ferry** is an often overlooked pleasure ride. The ten-minute journey is cheap, just RMB2 each way, and on a clear day offers superb waterborne panoramas. The views of the sky-reaching Pudong skyline and the Bund's cultured neoclassical and art deco architecture from the middle of the river are superb—and you'll share it mostly with locals crossing for business or shopping trips, as few tourists ever take the trip. On the Puxi riverbank, the ferry departs/arrives from a clearly marked pier at the south end of the Bund (opposite Jinling Road), while east of the river, the terminal is at Fucheng Road. Turn immediately left, and stroll along the riverbank for ten minutes in the direction of the Oriental Pearl TV Tower until you reach the heartbeat of Pudong.

The Three Megatowers

In Pudong, dominating the environs and visible from just about anywhere in Shanghai, rises a glittering tryptich of steel-and-glass towers: The Jinmao Tower, which now stands at 1,379 feet (421 m); Shanghai World Financial Center, standing 1,614 feet (492 m); and—tallest of all—the Shanghai Tower, which will rise to 2,073 feet (632 m), on completion in 2014.

In the 1990s, Shanghai drew up plans to create the three sky-towers to symbolize the soaring ambition of Pudong to become a global center of finance and commerce. The first to open—in 1998—was **Jinmao Tower** (Jinmao Dasha), which has 88 floors. High-speed elevators whisk visitors to the 88th-floor Observation Deck in less than a Shanghai minute, where (on a clear day) the views across Pudong and Puxi are worth the steep admission.

In a successful bid to blend modern and traditional Chinese architecture, the building rises through 16 distinct segments. Chicago architect Adrian Smith designed the structure to evoke a pagoda. The first 50 floors are given over to office space; above rises the Grand Hyatt Shanghai (Jinmao Kaiyue Dajiudian; *88 Century Avenue, tel 5049-1234*).

Right next door to the Jinmao Tower is a newer behemoth: The **Shanghai World Financial Center** (Shanghai Guoji Jinrong Zhongxin). This tops out at 101 stories. The center's original design featured a circular aperture atop the tower. This was hurriedly revised to avoid the finished structure resembling a Japanese flag. The Shanghai World Financial Center is home to the

Your rise to the top of Jinmao Tower is swift: 45 seconds, to be precise, from basement to Observation Deck.

vertigo-inducing 100th floor Sky Walk observation platoform.

Set to trump both its soaring counterparts in Pudong, the currently-under-construction **Shanghai Tower**—designed by Gensler—is slated to rise to a height of 2,073 feet (632 m) when completed in 2014. The top floors will feature a hotel managed by China's Jinjiang Group. ∎

Jinmao Tower

🅰 229 A2
✉ 88 Century Ave.
☎ 5047-5101
💲 $$

Shanghai World Financial Center

🅰 229 B2
✉ 100 Century Ave.
☎ 4001/100-555
💲 $

Cruise the Huangpu River

Cruises on the Huangpu leave hourly from the Pearl Dock at 1 Shiji Dadao (Century Avenue), next to the Oriental Pearl TV Tower, and from the Jinling Pier on the river's west side, near the southern end of the Bund. Shorter cruises (about 30 minutes) are ideal for an evening excursion, when the lights of the skyscrapers stage a fantastic show, while the longer cruises (up to 3.5 hours) are best in broad daylight for viewing the docks.

Comfy chairs cushion a cruise down the Huangpu River to the sea.

NOT TO BE MISSED:

Nanpu Bridge • Russian Consulate • Yangpu Bridge • Wusongkou

The cruise described here departs from Pudong's Pearl Dock. It heads upstream (south) first, passing the Bund on the starboard (right) side and offering fine views of Pudong Park and the skyscrapers of Lujiazui on the port (left) side. The boat passes beneath the vast bulk of **Nanpu Bridge** ❶ (see p. 212) then turns in midstream and heads downriver. Short cruises end at the Yangpu Bridge. Longer cruises sail all the way to the Yangtze River, a 35-mile (60 km) round-trip that includes refreshments.

Heading downstream from the Bund, the river passes **Suzhou Creek** and the historic **Waibaidu Bridge** ❷ on the left bank, then sweeps past the old **Russian Consulate,** the docks of Tilanqiao, and the hulking **Yangpu Bridge** ❸. Spanning the inconceivable distance of 8,373 yards or 4.7 miles (7,658 m or 7.6 km), this cable-stayed monster links Hongkou and north Shanghai to Pudong and the airport.

Farther downstream, the gritty personality of China's busiest port emerges. An estimated 2,000 oceangoing vessels and 18,000 river vessels dock here every year, and as you make your way downriver you're likely to spot every class, from pleasure craft and ferry boats to container ships, oil tankers, and Chinese naval vessels (which are off-limits to photography).

Beyond the Yangpu Bridge, giant **Fuxing Island** ❹ nestles against the left bank of the river and the northern suburb of Yangpu. It is being developed as a marina and a recreational area. Beyond Fuxing Island, on the left (west) bank of the Huangpu, you'll see one of Shanghai's largest wooded areas, **Gongqing Forest Park** ❺ (see p. 248).

Historic **Wusongkou** awaits at the mouth of the Huangpu, where this so-called "yellow creek" empties into the mighty Yangtze River. It was here that the British navy shelled the Qing batteries—the opening salvo of the First Opium War in 1842. The **Wusongkou Lighthouse** ❻ on the left (north) bank marks the Wusong Bar, traditionally deemed the start of the Yangtze proper. Beyond, in the middle distance, lie Chongming and Changxing Islands.

As you cruise back upriver, focus on the Pudong bank (the east side of the river). Here a thicket of cranes signals the frenetic pace of the docklands and of 21st-century Pudong as its skyline continues to rise and expand.

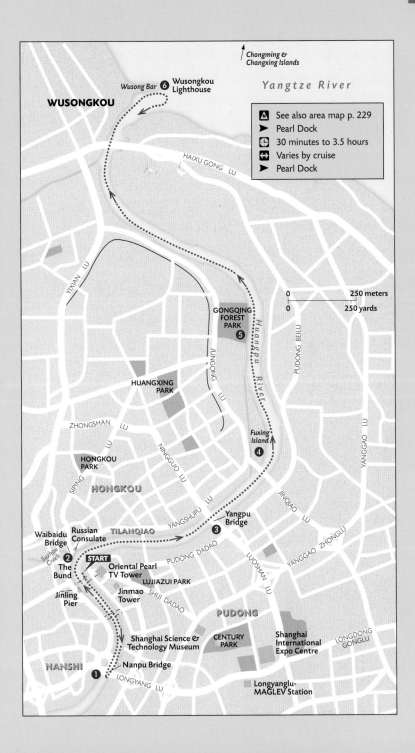

Chongming &
Changxing Islands

Yangtze River

Wusong Bar ❻ Wusongkou
Lighthouse

WUSONGKOU

HAIXU GONG LU

See also area map p. 229
Pearl Dock
30 minutes to 3.5 hours
Varies by cruise
Pearl Dock

YIXIAN LU

GONGQING
FOREST
PARK
❺

Huangpu River

JUNGONG LU

PUDONG BEILU

0   250 meters
0   250 yards

HUANGXING
PARK

ZHONGSHAN LU

NINGGUO LU

Fuxing
Island
❹

YANGGAO LU

HONGKOU
PARK

SIPING LU

HONGKOU

YANGSHUPU LU

JINQIAO LU

YANGGAO ZHONGLU

Yangpu
Bridge
❸

Waibaidu
Bridge

Russian
Consulate

TILANQIAO

PUDONG DADAO

LUOSHAN LU

Suzhou Creek

❷
The
Bund

START

Oriental Pearl
TV Tower

LUJIAZUI PARK

Jinling
Pier

Jinmao
Tower

SHUI DADAO

PUDONG

LONGDONG GONGLU

Shanghai Science &
Technology Museum

CENTURY
PARK

Shanghai
International
Expo Centre

NANSHI

❶

Nanpu Bridge

LONGYANG LU

Longyanglu-
MAGLEV Station

More Places to Visit in Pudong

The Himalayas Center

Opened in 2012, this eye-catching building was designed by Arata Isozaki and incorporates both the Himalayas Hotel and Shanghai's most innovative contemporary art museum, the Himalayas Art Museum.

✉ 1 Fangdian Road ☎ 6075-8555
💲 $$ 🚇 Metro: Huama Road

Qinci Yangdian Temple

Pudong's Qinci Yangdian Temple (Qinci Yangdian Si) is the largest Taoist temple in Shanghai. It likely dates from the Three Kingdoms period (220–280), though its present form is clearly a Qing dynasty restoration.

🗺 229 C1 ✉ 476 Yuanshen Road
☎ 5882-8689 💲 $ 🚇 Metro: Dongfang Road

Shanghai Oriental Art Center

Home to the Shanghai Symphony Orchestra, the Shanghai Oriental Art Center (Shanghai Dongfang Yishu Zhongxin) resembles a blossoming orchid flower and boasts the latest acoustics technology.

🗺 229 C1 ✉ 425 Dingxiang Road
☎ 6854-1234 💲 $$–$$$$ for performances 🚇 Metro: Shanghai Science and Technology Museum

Shanghai Stock Exchange Building

Rising over the southern end of Lujiazui Park is the steel-and-concrete mass of the Shanghai Stock Exchange Building (Shanghai Zhengquan Jiaoyisuo; *visitors not allowed on trading floor*). Mainland China's largest stock exchange, its striking shape is said to represent an antique Chinese coin: Circular with a square hole in the center.

✉ 528 Puong Nanlu 🕐 10 a.m.–5 p.m.
💲 $

Shanghai Wild Animal Park

The 500-acre (200 ha) Shanghai Wild Animal Park (Shanghai Yesheng Dongwuyuan) features predatory cats, imported species, and other exotic and unusual creatures. Visitors ride in small buses, but there are walking areas as well.

🗺 229 C1 ✉ Sanzao Village, Nanhui District ☎ 5803-6000 💲 $$$ 🚇 Taxi or bus No. 2 from Shanghai Stadium

Xinchang Ancient Town

Xinchang Ancient Town (Xinchang Gucheng), farther afield to the south of Pudong, is a sensitively restored water town dating from the Song dynasty (960–1279). At least 20 Ming- and Qing-dynasty mansions have been preserved, and a Cultural Exhibition Hall showcases the town's traditional way of life. 🗺 229 C1
✉ Xinchang Town, Nanhui District

The Maglev Line

The groundbreaking Shanghai Maglev Train (Shanghai Cifu Shifan Yunying Xian) is the world's first commercial high-speed magnetically levitated train. The train—floating on a magnetic cushion—covers the 18.75 miles (30 km) from Longyang Road Station to Pudong International Airport in a blazing 7 minutes 20 seconds; that's almost 270 miles an hour (431 kph).

Plans are now in place to extend the line to Hongqiao International Airport in the Puxi District.

The revitalized districts of Hongkou and Zhabei north of Suzhou Creek, now showcasing the city's literary and artistic scenes

North Shanghai

Introduction & Map   238–239

Hongkou   240–241

Jewish Shanghai Walk   242–243

Zhabei   244–246

Feature: Chinese Ceramics   247

More Places to Visit in
   North Shanghai   248

Hotels & Restaurants   311

A musician in Lu Xun Park

North Shanghai

At first glance, Shanghai's northern districts of Hongkou and Zhabei don't inspire the visitor as much as the better-known areas to the south of Suzhou Creek. Instead of the broad boulevards associated with the former French Concession and the aristocratic elegance of the Bund, north Shanghai seems both poorer and grittier. Yet both Hongkou and Zhabei abound in history—much of it tragic—and are deeply associated with the city's once large Jewish community. Hongkou also has a rich literary tradition.

Industrial Hongkou and Zhabei are immediately north of Suzhou Creek, with Hongkou situated to the east and Zhabei to the west. Shanghai Railway Station marks the far western edge of Zhabei, while Hongkou extends across the Hongkou Creek toward Yangpu.

In 1863, both Hongkou and Zhabei formed part of the International Settlement created by the merging of the British and American Concessions. With the area south of Suzhou Creek known as the Central District, Zhabei and part of Hongkou formed the Northern District, and the remainder of Hongkou stretched into the Eastern District.

While the bright lights of colonial Shanghai were the Central District and the neighboring French Concession, north Shanghai was more working class and decidedly less glamorous.

It drew relative latecomers to the ethnic and national smorgasbord of colonial Shanghai, including especially the Japanese soldiers to Zhabei and Jewish settlers to Hongkou.

The Japanese devastated this area in 1932

NOT TO BE MISSED:

Discovering north Shanghai's rich Jewish history **238**

Paging through the literary past of the Duolun Road district **241**

The Shanghai Jewish Refugees Museum and the Ohel Moishe Synagogue **243**

The vast range of art at the M50 Gallery District **245**

The Jade Buddha Temple **245–246**

Finding your tranquility at Peace Park **248**

with their artillery attack on the North Railway Station and again in 1937 when invading authorities put the area under command of a Naval Landing Party.

In Hongkou, however, sufficient reminders of the former Jewish presence remain to make a visit to "Jewish Shanghai" well worthwhile. Hongkou also has a considerable literary tradition, not least because Lu Xun, modern China's greatest writer, lived, wrote, died, and is buried here. His legacy, and those of its other famous scribes, has encouraged Duolun Road's recent reemergence as a center of literary excellence.

Zhabei has recovered from both the Imperial Japanese attacks and the grinding poverty of the first three decades of Chinese Communist Party rule. The district is now an area of rising prosperity, with parks, art galleries, and the spectacular Jade Buddha Temple, with its five courtyards and myriad halls filled with various representations of the Buddha.

Northern Hongkou and Zhabei house educational institutions, including Tongji and Fudan Universities, as well as Gongqing Forest Park and Shanghai Circus World. Both Hongkou and Zhabei have benefited from Shanghai's recent extraordinary economic prosperity, and Sichuan South Road (Sichuan Nanlu) has become North Shanghai's busiest shopping street. ■

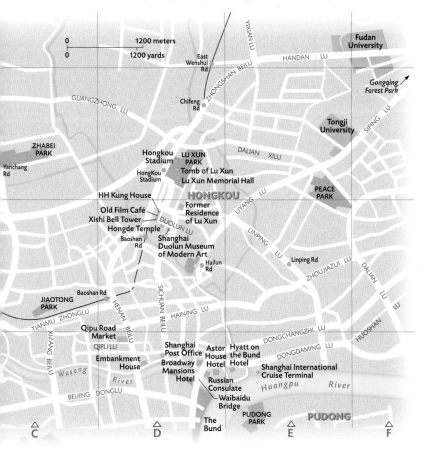

Hongkou

The iron girders of Waibaidu Bridge are generally seen as the northern gateway to the Bund, but they are also the southern gateway to the historic Hongkou District. While distant from the city center, this area is experiencing a revival. The Duolun Road Cultural Celebrities Street, a thriving arts scene, and nearby Fudan University give this area a less glitzy atmosphere than better known parts of Shanghai, but it is an interesting alternative to the tourist haunts downtown.

Shanghai Post Office (Shanghai Youzheng Ju)

🅐 239 D1

✉ 250 Suzhou South Road

☎ 6306-0438

Former Residence of Lu Xun (Lu Xun Guju)

🅐 239 D2

✉ 9 Lane 132, Shanying Road

☎ 5666-2608

💲 $

The area boasts some interesting architecture. Immediately beyond Waibaidu Bridge are two of colonial Shanghai's best known landmarks. Dominating the north side of Suzhou Creek, **Broadway Mansions Hotel** *(20 Suzhou South Road, tel 6324-6260, www.broadwaymansions .com)* was built in 1935 as an immense 19-story apartment building called Broadway Mansions. During the 1930s and '40s,

the upper floors functioned as the Shanghai Foreign Correspondents Club. The 18th-floor observation balcony still offers fabulous views south across the Bund and east toward Pudong.

Behind the Russian Consulate, the **Astor House Hotel** *(Pujiang Fandian, 15 Huangpu Road, tel 6324-6388, www.astorhousehotel.com)* was once Shanghai's premier hotel, attracting such glamorous guests as Ulysses S. Grant, Albert Einstein, and Charlie Chaplin.

Other fine buildings in the area include the 1924 **Shanghai Post Office,** with its classical lines and clock tower plus a postal museum and rooftop terrace. **Embankment House,** on Suzhou North Road (Suzhou Beilu), was built by Victor Sassoon in 1932 and was then the city's largest apartment building.

Lu Xun's Neighborhood

Once a locale for foreigners, Duolun Road and central Hongkou have become much associated with the writer Lu Xun (see sidebar p. 241). Widely acknowledged as the father of modern vernacular Chinese *(baihua)* literature, Lu Xun lived in this neighborhood between 1927 and 1936.

A short distance northeast is the **Former Residence of Lu Xun.**

Writer Lu Xun's tomb occupies peaceful Lu Xun Park, where locals stroll and do tai chi.

Duolun Road

North of Waibaidu Bridge along Sichuan South Road, Duolun Road is a lively center of creativity at the heart of Hongkou. Set in a restored area of *shikumen,* or stone gate housing, this area's official name is **Duolun Road Cultural Celebrities Street** (Duolun Lu Wenhua Jie), commemorating the literary circle that once lived here.

That circle included one of China's greatest literary figures, Lu Xun (1881–1936). An intellectual of pronounced left-wing sympathies, Lu Xun devoted himself to addressing his countrymen's spiritual woes in novels, essays, and short stories. His novella *The True Story of Ah Q* is considered a masterpiece. He also translated works from Russian and English. Other literary figures celebrated here include Guo Moruo (1892–1978), Feng Xuefeng (1903–1976), Ye Shengtao (1894–1988),

and Shen Yimo (1883–1971).

At the east end of the pedestrian zone stands the **Shanghai Duolun Museum of Modern Art** (Shanghai Duolun Xiandai Meishuguan; *27 Duolun Road, tel 6587-2530, www.duolunmoma.org., closed Mon., $*). Just off Duolun Road, the **China Left Wing Writers Museum** (Zhongguo Zuolian Bowuguan; *2 Lane 201, Duolun Road, $*) marks the site of the original League of Left-wing Writers established in 1930.

The distinctly Chinese upturned eaves of the **Hongde Temple** (Hongde Tang; *59 Duolun Road, Sun. services at 7 a.m. & 9:30 a.m.*) seem to indicate a Buddhist or Taoist structure, but this is a Christian church built in 1928. At the west end of Duolun Road is a stunning 1924 stone mansion featuring Moorish arches blended with neoclassical lines, former home to H. H. Kung, once the richest man in China.

INSIDER TIP:

Cafés are flourishing along Duolun Road. Try the Old Film Café *[No. 123],* next to the redbrick Xishi Bell Tower.

—ANDREW FORBES
National Geographic author

Born Zhou Shuren, he lived in this unpretentious three-story, redbrick-and-tile-house for six years. The residence acts as a museum, displaying his furniture and belongings. (The writer's library of 16,000 books is not here, however; it is preserved at the Lu Xun Museum in Beijing.)

Located a few minutes' walk north of the residence is **Lu Xun Park** (Lu Xun Gongyuan). This pleasant open space centers on a small lake, where locals come to exercise. It's also home to a bronze seated statue of Lu Xun and the **Tomb of Lu Xun** (Lu Xun Ling), as well as the **Lu Xun Memorial Hall** (*$*). The inscription on the tomb was Mao Zedong's tribute, while the trees on either side of it were planted by the Premier of the People's Republic of China Zhou Enlai and by Lu Xun's widow, Xu Guangping. The hall displays an extensive collection of Lu Xun memorabilia, including his horn-rimmed spectacles, pens, and hand-written essays.

On the northwest side of Lu Xun Park is **Hongkou Stadium,** a popular soccer venue with a capacity for 35,000 people. ∎

Hongkou Stadium (Hongkou Tiyuguan)
🅰 239 D3
✉ 444 Dongjiang-wan Road
🚇 Metro: Hongkou Stadium

Duolun Road
🅰 239 D2

Jewish Shanghai Walk

In the late 19th and early 20th centuries, Shanghai emerged as the center of Jewish settlement in the Far East. An initial wave of largely Sephardic Jewish emigrants from Baghdad via Bombay had arrived by the 1870s. A second wave of largely Ashkenazi Jewish emigrants arrived in the 1920s and '30s, following the Bolshevik Revolution in Russia and the subsequent rise of Nazism in Germany.

A residential street in Hongkou's former Jewish Quarter

By the late 1930s, Hongkou had become Shanghai's major area of Jewish settlement, with an estimated 20,000 Jewish residents, many of them stateless refugees. During the Japanese occupation of the city during World War II, they were ghettoized in the few blocks surrounding the old Hongkou synagogue. Most left after the war's end, and the community declined to just a few dozen people after the 1949 communist takeover. Although Shanghai's Jewish population is a far cry from what it once was, it's still possible to walk around Hongkou and get some idea of the area's Jewish history.

Head east from **Waibaidu Bridge** ❶ along Daming East Road–known as the "New Bund"–and featuring several modernistic buildings for about 1.2 miles (2 km) and turn northeast onto Huoshan Road. Halfway along this street is the Broadway Disco–once the **Broadway Theatre** ❷ (*65 Huoshan Road*),

NOT TO BE MISSED:

Broadway Theatre • Huoshan Park • Shanghai Jewish Refugees Museum

which housed the Jewish-owned Vienna Café. This was the only area of Hongkou to have lights at night during the '30s.

Continue east along Huoshan Road, passing a series of small town houses with gardens in front that were once owned by Jewish families. Enter tiny **Huoshan Park** (*6 a.m.–6 p.m.*) to view the stone plaque in Chinese, Hebrew, and English that commemorates the area's former role as a "haven for stateless refugees"–until 1939 Shanghai had no visa requirements. This monument was erected for the visit of Israel's

Prime Minister Yitzhak Rabin in 1993.

Turn north along Zhoushan Road, another street lined with small town houses—this area was once known as "Little Vienna" for its shops and cafés. Famous former residents include former U.S. Treasury Secretary Michael Blumenthal, movie mogul Michael Medavoy, and *Far Eastern Economic Review* founder Eric Halpern.

At tiny Changyang Road, turn west and continue to the recently refurbished **Ohel Moishe Synagogue ❸** (Moxi Huidang; *62 Changyang Road, weekdays 9 a.m.–4:30 p.m., $*), which forms part of the area's centerpiece, now called the **Shanghai Jewish Refugees Museum**. The synagogue was built in 1927 to serve the mainly Russian Ashkenazi Jewish community of Hongkou and was administered by Meir Ashkenazi, the chief rabbi of Shanghai from 1926 to 1949. No longer a place of worship, it serves as a center for remembering Shanghai's Jewish past. On various floors you'll find historic photographs

of Shanghai Jewish life and of recent visits by Jewish luminaries (Yitzhak Rabin's image takes pride of place), as well as furniture and everyday items from the pre-1949 period. Books on sale at the Memorial Hall include studies of Jewish Shanghai, along with a study of the much earlier Song dynasty Jewish settlement at Kaifeng in Henan Province (in English only).

For further information on the Jewish settlement in Hongkou, as well as the former Jewish presence elsewhere in Shanghai (notably in the French Concession), contact the **Shanghai Center for Jewish Studies** (Shanghai Youtai Yanjiu Zhongxin; *7 Lane 622, Huaihai Middle Road, tel 6384-4022*). **Dvir Bar Gal** runs Jewish History Tours of this area and other parts of Shanghai (*www.shanghai-jews.com*).

⚠	See also area map p. 239
►	Waibaidu Bridge
🕐	1.5 hours
↔	3 miles (4.8 km)
►	Ohel Moishe Synagogue

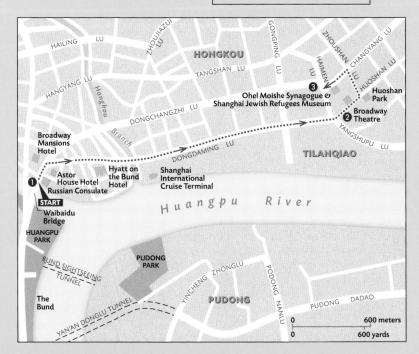

Zhabei

Although Zhabei is quieter than Hongkou, its neighbor to the west, there are still places of interest to visit here, as well as in neighboring Jingan, just on the other side of Suzhou Creek.

A well-stocked fruit market near Suzhou Creek tempts shoppers with color.

Suzhou Creek

 238–239
B2–D1

Suzhou Creek

Suzhou Creek (also known as the Wusong River) is a narrow waterway just 78 miles (125 km) long, which rises in Lake Tai to the west of Shanghai. Its small size belies its historic importance as an artery for all manner of waterborne trade in and out of Shanghai and as a frontier between the British and American Consessions in the 19th century. Lined with industrial and agricultural warehouses, by the early years of the 20th century, Suzhou Creek—locally known as the "stinking river"—was the city's most polluted stretch of water.

The waterway forms the southern boundary of Zhabei District. It is being gradually cleaned up as part of the Suzhou Creek Rehabilitation Project, which was launched in 1998 with a budget of 11.35 billion yuan ($1.37 billion). The warehouses, a protected heritage zone, are being restored to attract shopping plazas, restaurants, and bars, and to encourage the city's flourishing art scene. The ongoing project, which had met many of its targets by 2010, also includes new parks and 250 acres (100 ha) of greenbelt.

North of Suzhou Creek, about 700 yards (650 m) along Henan North Road, is **Qipu Road Market** (Qipu Lu Shihchang; *Henan Beilu at Qipu Road*), a huge market mainly selling shoes and clothing. This has inherited the mantle of the old Xiangyang Market.

Farther west looms the giant **Shanghai Railway Station** (Shanghai Huochezhan; *385 Meiyuan Road, tel 6317-9090*), the oldest of Shanghai's three major rail hubs, offering rail links across the country. This area is fairly rough, housing new migrants from the countryside.

INSIDER TIP:

If you're shopping at the Qipu Road Market, buyer beware! Fakes and knockoffs are common. That Gucci bag might be spelled with two *x*'s.

—JENNIFER ALLARD
National Geographic contributor

M50 Galleries

The M50 Art Gallery District is centered on Moganshan Road to the west of Suzhou Creek. This was formerly an area of bleak warehouses and textile mills that city authorities once planned to demolish and replace with high-rise apartments.

In the mid- to late 1990s, artists began to move into the area and set up galleries and studios in the old storehouses. The area prospered as a result, and the city began to encourage Moganshan Road to develop further as an arts district. Several converted industrial buildings and warehouses

now accommodate 50 galleries that feature painting, photography, sculpture, graphic design, and furniture-making. Moganshan Road has effectively become a pedestrian zone.

Some of the better-known galleries include **Art Scene Warehouse, Art Sea Studio and Gallery, Eastlink,** and **ShanghArt.** All are located in a complex that once made up the Xinhe Spinning Mill. There are so many galleries and so many artists not just from China but Europe, North America, Israel, and Japan, that it's well worth setting aside at least an afternoon to wander the corridors.

The historic **Sihang Warehouse** (*1 Guangfu Road*) by the junction of Xizang North Road (Xizang Beilu) and Guangfu Road played a key role in the Second Sino-Japanese War. Between October 26 and November 1, 1937, Chinese troops of the Nationalist 524th Regiment, the "800 heroes," held the building against repeated assaults by the elite Imperial Japanese Third Division in the most celebrated defense of Zhabei against the invaders. In 2001, the building was designated the Sihang New Creative Warehouse and became galleries and studios.

Jade Buddha Temple

The celebrated Jade Buddha Temple is located on the west bank of Suzhou Creek, not far south of Moganshan Road. Completed in 1918 in traditional style and centered on five courtyards, it is one of Shanghai's most active and most revered

M50 Art Gallery District
🅰 238 B2

Art Scene Warehouse
✉ Building 4
50 Moganshan Road
☎ 6277-4940
www.artscene
warehouse.com

Art Sea Studio and Gallery
✉ Building 9
50 Moganshan Road
☎ 6227-8380

Eastlink
✉ Building 6
50 Moganshan Road
☎ 6276-9932
www.eastlinkgallery
.cn

ShanghArt
✉ Building 16
50 Moganshan Road
☎ 6359-3923
www.shanghai
gallery.com

Jade Buddha Temple (Yufo Si)
🅰 238 B1
✉ 170 Anyuan Road
☎ 6266-3668
💲 $

Shanghai's celebrated Jade Buddha Temple provides a peaceful refuge in a busy city.

Buddhist temples. The Jade Buddha Temple's story begins in 1882, when a monk from Putuoshan Island named Huigen brought two valuable jade Buddha images from northern Burma.

Those images, probably from Kachin State's Mogaung Valley, were housed in the original Jade Buddha Temple, which was destroyed in the revolution that overthrew the Qing dynasty and established the Chinese Republic. Fortunately, the two jade Buddha images survived, and a new temple was constructed to house them on Anyuan Lu in 1918.

The **Hall of Heavenly Kings** (Tianwang Dian) contains a large image of Maitreya Buddha, represented as a laughing Buddha surrounded by heavenly kings as divine protectors. A paved courtyard leads to the **Great Treasure Hall** (Daxiong Baodian), which houses images of the Buddhas of the past, present, and future

seated on gilt thrones. Worshipers pass a bronze image of Guanyin, the female manifestation of Avalokitesvara—the goddess of mercy beloved by Chinese and Mahayana Buddhists everywhere. Beyond the temple's drum and bell lies the **Ten Thousand Buddhas Hall,** where services are held.

Also on the ground floor, the **Hall of the Reclining Buddha** houses one of the two statues Huigen brought back from Burma. The reclining image of Sakyamuni, carved from a single piece of jade 37 inches (96 cm) in length, is clearly of Southeast Asian, Theravada origin.

Upstairs, in the most revered of the temple chambers, the **Jade Buddha Hall,** is the main image and namesake of the temple, the Jade Buddha, or Yufo. Carved from a single piece of white jade, this seated image of Sakyamuni is 6 feet 3 inches (1.92 m) tall and weighs a remarkable 2,200 pounds (1,000 kg). ∎

Chinese Ceramics

Famed for centuries the world over, Chinas's porcelain enjoys a long and splendid heritage. Although designed as works of art, ceramics from the Middle Kingdom were also objects of utilitarian value.

Pottery fragments in China date back to Neolithic times, to a primitive society known as Yangshao in northern China. Surving specimens from the Shang dynasty reveal an evolution to the development of glaze, possibly during the Zhou dynasty. Pieces from the Han dynasty show growing mastery of glazing tecniques and stylistic energy, especially in statues and effigies.

Porcelain first appeared during the Tang dynasty as did colored glazes, most notably in the world-renowned *sancai* (tri-color) pieces that are typically green, yellow, brown, orange, and blue against an earthenware body. Song-dynasty ceramics are noted for their undeco-rated, monochromatic simplicity.

The Yuan dynasty saw the arrival from the Middle East of underglaze cobalt blue (*qinghua*, or blue-and-white), a technique that flourished under the Ming and Qing dynasties. The Qing dynasty is also notable for colored porcelain and complex decoration. The luxuriously painted, often spectacular pieces are balanced by restrained monochromatic works. Much Qing porcelain was destined for export to the European market, and consequently Western decorations were incorporated. Porcelain is still produced at numerous kilns today, but the golden age of porcelain production are over.

Symbols

At first glance, many ceramics are hidden behind a jungle of decorative motifs. An under-standing of the prominent decorative symbols used on Chinese ceramics will help apprecia-tion. The dragon often denotes the emperor and could indicate that the piece is imperial porcelain. The phoenix represents the empress. Peaches symbolize longevity, as do pine trees, tortoises, bamboo, and the bald-headed god of longevity. The Chinese character for long life (*shou*) is also a popular pattern.

Homophones are liberally used. Bats are common motifs; they are pronounced *fu*, the same sound as good fortune. Fish (*yu*) denote abundance. Other designs include landscapes, flowers, and historical scenes. Literature often embellishes later pieces with a poem or a piece of prose in appropriate calligraphy. Religious imagery includes the eight immortals (see pp. 116–117), the eight *I-Ching* trigams, and the eight Buddhist symbols.

INSIDER TIP:

Unless you're an expert, don't go looking to buy porcelain of historic value. Most of what you see in China's markets is fake. The real thing is found only in private collections around the world.

—DAMIEN HARPER
National Geographic author

Glaze & Mark

Chinese ceramics are categorized by their color and glaze. The most famous colored porcelain is cobalt underglaze (a technique of painting the ware before it is glazed and fired).

The mark, used to identify the date of man-ufacture, is found at the foot of the ceramic. This is typically square or circular, with the name of the dynasty preceding the emperor, read vertically from right to left. However it is very risky to date a piece by mark alone, as forgeries are manifold, and the quantity of fakes has grown to meet a worldwide demand.

More Places to Visit in North Shanghai

Daning Green Land Park

The largest park in northwestern Shanghai is Daning Green Land Park (Daning Lingshi Gongyuan) with 168 acres (68 ha) of gardens, woods, lakes, and waterfalls. The annual Zhabei Tourism Festival is held here in October and features concerts, laser shows, fireworks, skydiving, and water sports. [M] 238 B3 [✉] 288 Guangzhong West Road (Guangzhong Xilu) [☎] 6652-3698 [$] $ [🚇] Metro: Shanghai Circus World

Feng Shui

Feng shui translates literally as "wind water." A popular practice with just about everyone in China, feng shui offers a clear set of guidelines to help people live in harmony with the environment and flow of energy (qi). Historically, it has been most commonly used to locate burial sites and provide guidance for the construction of new and renovated buildings. Although generally regarded as superstition, many of its teachings are nevertheless rooted in practicality, and it has exerted massive influence on all aspects of traditional Chinese architecture.

The **Expat Learning Center of Shanghai** offers ten-week courses in feng shui (*Building No. 1, Lane 152 Kangping Road, Xuhui District, 5588-9133, www.shanghai-classes.com/fengshui*).

Gongqing Forest Park

Located on the west bank of the Huangpu River north of Zhabei, Gongqing Forest Park (Gongqing Senlin Gongyuan) is a pleasant retreat. Activities include boating, fishing, horseback riding, rock climbing (on an artificial wall), and soccer. Children may enjoy an adventure playground, roller coaster, and fun fair. The park gets busy on weekends and holidays. [M] 239 F3 [✉] 2000 Jungong Road [☎] 6532-8194 [$] $ [🚕] Taxi or bus No. 8

Peace Park

Shanghai's Peace Park (Heping Gongyuan) covers 50 acres (20 ha) in northeastern Hongkou and includes an artificial lake, bird and wildlife sanctuaries, and a Sea World show featuring sea lions and dolphins. It's also the venue for buffalo and cock fighting, plus piglet Olympics on the May Day national holiday. [M] 239 E2–E3 [✉] 891 Tianbao Road [☎] 6272-7912 [$] $ [🚇] Metro: Linping Road

Shanghai Circus World

Shanghai Circus World (Shanghai Maxi Cheng) is the main venue for traditional circus entertainment in Shanghai, featuring extraordinary acrobatics, tightrope walking, death-defying trapeze artists, performing lions, tigers, and pandas—everything associated with the circus. Home to the Shanghai Acrobatic Troupe, the venue features a revolving stage and state-of-the-art lighting and acoustics. [M] 238 C3 [✉] 2266 Gonghe New Road [☎] 5665-3646 [$] $–$$$$ [🚇] Metro: Shanghai Circus World

Zhabei Park

Zhabei Park (Zhabei Gongyuan) opened in 1914 as Song Jiaoren Park in honor of the anti-Qing nationalist. The revolutionary first president of the Kuomintang (KMT) was assassinated at Shanghai North Station in 1913 and subsequently buried here. The park is also associated with tea and regularly hosts the International Tea Culture Festival. A giant golden teapot marks the park's entrance, and an exhibition hall on the grounds chronicles the long history of tea. [M] 239 C3 [✉] 1555 Gonghe New Road [☎] 5633-4565 [$] $ [🚇] Metro: Yanchang Road

Suburbs offering shops, museums, public parks, and easy day trips to Jiading, Sheshan, and Songjiang

West Shanghai

Introduction & Map   250–251

Jingan   252

Hongqiao   253

Changning   254

Sheshan   255

Experience: Practice Early Morning Tai Chi   255

Feature: Western Architecture in Shanghai   256–257

Experience: Exploring Shanghai's Lilong Lanes   257

More Places to Visit in West Shanghai   258

Hotels & Restaurants   311–314

Confucius Temple detail, Jiading

West Shanghai

West Shanghai covers a huge area, extending from upscale, bustling Jingan to the affluent residential area of Changning to Hongqiao and Gubei to the west of the Inner Ring Road (Zhongshan Road). Still more distant, the western suburbs of Jiading, Qingpu, and Songjiang are far enough from downtown Shanghai to move at a slower pace and offer a genuine rural feel.

Jingan has long been associated with wealth, notably during colonial times when it was home to Shanghai's Sephardic Jewish magnates and Ohel Rachel, Shanghai's second oldest surviving synagogue. Though the many Jewish families moved to Israel or the United

States, an upwardly mobile neighborhood of malls and offices remains. It's also home to Jingan Temple, one of the city's most important Buddhist temples.

Farther west, affluent Changning enjoys the green spaces of Zhongshan and Changfeng

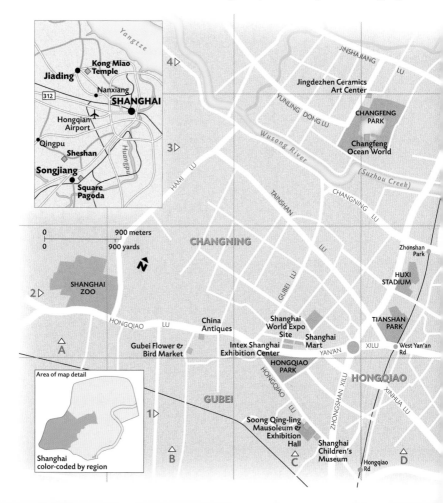

Parks. Nearby Zhongshan are the Revolutionary Historical Relic Exhibition Hall and the No. 3 Girls Middle School. The Jingdezhen Ceramics Art Center and the city's first aquarium are in the Changfeng Park neighborhood.

Hongqiao and Gubei are known for the Shanghai Zoo, the Shanghai Children's Museum, and the neighboring Soong Qing-ling Mausoleum in addition to its expatriate residents, shops, and bird market.

The district of Jiading includes Nanxiang, known for its Garden of Ancient Splendor and *xiao long bao* dumplings (see sidebar p. 258). Jiading is a canal town with a Confucian temple and museum.

To the southwest of Shanghai, Sheshan's highlights include its observatory, the Basilica of Notre Dame, the Xiudaozhe Pagoda, and the tilting pagoda at Huzhu Ta. Neighboring Songjiang

features the Square Pagoda and the Garden of the Poet Bai Juyi. The Chinese-style Zhenjiao Mosque, built in the mid-14th century, is one of the oldest mosques in China. ∎

NOT TO BE MISSED:

The beauty of Jingan Temple   252

Exploring the Soong Qing-ling Exhibition Hall ⅋ reading the international cast of names in Wangou Cemetery   253

The Jingdezhen Ceramics Art Center in Changning   254

Sheshan's rich Jesuit history   255

Enjoying early morning tai chi   255

Wandering through the *lilong* lanes of the city   257

Dumpling heaven in Nanxiang   258

Jinshajiang Rd

WUNING LU

JIANGSU BEILU

Wusong River

CHANGSHOU LU

WANHANGDU LU

ZHONGSHAN (SUN YAT-SEN) PARK

Zhonshan Park

CHANGNING LU

WUDING XILU

JIANGNING LU

JINGAN

Hua Xia Sex Culture Museum

Revolutionary Historical Relic Exhibition Hall

No. 3 Girls Middle School

Jiangsu Rd

SHANXI BEILU

JIANGSU LU

YUYUAN LU

BEIJING XILU

Ohel Rachel Synagogue

Jingan Temple

Jing'an Temple

Shanghai Centre

Plaza 66

Westgate Mall

NANJING XILU

Park Place Mall

YAN'AN XILU

Wheelock Place Tower

JINGAN PARK

YAN'AN

The PuLi Spa and Hotel

CITIC Square

Shanghai Exhibition Centre

ZHONGLU

HUASHAN LU

Xingguo Binguan

DING XIANG GARDEN

E

F

XIANGYANG PARK

G

Jingan

Jingan was always a wealthy area, home to some of Shanghai's richest *taipans* (foreign business-men). It was also a favored shopping district for their wives. Even today, Jingan is the place to go for fine silks and couturier clothing.

Jingan
🔼 251

Ohel Rachel Synagogue (Youtai Jiaotong)
🔼 251 G2
✉ 500 Shaanxi North Road
🕐 By special arrangement

Jingan Temple (Jingan Si)
🔼 251 F2
✉ 1686 Nanjing West Road (Nanjing Xilu)
☎ 5213-1586
💲 $

On the north side of Nanjing West Road (Nanjing Xilu), **West-gate Mall, CITIC Square, Plaza 66,** and **Shanghai Centre** attest to the area's continuing affluence. Just north along Shaanxi North Road, beyond CITIC Square, the former **Ohel Rachel Synagogue** survives. Built by banker Jacob Sassoon in 1920, this synagogue has been refurbished. Though it remains consecrated, it now serves as a museum (see p. 218; *open to the public only by special arrangement with the Shanghai Center for Jewish Studies; tel 6/384-4022, email ohelrachel@chinajewish.org*).

South of Nanjing West Road, the **Shanghai Exhibition Centre** (Shanghai Zhanlan Zhongxin; *1000 Yan'an Road*) on the former estate of Silas Hardoon—once the city's richest man—is a fine example of high socialist-realist

Be sure to visit the Jade Buddha Hall in Jingan Temple to marvel at the 12.5-foot (3.8 m) statue, the largest sitting jade Buddha in China.

—LARRY PORGES
National Geographic Travel Books editor

kitsch from the days of Sino–Soviet solidarity in the early 1950s. Designed by a Soviet architect, the Christmas cake–like structure combines a five-pointed commu-nist star atop classical pillars and floral wreaths with elements of Eastern Orthodox church architec-ture, including a gilded steeple.

Near the western end of Nan-jing West Road, **Jingan Temple** is said to have been built in A.D. 247, but it has been restored and re-built down the ages. Dedicated to Sakyamuni Buddha, it now seems equally dedicated to commerce, with a shopping mall located within the temple precincts. In the 1930s, Jingan Si was the richest Buddhist temple in Shanghai and the preserve of the abbot Khi Vehdu, who was 6 feet 6 inches (2 m) tall. Protected by White Russian bodyguards, he reportedly kept seven concubines, each with her own house and car! ■

Bubbling Well Road

Bubbling Well Road was once the name of Jingan's Nanjing West Road (Nanjing Xilu). A carbonated spring that stood at the intersection of Nanjing West Road and Wanhang Road was paved over long ago, but a re-creation of the spring is in **Jingan Park** (Jingan Gongyuan), the former Bubbling Well Cemetery. In dry weather, calligraphers practice writing Chinese ideo-graphs on the stone flags using giant *maobi* brushes and water—a transient art form.

Hongqiao

South of Changning and west of Zhongshan Road, Hongqiao is an area of high-rise office blocks, conference centers, trade exhibitions, and expensive shops. It's also home to many of Shanghai's expatriate residents—not just Westerners, but also Taiwanese, Japanese, and Koreans.

Set in the center of the old International Cemetery, Hongqiao's most revered monument is the unassuming **Soong Qing-ling Mausoleum** (Soong Qing-ling Ling-yuan). Also known as Madame Sun Yat-sen, Soong Qing-ling married the father of modern China in 1915.

She remained politically active after her husband's death in 1925 and continued to support the communists against Chiang Kai-shek. She became vice president of the People's Republic of China in 1949 and was made honorary president of the People's Republic of China in 1981.

The much larger **Soong Qing-ling Exhibition Hall** displays memorabilia, including clothing, textbooks, and photographs. The surrounding **Wangou Cemetery** is now Shanghai's only cemetery for foreign nationals.

Just east of the cemetery stands the **Shanghai Children's Museum** and its partner the **Shanghai Discovery Children's Museum,** both dedicated to the scientific education of China's next generation.

Northwest of the cemetery, Hongqiao Lu leads past **Hongqiao Park** (Hongqiao Gongyuan) through an area known for its reputable antiques shops, like **China Antiques** (No. 1660, tel 6270-1023), **Wan Bo Arts and Crafts** (No. 1430, tel 6208-9581),

Shanghai Children's Museum offers a portal to China's future.

and **Alex's Antique Shop** (No. 1970, tel 6242-8734).

On the north side of the park, are the **Intex Shanghai Exhibition Center, Shanghai Mart,** and **Shanghai World Center** exhibition venues. The **Gubei Flower and Bird Market** (Gubei Hua Niao Shichang; 1778 Hongqiao Road) lies a little farther west.

One of Hongqiao's main attractions is the **Hongmei Road** bar and restaurant strip, where many of downtown Shanghai's most popular bars and eateries have now opened satellite branches. Hongmei Road runs south of the **Yan'an Road** elevated highway, about a mile (1.6 km) west of Shanghai Mart and Intex.

The western end of Hongqiao Road is the site of the **Shanghai Zoo,** maybe China's best zoo. ∎

Hongqiao

🗺 250

Soong Qing-ling Exhibition Hall (Song Qing-ling Chenlieguan)

🗺 250 C1
✉ 21 Songyuan Road
☎ 6275-8080
$ $

Shanghai Children's Museum (Shanghai Ertong Bowuguan)

🗺 250 C1
✉ 61 Songyuan Road
☎ 6278-3130
$ $

Changning

Like Jingan, Changning has long been one of Shanghai's wealthier districts. Several historical and cultural sights make it worth a visit.

Changning
 250–251

Changfeng Ocean World (Changfeng Haiyang Shijie)
🅰 250 D3
✉ 451 Daduhe Road
☎ 6223-5501
💲 $$$

Built by a British trading company to replicate an English country estate, Hazlewood became Mao's favored residence following the communist seizure of power in 1949. It now serves as the **Prosperous Kingdom Guesthouse** (Xingguo Binguan; *78 Xingguo Road, tel 6212-9998*).

North of the guesthouse is the prestigious **No. 3 Girls Middle School** (*Di San Nu Zhong; Lane 155 Jiangsu Road*), founded in 1890.

Back in central Changning, the **Revolutionary Historical Relic Exhibition Hall** (Changning Qu Geming Wenwu Chenlie Guan; *1376 Yuyuan Road, tel 6251-1415, closed Sun.*) displays books, maps,

pamphlets, posters, and other revolutionary literature.

A taxi is the best way to reach **Changfeng Park** (*Zhongshan Road*). At Gate 4 is the city's finest aquarium, **Changfeng Ocean World.** Its vast tanks house a variety of marine life, including whales, penguins, and sharks.

On the north side of the park at the **Jingdezhen Ceramics Art Center** (Jingdezhen Ciqi Yishu Zhongxin; *1253 Daduhe Road*), thousands of ceramic pieces from Jingdezhen and Yixing (see feature p. 247) are displayed. Here you can watch potters work and buy contemporary ceramics. ■

Children play at the popular adventure playground in Changning's Zhongshan Park.

Sheshan

The town of Sheshan, about 19 miles (30 km) west of Shanghai and almost due south of Jiading, is home to Sheshan Mountain, where the Jesuits established an observatory in 1898. You'll also find several other religious institutions that bear a closer look.

Start at the refurbished **Sheshan Observatory** (Sheshan Tianwen-tai; $), which houses a small museum dedicated to the history of Chinese astronomy.

The Jesuits are also responsible for erecting the impressive church next door that started life as the Cathedral of the Holy Mother in 1866. In 1935 it was replaced by the redbrick-and-stone Basilica of Notre Dame, more commonly called **Sheshan Cathedral** (Sheshan Shengmu Dadian; *Mount Sheshan, $*). Red Guard iconoclasts damaged the church during the Cultural Revolution, but it has been restored. Look for the letters "M" for Mary (the Mother of God) and "S" for Societas Jesu (the Society of Jesus) inscribed on the old gate.

To the east of the church stands a 65-foot-high (20 m), seven-story tower, the **Xiudao-zhe Pagoda** (Xiudaozhe Ta; $), said to have been constructed between 976 and 984 during the Song dynasty.

About 5 miles (8 km) distant from Sheshan is the "pagoda for guarding pearls," **Huzhu Pagoda** (Huzhu Ta; *Tianma Mountain, $*), a 62-foot-high (19 m) pagoda chiefly remarkable for its tilt—locals have dubbed it the "leaning tower of China." Though much smaller than the Leaning Tower of Pisa, the pagoda does tilt at a slightly greater angle and

therefore is no place for vertigo sufferers. It is claimed that the octagonal stone Huzhu Ta was originally built in 1079 but that its trademark slant did not develop until 1788, when villagers pulled out some supporting stones at the base while digging for treasure.

Sheshan is also home to the **Sheshan International Golf Club** (*Lane 288, New Linyin Avenue, tel 010/5779-8088, www .sheshangolf.com*), which hosts the World Gold Championship HSBC Masters each November. ∎

Sheshan

 250

EXPERIENCE: Practice Early Morning Tai Chi

Before visiting Shanghai, rumors of elderly early risers line dancing, hugging trees, and walking backward sound fanciful. But get up at dawn and head for **Jingan Park** (see map page 51) in the city center, and you'll see for yourself. Amid the trees, you'll spot individuals practicing the slow martial arts moves, plus ladies performing an energetic, leg-swinging line dance. Some early risers partake in meditative exercises while clinging to tree trunks, while others walk in reverse around the park, which is believed to soothe back pain. These are all traditional forms of early morning exercise. You may even be cajoled into joining in. As day turns to dusk, another good spot for tai chi watching is **Fuxing Park** (see pp. 216–217)—where you may even catch a male elder slow-motion shadow fighting with a real silver sword in hand.

Western Architecture in Shanghai

It's difficult to generalize about Western architecture in Shanghai because it's as varied as the people who settled in the city. Motivated by religion, some settlers erected fine churches, like St. Ignatius Cathedral in Xujiahui, the former Russian Orthodox Mission Church near Fuxing Park, and the Basilica of Notre Dame at Sheshan. Others were driven by commerce, erecting great temples to wealth, notably along the Bund.

Gazing down on the atrium of the Grand Hyatt Hotel, Jinmao Tower, Pudong

Many of the city's finest late 19th- and early 20th-century buildings were designed by the British architectural firm Palmer & Turner. Its landmark structures include the Bank of China, the Yokohama Specie Bank, the Customs House, and the Hong Kong and Shanghai Bank. When the latter opened in 1923, the six-floor, neoclassical building was the largest bank in East Asia and the second largest in the world after the Bank

of Scotland in the United Kingdom.

As foreign-concession Shanghai grew wealthier, grand hotels were built to house the travelers and tourists who flocked to the city for its sophistication and style as well as for its dubious but compelling reputation. Palmer & Turner also played a role in the travel industry, designing signature buildings like Grosvenor House (now the Jinjiang Hotel). Another of Shanghai's great foreign architects, Hungarian

Ladislau Hudec designed nearly 40 buildings between 1918 and 1941. Among them is the 22-story Park Hotel, which remained the city's highest structure until 1983. Hudec employed various styles, ranging from neoclassical to baroque to his trademark art deco. Some of his best-known work includes the Moore Memorial Church near Renmin Square, the Grand Theater, and the Shanghai Museum of Arts and Crafts, aka Shanghai's "White House," on Fenyang Road.

Shanghai's great Jewish families also contributed to the city's emerging skyline, constructing such major apartment blocks as banking and real estate magnate Sir Victor Sassoon's Cathay Hotel (now Fairmont Peace Hotel) on Maoming Road and Embankment House beside Suzhon Creek. Some of the wealthier taipans were also rather eccentric, resulting in the bizarre Gothic castle architecture of Moller Villa on Shaanxi South Road. Solid, respectable consular buildings also went up, exemplified by the fine Russian Consulate near Waibaidu Bridge and also by the elegant French, Japanese, and American Consulates on Huaihai Middle Road.

INSIDER TIP:

Beautifully preserved, the early 20th-century Jinjiang Hotel [59 Maoming South Road] lies in the heart of the French Concession and is wonderfully evocative of concession-era Shanghai.

—DAMIEN HARPER
National Geographic author

The International Settlement, especially the area around the Bund and Nanjing East Road, acquired the distinct feel of New York or Chicago. The French Concession developed a Gallic charm that still exists in the broad, tree-lined boulevards and shuttered villas.

Today Shanghai is changing at an astonishing pace, and the new architecture—while sometimes making concessions to traditional Chinese form—is overwhelmingly international. Futuristic Pudong, especially, with its soaring skyscrapers, reflects Shanghai's overarching ambition to reign as an international powerhouse of commerce, shipping, and technology.

EXPERIENCE: Exploring Shanghai's *Lilong* Lanes

In terms of traditional architecture, Beijing has its *hutongs*, and Shanghai is proud of its *lilongs*—redbrick houses constructed around a network of narrow alleyways. As in Beijing, swathes of lilongs have been razed to make way for modern skyscrapers, but pockets of lane living—often identifiable by the ubiquitous rows of hanging washing from the windows (lilong houses don't usually have a garden)—give an insight into a slower-paced, more community-based style of life in a megacity. Few foreigners understand the architectural and technical history of Shanghai's lane neighborhoods better than **Spencer Doddington** (*www .spencerdoddington.com*). A longtime

Shanghai resident, U.S.-born Doddington is an architect who has renovated numerous lane houses and apartment blocks—and uses this insight in his specialist tours. Knowledgeable, witty, and fluent in Mandarin and Shanghainese, he is also a frequent writer and speaker on issues of Shanghai architecture and heritage conservation. **Shanghai Flaneur** (*www.shanghai-flaneur.com*) is a collective of experienced English- and German-speaking Shanghai walking tour guides who explain the intricacies of Shanghai architecture. In addition to personalized lilong walks, they offer regular themed public walks that range from the old walled city to Shanghai's modern skyline.

More Places to Visit in West Shanghai

Jiading

Farther out of Shanghai to the northwest, Jiading makes an excellent day trip away from the big city. The town offers a pleasant opportunity for the visitor to become acquainted with a more traditional aspect of China. Jiading's cobbled streets and canals retain considerable Old World charms. Jiading's spirtual heart is **Dragon-Meeting Pond Park,** where five small streams converge. Dating from 1588, it remains a placid garden park. To the west stands the **Confucious Temple** (183 Nanda Road, $) that dates from 1219, although it was added to and restored in the Yuan, Ming, and Qing dynasties. ⚠ 250

Nanxiang

Ten miles (16 km) northwest of Shanghai—located in Jiading District on the road to Jiading and therefore easily visited on the way there or back—lies the small town of Nanxiang. A formal, Suzhou-style garden designed by local bamboo sculptor Zhun Shansong, the lovely **Garden of Ancient Splendor** (218 Huyi Road, $) served as the private garden for a Ming-dynasty official. Highlights include a Song dynasty pagoda and a Tang dynasty (618–907) stele. **Yunxiang Temple** (8 Huyi Road, $) is said to be the only surviving Tang-dynasty temple in the Shanghai area. ⚠ 250

Songjiang

Just south of Sheshan, on the Huhang Expressway between Shanghai and Hangzhou, is the town of Songjiang, set in pleasant low-lying, rice-farming country transected by waterways. The town's best known monument is the **Square Pagoda** (Zhongshan Road, $), a 160-foot-high (48.5 m), nine-story tower built during the Song dynasty (960–1279). The screen in front of the pagoda portrays a tan—a monster with a deer's antlers, lion's tail, and bull's hooves—associated with greed in Buddhism.

Other attractions include the **Garden of the Poet Bai Juyi** (Zubaichi; Zhongshan Road, $), a traditional Suzhou-style garden built by Gu Dashen—a Qing-dynasty official and admirer of the celebrated Tang-dynasty poet Bai Juyi (772–846). Songjiang's history is reflected in the **Xilin Pagoda** (Xilin Ta; Zhongshan Middle Road & Xilin North Road, $), a 152-foot-high (46.5 m) pagoda within a recently renovated Buddhist temple. The pagoda, said to date from 1440, can be climbed ($) for fine views. Much older—in fact, supposedly the oldest Buddhist structure in the Shanghai area—is the **Toroni Sutra Stele** (Tang Jing Zhang, Zhongshan Xiaoxue, Zhongshan Middle Road). This 30-foot-high (9 m) structure is made of 21 stone blocks. Perhaps Songjiang's best attraction is the Yuan-dynasty **Zhenjiao Mosque** (Zhenjiao Qingzhensi; Zhongshan Middle Road), the oldest Islamic structure in the area. ⚠ 250

Dumpling Heaven

Nanxiang may be best known as the original home of the enduringly popular Shanghai culinary delicacy *xiao long bao*, or little basket bun. Traditionally steamed in small bamboo baskets, these bite-size treats can be filled with broth and ground pork or vegetables. But be careful biting into them, as the hot broth can scald your mouth. Although popular across China, experts agree that the Shanghai version of xiao long bao was originally prepared and sold at a restaurant next to Nanxiang's historic Guyi Gongyuan, from where its fame soon spread into the big city. Today, they are sold throughout Nanxiang (and indeed all points beyond) and make a delicious and satisfying lunch, especially in cold weather.

From the exotic south and inland mountain resort of Moganshan
to the water towns and classical gardens in the west

Excursions From Shanghai

Introduction & Map   260–261

Hangzhou   262–265

Experience: The Tea Harvest   264

Feature: Grand Canal   266–267

Moganshan   268

Putuoshan   269

Suzhou   270–273

Experience: Nature's Harmony in
  Suzhou Gardens   272

Feature: Water Towns   274–275

Nanjing   276–278

Huangshan   279–280

Hotels & Restauants   314–316

Detail of Ming-dynasty domestic
scene in Chen Residence, Zhouzhuang

Excursions From Shanghai

South of Shanghai, the historic city of Hangzhou—a major destination in its own right—is the gateway to historic Shaoxing, the Buddhist pilgrimage island of Putuoshan, and peaceful Moganshan. Along the way, breathtaking countryside makes you feel as if you've traveled far away from the urban bustle. In the region west and northwest of the city you'll discover traditional water towns, as well as the classical gardens of Suzhou and the city of Nanjing, replete with memories both glorious and terrible.

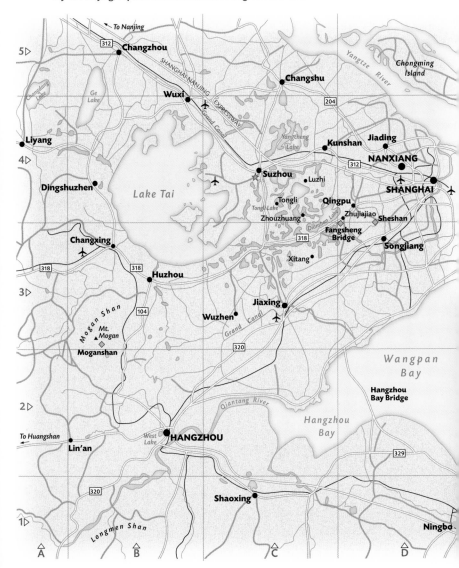

During the Southern Song dynasty (1127–1279), at a time when Shanghai was a sleepy fishing village, Hangzhou to the south served as the seat of government. This imperial tradition means that Hangzhou retains many of its ancient pagodas, temples, and other historic sites, as well as the world-famous Xi Hu, or West Lake, which the Chinese consider archetypal.

To the northwest of Hangzhou, Moganshan is an isolated area of hills and mountains celebrated for its bamboo groves, cool climate, fresh air, and natural beauty. It has long been a favored weekend retreat of wealthier Shanghainese—not to mention Western missionaries, local warlords, gangsters, and Kuomintang generals.

Putuoshan, south and east of Hangzhou, was affected particularly badly during the Cultural Revolution, when zealous Red Guards desecrated temples and smashed Buddha images. The resident population of Buddhist monks dwindled to fewer than 30, from a prerevolutionary high of about 2,000. Buddhism has made a comeback in China since the mid-1980s, and Putuoshan has reemerged as a popular pilgrimage center for Buddhists and other vacationers, who visit the island for

NOT TO BE MISSED:

West Lake and the hill temples of Hangzhou 262–265

Learning the secrets of the tea harvest 264

The long and winding history of the Grand Canal 266–267

Exploring the quiet valleys of Moganshan 268

The pilgrimage to the sacred Buddhist island of Putuoshan 269

Suzhou's classical gardens 272

The beauty of Suzhou silk 273

Charming traditional water towns 274–275

The mists of Huangshan 280

its temples, beaches, caves, and tranquil hills.

North of Shanghai, the fertile flatlands around Lake Tai are famed for a number of water towns that date back to imperial times. These peaceful, scenic villages feature picturesque bridges arching across willow-lined canals.

Like Hangzhou, the city of Suzhou, near Lake Tai's shores, has retained its ancient core. Surrounded by moats, it boasts the most exquisite collection of classical gardens in China, as well as numerous ancient temples and pagodas.

Some distance north and west of Suzhou, but readily accessible by high-speed train, the Ming capital of Nanjing is now a feasible day trip from Shanghai, though it is better experienced on a weekend break. Packed with historic sites, from the world's longest city wall to the Ming Tombs, it is also home to the magnificent Mausoleum of Sun Yat-sen, the founder of modern China. Other sites include a sobering memorial to the Nanjing Massacre of 1937–1938 and the Yangtze Great Bridge. ■

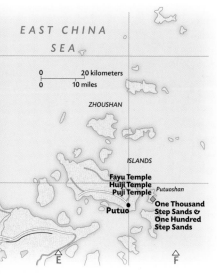

Hangzhou

Hangzhou is often described as an excursion from Shanghai, and that is precisely how most visitors will approach the city. It's not a small place, however, having a population of about 7 million people and a considerable history of its own, as well as extensive parkland to the south and west of the city center.

Hangzhou
260 B2, 263

**West Lake
(Xi Hu)**
260 B2, 263

The Venetian merchant Marco Polo visited Hangzhou in the late 13th century and described the city as "beyond dispute the finest and noblest in the world." In imperial times, much of the city's wealth was due to its position at the southern end of the Grand Canal, which runs for 1,115 miles (1,794 km) to connect with Beijing in the north. Although the city has also suffered disasters, most notably during the Taiping Rebellion in 1861 and the Cultural Revolution, many of its surviving cultural treasures have been carefully restored. The city is again wealthy, with an economy based on silk and textile production, electronics and other light industries, and green tea.

Tourism is increasing every year, as Chinese travelers and overseas visitors flock to see Hangzhou's ancient temples and pagodas, along with the willow-lined West Lake.

West Lake

West Lake (Xi Hu) is lovely enough, and large enough, to merit the better part of a day's exploration. You can walk around the 2.6-square-mile (6.8 sq km) lake, wander across it via two ancient causeways, and also explore the waters by boat, or by hiring a bicycle from one of hundreds of kiosks near the lake.

At the lake's northeastern shore, **Bai Causeway** (Bai Di) leads to **Sun Yat-sen Park** (Zhongshan Gongyuan) on **Gu Shan**, West Lake's largest island. Visitors flock here to enjoy fine teahouses and also Louwailou Fandian, the lake's

Wooded paths, bamboo groves, and small pagodas bedeck tranquil Tiger Dreaming Spring, a popular place to stroll.

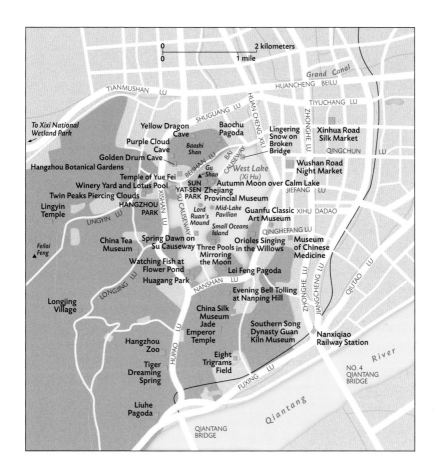

Map labels:

0 2 kilometers
0 1 mile

Grand Canal
HUANCHENG BEILU
TIANMUSHAN LU
TIYUCHANG LU
SHUGUANG LU
HUAN CHENG XILU
ZHONGHE LU
To Xixi National Wetland Park
Yellow Dragon Cave
Baochu Pagoda
Lingering Snow on Broken Bridge
Xinhua Road Silk Market
Purple Cloud Cave
Baoshi Shan
QINGCHUN LU
Golden Drum Cave
BEISHAN LU
BAI CAUSEWAY
West Lake (Xi Hu)
Wushan Road Night Market
Hangzhou Botanical Gardens
Gu Shan
Temple of Yue Fei
Winery Yard and Lotus Pool
SUN YAT-SEN PARK
Autumn Moon over Calm Lake
JIEFANG LU
Twin Peaks Piercing Clouds
Zhejiang Provincial Museum
XISHAN LU
SU CAUSEWAY
Lingyin Temple
HANGZHOU PARK
Lord Ruan's Mound
Mid-Lake Pavilion
Guanfu Classic Art Museum
XIHU DADAO
LINGYIN LU
Small Oceans Island
QINGHEFANG LU
Feilai Feng
China Tea Museum
Spring Dawn on Su Causeway
Three Pools Mirroring the Moon
Orioles Singing in the Willows
Museum of Chinese Medicine
ZHONGHE LU
JIANGCHENG LU
QIUTAO LU
Watching Fish at Flower Pond
Lei Feng Pagoda
NANSHAN LU
Huagang Park
LONGJING LU
Evening Bell Tolling at Nanping Hill
Longjing Village
China Silk Museum
Jade Emperor Temple
Southern Song Dynasty Guan Kiln Museum
Nanxiqiao Railway Station
Hangzhou Zoo
HUPAO LU
Eight Trigrams Field
Qiantang River
Tiger Dreaming Spring
FUXING LU
NO. 4 QIANTANG BRIDGE
Liuhe Pagoda
QIANTANG BRIDGE

famed restaurant. A stroll up Gu Shan, the hill that gives the island its name, leads to the **Huayanjing Pagoda** (Huayanjing Ta), which offers fine views across the lake.

South of Gu Shan, and accessible only by boat, are three smaller man-made islands. **Mid-Lake Pavilion** (Huxinting) and **Lord Ruan's Mound** (Ruangong-dun) are both wooded and tiny. Father to the south lies **Small**

Qinghefang Old Street

On the east side of West Lake, in the heart of downtown Hangzhou, Hefang Old Street has been part of the city's commercial district since the Tang dynasty. Its present incarnation dates from the 18th and 19th centuries. The pedestrian-only shopping area was completely restored in 2001, and many of the buildings are in fact re-creations of Ming- and Qing-dynasty styles.

**Huagang Park
(Huagang
Guangyu)**
🅰 263

Lei Feng Pagoda
🅰 263

**Precious Stone
Hill (Baoshi
Shan)**
🅰 263

Oceans Island (Xiaoying Zhou), which is studded with pavilions and pagodas.

Paralleling the lake's western shore, **Su Causeway** runs south from Beishan Road at a point near the Temple of Yue Fei past Small Oceans Island to Nanshan Road. From there, it's a five-minute walk west to **Huagang Park**. Or head east to find one of West Lake's greatest attractions, **Lei Feng Pagoda** ($). Recently rebuilt in the traditional style, but with a sturdy, state-of-the-art steel-and-glass structure, the pagoda offers fantastic views across West Lake and Hangzhou City.

Precious Stone Hill

Along the north shore of West Lake, overlooking Beishan Road, is a rocky outcrop known as Precious Stone Hill. The hill has a number of historic sites, the

most important of which are the Temple and Tomb of Yue Fei.

Yue Fei (1103–1142) was a Song-dynasty military commander who fought bravely against the Jurchen Manchu, who had occupied the Song capital of Kaifeng and captured the Song emperor Qinzhong. As Yue Fei was about

EXPERIENCE: The Tea Harvest

Each year, China's tea drinkers eagerly anticipate the tea harvest in late March/early April. In Hangzhou, the first Longjing tea leaves of the season are greeted with the same buzz of expectation as a Beaujolais Nouveau in France. Vintage years come and go, but the taste of freshly picked and wok-dried Longjing tea is a cherished annual treat. Hotels in the city offer special tea harvest packages, notably the **Landison Longjing Resort** (www.longjingresort.com), beautifully situated on Lijilong Mountain amid a verdant tea plantation.

Watching pickers at work is an education, and the place to do it is **Longjing** (Dragonwell) village, source of this highly prized tea variety. Hangzhou hotels

arrange private tours to watch the tea picking and try your hand at drying the leaves in a large iron wok, followed by a Chinese tea ceremony. Alternatively, hire a cab for the morning to take you on the picturesque 30-minute drive south of Hangzhou, which winds up through the tea valleys to the village. You can buy tea leaves here, but be prepared to bargain hard. While in the vicinity, stop at the nearby **China National Tea Museum** (88 Longjin Road, tel 8796-4222, www.teamuseum.cn), in Shuangfeng village. It's set on a large tea estate, where you can watch the pickers in action, and learn about the history and medicinal properties of tea. A teahouse in the back garden serves the local brew in porcelain teapots.

The Qiantang River Bore

The Qiantang, the largest river in Zhejiang Province, flows from the borderlands of Anhui and Jiangxi east to Hangzhou Bay. The bay's bottleneck shape and the moon's gravitational pull combine to cause a tidal flow to rush into the river on the 18th day of the eighth lunar month. The result is the world's largest tidal bore: The waters rise up to 30 feet (9 m) and sweep past Hangzhou with a noise that resembles thunder or thousands of galloping horses.

to take back Kaifeng, Gaozong, the acting Song emperor, recalled him, fearing that he would lose power to Qinzhong if the Manchu were defeated. Yue Fei was executed in 1142 but officially exonerated in 1162, one year after the death of Emperor Gaozong, and reinterred with full honors beside West Lake.

At the **Temple of Yue Fei,** his memorial hall is generally filled with fresh flowers and coils of smoking incense. Murals relate key episodes from Yue Fei's life, and a walkway leads through a formal Song-style garden to the tombs of Yue Fei and his sons.

Immediately behind the tombs, a path leads to **Purple Cloud Cave** (Ziyun Dong), the oldest of several cave-temples in the area. From here, a ten-minute walk to the southeast brings you to the **Golden Drum Cave** (Jingu Dong), while **Yellow Dragon Cave** (Huanglong Dong; $) awaits at the end of a 20-minute stroll to the northeast.

Following the steep stone paths to the eastern part of Precious Stone Hill leads to **Baochu Pagoda** (Baochu Ta), a needle-pointed tower that can be seen from around West Lake.

Other Sites

Hangzhou Botanical Gardens covers nearly 500 acres (200 ha). The Garden of a Hundred Herbs (Baicao Yuan) actually features more than a thousand types of herbs.

Southwest of Lingyin Road is Hangzhou's most revered temple and one of China's richest: **Lingyin Temple.** At its entrance stands the seven-story Song-dynasty **Ligong Pagoda** (Ligong Ta). The temple climbs Lingyin Hill through five halls. The cliff south of the temple, **Feilai Feng,** or the Peak That Flew From Afar, is decorated with 470 Buddhist stone carvings dating from the 10th to 14th centuries.

In the west of the city, **Xixi Wetland,** created during the Han dynasty, is now China's first national wetlands park. A boat cruise along the urban wetlands offers insights into the unique flora and fauna of the region.

Father south, by the north bank of the Qiantang River, **Liuhe Pagoda** is impressive for its elegance and size. The octagonal pagoda is a great place to view the 4,767-foot-long (1,453 m) **Qiantang Bridge** and watch the annual bore (see sidebar above). ∎

Temple of Yue Fei (Yue Wang Miao)

- 🗺 263
- ✉ 1 Hougushan Road
- 💲 $

Hangzhou Botanical Gardens (Hangzhou Zhiwuyuan)

- 🗺 263
- ✉ 1 Taoyuanling
- 💲 $

Lingyin Temple (Lingyin Si)

- 🗺 263
- ✉ 1 Fayung Nong
- ☎ 8796-8665
- 💲 $

Xixi Wetland

- 🗺 263
- ✉ 518 Tianmushan Road
- **www.xixiwetland .com.cn**

Liuhe Pagoda (Liuhe Ta)

- 🗺 263
- ✉ 147 Nanshan Road
- ☎ 8659-1401
- 💲 $

Grand Canal

China's Grand Canal (Da Yunhe) is the oldest and longest man-made waterway in the world. Dating from the fifth century B.C., the canal links Beijing with the East China Sea at Hangzhou, winding a north–south path through the provinces of Hebei, Shandong, Jiangsu, and Zhejiang. It also crosses six major rivers: the Hai, Wei, Huang, Huai, Yangtze, and, finally, the Qiantang (see sidebar p. 265).

The busy, diverse traffic on the Grand Canal reflects China's rapid industrialization and growing need for transportation.

The founding of the Grand Canal is generally attributed to Fu Chai, Duke of Wu—present-day Suzhou—who ordered the construction of a canal to transport soldiers in an attack on the neighboring state of Qi in 486 B.C., during the Warring States period. This initial canal was extended and improved under the Sui dynasty (A.D. 581–618), attaining approximately its current form around 610. After Beijing became the capital of the Yuan dynasty in 1279, a westward extension of the canal to Luoyang was abandoned. In the late 1200s, a new section was cut through hilly terrain in Shandong, considerably shortening the route between Hangzhou and Beijing. This addition effectively established the canal as it is today, with an overall length of 1,115 miles (1,794 km).

In 1855 the Huang He, or Yellow River, suffered particularly severe flooding and changed course. The Shandong section of the Grand Canal was severed and fell into a decline exacerbated by improvements in oceanic shipping routes and the subsequent introduction of railways. Reconstruction did not take place in any meaningful way until after the establishment of the communist People's Republic in 1949. Even today, only the section between Hangzhou and Jining in Shandong Province is navigable.

The main purpose of the Grand Canal in imperial times was to transport grain from southern and central China to Beijing. At its peak, records show that as many as 8,000 riverboats transported between 250,000 and 360,000 tons (226.8–326.6 kt) of grain annually to the capital. The canal was also used to transport other commodities, including luxury goods for use by the imperial court. Not surprisingly, the towns along its banks prospered.

The Grand Canal also served as an important cultural link between northern and southern China, helping to unify the state and to establish a sense of common cultural identity. Qing emperors, notably Kangxi (1661–1722) and Qianlong (1735–1796), used its waters to make inspection tours of the south. It was also traveled by early European visitors, including Marco Polo (13th century) and Matteo Ricci (16th century). Some skeptics have raised

INSIDER TIP:

In Hangzhou, you can catch a half-hour cruise of the Grand Canal from Wulinmen Dock *(138 Huancheng North Road)*, Gongchenqiao Wharf, Xinyifang Wharf, or Genshanmen Wharf *($)*.

—KENNY LING
National Geographic contributor

doubts that Polo ever visited China, but his accounts of Hangzhou as well as of Suzhou seem very authentic to most readers, as does his description of the Grand Canal's arched bridges, prosperous trade, and many great warehouses.

Today the navigable sections of the Grand Canal handle cargo that neither Marco Polo nor the emperors Kangxi and Qianlong could possibly have imagined. Vast quantities of heavy goods—sand, gravel, coal, bricks, fuel oil—traverse its waters. The Jianbi locks at the junction with the Yangtze handle 75 million tons (68,040 kt) of cargo each year, and the Li Section in Jiangsu Province is projected to reach a staggering 100 million tons (90,720 kt) of cargo handled per year in the near future. The Grand Canal's founder, Fu Chai, would doubtless have been amazed and, one hopes, more than a little proud.

Hangzhou's Modern Economy

Historically, Hangzhou earned much of its wealth through connections with water. The Grand Canal transported tea, agricultural goods, and silks all the way to Beijing, while West Lake has always been the centerpiece of a profitable tourism industry. Today, Hangzhou is an affluent city that regularly tops polls of the best location in China to do business. In the outlying districts, numerous successful manufacturing businesses grew up in the 1990s to profit from Hangzhou's auspicious location and lower labor costs. More recently, e-commerce has become a defining feature of the Hangzhou economy—due partly to governmental support of start-up firms in the large high-tech parks on the city's outskirts, and a large tech-literate workforce of university graduates. Among Hangzhou's biggest names is online trading conglomerate Alibaba, founded by entrepreneur Jack Ma, which retains its global headquarters in the city.

Moganshan

With its cool climate and quiet valleys, the mountain resort of Moganshan—located 125 miles (200 km) southwest of Shanghai—is an appealing weekend getaway for city dwellers. Part of the pleasure of visiting this small, isolated settlement is the journey up the hills. Some still approach the old-fashioned way—by sedan chair.

Early 20th-century artwork on display in Moganshan

Moganshan
🅐 260 B3

Bamboo Museum (Zhuzi Bowuguan)
✉ Yinshan Road
💲 $

You'll find most of the places to stay and eat along **Yinshan Jie,** the main street. From here, you can explore the whole town in an hour or two.

Begin at the small **Bamboo Museum,** which honors the area's main crop. Beyond the museum, at 126 Yinshan Jie, stands a rather nondescript gray stone house, where Chairman

Mao once stayed. Other historic houses on Yinshan Jie include **No. 546** and **No. 547;** the latter is now an upscale guesthouse.

Beyond Yinshan, on the far side of the mountain, is the former retreat of Chiang Kaishek and Soong Meiling, who honeymooned here in 1927 at a house called **White Cloud Castle,** now part of the Baiyun Hotel (see p. 315)

The Moganshan skyline is dominated by the former **Protestant Church** and the former **Assembly Hall,** whose crenellated tower recalls a medieval keep. Still active, in contrast to the church and the hall, is the tiny **Yellow Temple** (Huang Si).

Other attractions include the **Sword Pond** (Jian Chi), set in a lovely gully, and the adjacent **Sword Pond Falls.** According to local legend, a smith forged two swords that made their bearers undefeated in battle at this spot during the Spring and Autumn Period (722–481 B.C.).

Carefully maintained stone paths wind around and across Moganshan, leading to such scenic spots as **Strange Stone Corner** (Guai Shi Jiao). Below the famous overlook, the **Qingcaotang Tea Plantation** *(open by special arrangement with the estate manager)* offers tours. ∎

Putuoshan

For centuries, Buddhists have been making pilgrimages to Putuoshan—Mount Putuo—a sacred Buddhist mountain located on an island of the same name in the Zhoushan Archipelago. You can reach the site via an hour-long ferry ride or the 22.5-mile-long (36 km) Hangzhou Bay Bridge. Sights are close enough to one another to explore on foot; otherwise, minibuses connect the attractions as well. Putuoshan is also revered for its seafood restaurants.

The Temples

Established in 1080, but rebuilt several times, **Puji Temple** (Puji Si; $) is a lovely complex of pavilions, pagodas, and lotus ponds. Standing near the back of the temple, and especially venerated, is a golden statue of Guanyin.

To the north of Puji stands the **Fayu Temple** (Fayu Si; $). Dating from the Ming dynasty (1368–1644), the large temple extends through six levels up Foding Mountain (Foding Shan). The most important building is the Dayuan Hall (Dayuan Tang), which houses another venerated Guanyin image. Exquisitely carved, intertwining wooden dragons decorate the hall's dome.

Huiji Temple (Huiji Si; $) lies still farther to the north, near the summit of Foding Shan. Dating from the Ming era, the temple offers panoramic views across the island. Although a cable car now whisks visitors to the summit, you can still walk the beautiful wooded path up the mountain. The walk takes about an hour.

More Sights to See

Far from Huiji, at the southern tip of the island, the **South Seas Guanyin** (Nanhai Guanyin) is a 108-foot-tall (33 m) gilded statue of the goddess of mercy. Her right hand is raised in blessing and her left hand holds what is probably intended to be a *darmachakra*, or Buddhist wheel of law. The icon-packed hall in which the statue stands is decorated with wooden murals depicting Guanyin rescuing shipwrecked seafarers.

Dasheng Nunnery (Dasheng An) houses the island's largest Reclining Buddha and a wealth of other Buddha images. Near Puji, the three-story **Duobao Pagoda** (Duobao Ta, or Many Treasures Pagoda), built in 1334, dates from the Yuan dynasty. ∎

Putuoshan
- 261 F1

Visitor Information
- CITS, 115 Meigin Road
- 0580/663-1037

Beaches & Beyond

Although Putuoshan is a small island, just 3.5 miles (5.5 km) long and 2 miles (3 km) wide, it has two attractive beaches: **One Thousand Step Sands** (Qianbusha) and **One Hundred Step Sands** (Baibusha).

South of Baibusha, a small promontory, the **Hall of the Unwilling to Depart Guanyin** (Bukenqu Guanyinyuan) awaits. Nearby is the **Sound of Tides Cave** (Chaoyindong), where the waves thunder into the hollowed-out cliff. Visions of the Guanyin have appeared at this spot to the pious over the centuries.

Other caves worth exploring include **Buddhist Tidings Cave** (Fanyindong), with a small Guanyin temple, and **Morning Sun Cave** (Zhaoyangdong), located between the two stretches of beach.

Suzhou

With a population of 6 million, the city of Suzhou, 50 miles (80 km) northwest of Shanghai, is smaller than Hangzhou or Shanghai. But it is still substantial. Founded at least as early as 514 B.C., Suzhou peaked under the Ming and Qing dynasties, when most of the famous gardens were built (see p. 272). Today, it is one of China's richest cities, with the most celebrated group of classical gardens anywhere in China, numerous pagodas, and a thriving silk industry.

Suzhou

🗺 260 C4

Kunqu Opera Museum (Kunchu Bowuguan

✉ Xhongzhangjia Xiang

Throughout Suzhou's long and varied history, the core of the ancient walled city survived remarkably well. Despite the loss of the former royal city and, more recently, the ancient city walls, much remains for the visitor to see. Most sites of interest lie within the moats in the protected historic heart of town, ringed by canals and waterways crisscrossed by about 200 arched stone bridges.

Reading outside Suzhou's Shuang Ta Twin Pagodas

Pingtan Museum (Pingtan Bowuguan)

✉ Xhongzhangjia Xiang

Confucius Temple

Founded in 1035, the intriguing Confucius Temple (Wen Miao; *Renmin Road*) is one of the city's oldest temples. Long the venue for imperial examinations, it is filled with steles recording the names of past doctoral graduates.

A fine stone statue of Confucius stands in the courtyard, surrounded by centuries-old trees. Behind him, the rust-red temple rises, supporting a magnificent two-level tile roof. The temple houses Confucius-related artifacts and musical instruments, including a large, well-preserved set of bells, which temple attendants play several times a day. An **antiques market** also operates on the temple grounds.

Suzhou's Museums

Suzhou has a number of excellent museums focusing on local arts and traditions. They are all well worth visiting, though the Silk Museum takes pride of place.

Kunqu Opera Museum: One of the oldest forms of Chinese opera, *Kunqu* dates back at least 600 years, reaching its zenith in the 16th to 18th centuries. Housed in elegantly carved buildings from the Ming dynasty, the museum features objects related to the opera's history. Performances are given daily.

Pingtan Museum: Across from the Kunqu Opera Museum, this associated institution relates the history of *pingtan*, a locally celebrated music genre that mixes

I. M. Pei's Suzhou Museum

Meandering among Suzhou's traditional whitewashed cottages with slate roofs and feng shui–compliant gardens is an appealing pleasure. Modernizing this time-honored style of landscaping for 21st-century visitors to the Suzhou Museum *(tel 0512/6757-5666, www .szmuseum.com)* was a challenge Chinese-born architect I. M. Pei could not turn down. Pei spent childhood summers with family in Suzhou and understood the cultural connection between constructive elements and natural features. Visitors now come as much for Pei's creative take on ancient Chinese architecture as for the exhibits. Pei's vision is evident from the front courtyard and throughout the interiors, but venture to the deliberately minimalist garden at the back for his finest

achievement. Here, sliced open Chinese pagoda roofs and an angular goldfish pond are offset only by some wisteria trees and a historic whitewashed wall enclosing the compound. Inside, Pei deploys one of his favorite materials, glass (it was his idea to graft glass pyramids onto the Louvre in Paris) to flood light into the modern-meets-traditional building. This naturally illuminates the museum's vast collection of ancient porcelain, coins, jade sculptures, and paintings. A twisting waterfall running down the central atrium suffuses a becalming sound of running water through the galleries. The museum is located near many of the ancient Chinese gardens, and visiting those first before entering Pei's reverent, yet updated version is the best way to experience the Suzhou Museum.

singing with spoken dialogue. Two-hour performances take place daily at 1:30 p.m.

Suzhou Silk Museum: This well-displayed museum covers just about everything there is to know about Suzhou's most famous product, silk (see sidebar p. 273). Its exhibit halls include Ancient Hall (which looks at the history of the Silk Road in China), Silkworm Rearing Hall, Silk Weaving Hall, and Modern Hall.

Adjacent stores built in Ming- and Qing-dynasty styles represent silk-selling from the past to the present, purveying a wide range of silk products.

Suzhou's Pagodas

All of Suzhou's pagodas are historically fascinating, and several of them are among the finest in

INSIDER TIP:

To gain merit, local believers release fish and turtles into the ponds and waterways surrounding Suzhou's West Garden Temple.

—ANDREW FORBES
National Geographic author

China. **North Temple Pagoda,** in the northern part of the old city, was founded in the third century A.D. It was rebuilt in 1582 and again after a fire. The tallest historic pagoda south of the Yangtze River, it stands a dizzying 250 feet (76 m) high.

Tall, narrow, and elegant, the iconic **Twin Pagodas**—dating from the Northern Song dynasty—are

Suzhou Museum (Suzhou Bowuguan)
✉ 204 Dongbei Road, Pingjiang, Suzhou
💲 $
www.szmuseum.com

Suzhou Silk Museum (Suzhou Sichou Bowuguan)
✉ 2001 Renmin Road
💲 $
www.szsilk museum.com

North Temple Pagoda (Bei Si Ta)
✉ Xibei Jie
💲 $

West Garden Temple
✉ Tongjing Road & Fengqiao Road
💲 $

EXPERIENCE: Nature's Harmony in Suzhou Gardens

The classical gardens of Suzhou, established by affluent Confucian mandarins, offer oases of tranquility and a deep immersion in Chinese tradition. Some advance reading will enrich your experience: *The Craft of Gardens: The Classic Chinese Text on Garden Design* by Ji Cheng (translated by Alison Hardie) is the definitive text (with modern-day photography), while *The Gardens of Suzhou* by Ron Henderson offers fresh perspectives. The gardens are based on the principles of *shan-shui*, or mountains and waters, dovetailing with Taoist concepts of natural harmony. The Suzhou Gardens should not be rushed through: Take a full morning or afternoon for quiet reflection and meditation.

The beauty of the Blue Wave Pavilion is its harmonic intermingling of man-made buildings with the natural environment.

Whether you spend a day or longer at the gardens, your time will be rewarded. From Shanghai, **Luxury Concierge** *(tel 1350/166-2908, www .luxuryconciergechina.com)* runs private, one-day tours, to Suzhou that include the Suzhou Museum, a couple of the gardens, and lunch.

If you stay overnight in Suzhou, **Hotel Soul** *(27 Qiaosikong Alley, Pingjiang, Suzhou, tel 0512/6777-0777, www.hotelsoul.com.cn)* offers half-day excursions in summer for guests, with guided tours of three gardens and a picnic lunch.

Small and lovely, the **Master of the Nets Garden** *(Off Shiquan Jie, www.szwsy .com/en/home, 7:30 a.m.–5:30 p.m., $)* dates from the 12th century. Just over an acre

(0.4 ha) and the smallest of Suzhou's residential gardens, this garden presents an illusion of space, tranquility, and harmony. An evening visit offers a chance to experience traditional Suzhou folk songs, dance, and Kun opera. From March to November, ten-minute shows run from 7:30 p.m. to 10 p.m., with visitors encouraged to join in.

Nearby, the **Blue Wave Pavilion** *(Canglangting Jie, off Remin Lu, 7:30 a.m.–5:30 p.m., $)* dates from 1696. This was once the home of the classical scholar Su Zimei. It extends across 2.5 acres (1 ha) but seems larger due to an illusion of distant hills. Follow its paths that rise and fall in a suggestion of rocky hills.

The enchanting **Garden of Harmony** *(Off Remin Road,*

7:30 a.m.–5:30 p.m., $) was the property of Wu Kuan, a Ming dynasty chancellor, though its present form dates from the late 19th century.

At the start of the 16th century, the Ming-dynasty mandarin Wang Xianchen laid out the **Humble Administrator's Garden** *(Dongbei Jie, 7:30 a.m.–5:30 p.m., $$)*. This luxuriant garden extends over 11.5 acres (5 ha) of streams, ponds, and pagodas. Wander its bamboo-covered islands, connected by bridges and causeways. The bonsai garden and garden museum are included in the admission.

To the south, the rock-sculpted **Lion Grove** *(Yuanyin Lu, www.szszl.com/en, 7:30 a.m.–5:30 p.m., $)* is named for its lion-shaped rock.

The Couples Garden *(Off Cang Jie, 7:30 a.m.–5:30 p.m., $)* is located in the east of the old city. Surrounded by water on three sides, it was designed by a former governor of Anhui Province during the Qing dynasty.

To the west, the remote **Garden for Lingering In** *(Liuyuan Road, www.gardenly .com/EN/, 7:30 a.m.–5:30 p.m., $$)* offers pagodas, an impressive bonsai collection, and courtyard Suzhou Opera in spring and summer.

identical, seven-story octagonal brick structures set amid gardens and a tea terrace.

In the southwest part of the old city, in what is now Pan Men Scenic Area, the 1,000-year-old **Ruiguang Pagoda** (Ruiguang Ta, $) is said to be the oldest pagoda in Jiangsu. Standing 142 feet (43 m) high, the restored octagonal brick structure is embellished with finely carved eaves, banisters, and balconies.

To the west of town, on top of Tiger Hill (Huqiu Shan), **Yunyan Pagoda** is chiefly celebrated for its disconcerting incline. The blue-brick octagonal structure was erected in the tenth century on ground that was partly rock and partly softer soil. Over time, the 154-foot (47 m) tower began to tilt. Though it has been restored and repaired since, the tilt has not been fixed.

Other Sights

Anchoring the southwest center of the Main Canal, **Pan Men**—the Coiled Gate—is Suzhou's most ancient entranceway, dating back to the Warring States period.

The gateway is now part of the popular **Pan Men Scenic Area,** a beautifully maintained park set amid attractive canals. Other must-see landmarks here include the **Ruiguang Pagoda** and the delightful **Wumen Bridge.**

Northwest of the old city, **Tiger Hill** is a popular escape from the suburbs of Suzhou. The main attraction is the leaning **Yunyan Pagoda,** but the park holds a number of historic attractions, including the supposed **Tomb of King He Lu,** who died in 496 B.C. Look for the **Sword Testing Stone** and **Sword Pool,** both associated with the warrior king; the **Lu Yu Well,** celebrated for the quality of its water; and the 19th-century **Verdant Mountain Villa** (Yongcui Shanzhuang).

Founded in the third century A.D., the **Xuanmiao Temple** is Suzhou's most important and most popular Taoist place of worship. The temple is well worth visiting for its fine collections of sculptures, which date from the Tang and Song dynasties. ∎

Twin Pagodas (Shuang Ta)
- ✉ Dingshuishi Alley (off Fenghuang Road)
- 💲 $

Yunyan Pagoda (Yunyan Ta)
- ✉ Huqiu Road
- 💲 $$

Pan Men Scenic Area
- ✉ 49 Dongda Road
- ☎ 6526-0004
- 💲 $

Tiger Hill
- ✉ Huqiu Road
- ☎ 6532-3488
- 💲 $$

Xuanmiao Temple (Xuanmiao Guan)
- ✉ Guanqian Road
- 💲 $

Suzhou Silk

An antique Chinese name for Suzhou is Capital of Silk. It has long been the most famous center of silk production in China. Since at least as early as Tang dynasty times, the city has been renowned for its high-grade silk, woven locally from silkworms that are raised on Jiangsu mulberry leaves.

In times past, much of Suzhou's silk was destined for the imperial court. In the 13th century, Marco Polo commented on the great quantities of silk produced in Suzhou, as well as on the "gold brocade and other stuffs" made here.

Suzhou is also famous for its handmade silk embroidery, one of four traditional styles of embroidery in China.

Today, numerous factories continue to produce silk, and shops selling silk fabric and garments are everywhere. A particularly appealing place to go shopping for silk is **Shiquan Street** (Shiquan Jie) to the southeast of Suzhou's old city, near the Master of the Nets Garden.

Water Towns

West of Shanghai, an arc of small towns and villages known in Chinese as *shui xiang,* or water towns, extends from Wuzhen in the south to Changzhou on the Grand Canal in the north. Acclaimed for their arched bridges, ancient buildings, and serene waterways, these are living towns, where daily life goes on: Coppersmiths and silk spinners work at their age-old crafts, people carry water, tend gardens, and congregate at the squares to chat.

Ancient whitewashed buildings and flagstone streets edge Tongli's main canal, giving credence to the town's naming by the *China Daily* as one of the "Top Ten Charming Chinese Towns."

The water towns make an easy day trip from Shanghai (Suzhou makes a good alternative base). The easiest and cheapest way is to take a tour (inquire at your hotel). Alternatively, you can take a bus or taxi from Shanghai (or Hangzhou or Suzhou). Few people choose to visit more than two or three water towns total, sticking to one a day.

Keep in mind that the towns can be crowded during the day, and for this reason an overnight is preferable. In the evenings and early mornings, after the visitors have left, the waterways become calm, mirroring the ancient houses in a scene straight out of old China. With the place to yourself, rent a boat and explore the narrow back canals and surrounding countryside.

Zhouzhuang

Of all the water towns, beautiful Zhouzhuang *(map 260 C4, visitor information: tel 86512/5721-1699, www.zhouzhuang.com, $$$, single entry ticket for all attractions),* located near Lake Tai's eastern shore and dating from the Warring States period (fourth and third centuries B.C.), is the most developed and best known. It's also the busiest, so avoid visiting on weekends and holidays, when the ancient narrow streets are jam-packed. Surrounded by lakes on four sides and laced with canals and waterways, it's no wonder Zhouzhuang calls itself the Venice of China. Little remains from the ancient period; the majority of what you see today dates from the Ming and Qing eras.

Tongli

Tongli *(map 260 C4, visitor information: Tongli Tourist Information Center, tel 0512/6333-1140, $$$, single entry ticket for all attractions)* sits on a complex of canals and rivers on the western shore of Tongli Lake (Tongli Hu). The town is neither as famous as Zhouzhuang nor as crowded with visitors, although Chinese filmmakers have favored the city since the mid-1980s. Tongli is surrounded by five lakes and divided into seven districts by 15 rivers and canals. These are crossed by 49 ancient bridges, most of them arched and one a triple bridge.

Changzhou

Located in Jiangsu Province to the northwest of Lake Tai, Changzhou *(map 260 B5, visitor information: Changzhou Visitor Center, 518 Yanling Dong Lu, Changzhou, tel 0519/8668-9445)* differs from the water towns on the lake's eastern shores: It's a city, not a town, and the busy **Grand Canal** (Da Yunhe; see pp. 266–267) runs through its heart. The city is friendly and accessible and will satisfy anyone seeking waterborne exploration with many canals and four interconnected rivers— the Tanghe, Baidang, Guanhe, and Beitang.

Xitang

Until 2005, the lovely village of Xitang *(visitor information: Xitang Town Tourism, www.xitang.com.cn, Jijia Xiang Youdian Road, $$, single entry ticket for all attractions)* near the eastern shore of Lake Tai was, perhaps, the quietest of the water towns. That changed after it appeared in *Mission Impossible III* (depicting old Shanghai), and tourism soared. The town dates back to the Warring States period and prospered during the Ming and Qing dynasties. This quintessential water town lies on flat land latticed by nine small rivers that divide the town into eight sections connected by 104 bridges. Local authorities claim there are 122 lanes and roads in the township, most of which are covered walkways strung with red lanterns.

Luzhi

One of the lesser known water towns, and one of the smallest, picturesque Luzhi *(map 260 C4, $$, single entry ticket for all attractions)*, east of Suzhou, is at least 1,400 years old. Despite its size (about 1 square mile/2.6 sq km), the town has a distinguished literary tradition. It is also noted for its traditional women's costume: embroidered cloth shoes, black cotton trousers, a pale blue cotton blouse, and a black turban elaborately decorated with red pom-poms and flowers.

INSIDER TIP:

In Luzhi, treat yourself to a local delicacy of Puli trotters or Puli duck, prepared to the recipe of Tang-dynasty poet Lu Guimong, a.k.a. Mr. Puli.

—LARRY PORGES
National Geographic Travel Books editor

Wuzhen

Sandwiched between Shanghai and Huzhou, Wuzhen *(map 260 C3, visitor information: Tongxiang Wuzhen Tourism, www.wuzhen.com.cn, 18 Shifo Nanlu, Wuzhen, $$, single entry ticket for all attractions)* has ancient timber buildings, dating from Qing times (1644–1911).

Zhujiajiao

The Ming dynasty water town of Zhujiajiao is a panorama of narrow lanes, ancient arched bridges, and temples. A crop of guesthouses have recently opened, so spending the night away from Shanghai is a treat. Buses depart in the morning for Zhujiajiao from the Shanghai Sightseeing Bus Center in Shanghai Stadium *(map 260 D4, tel 021/5351-4830, www.zhujiajiao.com)*.

Nanjing

With a population of around 8 million, Nanjing is a major metropolis by any standards. It's a cultural and intellectual city packed with interesting and vibrant sites, from the longest city wall in the world to the Sun Yat-sen mausoleum, from the Yangtze Great Bridge to the 1,475-foot (450 m) Zifeng Tower, which now dominates the city. The tower's 77th-floor observatory offers visitors superb views of both the old and the new across the city of Nanjing .

A perfect picture at Dr. Sun Yat-sen's mausoleum

Nanjing

🔼 260 B5 & 277

Presidential Palace (Zongtong Fu)

🔼 277

✉ Shangjiang Road

💲 $$

Zifeng Tower Observatory

🔼 277

✉ 2 Zhongshan Road

www.zifengtower.com

Begin your tour in the heart of downtown at the massive **Presidential Palace**, loosely modeled on the Forbidden City in Beijing. After the 1911 revolution, which overthrew the Qing, Sun Yat-sen, first president of the new Chinese Republic, chose this location for the government buildings. Today the palace serves as a repository for many of the city's cultural artifacts.

The former Kuomintang (Nationalist) buildings now function as the **Nanjing Museum for Modern History,** with exhibits dedicated to the late Qing dynasty and Republic of China and historical materials relating to Sun Yat-sen and the Presidential Palace. The museum is located near **Zhongshan Gate** (Zhongshan Men), the greatest of the city's nine surviving gates.

Even more overwhelming is the **Ming City Wall.** Built between 1368 and 1389, the 20.6-mile-long (33 km) wall curves and loops through the old city, but the best place to see the Ming battlements is in **Xuanwu Lake Park** (Zuan Hu Gongyuan; $).

A short walk south of the park leads to the **Former Residence of Zhou Enlai** and the **Zhou Enlai Library** (Zhou Enlai Tushuguan, Plum Blossom New Village, Changjiang Lu; $).

Purple-Gold Mountain

Nanjing's most celebrated sight might be **Zijin Shan,** the Purple-Gold Mountain to the east of the city. A cable car runs from Taiping Men Road on the east side of Xuanwu Lake to the mountain's summit. Much of the park is best explored on foot, but it takes at least a day.

The **Mausoleum of Sun Yat-sen** (Zhongshan Ling; $$) faces south on the mountain's flank. It's a major pilgrimage site, and on most days, the 392 steps to the **Sun Yat-sen Memorial Hall** are filled with visitors. The hall houses a 16-foot-high (5 m) seated statue

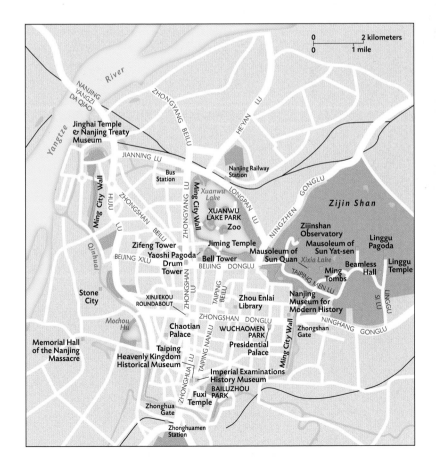

Yangtze Great Bridge

Crossing the Yangtze River just north of Nanjing is the Yangtze Great Bridge (Nanjing Yangzi Da Qiao), a visually impressive, if architecturally dated, tribute to Maoist autarchy and the "great days" of socialist construction. Completed in 1968 in the face of Sino-Soviet rivalry and Moscow's withdrawal of funding and experts, the bridge is only the second to cross the Yangtze. It was hailed by Mao as a symbol of China's ability to "go it alone."

Upon its completion, the 22,212-foot-long (6,772 m) span provided the first direct rail link between Beijing, Nanjing, and Shanghai. It's worth visiting for the sheer scale of the structure itself, for the fine—if dizzying—views it offers of the Yangtze River and its shipping far below, and for the massively muscled socialist-realist statues standing at either side of the bridge, featuring workers, soldiers, and peasants clutching weapons, tools, and Mao's little red book.

A second bridge, Nanjing Dasheng-guan Yangtze River Bridge, opened in late 2011 to facilitate the super high-speed rail link between Shanghai–Nanjing–Beijing.

Sacred Way (Shandao)

🗺 277

✉ Shixiang Road

Ming Tombs (Ming Xiaoliang)

🗺 277

💲 $$

Zijinshan Observatory (Zijin Shan Tianwentai)

🗺 277

💲 $

Memorial Hall of the Nanjing Massacre

🗺 277

✉ 418 Shuiximen Dajie

🕐 8 a.m.–5:30 p.m.

💲 $

www.nj1937.org

of Sun, while in the tomb a carved marble figure of the great man lies on top of the stone reliquary.

To the west of the mausoleum, the 1,970-yard (1,800 m) **Sacred Way**—lined with 12 pairs of Ming-dynasty stone animals—leads to the **Ming Tombs,** the last resting place of the Hongwu emperor Zhu Yuanzhang, founder of the Ming dynasty. His tomb was completed in 1405, seven years after his death, having taken 24 years to complete.

Beyond, a path leads through the forest to the **Mausoleum of Sun Quan,** Monarch of Wu during the Three Kingdoms period (220–265). In 2003, together with the other Ming Tombs just north of Beijing, the complex was registered by UNESCO as a World Heritage site. The mausoleum is marked by the **Ling Ta Altar Tower.**

West of the Ming Tombs, along Taiping Men Road and up a steep path to the north, stands **Zijinshan Observatory,** which houses a museum documenting the development of astronomy in China.

Memorial Hall of the Nanjing Massacre

Not for the faint-hearted, but definitely essential to understanding China's recent history and contemporary Chinese attitudes toward Imperial Japan, the **Memorial Hall of the Nanjing Massacre** (Nanjing Datusha Jinianguan) makes compelling, if disturbing, viewing.

Between mid-December 1937 and early February 1938, the Imperial Japanese Army systematically raped and killed between 150,000 and 300,000 Chinese soldiers and civilians, a crime that Japanese history books continue to downplay.

The Nanjing memorial hall is designed to document the atrocity and to categorically confirm that the massacre did indeed happen, a contention supported by masses of witness accounts and photographs. Most convincing of all is the public viewing hall erected over skeletons of massacre victims in a mass grave. ■

Huangshan

Adorning piles of coffee-table books on China is stunning, pine tree–clad Huangshan in south Anhui Province, China's most famous, probably most beautiful mountain.

The 160-mile-long (257 km) Huangshan range is a dramatic panorama of 72 peaks, capped by Lotus Flower Peak (Lianhuafeng). During the Qin dynasty, the mountain was called Qianshan, but it was renamed Huangshan in A.D. 747, in honor of the Yellow Emperor (Huangdi). The mount was later the hideaway of Chan Buddhist recluses, who foraged for inspiration among the pines, waterfalls, and hot springs.

On the summit, Xihai ("west sea") and Beihai ("north sea") are famed for their jaw-dropping misty panoramas. The main loci of interest on Beihai are **Lion Peak** (Shizifeng), **Monkey Which Looks Out Over the Sea** (Houzi Guanhai), and an old, twisted pine tree charmingly labeled **Flowers Springing From a Dreaming Writing Brush** (Mengbi Shenghua). Come sunrise, bleary-eyed wayfarers muster in padded coats on **Refreshing Terrace** (Qingli-angtai) along the slopes of Lion Peak. If you have the time, spend the night at one of the hotels on the summit, where the view can be astonishing. From **Cloud-Dispelling Pavilion** (Paiyunt-ing) on Xihai, the view reaches out over layers of small peaks emerging through the clouds and mist.

Clouds settle on the fairy-tale archipelago of Huangshan's lofty peaks.

Climbing Huangshan

The first hurdle is the very steep entrance charge. Ahead lie various routes, the easiest being the eastern one. Ride up on the cable car to pursue the eastern route from the **Yungu Temple,** which marks the start of the trail. This is an option if you just

Huangshan
Visitor Information

- 🔺 260 A2
- ✉ 6 Xizhen Jie, Tunxi
- ☎ 0559/252-6184
- 💲 $$$$$ (cable car $$$)

can't face the walk, but your patience can wear thin after hours of waiting in line. Sedan chairs await the truly decadent.

The eastern ascent is a 5-mile (8 km) stretch, and this should take you about three hours to finish. There's less to see than on the western route, but the climb is far easier and it's pleasantly shaded.

INSIDER TIP:

Scenes from the movie *Crouching Tiger, Hidden Dragon* (2000) were filmed in Huangshan's spectacular bamboo-covered valley.

—MARY STEPHANOS
National Geographic contributor

The Mists of Huangshan

According to Chinese legend, Emperor Shennong discovered tea when tea leaves mysteriously fell into a pot of water his servant was boiling for drinking. Whether the story is apocryphal or real, it is often said that Chinese *cha* was first sipped amid the mists of Huangshan—and the mountainsides remain one of China's most famous tea-growing regions. Known as the "dreamy mists," the thick vapor clouds that hang over the rugged mountain valleys have been immortalized in scores of Chinese landscape paintings, and are a key attraction for the millions of hikers and tourists who climb Mount Huangshan each year. The photogenic mists with mountain peaks peering through are particularly beautiful at sunrise and sunset.

Tower Hotel (Yupinglou Binguan), with its spectacular vista. The path then winds around Lotus Flower Peak before grinding on to Bright Summit Peak (Guangmingding) and the summit proper.

Many visitors ascend by the eastern route and descend by the western trail. Guides are available, but they are unnecessary as exploration is straightforward and English signs numerous.

The best weather occurs when the peaks are shrouded in mist (which is much of the time), and the Chinese insist on climbing to the very top for the breathtaking views over the "sea of clouds" (see sidebar at left).

The thermometer can dip, so take warm, waterproof clothes and extra layers. Summer sees Huangshan infested with climbers and is best avoided, if possible.

The nearest town is Tunxi (Huangshan Shi), served by an airport from where buses reach Huangshan. Alternatively, stay in the pleasant village of Tangkou at the foot of Huangshan and climb early the next day. ∎

The western ascent is a gut-wrenching 10 miles (16 km); around every corner waits a further flight of steps, mocking your stamina and testing your endurance. Along the western trail are the Merciful Light Pavilion (Ciguangge) and, farther up, the Halfway Mountain Temple (Banshansi), now a hotel and restaurant. The dwarfing granite pinnacle of Tiandu Peak rises south of Jade Screen

Travelwise

Planning Your Trip: Beijing   282–283

How to Get to Beijing   283–284

Getting Around Beijing   284

Planning Your Trip: Shanghai   285

How to Get to Shanghai   285–286

Getting Around Shanghai   286–287

Traveling Outside Shanghai   287

China: Practical Advice   287–291

Emergencies   292

Health   292

Further Reading   293

Hotels & Restaurants: 294

Hotels & Restaurants:
Beijing   295–305

Hotels & Restaurants:
Shanghai   305–316

Beijing Shopping   317

Beijing Entertainment   318–322

Shanghai Shopping   323

Shanghai Entertainment   324–327

China's white high-speed bullet trains, as that neatly links Beijing and Shanghai

Language Guide   328

Menu Reader   329

Beijing Subway Map   330–331

Shanghai Metro Map   332–333

TRAVELWISE

PLANNING YOUR TRIP: BEIJING

When to Go

Summers are brutally hot and the winters are harsh, but Beijing can be visited year-round. The weather is most pleasant during the spring and fall, and there are fewer people at the major tourist sites. As China's economy has expanded, both domestic and international tourism have soared, resulting in overcrowded sites. This is especially noticeable between mid-July and the end of August, when Chinese students are on vacation. Although it does not snow often in Beijing, when it does, the peaceful, deserted grounds of the Forbidden City, with its arched rooftops and temples, take on a magical look.

Millions of Chinese and hordes of tourists are on the move during the two long national holidays—Chinese New Year/Spring Festival (late Jan.–early Feb.) and National Day (Oct. 1)—making them the least desirable times to visit Beijing and the hardest to book transportation, tours, and hotels.

Climate

September and October days are sunny, and the temperature is mild. Winters are cold and dry. Most hotels are well heated; restaurants, however, can be chilly, so it is wise to bring a sweater when eating out. April through June is most enjoyable, but July and August can be extremely hot and humid and come with the greatest chance of rain.

The average high temperatures are as follows:

January 54°F/12°C
February 64°F/17.8°C
March 82°F/27.8°C
April 90°F/32.2°C
May 99°F/37.2°C
June 104°F/40°C
July 104°F/40°F
August 107°F/41.7°C
September 92°F/33.3°C
October 84°F/28.9°C
November 75°F/23.9°C
December 66°F/18.9°C

What to Bring

The sun is strong in the summer months, so be prepared with sunblock, sunglasses, and a hat. In the winter you will want to have gloves, a hat, and a scarf. It is a good idea to wear layers, and you will need a good winter coat. A comfortable and sturdy pair of walking shoes or sneakers will also be good to have if you plan to do a lot of walking in the city. Casual dress is suitable. However, how you dress can determine how you are treated. Clothes should always be clean and neat. Appropriate covering is needed for most temples.

Any prescription or specifically required over-the-counter medicines should be carried with you, as not all foreign medicines are easy to find. Multinational cosmetic and toiletry manufacturers have discovered the Chinese market, so Western-brand soaps, toothpastes, etc. abound.

Book lovers should bring a good selection of reading material, since most of the English books for sale in China are geared to Chinese who are studying English. Weekly news magazines such as *Time, Newsweek,* and the *Economist* are available, as are the daily *International Herald Tribune, Asian Wall Street Journal,* and *South China Post,* except editions that carry articles critical of the government.

A Chinese phrase book is worthwhile and often essential. The Chinese love swapping business or name cards, so if you have some, bring them along (see p. 289).

Entry Formalities

Visas

All foreign passport holders require a visa in advance of travel to China—there is no visa-on-arrival provision.

Nonetheless, acquiring the standard one-month tourist visa (type L) is not difficult. You should apply to the Chinese embassy or consulate closest to your home. Your passport must be valid for six months from your proposed date of entry and contain two blank visa pages when you hand in the visa application. Visas for longer periods, business visas, or multiple-entry visas are also available, with a commensurate increase in the fee.

The standard one-month tourist visa can be extended for an additional month at any Public Security Bureau office for a small fee. The Beijing PSB office *(gonganju)* is located at No. 2 East Street, Anding Gate, Dongchen District, Beijing, tel 010/8401-5300 or 010-8402-0101, *(www.bjgaj.gov.cn/eng).*

Some embassies and consulates accept applications by mail, while others require that you either submit the application in person or use a visa service—contact the embassy or consulate for specific details.

Selected Chinese embassies and consulates are listed below; for a complete list check the Chinese Ministry of Foreign Affairs website: *www.fmprc.gov.cn/eng.*

All foreign visitors are required to carry their passport at all times.

If you are planning to stay for a long period, register your passport with your nearest embassy or consulate (see p. 292). You will need a letter of invitation from a host company if you want to work in China. For more information on applying for a Chinese visa, visit the official China Visa Service website: *www.visaforchina.org.*

Australia
15 Coronation Dr.
Yarralumla, ACT 2600
Canberra
Tel 02/6273-4780
Fax 02/6273-5848
www.au.china-embassy.org

39 Dunblane St.
Camperdown
NSW 2050
Tel 02/8595-8000
Fax 02/8595-8021

Canada
515 Patrick St.
Ottawa, ON K1N 5H3
Tel 613/789-3434
Fax 613/789-1911
www.ca.china-embassy.org

New Zealand
2–6 Glenmore St.
Wellington
Tel 04/474-9631
Fax 04/499-0419
www.chinaembassy.org.nz

United Kingdom
31 Portland Pl.
London W1N 3AG
Tel 020/7631-1430
Fax 020/7299-4049
www.chinese-embassy.org.uk

Denison House
71 Denison Rd.
Rusholme
Manchester M14 5RX
Tel 161/236-1070

United States
2201 Wisconsin Ave.
Room 110
Washington, DC 20007
Tel 202/338-6688
Fax 202/588-9760
www.china-embassy.org

443 Shatto Pl.
Los Angeles, CA 90020
Tel 213/807-8088
Fax 213/807-8091

100 West Erie St.
Chicago, IL 60610
Tel 312/803-0095
Fax 312/803-0110

Customs

Foreign visitors are allowed to bring all personal effects, such as cameras, video recorders, laptop computers, GPS systems, etc., into China. The duty-free allowance permits three bottles of alcoholic beverages and two cartons of cigarettes. Foreign currency exceeding the equivalent of $5,000 is supposed to be declared, but this stipulation is not strictly followed.

Avoid carrying books on sensitive political subjects, such as Tibet. Pornography and religious materials in Chinese are also unwelcome.

During periods of concern about contagious diseases, such as SARS or avian flu, arriving passengers may have their temperatures taken using touch sensors.

On departure, note that Chinese law stipulates antiques dating from 1795 to 1949 be accompanied by a certificate stating their provenance, and that antiques dating prior to 1795 may not be legally exported.

HOW TO GET TO BEIJING

By Airplane

Beijing Capital International Airport (PEK) is the only airport that serves international flights in Beijing (*tel 010/6454-1100*). The airport is about 30 to 40 minutes, or 16 miles (26 km), northwest of the city. A taxi to the center of Beijing will cost about 100–120RMB ($15–$19), including the 10RMB ($1.50) toll fee. Two taxi lines are outside the arrival area. In all airports avoid taxi drivers who approach you in arrivals, as often you'll be overcharged. There are also buses running between the airport and downtown Beijing, with the ride taking

about 40 to 90 minutes, depending on traffic and destination—there are four different routes. Bus tickets cost 20RMB ($3). The Airport-Beijing City express train connects terminals 1, 2, and 3 with Dongzhimen Station in Central Beijing and costs 25RMB ($3.95) one way.

The following airlines provide frequent service to China:

Air Canada
Tel US: 888/247-2262
Tel Beijing: 010/6463-0576
www.aircanada.com

Air China
Tel US: 800/882-8122
Tel Beijing & Shanghai: 010/95583
www.airchina.com.cn

Air France
Tel US: 800/237-2747
Tel Beijing & Shanghai:
4008/880-8808
www.airfrance.com

British Airways
Tel US: 800/247-9297
Tel Beijing & Shanghai:
010/6459-0081
www.britishairways.com

Cathay Pacific / Dragonair
Tel US: 800/233-2742
Tel Beijing & Shanghai:
400/888-6628
www.cathaypacific.com

Delta
Tel US: 800/221-1212
Tel Beijing & Shanghai:
800/265-0488
www.delta.com

Japan Airlines
Tel US: 800/525-3663
Tel Beijing & Shanghai:
4008/88-5301
www.jal.com

KLM Royal Dutch Airlines
Tel US: 866/434-0320
Tel Beijing & Shanghai:
4008/880-8222
www.klm.com

Lufthansa Airlines
Tel US: 800/399-5838
Tel Beijing: 010/6459-8866
Tel Shanghai: 021/5352-4999
www.lufthansa.com

Qantas
Tel US: 800/227-4500
Tel Beijing & Shanghai:
021/5353-4600
www.qantas.com.au
Singapore Airlines
Tel US: 800/742-3333
Tel Beijing: 010/6505-2233
Tel Shanghai: 021/6288-7999
www.singaporeair.com
United Airlines
Tel US: 800/864-8331
Tel Beijing & Shanghai:
010/8468-6666
www.united.com
Virgin Atlantic
Tel Beijing & Shanghai:
21/5353-4600
www.virgin-atlantic.com

By Train

Since October 2011, Shanghai and Beijing have been connected by a high-speed rail service. The 820-mile journey (1,318 km) between the cities takes between five and eight hours depending on the number of stops on the particular service. Trains depart frequently throughout the day and evening in both directions, from Shanghai Hongqiao Railway Station and Beijing South Railway Station. See the online train timetable at www .travelchinaguide.com/china-trains.

The high-speed rail network is bringing cities closer by shortening journey times, and thus train travel has overtaken bus/coach travel as the default travel option, especially for short-distance intercity travel. From Shanghai, Suzhou is just a 35-minute train journey, Hangzhou is 50 minutes, and Nanjing about an hour. The journey from Beijing to Tianjin takes 27 minutes.

GETTING AROUND BEIJING

Beijing's public transportation system was improved a great deal by the city's comprehensive

infrastructure upgrade for the 2008 Olympics, with new highways and overpasses, new metro lines, and an expanded airport.

By Automobile

Only foreign residents with a valid Chinese driver's license, passport, and a Beijing Residence Permit may drive in China. International driver's licenses are not recognized in China, so driving may not be an option on your visit to Beijing. Moreover, driving is not recommended, since traffic is chaotic and road signs aren't always in English. However, Avis (tel 010/8406 3343) offers cars with drivers as part of the rental package. Prices start around 740RMB ($115) per day.

By Bicycle

The bicycle is still considered an important mode of transportation for a lot of people in Beijing, and there are dedicated bicycle lanes on most avenues. The pollution and danger of collision with cars makes it less fun than it once was. If you're an experienced cyclist, give it a try. A new basic bicycle costs around 400RMB ($65) from any department store. Be sure to get a lock and park in the guarded bicycle parking lots that the locals use.

By Bus

Buses are the cheapest way to get around town. Most city buses are priced at 1RMB (15 cents), while some buses are charged by mileage—1RMB for the first 7.5 miles (12 km), an extra 0.5RMB for every additional 3.1 miles (5 km). Air-conditioned buses are priced from 2RMB (30 cents).

You may buy prepaid IC cards for public transport, at a 60 percent discount. Beijing Public Transport also issues three special passes for short-time visitors. A 3-day pass for 18 rides costs 10RMB ($1.50); a 42-ride/7-day pass is 20RMB

($3.15); or a 15-day pass is 40RMB ($6.30). Cards are sold at hotels and designated places; some short-time passes are sold at bus terminals.

Buses are often crowded and stops are not identified in English, so buses can be a challenge. Worse yet, you can get caught in Beijing's dense traffic jams. Limited English information is found at www.bjbus .com/english/default.htm.

By Metro

The metro system is clean, efficient, safe, and probably the fastest way to move around the city. Beijing has nine metro lines: 1, 2, 4, 5, 8, 9, 10, 13, and 15, as well as the Batong line, three extension lines, and the Airport Express Link (see pp. 330–331).

Metro entrances are clearly marked with a blue capital "D" within a circle. Metro tickets are 3RMB (45 cents), while tickets for the light rail are 2RMB (30 cents). If you plan to transfer between the two systems, you can purchase a combination ticket for 5RMB (80 cents). Stations are marked in Chinese and Pinyin, and the next station is announced in both Chinese and English. There are also maps inside each car listing stops and connections. The metro runs from 5 a.m. to 10:30 p.m. and the light rail from 6 a.m. to 11 p.m. For detailed information check www.explorebj.com.

By Taxi

In recent years, Beijing has introduced whole new fleets of modern and comfortable taxis, mainly bigger and roomier Hyundais and Volkswagens. The basic fare starts at 10RMB ($1.50) for the first 1.8 miles (3 km), and then rises by 2RMB (30 cents) for every additional 0.6 mile (1 km). A surcharge is added between 11 p.m. and 5 a.m. Few taxi drivers are fluent in English, so have your hotel or destination written down in Chinese.

PLANNING YOUR TRIP: SHANGHAI

When to Go

Given the choice, your trip to Shanghai should be timed to achieve temperate weather and to avoid the crowds.

Winters can be cold and wet, and summers hot and humid. Crowded periods are Chinese New Year (known as Spring Festival in China) and National Day, commemorating the founding of the People's Republic in 1949. Chinese New Year is based on a lunar calendar, thus the date is not fixed, although it usually falls in February. Nearly all employees and students are given time off and travel stipends, resulting in a massive wave of domestic travel throughout the country. Hotel prices soar, and planes, trains, and buses are booked solid. Many small restaurants and tourist attractions, such as museums, will close for the week beginning with the official holiday.

An ideal time to visit Shanghai would thus be in the spring between Chinese New Year/ Spring Festival (late Jan.–early Feb.) and Labor Day or in the fall after National Day (Oct. 1). All this said, if you find yourself safely ensconced in your hotel during either of the two holiday rushes, observing the locals discover their own country can be a real pleasure. In a country where travel beyond one's hometown was, until fairly recently, either forbidden or an unaffordable luxury, the excitement is palpable.

Climate

Members of older generations regale grandchildren with stories of Shanghai blanketed in snow, but increased urbanization and vehicular traffic have caused the temperatures to climb, so it's more likely to be rain that falls in Shanghai during the winter months. Summers are hot and humid; though air-conditioning is the rule, early mornings and evenings are still most agreeable for a stroll.

Shanghai is located at 31 degrees north latitude. Temperature and humidity ranges are not unlike the coastal regions of the southeastern United States, though it's more likely to rain in Shanghai during the summer months.

Temperature ranges are:
January 34°–46°F (1°–8°C)
April 50°–66°F (10°–19°C)
July 73°–90°F (23°–32°C)
October 57°–73°F (14°–23°C)

Rainfall is highest during the summer months, but it is sporadic and often brings a cooling relief from the heat.

What to Bring

Shanghai is China's capital of chic, so you will certainly feel more comfortable dressing smartly, especially in upmarket venues.

Since the weather in Shanghai varies dramatically by season, prepare accordingly. Winter is not as bitterly cold as in other parts of China, but warm clothes are necessary. The heat and humidity of summer call for loose-fitting, breathable cottons. The Chinese rarely wear shorts, but they are acceptable attire for foreigners, except in temples. A jacket with a waterproof shell and removable fleece liner will cover all outdoor weather eventualities.

Most of the world's high-tech outdoor wear, such as down and fleece jackets, is made in China, but it's best to buy at home; these aren't cheaper in China, unless you find a stall selling bargain overruns.

A folding travel raincoat or an umbrella is almost always handy. A pair of comfortable, water-resistant walking shoes is vital. In all seasons except winter, a sun hat, sunglasses, and a sunblock cream are useful.

Any prescription or specifically required over-the-counter medicines should be carried with you, as not all foreign medicines are easy to find. Multinational cosmetic and toiletry manufacturers have discovered the Chinese market, so Western-brand soaps, toothpastes, etc. abound.

Book lovers should bring a good selection of reading material, since most of the English books for sale in China are geared to Chinese who are studying English. Weekly newsmagazines such as *Time, Newsweek,* and the *Economist* are available, as are the daily *International Herald Tribune, Asian Wall Street Journal,* and *South China Post,* except editions that carry articles critical of the government.

A Chinese phrase book is worthwhile and often essential. The Chinese love swapping business or name cards, so if you have some, bring them along (see p. 289).

Entry Formalities

(See pages 282-283)

The Shanghai PSB office *(gonganju)* is located at 1500 Minsheng Road, tel 010/6834-6205 or 010/2895-1900.

HOW TO GET TO SHANGHAI

By Airplane

Note that many airlines practice "code sharing," meaning that even if you buy a ticket from your carrier of choice, you may well fly on a different airline entirely. Virtually all international flights arrive at Pudong International Airport (PVG; *tel 6834-7575*) 30 miles (45 km) from the city center, while some flights from Hong Kong, Japan, and other Asian destinations, plus most domestic flights, use Hongqiao International Airport (SHA), around 10 miles (16 km) from downtown. See pp. 283–284 for a list of airlines that provide frequent service to China. The city can be reached from SHA by taxi for 30–40RMB ($4.70–$6.30) or on Metro Line 2. This connects to the new Hongqiao Railway Station, with high-speed connections to major cities, including Beijing.

Top hotels offer private cars for a fee, but no airport shuttle buses. The easiest way to transfer from PVG is by taxi. Official taxis are found outside the airport and charge between 200RMB and 240RMB ($31–$38) for the trip to downtown Shanghai. The trip takes about one hour, depending on traffic. For hotels in Pudong, the time is much less.

Official airport buses serve all parts of Shanghai and can get you into town for about 30RMB ($4.70) depending on your destination. There are many routes, so get prior information from the airport bus service counter in the arrivals hall.

A final alternative is the high-speed magnetic levitation (Maglev) train, which leaves from Pudong every 15-20 minutes and travels at speeds of nearly 270 mph (431 kph). A one-way ticket on the Maglev costs 50RMB ($7.90). The Maglev is very convenient for travelers staying in Pudong, but is impractical for most travelers from the airport since it only reaches Longyang Road metro station, where you will need to transfer. It's best to save this high-speed adventure for later, once you've gotten rid of your luggage and your jet lag.

GETTING AROUND SHANGHAI

Like Beijing, Shanghai's public transport system was massively expanded ahead of the city's hosting a major international event, in this case the 2010 World Expo. New metro lines, roads, and bus routes were created, and taxis are now plentiful.

Useful terms are *lu* (road), *dadao* (avenue), and *xiang* (lane). By convention these are often subdivided according to the cardinal directions. Thus, Shanghai's famous Nanjing Road is divided into Nanjing Xilu, or Nanjing Road West, and Nanjing Donglu, or Nanjing Road East. Other variants are Henan Beilu (Henan Road North), Henan Zhonglu (Henan Road Central), and Henan Nanlu (Henan Road South). There is no numbering convention in Shanghai: Odd- and even-numbered buildings intermingle.

By Automobile

Only foreigners who hold a residence permit are allowed to apply for a Chinese driver's license, which is required to own or rent a car. This is a blessing in disguise, since Shanghai traffic is chaotic. If you wish to travel by private car, it should be with a driver. This can be arranged through your hotel; otherwise, rental cars with drivers are available from Hertz *(tel 6211 6381)* or Avis *(tel 6241 0215)*. Both of these companies have offices at Pudong International Airport and in the city.

By Bicycle

The days when everyone commuted by bicycle are well and truly gone in Shanghai. While millions still pedal through town, and dedicated bicycle lanes exist in some areas, pollution and traffic make cycling a hazardous experience.

Rentals are hard to come by and either worn out or pricey—it's best to spend 400RMB ($65) for a new basic model from any department store. Be sure to get a lock and park in the guarded bicycle parking lots that the locals use.

By Bus

The Shanghai bus system is cheap but crowded. Be vigilant of pickpockets, especially if you're carrying a handbag or backpack.

The system is also hard to navigate for non-Chinese speakers, unless you know the desired line and stop. To see the sights, take a taxi or walk.

One bus line in Shanghai is worth the ride: the double-decker buses imported from Hong Kong (Route 911), which ply Huaihai Road through the French Concession. These have an open upper deck and music to accompany the scenery. Board at the old city gate, just north of the Yuyuan Gardens.

By Metro

Shanghai's ever growing underground and light-rail mass transit system is probably the most efficient way to get around the city, since it is not affected by the notorious traffic congestion aboveground. The trains, however, do get crowded during the morning and evening rush hours, and obviously offer little in the way of scenery. Known as *ditie* in Chinese, there are route maps in each station and car (see pp. 332–333). Announcements are made in English, and the stored-value fare cards (Shanghai Public Transportation Card, or *jiaotongka*) can be used in taxis.

Metro Line 1: Runs from Fujin Road in the north to Xinzhuang in the south, passing through the Shanghai train station and Shanghai South Railway Station.

Metro Line 2: Runs east and west from East Xujing to Pudong Airport, passing through Hongqiao International Airport, the main shopping street of Nanjing, East Road, and Lujiazui.

Metro Line 3: Mainly aboveground and reaches the main train station and Shanghai South Railway Station.

Metro Line 4: Essentially a ring around the city, useful for travel from Pudong to the train station.

Metro Line 5: Connects Line 1 at Xinzhuang with the Minhang Development Zone.

Metro Line 6: Looping line that extends from Pudong's northern manufacturing districts to meet Line 8 at Oriental Sports Center.

Metro Line 7: L-shaped line connecting northern Meilan Lake with Central Changshu Road, Longyang Road, and Maglev Station.

Metro Line 8: Runs from Shiguan Road in the northeast to the Aerospace Museum in the deep south.

Metro Line 9: Runs from Songjiang to Middle Yangao Road.

Metro Line 10: Runs from Xingjiangwancheng in the north to Hongqiao International Airport in the west.

Metro Line 11: Runs from Jiangsu Road to Anting and Jiading.

For more information visit *www.exploreshanghai.com.*

By Taxi

Taxis in Shanghai are plentiful and comfortable, using mainly locally built Volkswagen Santana and Passat models. During rush hour and in the rain, finding a taxi is harder. The fare is 12RMB ($1.90) for the first 1.8 miles (3 km) and 2.40RMB ($0.37) for each additional 0.6 mile (1 km). Fares increase after 11 p.m.

Several taxi companies compete for your service, the largest and most reliable of which is the Da Zhong taxi fleet, characterized by its turquoise-colored vehicles. While most taxi drivers are honest, the usual caveats apply: The meter lever should be upright and lighted in red when you board and lowered when you start off. If not, say *"Qing da biao,"* or point at the meter. When boarding, it's a good idea to have your destination written in Chinese characters on a slip of paper. Also carry the card of your hotel for the return trip. When disembarking, ask for a receipt *(fapiao),* which is automatically printed by the meter, since it notes the taxi's number and the company's phone number should you forget something in the cab.

Tipping is not expected, and you can pay with the Shanghai Public Transportation Card, or *jiaotongka,* used in the subway. If you're paying in cash, be sure to have something smaller than a 100RMB note.

By Boat

A great way to distance yourself from the clamor of Shanghai is to take a boat cruise on the Huangpu River. This service is offered by **Huangpu River Cruises** *(239 Zhongshan Dong Er Road, tel 6374-4461).* Tours depart from the south end of the Bund. Both daytime and nighttime cruises are available and are usually an hour long, although trips of four hours can take you to the mouth of the Yangtze River. Prices range from 50–150RMB ($8–$23.50). For a more local experience, join the crowds on the passenger ferry that leaves from the southern end of the Bund and arrives at the southern end of Dongchang Road in Pudong. This costs 2RMB (about 30 cents).

TRAVELING OUTSIDE SHANGHAI
Guided Bus Tours

The Shanghai Bus Sightseeing Tour Center *(Shanghai Stadium, 666 Tianyaoqiao Road, Gate 12, Staircase 5, tel 6426-5555)* offers many tour options, both within Shanghai and beyond to such neighboring areas as Hangzhou and Suzhou. Some are day tours, others include an overnight stay.

For a comprehensive day tour of Shanghai, including the former French Concession, the Bund, Jade Buddha Temple, Yuyuan Gardens, and Pudong, try **Jinjiang Tours** *(161 Changle Road, Luwan District, tel 6415-1188).* Jinjiang's tour costs 250RMB ($39) and includes lunch. They can also arrange tours by private car for small groups.

Greyline Tours *(2 Henshan Road, Xuhui District, tel 135/1216-9650)* offers tours of both the city and outlying areas.

CHINA: PRACTICAL ADVICE
Safety

China is overall a very safe country to travel in with low crime rates and friendly, honest inhabitants. As in most heavily populated cities of the world, precautions against pickpockets should be taken, particularly in popular tourism areas, on public transport, and in cafés and tourism attractions. There is no need to carry large amounts of cash, so store as much as necessary in your hotel safe. Foreign visitors are required to carry their passport at all times, and although spot checks by the police are rare they do occur, so you should at least carry a color photocopy at all times.

Bargaining

Bargaining is essential, except in department stores and high-end shops. Foreigners are often grossly overcharged (especially in heavily touristed areas), so feel free to haggle. Be friendly but firm, and have fun. Once you have settled on an item, walk around and see what other vendors are asking for the same thing—prices can differ sharply. Begin by cutting the starting offer in half. If you hit an impasse, pretend to walk away. If the seller is willing to meet your price, he or she will run after you.

Communications

Language

Levels of English are fast improving in both Beijing and Shanghai, but not everyone will understand your mother tongue. While international hotels and restaurants have English-speaking staff, taxi drivers, local restaurants, stores, and cafés might not. Youth hostels always have English speakers, but cheaper hotels do not. Patience is an essential virtue. Don't expect restaurant staff to understand you, and expect to do a lot of pointing.

Shanghai upgraded all local signage in 2010 with street signs, metro stations, and public notices written in both English and Chinese characters. In Beijing, Chinese characters and Pinyin are used on street signs and metro stations, so you may quickly get lost amid Chinese signs with few recognizable English words. A phrase book is essential. See the Chinese language sections (pp. 290 & 328–329).

Internet

Most hotel rooms will offer an Internet connection for your laptop. Starbucks, Coffee Bean & Tea Leaf, Wagas, Element Fresh, and an expanding range of cafés and bars across both cities provide free Wi-Fi. If you don't have a laptop, cheap Internet cafés are scattered around both cities. Be prepared though. Strong Internet censorship exists—sites such as Facebook are blocked, and Internet speeds can be painfully slow. For up-to-date information on hot spots or cafés look at *www.chinapulse.com*.

Post Offices

Airmail letters to the United States, Britain, and Australia should take between four days and a week to reach their destinations. Mark envelopes "airmail/par avion." Stamps are sold at the post office counter;

there are no machines. Envelopes are often gumless, but glue is available at the post office. (Some staff speak simple English.)

Telephone

China's country code is 86. The Beijing code is 010 and Shanghai's is 021—eliminate the first 0 when dialing from overseas. When making calls from China, first dial 00 followed by the international code and then your telephone number.

Phone cards can be purchased at the airport and in small shops and newspaper stands for use with public telephones. You will also see telephones in small shops and at newspaper stands that are for public use for a small fee. A three-minute city call usually costs 0.5RMB (7 cents). If you're going to be in China for more than a few days, you may want to buy a secondhand mobile phone for under $40. An unlocked U.S. tri-band (GSM 1900/1800/900) phone can be used in China when you buy a new SIM card. Local directory assistance can be reached at 114. You'll be transferred to an English-speaking operator once they realize you're a foreigner.

Using the home country direct number, 108, you can connect with a local operator in your home country, from whom you can place a collect or credit card call. The following numbers are used:

Australia 108-610
Canada 108-186
Hong Kong 108-852
New Zealand 108-640
United Kingdom 108-440
United States 108-11

China Netcom issues Internet Protocol (IP) phone cards that can be used to call abroad at highly attractive rates, especially since the cards are sold at a discount from their face value.

Important: 800 numbers can not be accessed by cell phone. Some companies have toll-free

numbers initiated with 400. You may either call a non-800 number with a cell phone or use a fixed line.

Internet Skype calls are not blocked in China, and using Skype is a popular way to make calls both to phones and to other computers in China and around the world.

Conversions

Although a traditional measurement system exists, China now follows the metric system.

1 kilometer = 0.62 mile
1 meter = 1.09 yards
1 centimeter = 0.39 inch
1 kilogram = 2.2 pounds
1 gram = 0.035 ounce
1 liter = 0.76 pint
0°C = 32°F

Drugs & Narcotics

No illegal drugs, including marijuana, may be carried into or consumed in China. While foreigners will not usually be subjected to the penalties meted out to Chinese for such infractions, discovery of even small quantities of illegal drugs will doubtlessly lead to an unpleasant encounter with the judicial system, followed by deportation.

If you take medicine that has abuse potential, such as painkillers, diet pills, or sleeping pills, keep them in the container bearing a prescription label, and if possible carry a letter from your doctor.

Electricity

China uses a 220-volt electrical system. Although most electrical items intended for overseas travel (such as digital camera and laptop computer battery chargers) are automatically switched between 110 and 220 volts, be sure to check the manual or look for markings on the device before plugging it in. Hair dryers and electric shavers intended for use in the U.S. are usually 110 volt only. Transformers are available, but are either heavy or can overheat, creating a fire hazard. Plugs come in a variety of shapes, so a conversion plug is useful.

Holidays

Banks, companies, and government offices close on official holidays.

New Year's Day—January 1

Chinese New Year, also called Spring Festival, follows the lunar calendar. Dates for the next few years are as follows:

February 9, 2013

February 1, 2014

February 18, 2015

This date marks the beginning of a weeklong period of travel when the Chinese visit their hometowns or just take a trip. Expect transportation and accommodations to be limited.

International Women's Day—March 8

Qing Ming (Tomb Sweeping Day)—April 4. A two-day holiday.

Labor Day—May 1. Another week-long travel binge

Youth Day—May 4

Dragon Boat Festival—June 12

Anniversary of the Founding of the Chinese Communist Party—July 1

Anniversary of the Founding of the People's Liberation Army—August 1

China National Day: Anniversary of the Founding of the People's Republic of China—October 1. Like Chinese New Year, expect crowds and travel congestion throughout the week-long holiday that follows.

Insurance & Health

There are several foreign-run medical clinics in Beijing and Shanghai, but charges can be high, so health insurance is essential. Make sure that the medical coverage in your travel insurance is adequate and accepted in China. If planning an extended stay in China, take out internationally recognized medical insurance. Medical evacuation

policies are also available.

Bring any medicines you need, as it may be difficult to obtain them in China. Most over-the-counter and some prescription drugs can be purchased in branches of Watson's, which can be found around Beijing, or in any of the foreign clinics, but prices may be high in the clinics.

Language

Chinese is a tonal language, spoken by about 1.2 billion people. The majority speak Mandarin (*putonghua* or "common tongue"), a dialect spread over much of north China and used nationwide as a lingua franca.

You can use Mandarin in all parts of China (including Hong Kong and Macau), but as a rough guide, you'll find the farther away you are from Beijing, the more widespread the use of other dialects. In Shanghai most people speak the local Shanghainese dialect, which is impenetrable even to most Chinese. Mandarin is not easy to learn, but it's worth trying to pick some up during your trip.

Local Customs

Beggars

Chinese economic reforms have removed many safety nets for the impoverished. Rural hopefuls travel to large cities in search of work; some end up penniless and hungry. Foreigners are natural targets for beggars. Very young children frequently beg late into the evening, but their takings will be collected by nefarious adults claiming to be their "parents."

Business cards

It's well worthwhile printing up business cards with your name and company written in both English and Chinese. The ritual exchange of cards is much like a handshake and is more wide-spread than in the West.

The Chinese deliver their cards formally with both hands; it is polite to accept with both hands and to immediately read the card carefully as a mark of your respect.

Face

The concept of saving face (*mianzi*) is often a stumbling block for foreigners. Although it exists in the West, it is more important in China. Causing someone to lose face—that is, making them appear foolish or naive—should be avoided. It is advisable to remain respectful, making any complaints with decorum, peppered with firmness. As a general rule, never lose your temper. If you cause someone to publicly lose face by remonstrating with them, you will not regain their trust.

Guanxi

Guanxi (connection) has a distinct meaning in communist China. The code of guanxi is mutual assistance in procuring what you want and giving what others need. You may have what some Chinese want (a useful contact abroad); the offer of a business card signals a desire for guanxi.

Karaoke

The Chinese take karaoke very seriously. If you are entertained by the Chinese at a banquet, the karaoke equipment will inevitably be wheeled out, and you will be urged to sing the one Western song on the menu. If you are staying in one of the less expensive hotels, ask for the room farthest from the karaoke lounge if you want any sleep. Karaoke bars are known as "KTV" outlets (Karaoke by Television).

Lines

The Chinese are slowly learning the patient art of standing in line, but be prepared for a jostling mass, all elbows and bellowing voices. If you are waiting for a bus or train ticket, do not be alarmed if people walk in front of you. Politely let them know (or gesture) that you are in fact waiting in line, and they will back up.

Smoking

Nicotine addiction is widespread in China. Authorities have imposed smoking bans in some public places, but few restaurants have no-smoking zones. If you are allergic to smoke, China may be a hard place to visit.

Spitting

Fines are sporadically levied on offenders, but spitting carries on wholesale, even in crowded buses, trains, and even in restaurants. Do not take offense; it is acceptable behavior. But, apart from being unpleasant, this is a main transmission route for tuberculosis. Public education campaigns were widespread in Beijing prior to the 2008 Olympics and in Shanghai prior to the 2010 World Expo, and spitting is now being heavily discouraged.

Staring

Getting stared at by Chinese migrants from the provinces still happens to foreigners in Beijing and Shanghai. There is nothing threatening about it—it is simply curiosity—but it can be unnerving. Best learn to ignore it; overreacting will only magnify the intensity of the stare.

Taboos

Most Chinese avoid frank political discussions with Westerners. They keep their concerns private, and they may be sensitive to the implications of discussing such issues with you. You should avoid all sensitive political topics.

Written Chinese

Alphabets use letters to make up the sounds of words. Written Mandarin is the only major language without an alphabet. Instead it uses "pictures" or "characters" to describe the written word. Other dialects of Chinese also use pictures.

Pronunciation

This guide has used Chinese names in Pinyin to name places of note. Below are some of the Pinyin pronunciations you should pay attention to:

Vowel sounds

a	as in father
ai	as in fight
ao	as in cow
ang	as in sung
e	as in duh
ei	as in weigh
eng	as in lung
i	"ee"; "er" sound after r, c, ch, s, sh, zh, and z
ian	as in yen
ie	as in yellow
ou	as in oak
o	as in more
u	as in noodle
ui	as in way
uo	as in wart

Consonant sounds

c	as in cats
ch	as in catch
q	in between "ts" and "ch"
r	as in run
s	as in shine
x	"s" as in sing
z	"ds" as in duds
zh	"dge" as in dredge

Media

Newspapers & Magazines

English papers include the *China Daily*, *Global Times*, and *Shanghai Daily*. You can buy international newspapers at leading hotels usually one day after publication.

A number of magazines full of information on local restaurants and events also circulate. In Beijing these include *Time Out Beijing* (*www.timeout.com/travel/beijing*), *The Beijinger* (*www.thebeijinger.com*), and *City Weekend* (*www.cityweekend .com.cn/beijing*). In Shanghai look out for *Time Out Shanghai* (*www .timeout.com/travel/shanghai*), *That's Shanghai*, and *Shanghai Talk*.

Television & Radio

Medium- and high-end hotels all offer a number of satellite stations such as CNN, BBC, HBO, Star TV, and other international channels. CCTV9 broadcasts in English, as does ICS in Shanghai. China Radio International broadcasts daily in English.

Money Matters

The Chinese currency is known as yuan renminbi (RMB), which literally means "the people's currency." The basic unit is the yuan, commonly known as kuai. The yuan is divided into 10 jiao, also called mao, and each jiao is further divided into 10 fen, but you'll only see these in banks. Paper notes come in denominations of 100, 50, 20, 10, 5, and 1 yuan. Smaller notes are 5, 2, and 1 jiao. Coins circulate in 1 yuan and 1, 2, and 5 mao denominations.

Renminbi is not yet internationally convertible, so you will have to wait until you arrive in China to exchange your money. The best places to convert your dollars into yuan are at the front desk of your hotel or at a branch of a major bank, such as the Bank of China or CITIC. All of these operate with standardized government rates—anything cheaper is illegal and thus risky. You need to present your passport in order to change money. Save the receipts from your currency transaction. You will need to show this to change renminbi back to your own currency when departing China. The rate may vary, but as of publication time, it stands at 6.34 RMB to the dollar.

Carry a decent amount of cash with you at all times, and wear a money belt to thwart pickpockets.

ATMs
ATM cards are gaining ground in China, and it's now easy to find machines around the city that accept international cards. Maximum daily withdrawals differ, but are usually 5,000RMB to 6,000RMB ($785–$945). However, normally you can only withdraw 2,000RMB to 2,500RMB ($315–$395) per transaction, so to withdraw 6,000RMB you'll need to do three consecutive transactions. Look for stickers on the ATMs that say MasterCard, Visa, Plus, or Cirrus. The best ATMs are at the Bank of China, the Industrial and Commercial Bank of China (ICBC), CITIC, and China Merchants. International banks such as Citibank, HSBC, and Standard Chartered are often more reliable—there are Citibank and HSBC ATMs in the Beijing Capital International Airport. Beware: Machines often have technical problems, or run out of cash.

Debit cards or bank-issued cash cards are less likely to work in Chinese ATMs.

Opening Times
Banks, businesses, and government offices are open weekdays from roughly 8:30 a.m. to 5:30 p.m., with some closed for an hour for lunch. Many banks have branches that are open on Saturdays and Sundays. Temples, museums, zoos, and other tourist sites are generally open daily, from 8 a.m. or 9 a.m. to 5 p.m. Parks generally open earlier and close later.

Passports & Visas
You are technically required to have your passport with you at all times, but to prevent losing it, make a copy of the page with your photo and passport number and keep that in your wallet.

If you lose your passport, report it to the Foreign Affairs Section of the Beijing Public Security Bureau and your embassy or nearest consulate immediately. The PSB office (*gonganju*) in Beijing is located at No. 2, Andingmen Dong Dajie, tel 010/8402-0101; the nearest subway station is Yonghegong. The Shanghai PSB office is located at 1500 Minsheng Road, tel 010/6834-6205 or 010/2895-1900. You must go to PSB yourself to fill in a declaration form.

If you're planning an extended stay in China, it's advisable to register with your nearest embassy or consulate. Thirty-day tourist visas (type L) are usually issued, but longer periods may be granted. You can extend your L visa twice at the Public Security Bureau.

Rest Rooms
Public toilets can be quite dirty and offensive. Take toilet paper with you as it's often not available in the stalls. Most hotels, apart from the very cheapest, will provide a Western-style toilet. Beyond that, however, expect to acquaint yourself with the Chinese squat toilet.

Time Differences
Beijing and Shanghai are eight hours ahead of Greenwich mean time (GMT). Noon in either city is 11 p.m. in New York, 8 p.m. in Los Angeles, 5 a.m. in Paris, 4 a.m. in London, 2 p.m. in Melbourne, and 4 p.m. in Wellington.

Tipping
Tipping is not common in China. If you try to tip, the recipient may refuse, but try three times before giving up to make sure the person is not just being polite. Otherwise politely drop the matter. Many hotel staff, tour guides, and drivers survive on gratuities and will expect a tip. A 12 to 15 percent service charge is added to the bill in hotel dining rooms. A 15 percent service charge is usually added to your room bill, but bellboys will expect a tip for carrying your bags.

Tourist Offices
China is only starting to see the benefits of tourism and the revenues it generates. There are no tourist centers—replete with free maps and brochures, advice, and help—but some centers offering limited assistance have opened in both cities, though mainly aimed at domestic Chinese travelers.

Foreign Tourism Offices
The China National Tourism Administration (CNTA) has offices in many countries abroad. The information they provide is useful, like a list of specialized tour operators, but like government-owned newspapers, the idealized portrait of the country they offer can mislead. CNTA has 15 overseas tourist offices around the world including three in North America: New York, Los Angeles, and Toronto. For a complete list of overseas offices and contact details, visit *www.cnto.org/aboutcnto.asp*.

Travelers With Disabilities
Disabled travelers will find China inadequately equipped. Public transportation remains largely inaccessible, although newer metro stations and high-speed trains and airports are increasingly better equipped for the disabled. Only the best hotels and restaurants are fully prepared to host handicapped travelers. There are no sidewalks in many places, and the only way to cross streets is via an underground tunnel or an elevated stairway.

EMERGENCIES
Crime
Most travelers feel safe in Beijing and Shanghai, although crime is rising. Most serious crimes that occur do not involve foreigners.

Pickpocketing is a problem, however. Spread your money between a number of pockets, and wear a money belt. Never change money on the street—it is likely that you'll be cheated or end up with counterfeit notes. When traveling on buses and metros or walking on busy streets, keep a close eye on your bag.

Always ask for your receipt when you exit a taxi so that you can locate the driver if you leave anything behind.

Emergency Phone Numbers
Ambulance 120 or 999
Fire 119
Police 110
Traffic accident 122

Embassies & Consulates
Australia
Embassy 21 Dongzhimenwai Dajie, Chaoyang, Beijing
tel 010/5140-4111
www.china.embassy.gov.au

Consulate CITIC Square, 1168 Nanjing West Road (Nanjing Xilu), 22nd Floor, Shanghai, tel 021/2215-5200, www .shanghai.china.embassy.gov.au

Canada
Embassy 19 Dongzhimenwai Dajie, Chaoyang, Beijing
tel 010/5139-4000
fax 010/6532-4072
www.canada.international.gc.ca

France
Embassy 60 Tianze Road, Chaoyang, Beijing
tel 010/8531-2000
www.consulfrance-pekin.org

Consulate Haitong Securities Building, 2nd floor, Suite 201, 689 Guangdong Road, Shanghai
tel 021/6103-2200,
www.consulfrance-shanghai.org

Germany
Embassy 17 Dongzhimenwai Dajie, Chaoyang, Beijing
tel 010/8532-9000
www.peking.diplo.de

Consulate 181 Yongfu Road, Shanghai, tel 021/3401-0106

Japan
Embassy 7 Ritan Road, Beijing
tel 010/6532-2361
www.cn.emb-japan.go.jp

Consulate 8 Wanshan Road, Hongqiao, Shanghai
tel 021/6278-0788

U.K.
Embassy 11 Guanghua Road, Jianguomenwai Dajie
tel 010/5192-4000
fax 010/5192-4239
http://ukinchina.fco.gov.uk/en

Consulate, Shanghai Suite 301, Shanghai Center, 1376 Nanjing West Road, Jingan District
tel 021/3279-2000
fax 6279-7651
http://ukinchina.fco.gov.uk/en

U.S.
Embassy 55 An Jia Lou Lu 1
tel 010/8531-3000, http://beijing .usembassy-china.org.cn/

Consulate, Shanghai 8th Floor, Westgate Mall, 1038 Nanjing West Road, tel 3217-4650, http://shanghai.usembassy-china .org.cn/

Lost Credit Cards
American Express
852/2277-71010

Mastercard
852/8009-66677

Visa
852/8009-00782

HEALTH
The most common ailments to afflict travelers are either digestive (diarrhea or stomach cramps), caused by unfamiliar or unclean foods, or respiratory, either from infections such as the common cold or air pollution. Either will make traveling difficult and are best prevented.

Drink only bottled water and avoid street food. Don't overexert yourself and do be careful of rapid temperature changes. More serious conditions should be guarded against by immunization injections prior to travel. See your doctor three months in advance of your trip, since some injections must be given separately.

Medical Emergencies: Beijing
Beijing United Family Health Center
2 Jiangtai Lu,
Chaoyang District
Tel 010/5927-7000 or 010/5927-7120 for emergencies
www.ufh.com.cn

International SOS
Suite 105, Wing 1,
Kunsha Building 16 Xinyuanli,
Chaoyang District
Tel 010/6462 9112
www.internationalsos.com

Medical Emergencies: Shanghai
Parkway Health
203-4 West Retail Plaza,
The Shanghai Center,
1376 Nanjing West Road
Tel 021/6445-5999 (24 hours)
www.parkwayhealth.cn

Shanghai East International Medicine
150 Jimo Road, Pudong
Tel 021/5879-9999 (24 hours)
www.seimc.com.cn

FURTHER READING

Before traveling, it's worth reading a few titles to gain perspective on your destination. Suggestions for Beijing include:

The Classic of the Way and Its Power (Daode Jing) by Laozi. A Taoist classic.

The Hermit of Peking (2008) by Hugh Trevor Roper. Classic investigative scholarship into the colorful life of Edmund Backhouse, the eponymous hermit and Sinologist.

Midnight in Peking (2012) by Paul French. The murder of a British schoolgirl that haunted the last days of the old China.

Rickshaw: The Novel (1936) by Lao She. A socialist novel depicting the dehumanization of a worker in 1930s Peking.

When a Billion Chinese Jump (2010) by Jonathan Watts. A sober study of China's environmental travails by the *Guardian* journalist.

Shanghai is well represented in 20th-century literature, both in Chinese and in Western languages. The writers Lu Xun, Mao Dun, and Ba Jin are celebrated in the city's Duolun area, while Western writers, such as Noël Coward (*Private Lives*, 1930), André Malraux (*Man's Fate*, 1934), and J. G. Ballard (*Empire of the Sun*, 1984), wrote in or about the city.

Recommended reading about this colorful city includes:

A Short History of Shanghai (1928) by F. Hawks Potts. A well-informed history (reprinted) of the city up to 1928.

Becoming Madame Mao (2000) by Anchee Min. A sympathetic novel based on the life of Mao Zedong's fourth wife, Jiang Ching.

Bound Feet and Western Dress (1966) by Pang-Mei Chang. Biography of the author's aunt, who rejected traditional society to become a banker.

The Bund Shanghai: China Faces West (2007) by Peter Hibbard. A detailed examination of Shanghai's most celebrated thoroughfare then and now.

Candy (2003) by Mian Mian. A gritty look at drug addiction, prostitution, gambling, and vice in 1990s Shanghai, written by a former heroin addict.

Carl Crow—A Tough Old China Hand (2006) by Paul French. Portrait of the life and times of an American journalist in early 20th-century Shanghai.

Daughter of Shanghai (1994) by Tsai Chin. Raised in a liberal, Westernized home, the author left for London in 1949 but here rediscovers her roots.

Empire of the Sun (1984) by J. G. Ballard. A semi-autobiographical tale of the author's childhood internment in a Japanese prison camp in wartime Shanghai. Famously made into a movie, directed by Steven Spielberg.

The Fall of Shanghai: The Communist Takeover of 1949 (1974) by Noel Barber. A journalist's account of the historic events.

Frenchtown Shanghai (2000) by Tess Johnston and Deke Erh. The best historical and architectural account of the former French Concession.

Life and Death in Shanghai (1995) by Nien Cheng. A chilling insight into conditions during the Cultural Revolution, when the author was accused of espionage and jailed.

Man's Fate (1934) by André Malraux. Novel about Shanghai's White Terror in 1927 when Chiang Kai-shek and the Green Gang attacked the communists.

Midnight (1933) by Mao Dun. Novel exploring the commercial world of Shanghai from a working-class, socialist viewpoint.

New Shanghai: The Rocky Rebirth of China's Legendary City (2001) by Pamela Yatsko. A perceptive analysis by an American journalist.

Old Shanghai: Gangsters in Paradise (1984) by Lynn Pan. A very compelling account of Shanghai's underworld in the late 19th and early 20th centuries.

Opening Up: Youth, Sex Culture and Market Reform in Shanghai (2002) by James Farrer. A fascinating account of the changing mores of modern Shanghai.

The Rape of Nanking (1997) by Iris Chang. A harrowing historical account of Japan's worst wartime atrocity in China.

Red Azalea (2006) by Anchee Min. A powerful and well-written account of growing up in Shanghai during the Cultural Revolution.

The Shanghai Green Gang: Politics and Organized Crime 1919–1937 (1996) by Brian G. Martin. A compulsive, well-written page-turner.

Shanghai Journal (1969) by Neale Hunter. An eyewitness account of the Cultural Revolution in the power base of the Gang of Four.

The Soong Dynasty (1985) by Sterling Seagrave. Very readable account of relationships and politics among Shanghai's most influential 20th-century family.

Strange Haven: A Jewish Childhood in Wartime Shanghai (1999) by Sigmund Tobias. The story of a German-Jewish refugee family in wartime Hongkou.

Hotels & Restaurants

The combination of China's economic boom, the 2008 Beijing Olympics, and the 2010 World Expo fueled a rapid expansion in the number of hotels and restaurants in Beijing and Shanghai, providing visitors with unprecedented choices. Making the right one can turn a good visit into a great one.

HOTELS

As Beijing readied for the 2008 Olympics, many older hotels carried out extensive renovations while the number of new hotels surged—from top five-star hotels and quaint courtyard inns set up in ancient *hutongs* to comfortable and inexpensive budget hotels. This array of choices is a far cry from the 1970s, when the Beijing Hotel was the only option for foreign guests.

The Ritz-Carlton and the InterContinental are among the new high-end arrivals in Beijing's fast-rising Financial District, while the newly emerging Central Business District is home to the Regent and the posh Park Hyatt.

New boutique hotels include The Opposite House, a highly stylized hotel with a real "wow" factor, and The Orchid, a nicely renovated courtyard hotel. And then there are the small and simple hotels located within Buddhist temple grounds and along the Great Wall.

Shanghai's penchant for design-laden deluxe accommodations ranges from contemporary hotels in skytowers, such as Park Hyatt and the Ritz-Carlton Shanghai, Pudong, to stylish revamped heritage properties like Waldorf-Astoria Shanghai on the Bund and boutique-chic retreats like Jia Shanghai. Those traveling for pleasure may find the old French Concession a better bet. There, you'll find an alternative and affordable variety of accommodation is the restored 1930s building.

Those traveling on a tight budget now enjoy more and better options, such as Super 8, Home Inns, and Comfort Inns, which offer rooms for under $50 (including free Internet) at convenient locations in both cities. There's also a growing number of backpacker inns.

The busiest times of the year—and therefore the most expensive—are spring and fall, when the weather is at its best. If time is not an issue, consider visiting Beijing and Shanghai off-season, when prices drop and tourist sites are less crowded. Ctrip (*www.english.ctrip.com*) is a great place to compare prices. But no matter what, always ask for a discount.

RESTAURANTS

Beijing and Shanghai both offer visitors a plethora of exciting eateries. Over the past decade, a culinary renaissance in Beijing has revived the city's centuries-old reputation for food. Young entrepreneurs brought cuisines from all over China and opened new restaurants around the city, ranging from sleek, modern dining rooms in shiny new high-rises on Beijing's grand boulevards to small storefronts hidden in Beijing's old hutongs. Now you can dine on earthy Hakka cooking from southern China, specialties from Yunnan Province, lamb and yak dishes from Tibet, spicy foods from Sichuan, thick noodles from Shaanxi, and even imperial cuisine from the past. Discovering places to eat that are off the beaten track is part of the fun of any visit to Beijing.

Today's situation is even more remarkable when one considers that 20 years ago Beijing was a culinary desert. In the 1950s, Mao Zedong decided to cut off China's capitalist tails, a move that led private restaurants to close, including brand-name favorites (known as *laozihao* in Chinese), and to the disappearance of a generation of good chefs.

Shanghai also has world-class cuisine, but also offers many mid-range restaurants—notably the restored villas of the French Concession. Some of the best mid-range options are chains (including Zen and Shanghai Uncle). Likewise good, mid-priced food can be enjoyed in the eateries of the international chain hotels. One alternative for decent cheap eats is the ubiquitous food court found in most malls.

Some vegetarian options are noted in the menu reader (see p. 329). Although Buddhist temples and restaurants are the best places for meat-free food, most eateries will have a sufficient amount of vegetables on their menus. But be careful. Many dishes are prepared with meat-based cooking oils, and some waiters and waitresses will consider a dish vegetarian even if it has a small piece of diced meat in it. When ordering, be clear that you want NO meat. Sometimes you get what you ask for, but frequently you may find bits of dried shrimp or meat in your tofu or vegetables.

Listings

The hotels and restaurants listed here have been grouped first according to their district or area (as organized in the main guide), then listed alphabetically in descending order of price. For disabled access, it is recommended that you check with the establishments to verify the facilities.

Credit Cards

Most hotels and restaurants accept all cards. Abbreviations used are AE (American Express), DC (Diners Club), MC (Master-card), V (Visa).

PRICES

HOTELS

An indication of the cost of a double room in the high season is given by **$** signs.

$$$$$	Over $400 (Over 2,540 RMB)
$$$$	$300–$400 (1,900–2,540RMB)
$$$	$200–$300 (1,270–1,900RMB)
$$	$100–$200 (635–1,270RMB)
$	Under $100 (Under 635RMB)

RESTAURANTS

An indication of the cost of a three-course meal without drinks is given by **$** signs.

$$$$$	Over $100 (Over 635RMB)
$$$$$	$70–$100 (445–635RMB)
$$$	$40–$70 (255–445RMB)
$$	$20–$40 (125–255RMB)
$	Under $20 (Under 125RMB)

BEIJING

■ DONGCHENG

HOTELS

▦ PENINSULA BEIJING
❚❙ (WANGFU FANDIAN)
$$$$$
8 JINYU HUTONG
WANGFUJING DAJIE
TEL 010/8516-888
FAX 010/6510-6311
E-MAIL pbj@peninsula.com
www.beijing.peninsula.com
Formerly the Palace Hotel, this hotel, one of the finest in Beijing, is just a short stroll from Tiananmen Square and the Forbidden City. Guest rooms and suites boast teak and rosewood flooring and 42-inch (106 cm) flat-screen televisions. The Peninsula Academy offers tours as well as expert guidance on antiques, Chinese medicine, and tea. The **Huang Ting** restaurant (see p. 296) serves acclaimed Cantonese cusine. Also features a deluxe spa.
🛈 525 rooms, including 59 suites 🚇 Dengshikou
🅂 🅂 🕿 🎛
🅂 All major cards

▦ GRAND HYATT BEIJING
❚❙ (DONGFANG JUNYUE DAJIUDIAN)
$$$$
1 DONGCHANG'AN JIE
TEL 010/8518-1234
FAX 010/8518-0000
E-MAIL reservation.beigh@hyattintl.com
www.beijing.grand.hyatt.com
The stylish Grand Hyatt is one of the best places to stay in town. The rooms are state of the art, many with floor-to-ceiling windows overlooking one of the city's historic districts. Just a ten-minute walk from the Forbidden City and Tiananmen Square, the hotel stands above one of Beijing's shopping landmarks, Oriental Plaza. The **Made in China** restaurant (see p. 296–297) is known for innovative cuisine.
🛈 825 rooms, including 155 suites 🚇 Wangfujing 🅂 🅂
🅂 🕿 🎛 🅂 All major cards

▦ RED CAPITAL RESIDENCE (XINHONGZI KEZHAN)
$$$
9 DONGSI LIUTIAO
TEL 010/8403-5308
FAX 010/8403-5303
www.redcapitalclub.com
One of Beijing's few authentic courtyard hotels, the Red Capital Residence offers just five rooms, each furnished with period pieces. You can choose from the Chairman's Suite, one of the Concubines' Private Courtyards, or an Author's Suite (one inspired by Edgar Snow, an American writer, the other by Han Suyin, a Eurasian novelist).
🛈 5 🚇 Zhangzizhonglu
🅂 🅂 All major cards

▦ REGENT HOTEL
❚❙ (BEIJING LIJING JIUDIAN)
$$$
99 JINBAO JIE
TEL 010/8522-1888
FAX 010/8522-1818
E-MAIL beijing@regenthotels.com
www.regenthotels.com
The Regent has a great location: one block from the Wangfujing shopping street and a short walk to the Forbidden City. Rooms have natural light and king-size beds, plus large desks for a pleasant working environment. The hotel has several restaurants, including **Daccapo,** an Italian dining room, and **Li Jing Xuan,** a good Cantonese and dim sum restaurant.
🛈 500 🚇 Dengshikou 🅂 🅂
🕿 🎛 🅂 All major cards

▦ HOTEL KAPOK
$$
16 DONGHUAMEN JIE
TEL 010/6525-9988
FAX 010/6525-0988
E-MAIL reservation@hotelkapok.com
www.rapokhotelbeijing.com
One of a handful of boutique hotels, Hotel Kapok is the creation of Beijing architect, Pei Zhu. The New York Times praised the hotel's "spartanly stylish rooms in a five-story minimalist box wrapped in a diaphanous fiberglass grid." The design includes a bamboo-and-pebble garden in

front of every room. The hotel is within walking distance of the Forbidden City and Wangfujing shopping street.
🛏 89 🚇 Wangfujing 🅂
💳 🅂 All major cards

🏨 HILTON WANGFUJING
$$
8 WANGFUJING DONGDAJIE
TEL 010/5812-8888
www.hilton.com
This contemporary themed hotel enjoys a central location adjacent to Wangfujing shopping street and a 20-minute walk from the Forbidden City. The spacious rooms are well equipped with modern amenities and service is excellent. Diverse eating and drinking offerings include a Mediterranean-themed buffet restaurant, pan-Chinese fine dining, and Flames bar, which serves both traditional and mixology cocktails. There's also a stylish spa, and a fitness center.
🛏 255 🚇 Wangfujing 🅂
💳 🅂 All major cards

🏨 THE ORCHID
$$
65 BAOCHAO HUTONG
TEL 010/8404-4818
FAX 010/8418-1987
E-MAIL info@theorchid beijing.com
www.theorchidbeijing.com
This intimate and stylish boutique residence owned by a Canadian-Tibetan couple occupies a converted *hutong* home. There are ten wood-beamed rooms with rain forest shower and underfloor heating set around two inner courtyards. Free Wi-Fi is offered, and bicycles can be rented to explore the neighboring hutongs. The rooftop bar affords lovely nighttime views over the low-rise rooftops toward the Drum Tower.
🛏 10 🚇 Dengshikou 🅂

SOMETHING SPECIAL

🏨 RAFFLES BEIJING
🍴 $$
33 DONGCHANG'AN DAJIE
TEL 010/ 6526-3388
FAX 010/8500-4380
E-MAIL Beijing@raffles.com
www.raffles.com/beijing
Occupying a wing of the Beijing Hotel, this classically styled hotel is a Beijing institution. It enjoys an excellent location, just a short walk from Tiananmen Square and Wangfujing shopping street. The lobby's European chandeliers and antique furnishings set a sophisticated tone, and the magnificent rooms and suites—with four poster beds, satin drapes, comfy sofas, and marble bathrooms—could easily be Parisian. **Jaan** is an acclaimed European fine-dining restaurant, and afternoon tea in the historic **Writer's Bar** is a real treat.
🛏 171 🚇 Wangfujing
🚈 🅂 All major cards

🏨 LUSONGYUAN (LUSONGYUAN BINGUAN)
$
22 BANCHANG HUTONG KUANJIE
TEL 010/6404-0436
FAX 010/6403-0418
www.lusongyuanhotel.com
Lusongyuan, set in a traditional courtyard, is said to have been built by a Mongolian general during the Qing dynasty. It still retains much of its old charm and the rooms are exquisitely styled with period Chinese furnishings and design motifs.
🛏 57 🚇 Zhangzizhonglu
🅂 🅂 All major cards

RESTAURANTS

SOMETHING SPECIAL

🍴 MAISON BOULUD
$$$$$
CHI'ENMEN 23, QIANMEN DONGDAJIE
TEL 010/6559 9200
www.danielnyc.com/ maisonboulud
New York–based French celebrity chef Daniel Boulud's first China restaurant location: The handsome former U.S. Embassy building in Qianmen makes for an elegant setting, and the extravagant interior design more than matches the classical facade. Maison Boulud's refined modern French cooking, including seasonal tasting menus, is as good as it gets in Beijing, and combined with the artistic decor make this a top-class—if rather pricey—dining experience.
🚇 Qianmen 🅂
🅂 All major cards

🍴 HUANG TING
$$$$
PENINSULA BEIJING
8 JINYU HUTONG
WANGFUJING DAJIE
TEL 010/6510-6707
Huang Ting is a Cantonese restaurant operated by the Peninsula Beijing. The stunning decor is made up of bricks from dismantled courtyard houses and antiquated screens and panels from an old Suzhou mansion. Huang Ting's excellent dim sum should be enjoyed with a pot of oolong, pu'er, or jasmine tea.
🍽 100 🚇 Dengshikou
🅂 All major cards

🍴 MADE IN CHINA
$$$$
GRAND HYATT BEIJING
1 DONGCHANG'AN JIE
TEL 010/8518-1234 EXT 6024
Made in China's open-style

---

kitchen provides diners with front-row seats to watch all the action. Flames shoot up from beneath giant woks as chefs stir-fry Sichuan-style green beans, while others perform the deft task of stuffing and folding dumplings. You can also get a peek at your own Peking duck as it roasts in a brick oven just steps away.
🍴 100 🚇 Wangfujing
💳 All major cards

🍴 TIANDI YIJIA
$$$$
140 NACHIZI DAJIE
(CLOSE TO CHANGPU
RIVER PARK)
TEL 010/8511-5556
This place is nestled in the shadows of the Forbidden City. Mythological *qilins* stare from the traditional stone screen wall as you enter. The yellow parasols overhead and the calligraphy carefully positioned around the restaurant lend the place a harmonious feeling. The menu is pan-Chinese cuisine and runs the gamut from home-style dishes to shark's fin, abalone, bird's nest, and sea cucumber. Whet your appetite with the goose liver marinated in sake and served on a bed of crispy French beans (*qingjiu e'gan*).
🍴 200 🚇 Tiananmen East, Exit B, 3-min. walk
💳 All major cards

🍴 LEI GARDEN (LI YUAN)
$$$
3/F JINBAO TOWER
89 JINBAO JIE
TEL 010/8522-1212
www.leigarden.com.hk
Lei Garden is the Beijing branch of the upscale Hong Kong–based Cantonese chain. This restaurant is famous for its baked soft-shell crabs, Lei Garden also offers beef fillet sauteed with *sacha* sauce, spareribs in black-bean sauce, and stir-fried rice noodles—all

traditionally prepared.
🍴 400 🚇 Mishi Dajie
💳 All major cards

🍴 MOREL'S
$$$
(MOLAO XICANTING)
1ST FLOOR, BLDG. 5
XINZHONG JIE (OPPOSITE
WORKERS' GYMNASIUM)
TEL 010/6416-8802
Lively and packed with "local" residents of all nationalities, Morel's is remarkable not only for its pot mussels and superb locally bred steak but also for its ambience. It offers an extensive list of Belgian beers, and the Belgian waffle topped with strawberries makes a perfect end to any meal. Reservations recommended.
🍴 80 🚇 Dongsishitiao
🕐 Closed Mon.
💳 All major cards

🍴 MY HUMBLE HOUSE
$$$
1/F ORIENTAL PLAZA,
I DONGCHANG'AN DAJIE
TEL 010/8518-8811
www.myhumblehouse.com.sg
Part of a small chain with eateries in Singapore, Japan, and India, this is one of the few Chinese restaurants that have succeeded in the "Chinese fusion" experiment. Andrew Tjioe, the Indonesian-Chinese owner prefers to call it "contemporary Chinese." The food is incredibly tongue pleasing, using carefully picked spices and ingredients that marry well.
🍴 80 🚇 Wangfujing
💳 MC, V

🍴 RED CAPITAL CLUB
(XINHONGZI JULEBU)
$$$
66 DONGSI JIUTIAO
TEL 010/8401-6152
FAX 010/6402-7153
www.redcapitalclub.com.cn
Dining outdoors in the court-

yard of the Red Capital Club, a beautifully restored, 200-year-old courtyard house, you feel like you are miles away from the city and decades earlier. The restaurant features what owner Laurence Brahm calls "Zhongnanhai" cuisine, based on the favorite dishes of past Communist officials. South of the Clouds, a filleted fish covered with scallions and spices and baked between pieces of bamboo netting, was the favorite of one official who sampled it during the epic Long March. Guests are welcome to squeeze down the narrow steps in the courtyard for a look at the wine cellar.
🍴 65 🚇 Zhangzizhonglu
🕐 Dinner only
💳 All major cards

🍴 TEMPLE RESTAURANT
BEIJING
$$$
23 SONGZHUSI, SHATAN BEIJIE
TEL 010/8400-2232
www.temple-restaurant.com
Tucked down a *hutong* lane on a walled compound featuring a 600-year old Tibetan temple, this is among Beijing's hottest tables. It serves contemporary European cuisine in a restyled former factory building, with floor-to-ceiling windows overlooking the temple courtyard. Degustation and a la carte menus offer dishes including roasted turbot with basil crust, crustacean jus with crab and saffron, and confit of suckling pig with mashed potato and spiced apples, and the wine list is excellent. Reservations are essential.
🚇 Dongsi Shitiao 💳
💳 All major cards

🍴 DALI COURTYARD
$$
67 XIAO JINGCHANG HUTONG
GULOU DONG DAJIE
TEL 010/8404-1430
This lovely restaurant was

once a courtyard house. There are no menus; you are served the dish of the day, which includes a cold appetizer, soup, vegetables, and meat or fish. Each meal is a specialty of the ethnic Bai who reside in Dali, a quaint town in Yunnan Province, served either in the old home dining room or on the plant-filled outdoor terrace.

🪑 50 🚇 Andingmen
🃁 Cash only

🍴 VINEYARD CAFÉ

$$

31 WUDAOYING HUTONG
(NEAR LAMA TEMPLE)
TEL 010/6402-7961
www.vineyardcafe.cn

Hidden in small *hutong* close to the Lama Temple, this café offers simple Western food. There is a grapevine-adorned courtyard that doubles as a lounge area. Café Vineyard serves a hearty British brunch on the weekends—eggs, bangers, sautéed mushrooms, fried potatoes, baked beans, and fresh orange juice.

🪑 60 🚇 Yonghegong
🕐 Closed Mon.
🃁 All major cards

■ XICHENG

HOTELS

SOMETHING SPECIAL

🏨 RITZ-CARLTON BEIJING
🍴 (LISI KA'ERDUN JIUDIAN)

$$$$$

18 FINANCIAL ST.
TEL 010/6601-6666
FAX 010/6601-6029
www.ritzcarlton.com

New and old Chinese art brightens up the walls in the lobby of this smart new hotel, while in the **Tea Apothecary** waitresses clad in yellow silk *qipao* serve tea

and coffee. In the large rooms you will find state-of-the-art amenities such as Wi-Fi and LCD televisions, as well as Tang-dynasty wood-block reproductions on the walls. The restaurant **Cepe** (see below) serves up creative Italian cuisine.

🛏 253 🚇 Fuxingmen, 15-min. walk 🔄 🅢 🆂
📶 📺 🚭 All major cards

🏨 INTERCONTINENTAL BEIJING FINANCIAL STREET (JINRONGJIE ZHOUJI JIUDIAN)

$$$$

11 FINANCIAL ST.
TEL 010/5852-5888
FAX 010/5852-5999

The Chinese flagship of the InterContinental chain, this was the first international luxury hotel to open on Beijing's fast-rising Financial Street in the city's northwest corner. The hotel has a 24-hour business center.

🛏 330 🚇 Fuchengmen
🔄 🅢 🆂 🏊 📺
🃁 All major cards

🏨 WESTIN FINANCIAL STREET

$$$

9B FINANCIAL ST.
TEL 010/6606-8866
FAX 010/6606-8899
E-MAIL Reservation.beijing@westin.com
www.starwoodhotels.com

The location west of Tiananmen Square in Beijing's financial district favors business travelers, but this is a good option for a weekend stay. It offers all the facilities of a top city hotel, including a spa, fitness center, and indoor pool, Cantonese, Italian, and international buffet restaurants, plus a cocktail

PRICES

HOTELS

An indication of the cost of a double room in the high season is given by **$** signs.

$$$$$	Over $400 (Over 2,540 RMB)
$$$$	$300–$400 (1,900–2,540RMB)
$$$	$200–$300 (1,270–1,900RMB)
$$	$100–$200 (635–1,270RMB)
$	Under $100 (Under 635RMB)

RESTAURANTS

An indication of the cost of a three-course meal without drinks is given by $ signs.

$$$$$	Over $100 (Over 635RMB)
$$$$$	$70–$100 (445–635RMB)
$$$	$40–$70 (255–445RMB)
$$	$20–$40 (125–255RMB)
$	Under $20 (Under 125RMB)

lounge with live DJ sets. All rooms are in a contemporary style and the views from the Club floors (22nd–26th) are excellent.

🚇 Fuchengmen

RESTAURANTS

🍴 CEPE (YIWEI XUAN)

$$$$

1/F RITZ-CARLTON HOTEL
18 FINANCIAL ST.
TEL 010/6601-6666
FAX 010/6601-6029

Chef Giovanni Terracciano, a native of Naples, Italy, is the brains behind Cepe, whose specialties include roasted pork tenderloin filled with

black truffles and pasta served with fungi sauce. The highlight is Terracciano's homemade limoncello. The fresh lemon drink, with a little kick of vodka, is a pleasure.

🛏 60 🚇 Fuxingmen, 15-min. walk 🚭 🚯 All major cards

🍴 FANGSHAN
$$$

1 WENJIN JIE
(INSIDE BEIHAI PARK)
TEL 010/6401-1879

Imperial court cuisine is a style of cooking based on the foods served to the emperor and his court. The Man-Han banquet consists of 134 imperial dishes, served over six days. With a minimum of ten people, the cost is 10,800RMB ($1,438) each. The cheaper version starts at 200RMB ($27). This restaurant started as a teahouse with several former imperial chefs. In 1956, the place was reborn serving a full Man-Han imperial banquet in Beihai Park. Dining in this imperial structure, and being served by waitresses decked out in elaborate Qing-dynasty Manchu outfits, is a treat.

🛏 500 🚯 All major cards

SOMETHING SPECIAL

🍴 ZHANGQUN'S HOME (ZHANGQUN JIA)
$$$

5 YANDAI XIEJIE
TEL 010/8404-6662

This single-table restaurant was originally used as a meeting place for friends but was soon converted into an exclusive place to eat. The dining area is small, but the natural light penetrating through the skylight creates a warm and welcoming feeling.

🛏 4–10 🚇 Di'anmen Wai
🚯 No credit cards

■ CHONGWEN

🏨 NOVOTEL BEIJING XIN
🍴 QIAO (XINQIAO FANDIAN)
$$

2 DONGJIAOMINXIANG
TEL 010/6513-3366
FAX 010/6512-5126
E-MAIL rsvn@novotel xinqiaobj.com

This hotel enjoys an excellent location with easy transportation; both Tiananmen Square and the Temple of Heaven are within a ten-minute drive. **Tang Palace,** famous for its Hong Kong-style dim sum, is also a good place to taste Cantonese cuisine.

ℹ 700 🚇 Chongwenmen
🚮 🚭 🏋 🚯 All major cards

SOMETHING SPECIAL

🍴 LI QUN ROAST DUCK (LIQUN KAOYA DIAN)
$

11 BEIXIANGFENG
ZHENGYI LU
TEL 010/6705-5578

Despite the run-down neighborhood, Li Qun Roast Duck is always full. The entrance has been turned into a furnace for roasting ducks and the rooms made suitable for dining. Li Qun may not have the orderliness of other restaurants, but its appealing roast duck, with little fat between the crispy skin and tender meat, is among the best around.

🛏 60 🚯 All major cards

■ XUANWU

HOTELS

🏨 GRAND MERCURE BEIJING CENTRAL
$

6 XUANWUMEN NEI DAJIE
TEL 010/6603-6688
FAX 010/6603-1481

E-MAIL info@grandmercure beijing.com
www.mercure.com

Good value modern hotel in a district not very well served by the hospitality sector. Offers easy access to the Beijing metro and is walking distance from Tiananmen Square and the Forbidden City. Its bright, contemporary rooms, three bars and restaurants, and fitness center and pool are usually occupied by business travelers on weeknights and leisure guests on weekends.

ℹ 290 🚇 Xuanwumen 🚭
🚯 All major cards

RESTAURANTS

🍴 CAPITAL M
$$$$

3/F, NO. 2 QIANMEN DAJIE
010/6702-2727
www.m-restaurantgroup.com

Sister abode to Shanghai's M on the Bund, this classy restaurant, bar, and tea lounge features a terrace overlooking Tiananmen Square. The artsy interior blends parquet-tiled flooring, antique furnishings, wall murals, table silverware, and Chinese porcelain. The modern European menu features M on the Bund favorites like slowly baked, salt-encased selected leg of lamb and M's very famous pavlova. It also hosts regular literary events on Sunday afternoons.

🚇 Qianmen
🚯 All major cards

🍴 LAO SHE TEAHOUSE
$$

3 QIANMEN XIDAJIE
TEL 010/6303-6830
www.laosheteahouse.com

This thriving teahouse, restaurant, theater, and opera house is a mainstay of Beijing legend. Located just beyond the old city walls, it was once a popular meeting place for actors

---

🚭 Nonsmoking   🚯 Air-conditioning   🏊 Indoor Pool   🏊 Outdoor Pool   🏋 Health Club   🚯 Credit Cards

and Beijing opera stars. Today, it is rather pricey and often filled with tourists, but pleasingly retains its links to Beijing traditions that have almost ceased to exist elsewhere.

🚇 Qianmen 💳 All major cards

🍴 QUANJUDE ROAST DUCK RESTAURANT
$$
14 QIANMEN XIDAJIE
TEL 010/6304-8987
Beijing's most renowned roast meat dish is served in all its crisp-skinned, tenderized flesh glory at this popular restaurant. In fact, Quanjude's fruitwood-fired roast duck is served in numerous different ways—with various parts of the body marinated and flavored in traditional Beijing style. For first-time diners, the whole duck, cooked by hanging it on a hook over a roasted flame, is a fine introduction.

🚇 Qianmen 💳 All major cards

▪ CHAOYANG

HOTELS

🏨 PARK HYATT BEIJING
$$$$$
2 JIANGUOMENWAI DAJIE
TEL 010/8567-1234
FAX 010/8567-1000
E-MAIL parkhyattbeijing@
hyattintl.com
www.beijing.park.hyatt.com
The Park Hyatt located in the impressive Beijing Yintai Center is a boutique hotel. It combines Asian aesthetics with sleek, contemporary design. Rooms are situated on floors 37 to 49. The hotel's rooftop bar, designed to resemble a Chinese lantern, has dramatic views of the city.

ⓘ 219 rooms, including 18 suites 🚇 Guomao 🔧 🚭
🛗 🏊 📺 🛎 💳 All major cards

🏨 RITZ-CARLTON BEIJING, CENTRAL PLACE
$$$$
83A JIANGUO DAJIE
TEL 010/5908-8888
FAX 010/5908-8899
E-MAIL Rc.bjsrz.leads@
ritzcarlton.com
www.ritzcarlton.com
The better located of Beijing's two Ritz-Carltons sits at the east end of the CBD with easy metro access to downtown and the historic attractions. Guests should expect superlative service and rooms dressed with classical furnishings and high-tech amenities. The suites are luxurious with separate rooms featuring comfy sofas and TVs, lounge tables, and a marble bathroom with outsized bathtub. The dining options are excellent, and the opulent spa is one of Beijing's best.

ⓘ 305 🚇 Dawanglu
🚭 🔧 🛗 🏊 📺 🛎
💳 All major cards

🏨🍴 SOFITEL WANDA BEIJING
$$$$
93 JIANGUO LU
TEL 010/8599-6666
FAX 010/8599-6686
E-MAIL sofitel@sofitel
wandabj.com
www.sofitel.com
The Sofitel Wanda Beijing opened its doors in the summer of 2007 to rave reviews for its classic design, a blend of Tang-dynasty China with contemporary French style. The rooms feature Chinese motifs. Le Spa offers beauty treatments blending local plant life and traditional Chinese techniques. Sofitel is also known for its excellent French and Cantonese restaurants, notably **Le Pre Lenotre** (see p. 301).

ⓘ 417 rooms, including 63 suites 🚇 Dawang Lu, Exit A
🚭 🔧 🛗 🏊 📺
💳 All major cards

🏨🍴 CHINA WORLD SUMMIT TOWER
$$$
1 JIANGUOMENWAI AVENUE
TEL 010/6505-2299
FAX 010/6505-8811
www.shangri-la.com/beijing
The capital's highest hotel occupies the top 16 floors of a glassy megatower that is centrally located at the China World convention, shopping, and hotel complex. Managed by Shangri-La Hotels, it boasts superb 360-degree city views from the lobby, rooms, bars, and restaurants. Guest rooms occupy the 67th–77th floors, and feature gold-inspired decor, wall-hung plasma TV, free Wi-Fi and spacious bathroom with rain forest shower. The Adam Tihany–designed **Grill 79** restaurant and 80th-floor **Atmosphere** cocktail lounge are the crowning glories.

ⓘ 278 🚇 Guomao
🅿 🚭 🔧 🛗 🏊 V, MC

SOMETHING SPECIAL

🏨🍴 THE OPPOSITE HOUSE
$$$
11 SANLITUN LU
TEL 010/6417-6688
FAX 010/6417-7799
E-MAIL reservations@the
oppositehouse.com
www.theoppositehouse.com
Designed by Japanese architect Kengo Kuma, this is Beijing's sleekest boutique hotel. The art museum–style lobby features installations, hanging artworks, and a glass-floor panel overlooking the stainless-steel swimming pool. Understated, minimalist rooms feature blond-wood floors and white retro furnishings, spa-style bathrooms, and free Wi-Fi. Dining options are equally hip, including **Bei** for award-winning northeast Asian cuisine, while **Mesh** is a popular cocktail lounge with Beijing fashionistas.

(1) 99 rooms 🏠 Tuanjiehu
⬆️ 🚭 🌀 🏊 📺
🗝 All major cards

🏨 GRACE BEIJING
$$

JIUXIANQIAO ROAD,
2 HAO YUAN,
706 HOU JIE 1 HAO,
798 YISHUQU
TEL 010/6436-1818
www.gracebeijing.com
Sleek art-themed boutique
hotel located at Beijing's
celebrated 798 Art District.
This peaceful retreat features
the acclaimed Yi House
French bistro with a large
patio garden, an elegant
cocktail bar, plus a small gym.
Contemporary works by
international artists hang in
the whitewashed lobby, and
the Boers–Li art gallery is
adjacent to the entrance. Each
room is smartly styled with
blond-wood floors and white-
tiled bathrooms, plus modern
comforts including free Wi-Fi,
satellite TV, and iPod dock.
(1) 30 ⬆️ 🚭 🌀 📺
🗝 All major cards

🏨 HOTEL G
$$

7 GO22NGTI XILU
TEL 010/6552-3600
FAX 010/6552-3606
E-MAIL info@hotel-g.com
www.hotel-g.com
Tucked behind Workers'
Stadium just off Gongti Bei
Road, Hotel G is a funky,
upbeat boutique hotel
targeting a fashion-conscious
clientele. There's an innate
sense of humor, too, with the
four retro-hip room categories
titled Good, Great, Greater,
and Greatest, and each room
offering a choice of window
light colors that create a
nighttime tapestry effect on
the facade. The artsy rooms
combine photo art imprinted
on bare concrete walls and

a purple, scarlet, and gray
color palette, chic lamps, and
patterned sofas. There's also a
smart Japanese restaurant and
a tapas lounge.
🏠 Chaoyangmen

🏨 METRO PARK LIDO
$$

6 JIANGTAI LU
TEL 010/6437-6688
FAX 010/6437-6237
www.hotellidobeijing.com
Originally built in 1986 as
China's first Holiday Inn
Lido, this rebranded hotel
continues to attract business
travelers looking for comfort
and familiarity, but the
location—20 minutes by taxi
from the airport—makes it
difficult for tourists visiting
historic sites. The 400-odd
rooms have been upgraded
and refurbished, but the
hotel's restaurants (Chinese,
Tex-Mex, and an English-style
pub) inject a bit of color.
(1) 433 rooms, including
24 suites ⬆️ 🚭 🌀 🏊 📺
🗝 All major cards

RESTAURANTS

🍴 LE PRE LENOTRE
$$$$

6/F SOFITEL WANDA BEIJING
93 JIANGUO LU
TEL 010/8599-6666
Le Pre Lenotre, the sister of
notable Le Pre Catelan, has
brought authentic French
cuisine to Beijing, adding
to the excitement of the
city's increasingly mixed-
bag culinary scene. The cod
studded with bits of smoked
salmon served with eggplant
marmalade is wonderful. The
restaurant serves small bri-
oches, reminiscent of Parisian
baguettes. Elegant and
romantic the Lenotre is
the perfect locale for an
intimate dinner.
🍴 100 🏠 Dawang Lu, Exit A
🗝 All major cards

🍴 AGUA
$$$

4/F, NALI PATIO, 81 SANLITUN
BEILU
TEL 010/5208-6188
www.aqua.com.hk
This intimate restaurant
dressed in warm brown and
scarlet drapes and Moorish
lampshades serves award-
winning, fine Spanish cuisine
by Barcelona-born chef
Jordi Valles. Very strong on
contemporary Spanish meat
and seafood dishes, Valles has
also introduced a few vegetarian dishes. The lunch sets are
good value, though the dinner
menu is rather pricier.
🏠 Tuanjiehu 🗝 V, MC

🍴 BEI
$$$

THE OPPOSITE HOUSE,
11 SANLITUN LU
TEL 010/6410-5239
www.beirestaurant.com
Talented chef Max Levy com-
bines the cuisines of northern
China, Japan, and Korea (Bei
means north in Mandarin) in
his innovative restaurant at
the Opposite House hotel.
Befitting the boutique hotel
location, the decor is highly
contemporary and styled
with purple backlit paneling
and ceiling-hung mini-lights
reaching down over the
tables. One of Beijing's "talk
of the town" restaurants, Bei
offers a meticulously crafted
menu featuring treats such
as blackened miso pork belly
with baby taro and tatsoi, and
kyushu amberjack sashimi
with garlic oil, ponzu vinegar,
oak leaf, and radish.
🕐 Dinner only 🏠 Tuanjiehu
🗝 All major cards

SOMETHING SPECIAL

🍴 DUCK DE CHINE
$$$
1949 HIDDEN CITY, GONGTI
BEILU
TEL 010/6501-8881
www.elite-concepts.com
The Gallic name is an indicator
of what awaits at this popular
eaterie dressed like a rustic
chic French brasserie, with un-
covered brick, heavy wooden
tables, and large chandeliers.
The menu features sev-
eral duck dishes, such as duck
confit, given a French twist,
plus the signature roasted
Peking duck. The wine list is
impressive. Duck de Chine
also features the first Bollinger
Champagne Bar in China.
🚇 Tuanjiehu 🔆
🍴 All major cards

🍴 TRANSIT
$$$
4-36, 3RD FLOOR, THE VILLAGE
NORTH, SANLITUN LU
TEL 010/6417-9090
Chili-pepper laden Sichuan
hot pots are usually served
in kitchen-style diners, but
Transit elevates the experience
several levels. The sophisticated decor is aimed at affluent diners with a penchant for
highly spiced food. A signature
chicken in red chili oil is
tongue-numbingly hot, while
mapo doufu—a Sichuan dish
of tofu in a peppery sauce—is
slightly less eye-watering.
🚇 Tuanjiehu 🍴 V, MC

🍴 YUAN YUAN
$$$
16 TUANJIEHU PARK
(WEST GATE)
DONG SANHUAN
TEL 010/6508-2202
Yuan Yuan was the winner of
the Golden Chopstick award
for its braised pork *(hongshao
rou)* in the 2006 Shanghai
New Cuisine competition.

The caramelized belly pork,
which melts in your mouth,
is a Shanghainese signature
dish, and an all-time favorite.
Other well-known dishes not
to be missed are stir-fried
glutinous rice cake, bean-curd
thread in chicken consommé,
scrumptious wild vegetables in
sesame oil, and peanuts mixed
with bean curd tossed in light
soy dressing.
🪑 150 🍴 MC, V

🍴 NOODLE LOFT
$$
20 XIDAWANG LU
TEL 010/6774-9950
The freshly hand-pulled
noodles here are second to
none. The noodles are cooked
al dente and have a chewy
texture. The varieties is endless. Try knife-shaved noodles,
one strand noodle, cat's ears,
or *kao laolao*, a honeycomb-
like noodle served with the
sauce of your choice: minced
meat sauce, or a vinegar and
soy sauce combination.
🪑 150 🚇 Dawanglu
🍴 MC, V

🍴 PURE LOTUS
$$
TONGGUANG BUILDING, 12
NONGZHANGUAN NAN LU
TEL 010/6592-3627
Beijing's quirkiest and most in-
ventive vegetarian restaurant
is also its most visually stun-
ning. The interior resembles
a movie set version of a
Buddhist temple, and real-life
monks serve the food. Each
dish—the tomato dumplings
and stir-fried mixed mush-
rooms are especially good—is
presented on wooden platters.
They even do a vegetarian
version of the city's roasted
Peking duck.
🚇 Tuanjiehu

PRICES

HOTELS
An indication of the cost of
a double room in the high
season is given by **$** signs.

$$$$$	Over $400 (Over 2,540 RMB)
$$$$	$300–$400 (1,900–2,540RMB)
$$$	$200–$300 (1,270–1,900RMB)
$$	$100–$200 (635–1,270RMB)
$	Under $100 (Under 635RMB)

RESTAURANTS
An indication of the cost of
a three-course meal without
drinks is given by $ signs.

$$$$$	Over $100 (Over 635RMB)
$$$$	$70–$100 (445–635RMB)
$$$	$40–$70 (255–445RMB)
$$	$20–$40 (125–255RMB)
$	Under $20 (Under 125RMB)

▦ HAIDIAN

HOTELS

SOMETHING SPECIAL

🏨 AMAN AT SUMMER
🍴 PALACE
$$$$$
1 GONGMENQIAN ST.
TEL 010/5987-9999
FAX 010/5987-9900
E-MAIL amanatsummer
palace@amanresorts.com
www.amanresorts.com/
amanatsummerpalace
Seclusion and privacy are
guaranteed at this intimate
resort that boasts private
access to the UNESCO World
Heritage listed Summer

🏨 Hotel 🍴 Restaurant ⓘ No. of Guest Rooms 🪑 No. of Seats 🅿 Parking 🚇 Metro 🕐 Closed 🛗 Elevator

Palace. The focal point of this private estate that was once reserved for guests visiting China's Empress Dowager is a peaceful lake, beside which Chinese musicians play in the afternoon. The residential-style suites are large and decorated in modern-meets-ancient Chinese style, and feature a separate lounge, bathroom, and bedroom. Resort facilities include fine Chinese and Japanese restaurants including **Naoki,** a lakeside lounge, and an Aman Spa.
☎ 54 🔲 🚭 🈴
🍽 All major cards

🏨 SHANGRI-LA HOTEL (XIANGGE LILA FANDIAN)
$$
29 ZIZHUYUAN LU
TEL 010/6841-2211
FAX 010/6841-8002
www.shangri-la.com
E-MAIL slb@shangri-la.com
Located in Beijing's new financial district, the Shangri-La is surrounded by charming landscaped gardens. From its western location, guests can easily access the nearby exhibition centers and high-tech zone (Beijing's Silicon Valley). Of greater interest to tourists is its proximity to major attractions in northwest Beijing, including the Summer Palace. ☎ 670
🈴 Wanshousi 🔲 🚭
🏊 🎽 🍽 All major cards

RESTAURANTS

SOMETHING SPECIAL

🍴 S.T.A.Y.
$$$$$
SHANGRI-LA HOTEL,
29 ZIZHUYUAN ROAD
TEL 010/6841-2211 EXT 6727
The name is an acronym for Simple Table Alléno Yannick.

The inventive French chef, who has received five Michelin stars during his career, has inverted his own name but keeps a steady hand in the kitchen. Yannick's highly stylized—and high-priced—modern food ranges from signature quail eggs with sea urchin and Schrenckii caviar to chicken pot au feu and buttered fettucine with black truffles. 🈴 Wanshousi
🚭 🍽 All major cards

🍴 NAOKI
$$$$
AMAN AT SUMMER PALACE,
1 GONGMENQIAN ST.
TEL 010/5987-9999
Naoki is a sumptuously designed, feng shui–inspired restaurant designed around a Zen reflecting pool at Aman at Summer Palace. Diners sit at a Japanese-style counter, and are served inventive *kaiseki* menus, Japanese fine dining that incorporates French techniques.
🚭 🍽 All major cards

🍴 GOLDEN PEACOCK (JIN KONGQUE)
$
16 MINZU DAXUE BEILU WEIGONGCUN
TEL 010/6893-2030
Golden Peacock serves the food of the Dai people, an ethnic group from Yunnan Province in southwest China. The restaurant is always packed with customers who miss their hometown cooking.
🔲 60 🈴 Minzu Daxue
🍽 Cash only

■ EXCURSIONS NORTH TO THE GREAT WALL

HOTELS

🏨 COMMUNE BY THE 🍴 GREAT WALL
$$$$$
GREAT WALL EXIT 53 AT SHUI-GUAN, BADALING HWY.
TEL 010/8118-1888
FAX 010/8118-1866
www.commune.com.cn
This boutique hotel cum semi-architectural museum is the brainchild of Zhang Xin and Pan Shiyi. Set amid the peaceful green mountains near the Shuiguan section of the Great Wall, the place is a collection of contemporary architecture designed by 12 Asian architects. There are 42 villas with unique designs spread out across the steep valley plus smaller rooms in a hotel-style building with views of the nearby Great Wall. The Club House includes the **Courtyard Restaurant** (worth the trip alone), Kids' Club, and a spa.
☎ 46 🔲 🚭 🎽
🍽 All major cards

🏨 RED CAPITAL RANCH (WANSHOU GONG)
$$$$
28 XIAGUANDI VILLAGE
YANXI TOWNSHIP
HUAIROU COUNTY
TEL 010/8401-8886
www.redcapitalclub.com.cn
Nestled between a small river and a wild section of the Great Wall, this beautifully restored Manchurian hunting lodge is made up of individual lodges, equipped with modern facilities. The dining room serves Manchu dishes and locally picked wild vegetables. The bar has colorful furniture and rugs and overlooks the stream. The hotel offers spa services, including Tibetan massage. Transportation from Beijing is included in the price.
☎ 10 🚭 Ceiling fans
🍽 All major cards

🚭 Nonsmoking   🔲 Air-conditioning   🏊 Indoor Pool   🏊 Outdoor Pool   🎽 Health Club   🍽 Credit Cards

🏨 **THE SCHOOLHOUSE**
$$$$
12 MUTIANYU VILLAGE
TEL 010/6162-6506
E-MAIL info@theschoolhouse
atmutianyu.com
www.theschoolhouseat
mutianyu.com
The Schoolhouse at Mutianyu
is a sustainable tourism village
at the base of the Great Wall. It
offers boutique inn accommodation in a converted glazed-tile
factory, and operates guided
tours of the wall and nearby
villages. The restaurant cooks
up regional cuisine using locally
grown ingredients, and there
is also an art glass studio and
gallery.

RESTAURANTS

🍴 **XIAOLUMIAN**
$
130 YINGBEIGOU CUN
HUAIROU DISTRICT
TEL 010/6162-5006
Xiaolumian focuses on noodles,
with a selection of buckwheat
and veggie noodles flavored
with spinach, carrot, or
wormwood artemisia. Set in a
weathered stone farmhouse
surrounded by a walled orchard
in the shadow of the Great
Wall, this is an ideal place to
stop for lunch.
🪑 20 inside plus 60 terrace
🕐 Closed Mon.–Fri.
💳 All major cards

◼ EXCURSIONS SOUTH

HOTELS

SOMETHING SPECIAL

🏨 **THE ASTOR HOTEL TIAN-
JIN
(LISHUNDE
DAFANDIAN)
$$**

33 TAI'ERZHUANG LU
TEL 022/2331-1688
FAX 022/2331-6282
www.starwoodhotels.com
One of Tianjin's most historic
hotels, the Astor was built in
1863. Puyi (the last emperor),
Sun Yat-sen, and Yuan Shikai
have stayed here. Situated
near the Hai River, it was
the first to use electric lights
in Tianjin during the Qing
dynasty. Fragments of history
remain inside: The original
American Otis elevators
are there, mid-19th-century
furniture remains, and you can
find the radio used by Puyi.
If you can afford it, stay in
the Sun Zhongshan (Yat-sen)
Presidential Suite and enjoy
a sumptuous afternoon tea
in the Victorian Lounge.
This 147-year-old hotel was
recently extensively refur-
bished and upgraded and now
includes a hotel museum and
the 1863 Bistro & Terrace.
🛏 152 💳 All major cards

🏨 **BANYAN TREE TIANJIN
RIVERSIDE
$$**
34 HAIHE EAST ROAD
TEL 022/5888-5896
FAX: 022/5861-9998
www.banyantree.com
Opened in fall 2012, Banyan
Tree's first "urban resort" in
mainland China is located
beside the Hai River in central
Tianjin. Guest rooms draw
their inspiration from the
muted tones and refined
aesthetic of traditional
Chinese ink paintings, while
the restaurants serve Cantonese, classic Thai, and barbecue
cuisines. The Banyan Tree Spa
specializes in wellness treatments based on natural Asian
healing therapies.
🛏 159 💳 💱
💳 All major cards

🏨 **WESTIN TIANJIN**
$$
101 NANJING ROAD
TEL 022/2389-0088
FAX 022/2389-0099
E-MAIL westin.tianjin@westin
.com
www.starwoodhotels.com
A comfortable modern hotel
with great facilities in the
heart of Tianjin's business
district. It's also near to the
main shopping center and sev-
eral attractions. The rooms are
well appointed for business
and leisure travelers, and there
are three restaurants, a large
fitness center, a fully equipped
business center, and a spa.
🛏 275 🅿 💱 💳 💱
💳 V, MC

RESTAURANTS

🍴 **GOUBULI**
$
77 SHANDONG ROAD
TEL 022/2730-2540
The famous Goubuli, located
just off the shopping drag of
Binjiang Dadao, has been serv-
ing up its trademark specialty
steamed buns (baozi) for over
a hundred years. The appe-
tizing buns come in almost
100 varieties (pork, chicken,
shrimp, vegetable, and more)
and a selection of tasty and
good-value set meals is also
available. There are other
branches dotted around town,
Beijing, and beyond.
🪑 300 💳 Cash only

🍴 **LITTLE SHEEP
(XIAOFEIYANG)
$**
RONGYE DAJIE
TEL 022/2730-8318
Warm up cold Tianjin
winter days with a steaming
Mongolian lamb hot pot
at this branch of the nation-
wide chain.
🪑 500 💳 Cash only

🍴 XIANG WEI ZHAI

$

HYATT HOTEL TIANJIN
219 JIEFANG BEILU
TEL 022/2331-8888

This pleasantly designed dumpling restaurant is a joy. The name means "country-side flavor," pointing to its emphasis on traditional simplicity. Try the crab and chive dumpling or the seafood and noodle soup, and wash it down with Chinese tea. Inexpensive and all very worthwhile. Service charge included. English menu.

🔲 44 🅢 All major cards

SHANGHAI

■ THE BUND TO PEOPLE'S SQUARE

HOTELS

🏨 THE WESTIN BUND
🍴 CENTER (WEISITING DAFANDIAN)

$$$$$

88 HENAN MIDDLE ROAD
TEL 6335-1888
FAX 6335-2888
E-MAIL rsvns-shanghai@
westin.com
www.starwoodhotels.com

Three blocks off the Bund, in the 50-story Bund Center, the Westin is a business traveler's favorite, with an atrium lobby, and restaurants serving Italian, Thai, Japanese, and Chinese cuisine. While the luxurious Banyan Tree Spa is located on the premises, those on a tight schedule can book rooms with built-in aerobic exercise machines. The modern rooms are located across two towers and tastefully decorated, the service ultraefficient.

🅘 570 🚞 East Nanjing Road
🅢 🅢 🚪 🆈 🅢 All major cards

🏨 FAIRMONT PEACE HOTEL

$$$$

20 NANJING EAST ROAD
TEL 6321-6888
FAX 6329-1888
E-MAIL peacehotel@fairmont
.com
www.fairmont.com/peace
hotel

Shanghai's most famous hotel reopened in 2010 under the Fairmont brand after three years of renovations. Built by Sir Victor Sassoon in the 1920s, and famed for its green copper tower, the art deco facade and interior design were unmatched in Shanghai. The updated hotel retains the fine period detailing, and has resuscitated star features such as the Nine Nations Suites and live evening music in the Jazz Bar. A museum on the second floor retells the fabled history of this Shanghai institution.

🅘 270 🚞 East Nanjing Road
🅢 🅢 🚪 🆈 🅢 All major cards

🏨 THE PENINSULA
🍴 SHANGHAI

$$$$

32 THE BUND
TEL 2327-2888
FAX 2327-2000
E-MAIL psh@peninsula.com
www.peninsula.com/
Shanghai

The Peninsula Shanghai represents both an homage to the city's art deco heritage and superlative contemporary luxury. Cutting-edge in-room technology includes spa-style bathroom lighting, cable TV, and 1,000-channel Internet radio. The riverview **Sir Elly's Terrace** is perfect for sunset cocktails, while the exquisite Peninsula Spa is among the city's most luxurious wellness retreats. The award-winning **Yi Long Court** serves fine Cantonese cuisine in a restaurant styled like a 1930s Shanghai nobleman's home.

🅘 235 🚞 East Nanjing Road
🅢 🅢 🚪 🆈 🅢 All major cards

SOMETHING SPECIAL

🏨 WALDORF ASTORIA SHANGHAI ON THE BUND

$$$$

2 THE BUND
TEL 6322-9988
FAX 6321-9888
E-MAIL shawa.info@
waldorfastoria.com
www.waldorfastoriashanghai
.com

Housed in the neoclassical Shanghai Club dating from 1911, the Bund-front heritage building houses 20 deluxe club suites designed like traditional Shang-hainese residences—but with contemporary in-room tech-nologies. A new tower offers 237 rooms and suites with fine river views. The lavishly re-created **Long Bar**—the signature venue of the original Club—features a 110-foot-long bar counter and an oyster bar, while the satin-draped **Salon de Ville** is an elegant venue for afternoon tea.

🅘 260 🅿 🚞 East Nanjing Road
🅢 🚪 🅢 All major cards

🏨 ASTOR HOUSE HOTEL
🍴 $$$ (PUJIANG FANDIAN)

15 HUANGPU ROAD
TEL 6324 6388
FAX 6324-3179
www.astorhousehotel.com
E-MAIL sales@astorhouse
hotel.com

This fallen five-star from the decadent 1920s was recently rescued by a renovation. The likes of Charlie Chaplin and Albert Einstein once stayed here, and Shanghai's first elec-tric lightbulbs were installed in 1886. Full of atmosphere, great location on the Bund.

🅘 116 🚞 North end of East Nanjing Road
🅢 All major cards

🅢 Nonsmoking 🅢 Air-conditioning 🚞 Indoor Pool 🅿 Outdoor Pool 🆈 Health Club 🅢 Credit Cards

🏨 LES SUITES ORIENT
$$$
1 JINLING EAST ROAD
TEL 6320-0088
FAX 6320-3399
E-MAIL RSVN@lessuites
orient.com
www.hotelsuitesorient.com
Located at the south end of
the Bund with fine river views,
this boutique-style hotel features art deco theming and
museum-style displays of
antiques and memorabilia.
The rooms are decorated with
cool marble and hardwoods,
and feature exceptional
in-room amenities, including
complimentary Wi-Fi and a
free smartphone for making
local calls and containing a
selection of maps and city
information. A library lounge
serves tea and refreshments
for all guests.
ⓘ 168 🅿 🔁 🔲
🃏 All major cards

🏨 🍴 WATERHOUSE AT SOUTH BUND
$$$
1-3 MAOJIAYUAN ROAD
TEL 6080-2988
FAX 6080-2999
E-MAIL reservations@water
houseshanghai.com
www.waterhouseshanghai
.com
This design-led, 19-room
hotel is housed in a radically
renovated former warehouse
south of the Bund and is
popular with visiting celebrities. Each individually themed
room features bare concrete
walls, minimalist furnishings,
and graphic artworks. The
rooftop terrace is home to a
terrace bar, and **Table No. 1**
is a hip restaurant created by
high-profile British chef
Jason Atherton.
ⓘ 19 🚇 Yuyuan Gardens 🔲
🃏 All major cards

🏨 CAPTAIN HOSTEL (CHUANZHANG QINGNIAN JIUDIAN)
$$
37 FUZHOU ROAD
HUANG PU DISTRICT
TEL 400/001-9990
FAX 6321-9331
E-MAIL captainhostel@
hotmail.com
www.captainhostel.com.cn
For those seeking a respite
from modern luxury, this
favorite of backpackers of all
ages is perfect. Located in a
1920s art deco building just off
the Bund, the Captain offers
not just dorm beds but a selection of double rooms with
attached bathrooms. Only
some rooms have a television.
The rooftop bar has the same
great views of the river as its
neighbors at a fraction of the
cost. The hostel offers a variety
of activities for its guests, such
as classes in Chinese cooking and handicraft making.
Bicycles are available for rent
and there's an Internet café in
the lobby.
ⓘ 21 🚇 East Nanjing Road
🃏 All major cards

RESTAURANTS

🍴 JEAN GEORGES
$$$$
3 THE BUND, 4TH FLOOR
TEL 6321-7733
www.threeonthebund.com
This citadel of haute cuisine
was opened by Jean-Georges
Vongerichten in 2004 fol-
lowing his successful New
York restaurant. French-Asian
fusion with a continental
flair is the theme, both in
decor and cuisine. Specialties
include foie gras brûlée, sea
scallops, kingfish sashimi, and
lamb loin with black trumpet
mushrooms, all prepared in
unique styles. Both set and a
la carte menus are presented.
Ambience is elegant and many

consider this Shanghai's best
Western restaurant. Prices are
high, but proportional to the
overall value. Book ahead.
🍴 190 🅿 🚇 East Nanjing
Road 🔁 🔲 🔲
🃏 All major cards

🍴 M ON THE BUND (MISHI XICANTING)
$$$$
THE BUND, 5TH FLOOR
TEL 6350-9988
www.m-restaurantgroup.com
This is where, in 1999,
Shanghai's Western gourmet
tradition began. While locals
and expats may have moved
on in search of the next big
thing, M on the Bund still
prepares excellent food in

---

a great setting. It is located on the seventh floor of a concession-era building (enter from the side at 20 Guangdong Road) and maintains an elegant art deco atmosphere, coupled with views from the terrace over the river and Huangpu. The menu varies by season, but is concise, and while decidedly continental, has Mediterranean and North African influences. House specialties include leg of lamb and the signature Pavlova dessert. Advance reservations required. One floor down is the uber-chic Glamour Bar cocktail lounge and champagne bar, a Shanghai institution.

🔢 250 🚇 East Nanjing Road 🚭 🅰 🅲 All major cards

SOMETHING SPECIAL

🍴 MR & MRS BUND
$$$$

6/F, 18 THE BUND
TEL 6323-9898
www.mmbund.com

Created by enigmatic French chef Paul Pairet, this fashionable Bund-front restaurant is strictly reservations only. Shanghai's movers and shakers fill the place each night. A huge menu veers from Pairet's signature molecular gastronomy to heartier modern European fare with distinctive Asian influences. The brightly colored cocktail bar and modern interior design enliven the heritage building setting, and the window tables offer great views over the Bund and river. The whole experience neatly defines the early 21st-century Shanghai zeitgeist.

🚇 East Nanjing Road 🅰
🅲 All major cards

🍴 LOST HEAVEN
$$$

17 YAN'AN EAST ROAD
TEL 6330-0967
www.lostheaven.com.cn

Set over three floors, with an open-deck lounge on top, this is one of Shanghai's hottest tables. Its semi-spicy mountain Mekong cuisine is a fusion of cooking styles and ingredients from the southwestern province of Yunnan, and neighboring Burma and Thailand. The striking black and scarlet decor is embellished with specially commissioned photos from Yunnan villages and ethnic adornments from the region's Dai, Bai, and Miao minorities. Reservations essential.

🚇 East Nanjing Road
🅰 🅲 All major cards

🍴 SHANGHAI UNCLE (HAISHANG ASHU)
$$$

222 YAN'AN EAST ROAD
BUND CENTER, NEAR HENAN
MIDDLE ROAD
TEL 6339-1977

Owned by a Shanghainese American, this restaurant offers Shanghainese food with some interesting twists. In addition to the house specialty of Uncle's crispy pork of flame, try the traditional Shanghai dish of cold smoked fish or Peking pancakes with scallops and XO sauce. The restaurant is located in the basement of the Bund Center, so the only views are of the amusing decor and lively patrons, best seen from booths on the mezzanine. There's a second location on the Pudong side of the river. Reservations recommended.

🔢 500 🚇 East Nanjing Road
🅰 🅲 All major cards

■ FUXING ROAD TO HUAIHAI ROAD

HOTELS
SOMETHING SPECIAL

🏨 THE LANGHAM XINTIANDI
$$$$$

99 MADANG ROAD
TEL 2330-2288
FAX 2330-2233
E-MAIL tlxd.resv@langham hotels.com
www.xintiandi.langhamhotels .com

Centrally located in the Xintiandi dining and shopping district, this is one of Shanghai's newer upscale hotels. Elegant luxury reigns at **Ming Court**, the signature Cantonese restaurant, and the **Club Lounge**. Service is highly personable, and the decadent Chuan Spa provides a serene environment for deluxe wellness treatments. In addition, Langham Hotels also manages the 53-room boutique-style 88 Xintiandi hotel across the street.

ℹ 357 🅿 🚇 South Huangpi Road 🅲 🚇
🅰 All major cards

🏨 88 XINTIANDI
$$$$

380 HUANGPI SOUTH ROAD
TEL 5383-8833
FAX 5383-8877
E-MAIL enquiry@88xintiandi .com
www.88xintiandi.com

Now managed by Langham Hotels, this 53-room boutique hotel in the Xintiandi complex re-creates the *shikumen*, or stone gate houses, of old Shanghai. The tastefully done rooms are all suites, or at least contain a small kitchenette. Some rooms have lake views, but if your balcony overlooks the shopping area, make sure it's on a high floor, since the activities below can go late.

ℹ 53 🅿 🚇 South Huangpi Road 🚭 🅲 🅾 🚇 🏋
🅰 All major cards

🅲 Nonsmoking 🅲 Air-conditioning 🏊 Indoor Pool 🏊 Outdoor Pool 🏋 Health Club 🅰 Credit Cards

🏨 OKURA GARDEN HOTEL (HUAYUAN FANDIAN)
$$$$

58 MAOMING SOUTH ROAD
TEL 6415-1111
FAX 6415-8866
E-MAIL rmresv@garden
hotelshanghai.com
www.gardenhotelshanghai
.com

Situated on the grounds of the former French Sporting Club, the Okura uses the spectacular, old three-story building for its lobby, restaurants, and function rooms. After the French departed, the sweeping staircases, crystal chandeliers, and grand ballroom with a stained-glass dome ceiling appealed to the tastes of Chairman Mao and his top associates, who held regular conferences here. The guests are mainly Japanese, but the staff speaks English. The recently refurbished guest rooms are in the less inspiring 33-story annex and have a distinct Japanese feeling to them (i.e., tasteful minimalist style).

ℹ️ 500 🅿️ 🚇 South Shanxi Road 🚳 🚫 ⛱️ 🏧
🃏 All major cards

🏨 JINJIANG HOTEL (JIN JIANG FANDIAN)
$$–$$$$

59 MAOMING SOUTH ROAD
TEL 3218-9888
FAX 6472-5588
E-MAIL bc@jinjianghotels
.com
www.jinjianghotels.com

First opened in the 1920s and called the Cathay Mansions, this complex now comprises the original Cathay, as well as the 1930s Grosvenor House, which has been converted into an all-suite hotel, and the recently renovated South Building. The gardens are magnificent, and the restaurants range from Thai to Mexican. Classical music

concerts are held in the Grand Hall of the former Cathay Mansions.

ℹ️ 328 🅿️ 🚇 South Shanxi Road 🚳 🚫 🚳 ⛱️ 🏧
🃏 All major cards

🏨 HENGSHAN MOLLER VILLA (HENGSHAN MALE BIESHU FANDIAN)
$$–$$$

30 SHAANXI SOUTH ROAD
TEL 6247-8881
FAX 6289-1020
E-MAIL sde@mollervilla.com
www.mollervilla.com

Once the private residence of a British real estate magnate with a penchant for horse racing. He built this castlelike structure to fulfill the dreams of his youngest daughter. The architecture can only be described as eccentrically pleasing. Steeples and spires, with a leafy garden complete with bronze statuary and meteorites as decor, all somehow fit in with the chandeliers and ornate European-style furniture in the wood-paneled rooms. There are 11 rooms in the original building. The adjacent three-story block is cheaper but not the original.

ℹ️ 40 🚇 South Shanxi Road 🚳 🚫 🚳 ⛱️
🃏 All major cards

🏨 DONGHU HOTEL
$$

70 DONGHU ROAD
TEL 6415-8158
FAX 6415-7142
www.donghuhotel.com

Visitors with an interest in old Shanghai should find this converted mansion set in a walled compound with attractive shaded gardens of interest. It once belonged to Du Yuesheng, the notorious Green Gang boss and Shanghai mobster. The main building is surrounded by seven smaller

villas, which once were home to some of Du's numerous mistresses. Well appointed with all the usual amenities, it's conveniently close to the restaurants of Donghu, Xinle, and Huaihai Roads.

ℹ️ 310 🅿️ 🚇 Changshu Road or South Shanxi Road 🚳 🚫 🚳 🚁 ⛱️ 🃏 All major cards

🏨 🍽️ OLD HOUSE INN (LAOSHI GUANG LAO SHIGUANG JIUDIAN)
$$

NO. 16, 351 LANE
HUASHAN ROAD
TEL 6428-6118
FAX 6429-6869
E-MAIL info@oldhouse.cn
www.oldhouse.cn

Located down a residential alley, this 12-room inn has the feel of the old family home it once was. It is owned and managed by a local architect and has rooms in Chinese style with warm wood paneling. Intimate and charming.

ℹ️ 12 🚇 Changshu Road
🚫 🃏 All major cards

RESTAURANTS

🍽️ MR WILLIS
$$$$

195 ANFU ROAD
TEL 5404 0200
www.mrwillis.com.cn

Talented chef Craig Willis greets guests from the open kitchen as he cooks up modern Australian classics with seasonal leanings in this loft-style restaurant. Located on a pretty former French Concession street, Mr Willis has built up a loyal following, so reservations are required. Downstairs is his more casual pizza and wine parlor, La Strada.

🚇 Changshu Road 🚫
🃏 All major cards

🏨 Hotel   🍽️ Restaurant   ℹ️ No. of Guest Rooms   🚇 No. of Seats   🅿️ Parking   🚇 Metro   🕐 Closed   🛗 Elevator

¶ T8

$$$–$$$$

HOUSE 8, NORTH BLOCK
XINTIANDI
181 TAICANG ROAD
TEL 6355-8999

Located in a Xintiandi *shiku-men* that has been decorated with a mixture of traditional and contemporary motifs, the swish T8 caters to a celebrity clientele. The Spanish chef's fusion cuisine takes Chinese and Thai flavors and uses them in European-style creations. Everything from a lobster oxtail ravioli starter to slow-cooked lamb and suckling pig—and the wine list—is superb. Advance dinner reservations suggested.
⊞ 106 🚇 South Huangpi Road ⬡ ⬡ All major cards

¶ BELLA NAPOLI

$$$

LANE 946, CHANGLE ROAD
TEL 6253-8358
www.bellanapoli-sh.com

Justifiably laying claim to making Shanghai's best thin-crust Italian pizza, Bella Napoli also serves a large selection of handmade pastas. Tucked away in an old villa down a narrow lane, the no-frills interior opens onto a lovely garden terrace. Owner Guido ensures the service is efficient and friendly—and the Italian wines and limoncino flow freely.
🚇 Changshu Road ⬡ ⬡ All major cards

¶ SICHUAN CITIZEN

$$$

30 DONGHU ROAD
TEL 5404-1235
www.citizenshanghai.com

Shanghai diners adore the seductively spicy flavors of Sichuan Province, and this smart restaurant updates the genre for the city's style-conscious set. Decorated like an updated 1930s Shanghai

café, its serves a large menu of pepper-laden Sichuan hot pots and meaty stews plus an excellent cocktail menu—and ice-cold beer to becalm numbed tongues. Vegetarian versions of many dishes are served on request.
🚇 South Huangpi Road ⬡ ⬡ All major cards

¶ ZEN

$$$

RM 2 SOUTH BLOCK XINTIANDI, LANE 123
TEL 6385-6385

Although part of a chain that specializes in Cantonese food, here the emphasis is on taste and good service. Choices include the pomelo salad, crispy roast pork, and steamed crab in rice wine sauce. A choice selection of wines is available. The excellent Sunday dim sum lunch requires reservations several days prior.
⊞ 320 🚇 South Huangpi Road ⬡ ⬡ All major cards

¶ CRYSTAL JADE RESTAURANT (FEICUI JIUJIA)

$$

HOUSE 6–7, LANE 123
XINGYE ROAD
XINTIANDI
TEL 6385-8752

If it's made from or wrapped in rice flour, they have it. The open kitchen lets you watch the dough being transformed into noodles, dumplings, and dim sum. The fillings are wide-ranging, from standard pork and chicken to shrimp, crab, and lobster. Heavier fare, such as roast pork and duck, is also served. This is one of several Shanghai branches of this popular restaurant, and one of the best places to sample the Shanghai favorite dumpling, called *xiao long bao*. Advance reservations

are recommended.
⊞ 200 🚇 South Huangpi Road ⬡ ⬡ All major cards

¶ HOT POT KING (LAIFU LOU)

$

1416 HUAIHAI MIDDLE ROAD
TEL 6474-6380

This is a good place to sample *huo guo*, a Chinese culinary tradition in which a selection of meat, seafood, dumplings, and vegetables are brought to your table uncooked, then simmered in a communal pot of broth. After cooking, you dip them in a selection of sauces. Especially attractive on a cold and rainy Shanghai day. The chain has several branches throughout the city; call for the one nearest you, or if you see the sign, stop in.
⊞ 290 🚇 Changshu Road ⬡ ⬡ All major cards

■ PUDONG

HOTELS

⌂ GRAND HYATT (SHANGHAI JINMAO JINYUEJUNYUE DAJIUDIAN)

$$$$$

JINMAO TOWER
(54TH–88TH FLOORS)
88 CENTURY BOULEVARD
TEL 5049-1234
FAX 5049-1111
E-MAIL shanghai.grand@ hyatt.com
www.shanghai.grand.hyatt .com

Formerly billed as the world's highest hotel—it starts on the 54th floor of the deceptively 1950s-looking Jinmao Tower—the Grand Hyatt qualifies as a destination in itself. Beginning with the 33-floor atrium lobby, design is key, with every motif from futuristic to art deco to contemporary Chinese on show. Surprisingly, it all fits together, and the rooms, with floor-to-ceiling windows, give some incredible views if it's not cloudy. Food is superb as well, and the **Cloud Nine** bar on the 88th floor is fabled in Shanghai.

🛈 555 🅿 🚇 Lujiazui 🔁 🚾
🔁 🏊 📺 🍸 All major cards

🏨 PUDONG SHANGRI-LA (PUDONG XIANG-GELILA FANDIAN)
$$$$$

33 FUCHENG ROAD
TEL 6882-8888
FAX 6882-6688
E-MAIL slpu@shangri-la.com
www.shangri-la.com

The twin 28-story towers offer a less vertiginous but equally luxurious alternative for those wishing to stay in Pudong. Restrained elegance is the theme here, with traditional Chinese design elements and amber wood paneling. The guest rooms are said to be the largest in Shanghai and its suite of fine dining remains the best in Pudong. The CHI day spa is also one of the city's best.

🛈 981 🅿 🚇 Lujiazui 🔁 🚾
🔁 🏊 📺 🍸 All major cards

SOMETHING SPECIAL

🏨 🍴 PARK HYATT
$$$$$

100 CENTURY AVENUE
TEL 6888-1234
FAX 6888-3400
E-MAIL shanghai.park@hyatt.com
www.shanghai.park.hyatt.com

Hotel stays don't get much higher than this—or more deluxe. China's highest hotel occupies the 79th–93rd floors of the skyline-dominating Shanghai World Financial Centre. Floor-to-ceiling windows in each room optimize

the jaw-dropping views. The suite-style rooms are subdivided with separate bedroom, closet, bathroom, and entrance hall and are minimally designed with superior in-room technology. The Water's Edge Spa sits on the 85th floor, and the ultimate high is at **100 Century Avenue**, a restaurant and lounge spanning the 91st–93rd floors.

🛈 174 🅿 🔁 🚾
🔁 🏊 📺 🍸 All major cards

🏨 RITZ-CARLTON
🍴 SHANGHAI, PUDONG
$$$$

SHANGHAI IFC TOWER,
8 CENTURY AVENUE
TEL 2020-1888
FAX 2020-1889
E-MAIL rc.shasz.leads@ritzcarlton.com
www.ritzcarlton.com

Shanghai's second Ritz-Carlton occupies the upper floors of Cesar Pelli's Shanghai IFC Tower. The rooms and public areas are designed in updated art deco style with floor-to-ceiling windows offering superb panoramas of Shanghai's cityscape. High-tech features include touchpad room controls and automatic sensors that detect when you are sleeping or absent and adjust the lighting and temperature. The 58th-floor **Flair** restaurant and bar (see below) is a glamorous terrace bar, and the ESPA spa perches on level 53.

🛈 285 🅿 🚇 Lujiazui 🔁 🚾
🔁 🏊 📺 🍸 All major cards

RESTAURANTS

SOMETHING SPECIAL

🍴 FLAIR
$$$$

58/F THE RITZ-CARLTON
8 CENTURY AVENUE

TEL 2020-1778
Extending into the air from the 58th floor of the Ritz-Carlton Shanghai, Pudong, this upscale restaurant and bar features a stepped terrace, so it is not for vertigo sufferers. The unforgettable views are served with pan-Asian tapas plates, such as Singaporean chili crab claws and pan-fried Shanghai dumplings, and cocktails. It's not cheap, but very popular, so reserve ahead.

🚇 Lujiazui 🍸 All major cards

🍴 JADE MANSION
$$$$

4/F IFC MALL,
8 CENTURY AVENUE
TEL 5012-7728

www.jade388.com
Upscale sibling to Shanghai's popular Jade Garden restaurant chain. Aimed at the city's affluent dining class, this elaborately overdesigned restaurant specializes in traditional Huaiyang cuisine, which hails from neighboring Jiangsu Province. Expect fine regional Chinese dining, with a heavy bias toward seafood, served at premium Shanghai prices.
🚇 Lujiazui 🅢
🅢 All major cards

🍴 BAKER & SPICE
$$
LG1-16 IFC MALL,
8 CENTURY AVENUE
TEL 5015-2375
www.bakerandspice.com.cn
Part of a small foreign-owned chain of gourmet bread stores that also serve excellent croissants, pastries, paninis, salads, and fresh-brewed coffee in a spacious café offering free Wi-Fi. Popular with Pudong's pre-work breakfast and quick-bite lunch crowd.
🚇 Lujiazui 🅢
🅢 All major cards

■ NORTH SHANGHAI

HOTELS

🏨 HYATT ON THE BUND
$$$
199 HUANGPU ROAD
TEL 6393-1234
FAX 6393-1313
E-MAIL shanghai.bund@hyatt.com
www.shanghai.bund.hyatt.com
This twin-towered hotel sits on the North Bund, adjacent to the new cruise terminal, with excellent room views over the Huangpu River flanked by the Bund and Pudong. Excellent dining options include Xindalu, a

swish contemporary eaterie serving traditional roasted Peking duck. The popular Vue Bar features an alfresco cocktail terrace on the 33rd floor.
ⓘ 631 🅟 🚇 Tiantong Road
🖨 🅢 🅢 🚿 🏋
🅢 All major cards

🏨 INTERCONTINENTAL SHANGHAI
$$
500 HENGFENG ROAD
TEL 5253-9999
FAX 5253-9998
E-MAIL puxi@interconti.com
www.ichotelsgroup.com
Located a stone's throw from the main Shanghai Railway Station in the Zhabei District. Targeting mostly business, convention, and meetings travelers, this large hotel offers smart facilities, including restaurants and bars, a fitness center, and an indoor pool. The executive club floors and lounge yield fine skyline views.
ⓘ 533 🅟 🚇 Shanghai Railway Station 🖨 🅢 🅢 🚿 🏋
🅢 All major cards

RESTAURANTS

SOMETHING SPECIAL

🍴 XINDALU
$$$
EXT 6318, HYATT ON THE BUND,
199 HUANGPU ROAD
TEL 6393-1234
As its name suggests, Peking duck is widely regarded as a dish best served in the Chinese capital. Patrons of Xindalu may agree, while arguing it's the next best option. This smartly designed restaurant is built around a traditional wood-fired roaster imported from Beijing, with the ducks sourced from the best farms in north China. The result is Shanghai's most

flavorful purveyor of Beijing's favorite roasted meat dish.
🚇 Taiantong Road 🅢
🅢 All major cards

🍴 OLD FILM CAFÉ
$
123 DUOLUN ROAD
TEL 5696-4753
Coffee, tea, and light meals served amid a decor of old movies, iconic images, and statues of Chinese and Western film idols.
ⓘ 40 🅢 Cash only

■ WEST SHANGHAI

HOTELS

🏨 FOUR SEASONS HOTEL (SHANGHAI SIJI JIUDIAN)
$$$$$
500 WEIHAI ROAD
TEL 6256-8888
FAX 6256-5678
www.fourseasons.com
No attempts at futurism here, just classic elegance. A fountain and palm trees in the lobby, offset by marble and rich wood paneling, it's a world away from nearby busy Nanjing West Road. Staff is welcoming but discreet and the rooms spacious and classic. A jazz club enlivens things on the top floor, and the Cantonese restaurant is one of the best in town.
ⓘ 439 🅟 🚇 West Nanjing Road No. 1 🖨 🅢 🅢 🚿 🏋
🅢 All major cards

🏨 PORTMAN RITZ-CARLTON (SHANGHAI BOTEMAN LIJIA DAJIUDIAN)
$$$$$
1376 NANJING WEST ROAD
TEL 6279-8888

FAX 6279-8800
www.ritzcarlton.com
Located in the Shanghai
Center and surrounded by
excellent restaurants and
shopping venues, the Port-
man Ritz-Carlton is restrained
in its elegance and, mainly
because of the service, consistently wins independent
hotel survey accolades. The
health club includes squash
courts, an indoor-outdoor
swimming pool, and covers
three floors of the 50-story
hotel. The restaurants and
bars attract both locals
and expats.
🛏 564 🅿 🚇 Jingan Temple
🛗 🚫 🚭 🚃 🛁 🛎
💳 All major cards

🏨 HILTON SHANGHAI HOTEL (JINGAN XIERDUN FANDIAN)
$$$$
250 HUASHAN ROAD
TEL 6248-0000
FAX 6248-3848
www.hilton.com
This 43-story hotel was
Shanghai's first foreign-owned
hotel. Recent renovations
have brought it back to its
original high standard. The
location is excellent, within
walking distance of Hengshan
Road and the French Con-
cession. A health spa and six
fine restaurants make it a
worthy choice.
🛏 700 🅿 🚇 Jingan Temple
🛗 🚫 🚭 🛁 🛎
💳 All major cards

🏨 J.W. MARRIOTT
🍴 $$$$
TOMORROW SQUARE
399 NANJING WEST ROAD
TEL 5359-4969
FAX 6375-5988
www.marriott.com
The hotel, which opened in
2003, rises above one of the
city's best locations, People's

Park, and occupies the top 24
floors of the giant 60-story
Tomorrow Square tower. The
facilities are excellent and
include hydraulic massage
showers in the well-appointed
bathrooms, squash courts, a
deluxe Mandara spa, a number of fine restaurants, and
the world's highest library.
🛏 342 🅿 🚇 People's Square
🛗 🚫 🚭 🚃 🛁 🛎
💳 All major cards

🏨 MANSION HOTEL
$$$
82 XINLE ROAD
TEL 5403-9888
FAX 5403-7077
E-MAIL info@chinamansion
hotel.com
www.chinamansionhotel.com
Exuding history, this 1920s
building was once the den of
a notorious Shanghai gangster
and is now repurposed as
a 1920s-themed boutique
hotel. The lobby sets the
tone with a superb collection
of historic Shanghai photos,
artifacts, and artworks. The
spacious, classically decorated
rooms feature stone terraces
overlooking the courtyard,
and the top-floor terrace
bar and restaurant affords
unobstructed views of the city
skyline.
🛏 30 🍴 🅿 🚇 Changshu
Road 🛗 🚫 🚭 🚃 🛁 🛎
💳 V, MC

🏨 PARK HOTEL (GUOJI FANDIAN)
$$$
170 NANJING WEST ROAD
TEL 6327-5225
FAX 6327-6958
E-MAIL parkhtl@parkhotel
.com.cn
www.parkhotelshanghai.cn
A historic hotel overlooking People's Square. When
it was built in 1934, it was
the tallest building in Asia.
The Chinese government
now recognizes the hotel as

an official cultural relic and
as the official geographic
center of Shanghai. Art deco
architecture sets the tone. The
Park is one of the old guard—
not the most sophisticated of
hotels, but very distinguished.
Includes Chinese and Western
restaurants, a hotel museum,
and shopping arcade.
🛏 250 🚇 People's Square
🛗 🚫 🚭 🛁 💳 All major cards

SOMETHING SPECIAL

🏨 THE PULI HOTEL & SPA
$$$
1 CHANGDE ROAD
TEL 3203-9999
FAX 3251-8989
E-MAIL information@thepuli
.com
www.thepuli.com
Characterized by an eye-
catching fusion of Southeast
Asian and Chinese design
styles, this hip downtown ho-
tel features a sleek Anantara
spa and Jing An restaurant,
which serves highly inventive
comfort food. All rooms
are decorated with Asian
artworks and Chinese period
furnishings and offer a free
mobile phone. Located adja-
cent to fashionable Nanjing
West Road, it is popular with
both business and leisure
travelers.
🛏 193 🅿 🚇 Jingan Temple
🛗 🚫 🚭 🛁 🛎
💳 All major cards

🏨 RENAISSANCE ZHONGSHAN PARK
$$
1018 CHANGING ROAD
TEL 6115-8888
FAX 6115-8999
www.marriott.com
A soaring, 31-floor hotel in
the rapidly emerging business
and leisure district around
Zhongshan Park. Located
above the metro station, it
offers easy access to both

---

downtown and Hongqiao Airport. Designed in upbeat colors and styling, it offers two restaurants, a wine bar, tea lounge, and juice bar. Rooms feature all the necessary in-room requirements for its predominantly business traveler clientele.

🛈 665 🍴 🅿 🚈 Zhongshan Park 🚭 🄢 🄢 🏊 🏋 🎽
🄢 All major cards

RESTAURANTS

SOMETHING SPECIAL

🍴 FU 1088
$$$$
375 ZHENNING ROAD
TEL 5239-7878
Classic Shanghai chic rules throughout this heritage mansion formerly owned by a powerful general. The numerous dining rooms are decorated with period antiques, and the timeless ambience provides a suitable backdrop for the refined Shanghainese cooking. Menu favorites such as red-braised pork belly, drunken chicken marinated in Shaoxing rice wine, and sautéed river shrimps are eagerly devoured by the city's affluent set. Reserve in advance.
🚇 112 🚈 Jiangsu Road
🄢 No cards

🍴 SHINTORI NULL II (XINDULI WUER DIAN)
$$$$
803 JULU ROAD
TEL 5404-5252
Some find it incredibly cool, others just plain cold, but no one leaves this postmodern Japanese restaurant without strong impressions. After you pass through the tunnel-like entryway, translucent doors sweep open to admit you. The decor is stark, as in chrome and polished con-

crete; the main dining area is like a sunken pool; and the presentation includes sashimi on polished stone platters and cold noodles served in bowls of solid ice. The mezzanine tables are more intimate. Opinions vary on the scene, but no one can fault the food. Reservations are required.
🚇 130 🚈 Changshu Road
🄢 🄢 🄢 All major cards

🍴 BARBAROSSA
$$$
231 NANJING XILU
TEL 6318-0220
This North African–themed pleasure dome mixes restaurant, club, and sheesha bar in a three-story, domed-roof venue with an outdoor terrace in once proletarian People's Park. The Middle Eastern cuisine, such as lamb couscous and Tunisian-style tuna, are really quite good, but most diners are here for the arabesque music and the novelty of it all. Quite a scene. Reservations recommended.
🚇 300 🚈 People's Square
🄢 🄢 🄢 All major cards

🍴 1221 (YI ER ER YI)
$$–$$$
1221 YAN'AN WEST ROAD
TEL 6213-6585
Quite popular among expats and visiting businessmen, it's well known for its moderately priced and diverse Chinese cuisine served in a smart atmosphere. Standard favorites include the drunken chicken, Shanghai smoked fish, and spicy Sichuan beef. The tea you see being poured from incongruously long spouts is *babaocha* (eight treasures tea), which is flavored with dried fruits and nuts. Reserve well in advance.
🚇 120 🄢 🄢
🄢 All major cards

🍴 ELEMENT FRESH
$$
1/F SHANGHAI CENTRE, 1376 NANJING WEST ROAD
TEL 6279-8682
www.elementfresh.com
In a prime central location, this is the flagship of a small Shanghai-based chain of café-restaurants serving Asian and Western breakfasts, gourmet salads, lunch plates, desserts, juices, and smoothies. By day, the vibe is casual and relaxed, attracting a mixed clientele of locals, expats, and visitors. By evening the lights are lowered and the menu becomes a little more upscale, white tablecloths are unveiled, and the prices get more elevated.
🚈 Jingan Temple 🄢
🄢 All major cards

🍴 GOURMET CAFÉ
$$
1/F SHANGHAI CENTRE, 1376 NANJING WEST ROAD
TEL 6289 5733
www.gourmet-cafe.com
For burger cravings in Shanghai, look no further. British-owned Gourmet Café serves up a mean menu of gourmet Black Angus beef and char-grilled chicken burgers with names like Super Bad Chili Monster, Holy Guacamole, and Pollo Mejicano, and offers a plentiful selection of beers, cocktails, and smoothies. Vegetarian options are also offered. The downtown Shanghai Centre location means this smart diner is rarely empty.
🚈 Jingan Temple 🄢
🄢 All major cards

🍴 LYNN
$$
99-1 XIKANG ROAD
TEL 6247-0101
Shanghainese dining is largely restricted to unappealingly decorated cafés, but this

stylish restaurant adjacent to the Nanjing Road's Shanghai Centre bucks that trend. It serves both traditional and updated Shanghai classic dishes, such as shrimp dumplings and minced chicken with pine nuts, in a comfortable downtown locale. Book ahead for the highly popular unlimited weekend *dim sum* lunch.

🚇 West Nanjing Road
⬛ 🔌 🃏 All major cards

🍴 VEGETARIAN LIFE-STYLE

$

258 FENGXIAN ROAD
TEL 6215-7566

Shanghai's most popular vegetarian restaurant serves Chinese dishes replicating meaty counterparts using tofu, gluten, and mushroom protein, plus stir-fried noodles and rice, soups, and stews that are also free of dairy and MSG. The large menu includes veggie versions of regional favorites like spicy Sichuan *mapo doufu*, Shanghainese fried dumplings, and Hunanese peppered chicken. No alcohol is served, but all diners receive a complimentary refillable pot of Chinese tea.

🪑 112 🃏 No cards

⬛ EXCURSIONS FROM SHANGHAI

HANGZHOU

🏨 AMANFAYUN
$$$$$

22 FAYUN NONG, XIHUJIEDAO
XIHUFENGJINGMINGSHENG
TEL 0571/8732-9999
FAX 0571/8732-9900
E-MAIL amanfayun@
amanresorts.com
www.amanresorts.com
Opened in 2010, Amanfa-

yun occupies a Tang-dynasty tea village set in a mountain valley west of West Lake. It sits on a pilgrim pathway that Buddhist monks have historically followed to five nearby temples. Guests can step off the peaceful path into Zen-inspired farmhouse villas with thatched ceilings, an Aman spa, heated pool, rustic-chic Hangzhounese and vegetarian eateries, and a Chinese teahouse.

🚇 🃏 All major cards

🏨 FUCHUN RESORT
🍴 $$$$$

FUYANG SECTION, HANGFU
YANJIANG ROAD,
TEL 0571/6346-1111
FAX 0571/6346-1222
E-MAIL reservation@fuchun
resort.com
www.fuchunresort.com

Set amid tea plantations and rolling hills on the banks of Fuchun River beyond the city, Fuchun Resort is a visually stunning resort. Its magnificently meditative halls overlook a serene lake, pavilions, and an 18-hole golf course. The gourmet restaurants are beautifully designed in imperial Chinese style, the spa and swimming pool are photogenic attractions, and the large suite rooms are supremely luxurious. All this comes at a price, but as an upscale retreat it has few peers in China.

ⓘ 87 🅿 ⬛ 🔌 🃏 🏊 📺
🃏 V, MC

SOMETHING SPECIAL

🏨 FOUR SEASONS WEST
🍴 LAKE
$$$$

5 LINGYIN ROAD
TEL 0571/8829-8888
FAX 0571/8829-2298
www.fourseasons.com/
hangzhou

Hangzhou's stateliest five-star hotel is set beside the city's primary attraction, West Lake. The elegant suites and villas, many of which feature private terraces, are set amid Chinese gardens, with rockeries, ponds, and a walled courtyard—and all offer private butler service. The Chinese restaurant boasts individually themed dining pavilions with lanterns, period furnishing, and latticed wood paneling overlooking the gardens, while the deluxe day spa—decorated with imperial grandeur—must be seen to be believed.

ⓘ 73 🅿 ⬛ 🔌 🃏 🏊 📺
🃏 All major cards

HYATT REGENCY HANGZHOU (HANGZHOU KAIYUE JIUDIAN)

$$$$

28 HU BIN LU
TEL 0571/8779-1234
FAX 0571/8779-1818
E-MAIL hangzhou.regency@
hyatt.com
www.hangzhou.regency
.hyatt.com

Fronting West Lake, the newer Hyatt Regency is part of an upmarket residential complex with a shopping mall conveniently attached. The rooms were recently refurbished and the period-style **28 Hubin Road** serves excellent local Hangzhounese cuisine.

🛏 390 🅿 🔄 🚭 🅰 ☀ 🏥
🏨 All major cards

J.W. MARRIOTT

$$$

28 HUSHU SOUTH ROAD
TEL: 0571/8578-8888
FAX: 0571/8578-6999
www.marriott.co.uk

One of Hangzhou's leading business hotels, this is located in the heart of the city. Guest room designs are rather lacking a sense of place, but all are well equipped for business travelers, clean, and modern. Four restaurants include **Man Ho** for Cantonese fare and **CRU Steakhouse**, which serves up the best cuts of beefsteak in the city.

🛏 293 🅿 🔄 🚭 🅰 ☀ 🏥
🏨 V, MC

XIHU STATE GUEST HOTEL

$$$

7 XISHAN ROAD,
TEL 0571/8797-9889
FAX 0571/8797-2348
E-MAIL sales@xihusgh.com
www.xihusgh.com

Located on a 15-acre (6 ha) site on the west side of the

West Lake, the guest hotel is composed of eight buildings. Once a local millionaire's country estate, it has a 1.5-mile (2 km) stretch of lakefront and has been the favored retreat of China's political elites. It has an outdoor pool and a golf practice range. The property is managed by the local government, so don't expect facilities of an international standard, though the atmosphere compensates.

🛏 180 🅿 🔄 🚭 🅰 ☀ 🏥
🏨 All major cards

MOGANSHAN

BAIYUN HOTEL

$$$

502 MOGANSHAN
TEL 0572/803-3336 or 803-3382
FAX 0572/803-3274
www.mogan–mountain.com

Located at the top of the mountain in Hua Yang Park, this hotel has several buildings, ranging from adequately comfortable to luxurious.

🛏 80 🏥 🏨 All major cards

NAKED STABLES RESERVE

$$$

SANJIUWU, LAOLING VILLAGE
TEL 021/6431-8902
E-MAIL reservations@
nakedretreats.cn
www.nakedretreats.cn

Devised, designed, and built by a South African–Hong Kong married couple, this eco-friendly mountainside retreat is an hour's drive from Hangzhou. The luxurious treetop villas with deck balconies are nestled in a pine forest surrounded by tea plantations, bamboo glades, and a lake. Guests can saddle up one of the resort's own horses or rent a bike for an adventure ride through mountain trails. Less active visitors may prefer a dip in one of the infinity pools or

a relaxing spa treatment.

🛏 121 🅿 🔄 🚭 🅰 ☀ 🏥
🏨 🏨 V, MC

SOMETHING SPECIAL

LE PASSAGE MOHKAN SHAN

$$$

ZILING VILLAGE
TEL 0572/8052-958
E-MAIL reservations@
lepassagemoganshan.com
www.lepassagemoganshan
.com

An elegant French-owned country house retreat set in a picturesque valley surrounded by mountains, organic tea fields, and bamboo plantations. Guest rooms are individually designed in both classically chic and contemporary loft-style layouts, with distinctive French styling and period and modern furnishings. The restaurant serves home-style French cooking embellished by locally grown seasonal produce and boasts a cellar stocked with wines by boutique winemakers.

🛏 40 🅿 🚭 🅰 🏨 V,MC

PUTUOSHAN

PUTUOSHAN HOTEL

$

93 MEICEN LU
TEL 0580/609-2828

Near Puxi Temple and the harbor, the hotel is relatively modern and clean but not of the highest international standards.

🛏 150 🅿 🚭 🏥
🏨 All major cards

SUZHOU

HOTEL SOUL

$$$$$

27 QIAOSIKONG ALLEY,
PINGJIANG, SUZHOU
TEL 0512/6777-0777

🚭 Nonsmoking 🅰 Air-conditioning 🏊 Indoor Pool 🏊 Outdoor Pool 🏥 Health Club 🏨 Credit Cards

www.hotelsoul.com.cn
This small but stylish boutique hotel nestles at the center of the ancient, canal-laced city. The **Brasserie 101** restaurant offers French gourmet cuisine, and the 4th-floor roof garden is an oasis of calm with soothing water features. Guests are offered half-day excursions to the Suzhou Gardens (see p. 272) in summer, with guided tours of three of the gardens and a picnic lunch.

🛈 225 🅿 🛗 🌐 🛎
🅰 All major cards

🏨 PAN PACIFIC SUZHOU (SUZHOU WUGONG XI-LAIDENG DAJIUDIAN)
$$$$
388 XIN SHI LU
TEL 0512/6510-3388
FAX 0512/6510-0888
E-MAIL sheraton.suzhou@ starwoodhotels.com
www2.panpacific.com/ suzhou/overview
Located north of the Panmen scenic area, the Sheraton Suzhou is the best hotel in town, deftly embracing the local architectural vernacular with its upturned eaves, waterway bridges, and gorgeous gardens.

🛈 407 🅿 🛗 🌐 🛎
🅰 All major cards

🏨 PINGJIANG LODGE
🍴 $$
33 LIUJIA XIANG, PINJIANG QU
TEL 0512/6523-3888
FAX 0512/6523-3868
E-MAIL inquiry@pingjiang lodge.com
www.pjlodge.com
A small hotel located in a 450-year-old canal-side home. The ambience is pure "time-warp chic," with the rooms set across 11 courtyards, each named after Chinese landscape gardening styles, and dressed with ancient wooden beams, latticed window frames, and period

furnishings. There's a rockery garden, plus the remnants of Mao-era propagandist graffiti from the Cultural Revolution in the hallway.

🛈 52 🛗 🌐 🛎 No Cards

🏨 SUZHOU GARDEN HOTEL
$$
99 DAICHENGQIAO ROAD
TEL: 0512/6778-6778
FAX: 0512/6778-6888
E-MAIL office@gardenhotelsz .com
www.gardenhotelsz.com
Occupies a series of restored villas on a historic compound in the center of town, offering easy walking access to Suzhou's most popular landscaped gardens. Its guest list includes several ex-prime ministers and heads of state, such as U.S. President Carter. Recently refurbished, all rooms are contemporary in style with good in-room amenities. The leafy gardens, **Lotus Pavilion** restaurant serving Suzhou cuisine, and Thai-themed spa are the standout factors.

🛈 235 🅿 🛗 🌐 🛎 🚇 🛗
🅰 V, MC

NANJING

🏨 HILTON NANJING RIVERSIDE
$$
1 HUAIBIN ROAD
TEL 025/8315-8888
www.hilton.com
Opened in 2011, this hotel sits just outside the city center, offering easy access to the high-speed railway station. Its facilities and in-room amenities are targeted mainly at business travelers; it has a 24-hour fitness center and Cantonese and Huiyang restaurants.

🛈 411 🅿 🛗 🌐 🛎 🚇 🛗
🅰 All major cards

🏨 THE WESTIN NANJING
🍴 $$
201 ZHONGYANG ROAD
TEL 025/8556-8888
FAX 025/8556-9999
E-MAIL nj.reservation@ westin.com
www.starwoodhotels.com
Overlooking Xuanwu Lake, this modern hotel caters to both business and leisure travelers. The modern rooms are well equipped, offering pleasant lake and city views on the higher levels. Dining options include Cantonese and pan-Asian restaurants, and there's a spa and a fitness center to burn off the calories.

🛈 234 🅿 🛗 🌐 🌐 🚇 🛗
🅰 All major cards

HUANGSHAN

🏨 HAN YUE LOU VILLA
🍴 RESORT
$$$$$
YURUN HOLIDAY AREA, 78 YINGBIN AVENUE, TUNXI DISTRICT
TEL 0559/232-9888
FAX 0559/232-1616
www.hanyuelou.com
Located just in the mountain foothills, this deluxe all-villas resort opened in summer 2012. All 99 villas are spacious and exquisitely decorated with motifs from local Huizhou culture and offer personal butler service. **Fan Xing Lou** restaurant serves Huizhou cuisine, and there are two other Asian restaurants, a tea lounge, and the magnificent Moon Spa, which uses only organic spa products.

🛈 99 Private villas
🅿 🛗 🚇 🛎 🛗 🌐
🅰 All major cards

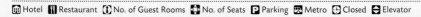

🏨 Hotel 🍴 Restaurant 🛈 No. of Guest Rooms 🛗 No. of Seats 🅿 Parking 🚇 Metro 🕐 Closed 🛗 Elevator

Beijing Shopping

Beijing is a treasure trove for shoppers. From antiques to silk, knock-offs to designers, the new economy has brought a multitude of consumer goods. The most interesting items may be found as you walk the lanes of the *hutongs* and the side streets away from other tourists. Do beware, however, that in the smaller places most shopkeepers will not be able to converse in English; prices are usually shown on calculators, and bargaining is expected.

Markets

Baoguo Temple Cultural Market (Baoguo Si Wenhua Shichang)

1 Baoguo Si,
Guang'anmennei,
Xuanwu District
Tel 010/6303-0976
Bus: Niujie/Baiguanglu Beikou
Founded in 1466 as a Buddhist complex, the Baoguo Temple is today a busy flea market, where hawkers display their goods on the ground, in bicycle carts, and in small makeshift rooms.

Panjiayuan Market (Panjiayuan Jiuhuo Shichang)

18 Huaweili,
West of Panjiayuan Bridge,
East Third Ring Road,
Chaoyang District
Tel 010/6775-2405
Bus: Panjiayuan Qiao/Jiuhuo Shichang
Open Mon.–Fri. 8:30 a.m.–6 p.m., Sat.–Sun. 4:30 a.m.–6 p.m.
Located on what looks like an abandoned building site, this is Beijing's premier flea market, with some 3,000 sellers. Here you'll find odd and interesting pieces apparently gathered from all over China. On any given day you may stumble across stone temple lions, Chinese bows, a leather Qing-dynasty saddle, or wooden grain boxes, worn smooth from generations of use.

Arcades & Malls

Dashilan Jie/Liulichang Xijie

Off Qianmen Dajie
Metro: Qianmen/Hepingmen
Connected chaotic lanes stuffed full of silk shops, herbal medicine stores, antique stores, art galleries, and an abundance of food and clothing specialists.

Oriental Plaza

1 Dongchang'an Dajie,
corner of Wangfujing Street
Metro: Wangfujing
www.orientalplaza.com
The heartbeat of Wangfujing shopping street is this vast mall connected to the metro station and just a short walk from Tiananmen Square. You'll find everything here from big name-brands, to a supermarket, ATMs, and coffee shops.

Silk Street

8 Xiushui Dongdajie
Tel 010/5169-9003
Metro: Yonganli
Floor after floor of silk, clothing, shoes, jewelry, and more. All run by garrulous vendors who love to haggle.

The Village at Sanlitun

6A Gongti Beilu
Tel 010/6417-6110
www.sanlitunvillage.com
The capital's most buzzing retail and lifestyle hub comprises a cluster of colorful buildings with more than 250 brand and local design stores, interspersed with smart restaurants, cafés, and bars.

Unique Shopping

The Bookworm (Shu Chong)

Behind Bldg. 4, Nan Sanlitun Road, Chaoyang District
Tel 010/6586-9507
Bus: Sanlitun
Open 9 a.m.–2 a.m.
Offering free Wi-Fi and plenty of space to work, the Bookworm is a bookstore, restaurant, and coffee shop rolled into one. It frequently hosts talks by local writers and authors passing through Beijing.

Mega Mega Vintage

241 Gulou Dongdajie,
Dongcheng District
Tel 010/8404-5637
Metro: Gulou Dajie
Popular with Beijing hipsters, this small store sells vintage fashions and street wear sourced from Korea, Japan, and Thailand.

Plastered

61 Nanluogu Xiang,
Dongcheng District
Tel 010/6407 8425
www.plasteredtshirts.com.
Plastered's edgy T-shirt designs have become a street institution, taking inspiration from everyday sights and sounds in the capital, including neon signs, skyscrapers, and political propaganda.

Spin

6 Fangyuan Xilu,
Chaoyang District
Tel 010/6437-8649
Adding a quirky update to traditional Jingdezhen pottery and ceramics, this smart store sells hand-painted porcelain tableware, vases, and ornaments.

Tranquil Tuesdays

71 Fangjia Hutong,
Dongcheng District
Tel 010/6407-1938
www.tranquiltuesdays.com
Metro: Andingmen
Tucked down a small lane this socially conscious store sells premium teas sourced from family-owned estates across China, plus hand-painted porcelain tea sets.

Beijing Entertainment

Even before the Olympics were granted to Beijing, the city was developing as the hottest art scene in Asia, and with money came international recognition. While the Beijing opera and acrobatics have been around for generations, the clubs and music scene are recent arrivals. For specific information on performances and times check out local publications, which are available free in many hotel lobbies, or visit *www.thebeijinger.com*.

Local Sources

For specific information on performances and times, plus the latest nightlife options check out *The Beijinger* and *Time Out Beijing* (both free, monthly), or *Agenda* and *City Weekend* (free, every two weeks), which can be picked up in hotel lobbies, bars, and cafés. Online options are *www.agenda beijing.com* and *www.thebeijinger .com*. Art Beijing *(www.artbeijing .net)* publishes a useful bimonthly Beijing art guide.

Art Galleries

Affordable Art Beijing

6 Babaokeng Hutong, Dongsi, Dongcheng District
Tel 010/6407-5314
www.affordableartchina.com
Hosted each May, the Affordable Art fair is one of Beijing's most popular art festivals, offering hundreds of works by emerging Chinese artists at value prices. AAB also sells art online and via its *hutong* base, and expanded to Shanghai in fall 2012.

Faurschou Gallery

2 Jiuxianqiao Lu, 798 Art District, Chaoyang District
Tel 010/5978-9316
www.faurschou.com
Sibling gallery to the Copenhagen original, it exhibits modern works by leading artists from Munch to Picasso, plus contemporary works from Europe, Asia, and the U.S.

Galerie Paris-Beijing

3 Qianyongkang Alley 5, Beixin-qiao Santiao, Dongcheng District

Tel 010/6401-8782
www.galerieparisbeijing.com
Owned by two French curators, and with a sister gallery in Paris, Beijing's best photographic gallery presents modern documentary showcases about changing urban and natural environments. The gallery store sells several superb photo books compiled from its exhibitions.

National Art Museum of China

1 Wusi Dajie, Dongcheng District
Tel 010/6400-6326
www.namoc.org
This vast state-owned museum in a cavernous building claims to own more than 100,000 Chinese artworks from throughout the dynasties, as well as modern and contemporary pieces. It also hosts some occasionally interesting large-scale international art exhibitions, such as a 2012 show on European constructivism.

Pace Gallery

2 Jiuxianqiao Lu, 798 Art District, Chaoyang District
Tel 010/5978-9781
www.pacebeijing.com
Established in 2008, and with galleries also in New York and London, Pace Gallery Beijing promotes the works of Chinese and Asian contemporary artists, and promotes its artists at international festivals and biennales.

Pekin Fine Arts

241 Art District,
Caochangdi Art District,
Caochangdi Village

Tel 010/5127-3220
www.pekinfinearts.com
Established by Beijing-based art collector and critic Meg Maggio in 2005, this 6458-square-foot (600 sq m) gallery in Caochangdi Art Village promotes innovative contemporary Asians working in a variety of art mediums, including painting, photography, installation, and video.

Redgate Gallery

Levels 1 & 4, Dongbianmen Watchtower Dongcheng District
Tel 010/6525-1005
www.redgategallery.com
Boasting a superb central location in the Dongbianmen Watchtower that formed part of the ancient city walls, Redgate Gallery is one of China's longest serving and most acclaimed galleries promoting Chinese contemporary artists.

ShangHart Gallery

261 Caochangdi Art District, Caochangdi Village
Tel 010/6432-3202
www.shanghartgallery.com
Established in Shanghai in 1996. One of the nation's most reputable galleries, promoting Chinese contemporary art in all its guises, it has opened this cool exhibition space in a gray-brick modern *hutong*-style building at Caochangdi.

Ullens Center for Contemporary Art

4 Jiuxianqiao Lu, 798 Art District, Chaoyang District
Tel 010/5780-0200

www.ucca.org.cn
Founded in 2007 by art collectors Guy and Myriam Ullens, this vast space occupies three 1950s factory buildings. It hosts cutting-edge exhibitions from leading Chinese and international artists, plus workshops and art events.

White Box Museum of Art
2 Jiuxianqiao Lu, 798 Art District, Chaoyang District
Tel 010/5978-4800
www.798whitebox.com
This impressive 8,610-square-foot (800 sq m) art space promotes works by leading Chinese contemporary artists, incorporating paintings, installation, video, and urban works. There is also an art store, café, and monthly art discussions and talks.

Theater & Opera
Beijing Concert Theater
1 Bei Xinhua Jie,
Liubukou
Tel 010/6605-7006
Metro: Xidan
Bus: Baijiazhuang
www.bjconcerthall.cn
Situated west of Tiananmen Square, this large concert hall and art gallery was built in 1985. This 1,000-seat arena hosts recitals and orchestral concerts by local and international performers.

Chang'an Grand Theater
(Chang'an Daxiyuan)
7 Jianguomen Neidajie,
Dongcheng District
Tel 010/6510-1310
Metro: Jianguomen
This modern and comfortable opera theater stages colorful performances of Beijing opera, with English subtitles appearing to the side of the stage.

Chaoyang Theater
(Chaoyang Juchang)
36 Dongsanhuan Beilu,
Chaoyang District
Tel 010/6507-2421
Metro: Hujialou
The Chaoyang Theater features traditional Chinese acrobatics and magic shows. There are two shows every night: 5:15 p.m. & 7:15 p.m.).

Concert Hall of Central Conservatory of Music
43 Baojia Jie,
Xicheng District
Tel 010/6641-4759
www.concerthall.ccom.edu.cn
Recently given a major uplift, this concert hall was reputedly the birthplace of Ding-dynasty emperor Kuang-hsu. China's finest musicians, including Liu Shikun, Xue Wei, Yuan Chenye, and Lang Lang, have performed here, as well as globally renowned musicians such as Yehudi Menuhin, Luciano Pavarotti, and Yo-Yo Ma. The Conservatory also hosts orchestras such as the Berlin Philharmonic Orchestra and the French National Symphony Orchestra.

Forbidden City Concert Hall
Xi Chang'anjie,
Inside Zhonghshan Park,
Dongcheng District
Tel 010/6559-8285
www.fcchbj.com (Chinese only)
Located in Zhongshan Park just west of the Forbidden City, this concert hall hosts an eclectic year-round program of orchestral and chamber performers, ranging from Salzburg's Mozarteum Orchestra and the Stuttgart Chamber Orchestra to the China Philharmonic Orchestra.

Imperial Granary Theater
22 Dongsishitiao
Tel 010/6409-6477
Metro: Dongsi Shitiao

www.imperialgranary.com.cn
Located in the restored 600-year-old stone-brick imperial granary, which was built in the same year as construction began on the Forbidden City, this arts and cultural center hosts regular Kunqu opera performances and Chinese musical concerts.

Lao She Teahouse
(Lao She Chaguan)
3 Qianmen Xi Dajie,
West of Qianmen
(South side of street)
Tel 010/6303-6830
Metro: Qianmen
This teahouse stages mini-performances of opera, martial arts, acrobatics, and comedy. Performances are held every day at 2:30 p.m. and 7:40 p.m. The hall is named after the late Lao She, one of China's most popular contemporary authors, who often wrote about Beijing.

National Center for the Performing Arts
2 Xichangan Dajie,
Xicheng District
Tel 010/6655-0989
Metro: Tiananmen West
www.chncpa.org
Housed in the controversial "glass egg" domed building just behind the Great Hall of the People, and designed by French architect Paul Andreu, this is one of Beijing's premier performance venues. It hosts year-round theater, dance, opera, and classical music concerts.

The Red Theatre
(Hong Juchang)
44 Xingfu Dajie,
Chongwen District
Tel 010/6710-3671
Metro: Tiantandongmen
The "Legend of Kung Fu" tells the story of a young boy and his dream of becoming a martial

arts master. Rather than dialogue, this spectacular show uses a combination of martial arts, acrobatics, and dance. Supertext in English is projected about the stage; it will help you follow the plot. Daily shows at 5:15 p.m. and 7:30 p.m.

Tianqiao Acrobatic Theatre (Tianqiao Zaji Juchang)

95 Tianqiao Shichang Road,
East end of Beiwei Road,
Xuanwu District
Tel 010/6303-7449
Metro: Hepingman
More than a hundred years old, this small theater gives the audience a chance to watch the acrobatics up close. Shows begin at 7:15 p.m. every day.

Bars & Night Clubs

Beijing is barging into the 21st century, and the bustling music scene—hip-hop, jazz, R&B, house, and techno—is just a small indication of the dramatic changes taking place. Sample the new China at one of the many bars and clubs opening up all over the city.

For the latest news about happenings on the Beijing bar and club scene, visit **Beijing Boyce** (www.beijingboyce.com), a blog written by one of Beijing's most knowledgeable bar hounds.

Apothecary

3/F, Nali Patio,
81 Sanlitun Nanlu,
Chaoyang District
New Orleans native Chef Max Levy has created something unique in Beijing—a signature cocktail bar that serves inventive cuisine. First to the cocktails—which showcase molecular mixing originality and traditional classics using house-made bitters and syrups. The Dark and Old Fashioned is already

semilegendary among Beijing's cocktail cognoscenti. Levy's Creole-inspired cooking is served until 1 a.m. on weekends, with a menu featuring dishes like dried oyster stew and panfried pork cheeks.

Atmosphere

80/F, China World Summit Wing Hotel, 1 Jianguomenwai Dajie,
Chaoyang District
Tel 010/6505-2299 ext 6432
Designed by Adam Tihany, this sleek bar peers down on the Chinese capital from the 80th floor of Beijing's highest tower. The superb 360-degree views and sleek interiors draw an affluent clientele of hotel guests and Beijing movers and shakers. Definitely a destination bar, and prices are set accordingly—but well worth visiting for the unmatched panoramas alone.

Bali Courtyard Bar

7/F, Zhongyu Plaza,
6 Gongti Bei Lu,
Chaoyang District
Tel 010/5975-2688
The skyscrapers of downtown Beijing seem a million miles from a Southeast Asian beach bar, but this hip lounge successfully re-creates a tropical poolside ambience on a Sanlitun rooftop. Comfy wicker chairs and beach-style daybeds are set around a central pool with thumping DJ music as an accompaniment. The nearest thing you'll find to a seaside nighttime vibe in China's landlocked capital.

Bed Bar (Chuang Ba)

17 Zhangwang Hutong,
Jiu Gulou Dajie,
Dongcheng District
Tel 010/8400-1554
Metro: Gulou Dajie
At the minimalist but chic Bed Bar, take your drinks lying down

on one of the Qing-style opium beds scattered around the place. The simple menu includes tapas and Asian snacks. House DJs play underground techno and house music on the weekends.

Centro

1/F Beijing Kerry Centre,
1 Guanghua Lu,
Xuanwu District
Tel 010/6561-8833 ext. 42
Metro: Guomao
Bus: Guanghua Lu
Who says hotel lobby bars are boring? Sleek and chic Centro is one the best and most polished bars in Beijing. The place is large, well designed, and comfortable, but don't plan on having a business meeting here: The live jazz music may be too loud.

Dada

206 Gulou Dong Dajia,
Dongcheng District
Tel 183/1108-0818
Opened near the Drum Tower in summer 2012, this DJ bar and club from Shanghai is one of the capital's coolest late-night hangouts. Eschewing much of the glitz and ostentation of 21st-century Beijing clubbing, Dada focuses more on developing and showcasing young, local DJ talent. Expect eclectic sets and plenty of experimental sounds, rather than global club beats.

Face

26 Dongcao Yuan,
Gongti Nanlu,
Chaoyang District
(behind Cervantes Institute)
Tel 010/6551-6788
Bus: Chaoyang Yiyuan/Shenlu Jie
A pricey but fun place for a drink before dinner, this bar

stirs up memories of author Rudyard Kipling's Asia, with Chinese, Indian, and Southeast Asian art juxtaposed with colonial furniture. Enjoy your drinks with a game of pool, or head onto the serene, intimate patio.

Fez

6/F, Nali Patio,
81 Sanlitun Bei Lu,
Chaoyang District
Tel 010/5208-6138
Imported from Hong Kong, this Mediterranean-themed rooftop bar in Sanlitun's Nali Patio is popular most evenings. This sleekly designed terrace bar is a great place to spend a warm spring or summer evening in the company of the capital's smart set. Serves a good range of cocktails and a range of Spanish tapas bites.

Glen

203 Taiyue Suites,
16 Sanlitun Nanlu
Tel 010/6591-1191
A fine collection of single malts behind the backlit counter gives the game away—this sophisticated but unstuffy lounge is based on a Japanese whiskey bar. For non whiskey-lovers, the large cocktail menu and comfy lounge sofas are more than enough reason to visit. Watching the mixologist at work is fascinating; as the ice is hand-chipped, the artist's eyes smile and the attention to detail is unerring.

Lan

4/F LG Twin Towers,
B12 Jianguomenwai
Dajie,Chaoyang District
Tel 010/5109-6012
Metro: Yong'anli
Designed by trendy French designer Philippe Starck, Beijing's hippest bar will make you feel like you've fallen down the rabbit hole. Lan offers a good selection of wines and an oyster bar, as well as DJs and live entertainment in the evenings. Try the Sichuan Mary cocktail.

Mesh

GF, Opposite House Hotel,
The Village, 11 Sanlitun Nanlu
Tel 010/6417-6688
www.theoppositehouse.com
Unapologetically a Beijing hipster's hangout, this modish lounge at the Opposite House boutique hotel is stylish in every sense. The decor features large outsized cranberry-colored sofas, blond-wood floors, and swooping meshed metal curtains hanging from the ceiling. The cocktails are well mixed and there is a good wine list. Prices are slightly high, but the atmosphere is always energetic and well-heeled.

Migas

5F Nali Patio, 81 Sanlitun Nanlu,
Choyang District
Tel 010/5208-6061
www.migasbj.com
Popular Latin-themed bar and lounge that comes alive mid-evening with live DJ sets. A lively party crowd enjoys cocktail specials and beer deals, plus tasty Spanish tapas bites. In spring and summer, the spacious rooftop deck terrace is one of the city's most popular locations. Decorated with cactus beds, and a wood-framed bar, the terrace yields spectacular views of the nighttime skyline.

Mix

Inside the Workers' Stadium,
North Gate,
Chaoyang District
Tel 010/6530-2889
Bus: Gongren Tiyuchang
If you want to mingle with Chinese bargoers, then the newly redesigned Mix—with its red glowing exterior—is the place to go. There are couches upstairs, while downstairs international DJs spin the latest hip-hop and R&B. On weekends you may have to squeeze your way onto the dance floor. The entrance fee Sunday through Thursday is 30RMB ($4.70); Friday and Saturday it's 50RMB ($7.90).

Q Bar

Top Floor, Eastern Inn Hotel,
6 Baijiazhuang Lu,
Chaoyang District
Tel 010/6595-9239
Bus: Zhongfangjie
Q Bar is especially famous for its mixed drinks, which are poured by two of Sanlitun's most experienced bartenders and said to be the best in Beijing. Try a martini or margarita. In the warmer months, relax on the rooftop patio.

Souk

West Gate of Chaoyang Park
(Opposite Kingda International Apartment),
Chaoyang District
Tel 010/6506-7309
This laid-back eatery cum bar offers inexpensive drinks as well as Mediterranean and Middle Eastern snacks. On Fridays enjoy cool acoustic sets by local bands.

Stone Boat Café

Southeast corner of Ritan Park,
Tel 010/6501-9986
Bus: Ritan Lu
Once a teahouse, this Qing-dynasty stone boat has been reincarnated as a lakefront bar and café. Sit under the shade of the trees and contemplate the world. On weekends enjoy an interesting range of live music, including blues, jazz, R&B, and exotic Chinese folk.

The Writer's Bar

GF, Raffles Beijing,
33 Donghang'an Dajie,
Dongcheng District
Tel 010/6526-3388
www.raffles.com/beijing
Sumptuous, classically styled
bar that pays homage to
literary culture. The walls are
adorned with photos of local
and global literary guests, plus
heads of state who have stayed
at the vast Beijing hotel in
which Raffles occupies a wing.
Leather sofas and patterned
rugs bestow a "drawing room"
atmosphere, and the Beijing
Sling cocktail references the
hotel's Singapore sibling, where
the famous drink was first
mixed.

Zajia

Jiugulou Dajie,
Hongen Daoist Temple,
23 Doufuchi Hutong,
Dongcheng District
Tucked away in a *hutong* lane
behind the Drum Tower, this
small split-level bar has bags
of atmosphere. It's the kind of
unpretentious bar that suits
Beijing's backstreets perfectly—
with a homely feel enhanced by
bench seats, wooden armchairs,
and potted plants. Drinks are
reasonably priced and the
welcome is always friendly.

Spas

Chi Spa

5F Shangri-La Hotel Beijing,
29 Zizhuyuan Lu,
Haidian District
Tel 010/6841-2211 ext 6748
www.shangri-la.com
Recently revamped, this is now
one of Beijing's chicest spas.
Warmly decorated with dark
wooden lattices and fragrant
candles, the relaxing ambience
is immediate. A large spa menu
ranges from hot-stone body
and detoxifying lymphatic
massages to body wraps and
scrubs to water therapies and
facials. The Signature Journeys
combine a range of deluxe
treatments.

Dragonfly

60 Donghuamen Jie,
Dongcheng District
Tel 010/6527-9368
www.dragonfly.net.cn
Located near the Forbidden
City, this is the most elegant
of the Shanghai-based spa
brand's three Beijing branches.
It offers Chinese, Japanese, and
Oriental massage treatments,
plus facials, waxing, and a nail
spa in becalming private suites
with Zen-infused Asian water
features, candles, lamps, and
music.

The Peninsula Spa

8 Goldfish Lane,
Wangfujing
Tel 010/6510-6090
www.peninsula.com
The indulgent design in dark,
warm tones is almost theatrical,
with hanging birdcages, carved
wooden tables, cushioned
banquettes, and latticed paneling. Half-day and full-day spa
journeys feature deluxe pam-
pering to the max, and there's
also a special men's spa menu.
For ultimate hot-cold body
invigoration, the crystal steam
room and ice fountain shower
is as good as it gets.

Ritz-Carlton Spa

Ritz-Carlton Beijing,
83A Jianguo Lu,
China Central Place,
Chaoyang District
Tel 010/5908-8888
Truly luxurious in every aspect,
the ten treatment rooms
include a couple's suite, an aqua
therapy room, a Vichy shower,
and six single rooms with private
balconies. Balinese and Chinese
massages are the standout offerings of a large spa menu, which
also features foot reflexology
and Sabai stone massage. The
naturally lit swimming pool with
lounge beds and crème marble
etching is stunning.

Tian Spa, Park Hyatt Beijing

2 Jianguomenwai Dajie,
Chaoyang District
Tel 010/8567-1234
www.beijing.park.hyatt.com
The Park Hyatt's super-deluxe
spa offers wellness treatments
based on tian chi, the balance of
yin and yang that is at the core
of Traditional Chinese Medicine.
Signature therapies include a
four-hand massage, green tea
and cucumber body renewal, a
jade stone harmony facial, and
Tian pedicure. Specially created
spa packages are also available
for men, women, and couples.

Shanghai Shopping

Shanghai is quite simply shopping crazy. Increasing affluence and a penchant for style means central malls and stores are pulsing from 10 a.m. to 10 p.m. seven days per week. The main shopping areas include Nanjing Road and Huaihai Road in Puxi and Lujiazui in Pudong. For local design boutiques and handicrafts, try Taikang Road's appealingly narrow *shikumen* lanes.

Markets

Dongtai Road Antiques Market

Off Xizang Road,
Luwan District
Metro: South Huangpi Road
Little you see in the dozens of stalls and small shops here is truly antique, but many interesting curios such as Mao era memorabilia, recently produced propaganda posters, ceramics, snuff bottles, and other small handicraft items are on offer.

South Bund Fabric Market

(Nan Waitan Qing Fang Mianliao Shichang)
399 Lujiabang Lu,
Dongjiadu District
Metro: Nanpudajiao
Called the Dongjiadu Fabric Market until it was moved indoors and to a new location in 2006, taxi drivers still use the old name, but know the new location, which is in the southeastern section of the old city (Nanshi). The major attractions here are the tailors who work from some of the shops. Bring a favorite item of clothing, chose a fabric from the huge selection available, and return in a week to pick up your new garment.

Arcades & Malls

Hong Kong Plaza

283 Huaihai Road
Tel 2327-8888
Metro: South Huangpi Road
In the heart of fashionable Huaihai Road, this eye-catching mall received a major revamp in 2010, and now features stores such as Gap, Apple, Coach and Tissot, plus some good dining options.

Plaza 66

1266 Nanjing West Road,
Huangpu District
Metro: West Nanjing Road
The most upmarket of Nanjing Lu's shopping malls. Tasteful displays, not crowded, and some excellent restaurants.

Shanghai ifc

8 Century Avenue, Pudong
Tel 6311-5588
Metro: Lujiazui
Pudong's glitziest plaza features a host of big-name flagship stores, such as, Apple, Gucci, Prada, Cartier, and Tiffany, plus Shanghai's best range of in-mall dining.

Tianzifang

Lane 200 Taikang Road
Metro: Dapuqiao
Shanghai's favorite hunting ground for handicrafts and local designer wares is Tianzifang, a labyrinth of alleys filled with jewelry, silk clothing, and accessories boutiques and cafés in former *shikumen* (stone-gated) homes. Although often crowded with tourists, it's an atmospheric alternative to Shanghai's mega malls.

Unique Shopping

Jooi Design

International Artist Factory,
Lane 210 Taikang Road
Tel 6473-6193
A Danish designer interprets Chinese traditional designs. Strong on accessories such as silk handbags and scarves.

Shanghai Museum Art Store

201 People's Avenue
Metro: People's Square
Part of the Shanghai Museum, the shop sells art books, cards, and prints too elegant to be called souvenirs. Also available are high-quality (and expensive) reproductions of the ceramic pieces found in the museum.

Shanghai Tang

North Block Xintiandi,
Lane 181 Taicang Raod
Tel 6384-1601
Metro: South Huangpi Road
Tel 5466-3006
Originally from Hong Kong, this citadel of chic is famous for its modern interpretations of the Chinese classics, *qipaos* for the ladies and jackets for men. Pricey.

Song Fang Maison de Thé

227 Yongjia Road
Tel 6433-8283
Created by a French former luxury brands executive with a penchant for *cha*, this lovely tea shop and teahouse sells an impressive selection of tea leaves from across China, which are packaged with 1950s-style Shanghai motifs.

Suzhou Cobblers

17 Fuzhou Road
Tel 6321-7087
Owned by local shoe designer Huang Mengqi, this tiny store sells colorful hand-stitched Chinese silk slippers, shoes, hats, and bags with patterns inspired by the glamour of 1930s Shanghai.

Shanghai Entertainment

Shanghai's entertainment scene is the most sophisticated, varied, and vibrant in China. After more than 40 years of repression, Shanghai's dining and nightlife scene underwent a renaissance from the late 1990s onward, and it refuses to look back. The people of Shanghai revel in their self-appointed status as the nation's arbiters of cool; and there are plenty of expats to help them ramp up the hip factor—as their numbers and their influence on the clubbing, music, and bar scene grow. The city has its fair share of theaters, opera houses, and cinemas as well as dance halls, clubs, and a very lively bar scene, notably around Xintiandi, Sinan Road, Fuxing Road, and Yongfu Road.

Local Sources

For specific information on performances and times, plus the latest nightlife options, check out *That's Shanghai* and *Time Out Shanghai* (both free, monthly) and *City Weekend* (free, every two weeks), which can be picked up in bars and cafés. Online options include www.thatsmags.com, www.timeoutshanghai.com, www.cityweekend.com.cn, www.smartsshanghai.com, and www.shanghaiist.com. For arts and culture events and listings, visit www.creativehunt.com and the free art map downloadable at www.shanghai-detour.org.

Theater & Opera

With several impressive venues, Shanghai's performing arts scene is truly of an international standard. Tickets are available in advance from the venue's box office, or through your hotel concierge. Avoid dealing with scalpers outside the venue; you're likely to be cheated.

Shanghai Concert Hall

523 Yan'an East Road
Tel 5386-6666
Metro: People's Square
This impressive neoclassical building from the 1930s hosts classical performances, from both local and foreign musicians.

Shanghai Grand Theatre

300 Renmin Avenue
Tel 6386-8686
Metro: People's Square

This is Shanghai's premier venue for Western opera, ballet, and Broadway musicals. In addition to visiting classical orchestras, it is the home of the Shanghai Philharmonic. Chinese opera performances round out the bill.

Shanghai Oriental Art Centre (Shanghai Dongfang Yishu Zhongxin)

425 Dingxiang Road
Tel 6854-1234
Metro: Shanghai Science and Technology Museum
Located in Pudong, this architecturally spectacular hall, shaped like a blooming lotus flower, with a steel-and-glass exterior mellowed by wooden interiors with superb acoustics in all its three halls, hosts major foreign troupes.

Opera Houses

Shanghai Centre Theatre

Shanghai Centre
1376 Nanjing West Road
Tel 6279-8948
Metro: Jingan Temple
A good alternative to Chinese opera is an acrobatic performance, and the Shanghai troupes are the best in China. Nightly performances feature tightrope walking, plate balancing, human pyramids, and magicians.

Yifu Theatre

701 Fuzhou Road,
People's Square
Tel 6322-5075
Metro: People's Square

Chinese opera is definitely an acquired taste. Needless to say, the plot will escape those who are not fluent in the language of archaic Chinese, and the music, using stringed instruments and gongs, can seem cacophonous. Still the costumes are beautiful and the acrobatic element needs no translation. The Yifu Theatre is Shanghai's top venue for the local version, *kunhu*, which is easier on the ear since it uses woodwind instruments.

Museums

Art Labor

Building 4, 570 Yongjia Road
Tel 3460-5331
www.artlaborgallery.com
A rare downtown location for a leading art gallery increases the appeal of this boundary-pushing contemporary art venue. Art Labor occupies a small former French Concession villa with unique movable walls and lighting. Its exhibitions feature both Chinese and international artists.

China Art Museum

China Pavilion,
World Expo Site
Tel 6327-2829
Open 9 a.m.–5 p.m.
Regularly changing exhibitions featuring Chinese and international artists, in both contemporary and classical styles.

Duolun Museum of Modern Art

27 Duolun Road,
Hongkou District
Tel 6587-2530
www.duolunmoma.org
Open Tues.–Sun.
10 a.m.–6 p.m.
Metro: East Baoxing Road
Publicly funded, noncommercial
museum, offering innovative and
genre-pushing displays of modern
Chinese art.

Eastlink

5/F, Building 6, 50 Moganshan
Road, M50 Art District
Tel 6276-9932
www.eastlinkgallery.cn
Established in 1999, this is one of
Shanghai's pioneering contemporary art galleries. It champions the
work of upcoming experimental
artists, many of whom have
become stars of the Chinese art
world. The 9,685-square-foot
(900 sq m) space presents some
of M50's most innovative and
eye-catching art.

Jewish Refugees Museum

62 Changyang Road,
Hongkou District
Tel 6327-9900
www.shanghaijews.org.cn
Open Mon.–Fri. 9 a.m.–11:30
a.m. & 1 p.m.–4 p.m.
Metro: East Baoxing Road
A museum dedicated to those
who lived in Shanghai's wartime
Jewish ghetto, which incorpo-
rated the renovated Ohel
Moshe Synagogue.

Lu Xun Museum

2288 Sichuan North Road,
Hongkou Park,
Hongkou District
Tel 6540-4378
Open 9 a.m.–4 p.m.
Metro: East Baoxing Road
Commemorates the leading
figure of Chinese modern

literature. Letters, photographs,
and period furniture.

Museum of Contemporary Art/MOCA

231 Nanjing West Road,
People's Park,
Huangpu District
Tel 6327-9900
www.mocashanghai.org
Open 10 a.m.–6 p.m.
(until 10 p.m. Wed.)
Metro: People's Square
Beautiful building in the heart
of the People's Park, displaying
an eclectic selection of Chinese,
Asian, and international
contemporary art.

Museum of the First Chinese Communist Party Congress

76 Xingye Road,
Luwan District
Tel 5382-2171
Open 9 a.m.–5 p.m.
Metro: South Huangpi Road
Located in a French villa on the
site where the future leaders of
China first met.

Propaganda Poster Art Center

868 Huashan Road,
Basement Level, Building B,
Changning District
Tel 6211-1845
Open 10 a.m.–3 p.m.
Huge collection of official govern-
ment propoganda posters and
artworks from the Mao era.
Both an exhibition and art gallery;
select pieces are for sale.

Shanghai Glass Museum

685 West Changning Road,
Baoshan District
Tel 6618-1970
www.shmog.org
Located in a converted glass fac-
tory in northern Baoshan District.
This fascinating museum charts
a path using interactive exhibits

and video screens through the
history of glass in both East and
West, journeying from ancient
Egypt and Middle Ages Europe to
China's space program. There's
also a superb collection of glass
art and sculpture from around the
world on the third floor.

Shanghai Museum

201 Renmin Avenue,
People's Square,
Huangpu District
Tel 6372-5300
www.shanghaimuseum.net
Open Sun.–Fri. 9 a.m.–5 p.m.
Metro: People's Square
Excellent display of Chinese
archaeological artifacts and art
encompassing 50 centuries.
Many consider this the best
museum in China.

Shanghai Science and Technology Museum (Shanghai Keji Guan)

2000 Century Avenue,
Pudong District
Tel 6862-2000
www.sstm.org.cn
Open Tues.–Sun. 9 a.m.–5 p.m.
Metro: Shanghai Science and
Technology Museum
With interactive robotics, a
simulated rain forest, and an
iWerks theater, this museum
brings science to life for the
young. World class, it is crowded
on weekends, and filled with
school excursions on most
weekday mornings.

Studio Rouge

Building 7, 50 Moganshan Road,
M50 Art District
Tel 5252-7856
www.studiorouge.cn
Highly acclaimed photographic
and contemporary art gallery
that expanded from its original
Bund location to M50 in 2006.
Its shows are among the most
engaging and visually accessible

in Shanghai for both collectors and casual observers, and often feature leading names from the Chinese art circuit.

Vanguard Gallery
Building 4, 50 Moganshan Road, M50 Art District
Tel 5252-2551
www.vanguardgallery.com
Focuses on the new works of emerging Asian artists who work across a variety of genres, including painting, installation, sculpture, video, printmaking, photography, and animation. It has also put its money where its mouth is by funding promising new artists with limited resources and presenting its artists' works at various exhibitions in China and overseas.

Nightlife
Shanghai's bar scene has something for everyone, from big band jazz to trance clubs, with a good middle ground of tasteful and comfortable venues catering to expats. Bars are supposed to close at 2 a.m., but the wilder carry on until dawn. Male travelers should be aware that some of the ladies they meet out on the town could be practicing the world's oldest profession.

Live Music
Cotton Club
1416 Huaihia Road, Xuhui District
Tel 6437-7110
www.cottonclub.cn
Metro: Changshu Road
A Shanghai institution, this is more relaxed than deluxe and has a good combination of jazz and blues, usually performed by the house musicians. Busy on weekends, with a mixed crowd of foreigners and Chinese.

House of Blues and Jazz
60 Fuzhou Road
Tel 6323-2779
www.houseofbluesandjazz.com
Metro: East Nanjing Road
Moved from the French Concession to a block back from the Bund, this oldtime favorite still keeps the beat. It's got an art deco atmosphere and a mixture of international jazz, soul, and blues bands.

Bars & Pubs
The Alchemist
Block 32, Sinan Mansions, 45 Sinan Road,
Old French Concession
Tel 6426-0660
www.alchemistbar.cn
Metro: South Shanxi Road
Smart cocktail bar and gastro-lounge at the revivalist Sinan Mansions nightlife district of adapted 1930s town houses. The molecular cocktails go down a storm, such as Yangtze River Tea, a sorbet-like concoction of Chinese *baijiu*, tequila, Captain Morgan, and citrus served alongside a demitasse of spiced jasmine tea. Menu selections include beetroot carpaccio, fiery prawns with chili and chorizo, and hot seared foie gras.

The Apartment
3/F, 47 Yongfu Road, Xuhui
Tel 6437-9478
www.theapartment-shanghai.com
Metro: Changshu Road
This casual-cool cocktail lounge and restaurant in a converted warehouse building features a spacious rooftop terrace that fills out most nights in spring and summer. Inside, the lounge offers comfy couches and leather chairs, while the lively 302 room offers nightly live DJ sets and a dance floor targeted to Shanghai's hipster crowd.

Bar Rouge
Bund 18, 7th Floor, Huangpu District
Tel 6339-1199
Metro: East Nanjing Road
A glamorous place for Shanghai's superchic to see and be seen. Great views, a cool terrace, inspired cocktail menu, and after 10 p.m., dancing.

Big Bamboo
132 Nanyang Road, Jingan
Tel 6256-2265
www.bigbamboo.asia
Metro: Jingan Temple
Shanghai's liveliest North American–style sports bar enjoys a propitious central location just behind the Ritz-Carlton Hotel on fashionable Nanjing Road. Two large floors feature numerous large screens and TVs showing live and recorded sports, and there are a couple of pool tables and dartboards on each level. Several tap and bottled beers are served, plus a large menu of hearty bar meals.

Cotton's
132 Anting Road, Old French Concession
Tel 6433-7995
www.cottons-shanghai.com
Metro: Hengshan Road
Owned and managed by convivial local entrepreneur Cotton Ding, this casual, unpretentious bar in an old French Concession villa is always popular. The cozy rooms and fireplaces over two floors are a great winter respite from the cold, but Cotton's really comes alive during warmer weather when the plant-filled garden terrace is packed every evening.

DR Bar

15 North Block
Xintiandi District
Tel 6311-0358
Metro: South Huangpi Road
A sleek and elegant martini bar
in trendy Xintiandi. Champagne
is also a favorite of the chic
clientele. The marble walls, black
furniture, and silver bar create a
sense of calm, enhanced by the
elegantly clad staff.

Dr Wine

177 Fumin Road, Jingan
Tel 5403-5717
Metro: Jingan Temple
Classy but friendly wine bar and
bistro split over two levels of a
converted town house. Owned by
a French wine importer, it serves
a good list of red and white wines
from global vineyards, with regular chalkboard specials, plus tapas
and meat and cheese platters.
This place is particularly popular
with downtown Shanghai's after-
work crowd.

The Long Bar

GF, Waldorf-Astoria Shanghai
on the Bund, 2 The Bund,
Huangpu
Tel 6322-9988
www.waldorfastoriashanghai.com
Metro: East Nanjing Road
In 1930s Shanghai, the Long Bar
was the city's most exclusive
private gentlemen's club.
Reopened in 2011 after being
carefully re-created using archival
photographs, this wood-paneled
lounge is again at the center of
Shanghai society—though now it
is open to all comers. It features
a replica of the original 110-foot
(34 m) bar counter plus an oyster
bar and nightly lounge music. It
serves fine wines, spirits, whiskies,
and Cuban cigars.

O'Malley's

42 Taojiang Road, Xuhui
Tel 6474-4533

Metro: Changshu Road
A Shanghai expat institution,
with smooth leather booths and
memorabilia on the wall, and, of
course, the obligatory draught
Guinness stout. Evenings feature
Irish music and major sporting
events on large screen. In summer, enjoy a beer on the terrace.

Sasha's

11 Dongping Road, Xuhui
Tel 6474-6628
www.sashas-shanghai.com
Metro: Changshu Road
Occupying a grand mansion once
home to the venerated Soong
family, Sasha's ranks among
Shanghai's most famous bars. The
huge terrace garden is a mainstay
of summer evening drinkers and
weekend brunch diners, while
regular nightly promotions, such
as buckets of mussels and Belgian
beer on Thursdays, keep the
strong regular clientele interested.
Sasha's serves excellent wood-
fired pizzas, too.

Spas

Anantara Spa

3F, Puli Hotel and Spa,
1 Changde Road, Jingan
Tel 3203-9999
www.thepuli.com
Metro: Jingan Temple
Resident at the superchic Puli
urban resort in central Jingan
District, Anantara Spa offers
five treatment suites that blend
Chinese, Indian, and Thai design
influences and healing therapies.
Signature treatments are inspired
by the naturally detoxifying and
healing properties of Chinese tea,
including a hydrating green tea
body wrap and a rose tea beau-
tification package designed to
restore your skin's natural luster.

Banyan Tree

Westin Hotel, 3rd Floor,
88 Henan Middle Road, Huangpu
Tel 6335-1888

Metro: East Nanjing Road
Among Shanghai's most luxurious
spas. In addition to massage, it
offers facials and body scrubs in
an atmosphere of ancient Asian
opulence. Prices? Don't ask.

CHI, The Spa

Pudong Shangri-La Hotel,
6th Floor, Tower 2,
33 Fucheng Road,
Pudong District
Tel 6882-8888 ext. 460
Metro: Lujiazui
The Tibetan motif carries into
the therapies themselves, which
include a scrub with *tsampa*, the
Tibetan staple made from roasted
barley. Facials, body wraps, and
healing hot-stone massages offer
a Shanghai indulgence in an
atmosphere of serenity.

Dragonfly

206 Xinle Road,
Luwan District
Tel 5403-9982
Metro: South Shanxi Road
This is the main location,
although there are now 11 Drag-
onfly branches in Shanghai. A
relaxing Zen atmosphere, with
a simple but comprehensive
treatment menu.

The Peninsula Spa

The Peninsula Shangai
32 The Bund, Huangpu
Tel 327-6599
www.peninsula.com
Treatments at what is the Bund's
most deluxe spa are inspired
by Oriental, European, and
Ayurvedic healing traditions and
are offered in spacious private
suites suitable for singles or
couples. Spa guests enjoy free
use of a private sauna, crystal
steam room, and ice fountain
shower for extra invigoration, and
the marble-edged skylit indoor
swimming pool opens onto a
spacious terrace serving Naturally
Peninsula spa cuisine.

Language Guide

Useful Words & Phrases

Hello   *nihao*
Goodbye   *zaijian*
Thank you   *xiexie*
Pardon me   *dui bu qi*
I   *wo*
We, us   *women*
You (sing.)   *ni*
You (plur.)   *nimen*
He, she   *ta*
Them, they   *tamen*
My name is...   *wo jiao...*
What is your name?   *ni gui xing?*
I want...   *wo yao...*
Do you have...?   *ni you mei you...?*
I do not have...   *wo mei you...*
I understand   *wo mingbai*
I don't understand   *wo bu mingbai*
No problem   *mei wenti*
I am American   *wo shi meiguoren*
I am English   *wo shi yingguoren*
I am Australian   *wo shi aodaliyaren*
America   *meiguo*
England   *yingguo*
Australia   *aodaliya*
Canada   *jianada*
New Zealand   *xinxilan*
China   *zhongguo*
France   *faguo*
Germany   *deguo*
Toilet   *cesuo*
Where is...?   *zai nar...?*
Where is the toilet?   *cesuo zai nar?*
How much is...?   *duoshao qian...?*
Water   *shui*
How much is the beer?   *pijiu duoshao qian?*
Too expensive   *tai gui le*
Vegetables   *cai*
Fruit   *shuiguo*
Money   *qian*
I don't like...   *wo bu xihuan...*

Numbers

one   *yi*
two   *er*
two (when followed by a noun)   *liang*
three   *san*
four   *si*
five   *wu*
six   *liu*
seven   *qi*
eight   *ba*
nine   *jiu*
ten   *shi*
11   *shiyi*
20   *ershi*
21   *ershiyi*
30   *sanshi*
100   *yi bai*
200   *liang bai*
1,000   *yi qian*
10,000   *yi wan*
1,000,000   *yi bai wan*
0   *ling*

Restaurant

Beef   *niurou*
Beer   *pijiu*
Chicken   *jirou*
Chopsticks   *kuaizi*
Coffee   *kafei*
Dumplings   *jiaozi*
Fork   *chazi*
Knife   *daozi*
Lamb   *yangrou*
Menu   *caipu/caidan*
Plate   *panzi*
Pork   *zhurou*
Tea   *cha*
Tofu   *doufu*
Waitress   *xiaojie*
Water   *shui*
Wine   *putaojiu*
I am vegetarian   *wo chisu*
Warm/hot   *re*
Cold   *leng*
The bill, please   *qing jiezhang/ mai dan*

Hotel

Do you have any rooms?   *you mei you kong fangjian?*
Bed   *chuangwei*
Check out   *tuifang*
Deluxe room   *haohuafang*
Double room   *shuangrenfang*
Passport   *huzhao*
Reception   *zongfuwutai*
Standard room   *biaozhunfang*
Toilet paper   *weishengzhi*

Time

Today   *jintian*
Tomorrow   *mingtian*
Yesterday   *zuotian*
What time is it?   *ji dian zhong?*

Getting Around

Airplane   *feiji*
Airport   *jichang*
Bicycle   *zixingche*
Boarding pass   *dengjika*
Bus   *gonggong qiche/bashi*
Car   *qiche*
Map   *ditu*
Medium-size bus   *zhongba*
Small bus   *xiaoba*
Subway   *ditie*
Taxi   *chuzu qiche*
Ticket   *piao*
Train   *huoche*
I want to go to...   *wo xiang qu...*
How far is it?   *duo yuan?*
Give me a receipt, OK?   *gei wo yi ge shoutiao, hao bu hao?*

Emergency

Ambulance   *jiuhuche*
Antibiotics   *kangjunsu*
Doctor   *yisheng*
Fire!   *zhao huo le!*
Help!   *jiuming a!*
Hospital   *yiyuan*
Police   *jingcha*
Public Security Bureau (PSB)   *gonganju*
I feel ill   *wo bu shufu*

Directions

North   *bei*
South   *nan*
East   *dong*
West   *xi*
Left   *zuo*
Right   *you*
Inside   *limian*
Outside   *waimian*

Post Office

Envelope   *xinfeng*
Letter   *xin*
Post office   *youju*
Telephone   *dianhua*

Sightseeing

Avenue   *dadao*
Lake   *hu*
Main street   *dajie*
Mountain   *shan*
River   *he, jiang*
Road   *lu*
Street   *jie*
Temple   *simiao/si/guan*

Menu Reader

Beijing (Peking), North, & Northeastern Dishes in Beijing & the North

Beijing duck	*Beijing kaoya*
Braised fish in soy sauce	*hongshao yu*
Braised spare ribs in soy sauce	*hongshao paigu*
Drunken crab	*zuixie*
Drunken shrimps	*zuixia*
Dumplings	*shuijiao*
Egg and tomato soup	*xihongshi jidan tang*
Hot pot	*huoguo*
Steamed crab	*qingzheng pangxie*
Stewed pork with rice noodles	*zhurou dun fentiao*
Stewed ribs with potatoes	*paigu dun tudou*

Shanghai/Eastern Chinese Dishes in Shanghai, Jiangsu, & Zhejiang Provinces

Beggar's chicken	*fugui ji*
Cold spiced beef	*xuxiang niurou*
Drunken pigeon with wine sauce	*zuixiang ruge*
Fried crab with salty egg	*xiandan chaoxie*
Quick-fried freshwater shrimps	*qingchao xiaren*
Shanghai crab in wine	*zuixie*
Shanghai dumplings	*xiaolongbao*
Smoked fresh yellow fish	*xun xinxian huangyu*

Cantonese/Chaozhou Dishes in Hong Kong, Macau, & the South (Cantonese in parentheses)

Barbecued pork buns	*cha shao bao (cha siu bao)*
Deep-fried shrimp	*suzha fengwei xia*
Fried dumplings	*guo tie (wok tit)*
Pork and shrimp dumplings	*shao mai (siu mai)*
Rice-flour rolls w/shrimp or pork	*chang fen (cheung fan)*
Shrimp dumplings	*xia jiao (ha gau)*
Spare ribs	*paigu (paigwat)*
Spring rolls	*chun juan (chun guen)*
Barbecued pork	*chashao (chasiu)*
Deep-fried stuffed chicken wings	*cuipi niang jiyi*
Roast crispy pigeon with soy sauce	*shengchou huang cuipi ruge*
Shark's fin soup	*dayuchi tang (daiyuchee tong)*
Steamed crab	*zhengxie (jinghai)*

Sichuan Dishes in Chengdu & Chongqing

Chicken with chili	*lazi jiding*
Eggplant in hot fish sauce	*yuxiang qiezi*
Fish and cabbage in spicy soup	*suancai yu*
Hot-and-sour soup	*suanla tang*
Mapo tofu (tofu with pork in spicy sauce)	*mapo doufu*
Meat strips in hot fish sauce	*yuxiang rousi*
Pork slices in chili	*shuizhu roupian*
Spicy noodles	*dandan mian*

Beijing Subway

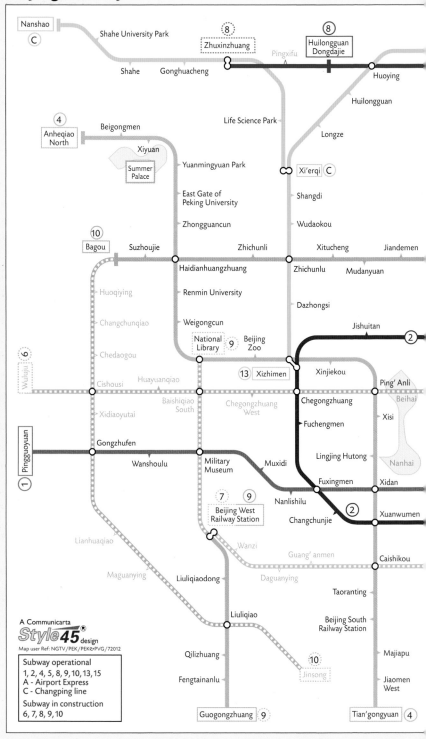

Nanshao
C

Shahe University Park
Shahe   Gonghuacheng

8
Zhuxinzhuang
Pingxifu

8
Huilongguan Dongdajie
Huoying

Huilongguan

4
Anheqiao North
Beigongmen
Xiyuan
Summer Palace
Yuanmingyuan Park
East Gate of Peking University
Zhongguancun

Life Science Park
Longze

Xi'erqi C
Shangdi
Wudaokou

10
Bagou
Suzhoujie
Zhichunli
Xitucheng   Jiandemen
Zhichunlu   Mudanyuan

Huoqiying
Changchunqiao
Chedaogou
Cishousi
6
Wuluju

Haidianhuangzhuang
Renmin University
Weigongcun
National Library   9   Beijing Zoo

Dazhongsi

Jishuitan

2

13   Xizhimen
Xinjiekou
Ping' Anli
Beihai

Huayuanqiao
Baishiqiao South
Chegongzhuang West
Chegongzhuang
Fuchengmen
Xisi

Nanhai

1
Pingguoyuan
Xidiaoyutai
Gongzhufen
Wanshoulu
Military Museum
Muxidi
Lingjing Hutong
Fuxingmen
Xidan

7   9
Beijing West Railway Station
Nanlishilu
Changchunjie
2
Xuanwumen

Lianhuaqiao
Wanzi
Guang' anmen
Caishikou

Maguanying
Liuliqiaodong
Daguanying

Taoranting

Liuliqiao
Beijing South Railway Station

A Communicarta
Style 45 ® design
Map user Ref: NGTV/PEK/PEK&PVG/72012

Subway operational
1, 2, 4, 5, 8, 9, 10, 13, 15
A - Airport Express
C - Changping line
Subway in construction
6, 7, 8, 9, 10

Qilizhuang

Fengtainanlu

10
Jinsong

Majiapu

Jiaomen West

Guogongzhuang   9

Tian'gongyuan   4

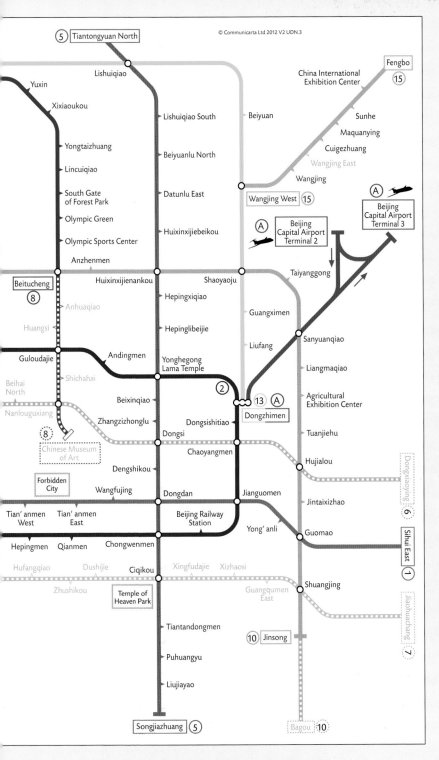

© Communicarta Ltd 2012 V2 UDN.3

5 Tiantongyuan North

Lishuiqiao

Yuxin

Xixiaoukou

Yongtaizhuang

Lincuiqiao

South Gate of Forest Park

Olympic Green

Olympic Sports Center

Anzhenmen

Beitucheng 8

Huixinxijienankou

Anhuaqiao

Huangsi

Guloudajie

Beihai North

Shichahai

Nanlouguxiang

8

Chinese Museum of Art

Forbidden City

Wangfujing

Tian'anmen West

Tian'anmen East

Hepingmen

Qianmen

Hufangqiao

Zhushikou

Dushijie

Lishuiqiao South

Beiyuanlu North

Datunlu East

Huixinxijiebeikou

Hepingxiqiao

Hepinglibeijie

Andingmen

Yonghegong Lama Temple

2

Beixinqiao

Zhangzizhonglu

Dongsi

Dengshikou

Dongdan

Beijing Railway Station

Chongwenmen

Ciqikou

Temple of Heaven Park

Tiantandongmen

Puhuangyu

Liujiayao

Songjiazhuang 5

Beiyuan

Shaoyaoju

Guangximen

Liufang

Dongsishitiao

Chaoyangmen

Jianguomen

Yong'anli

Xingfudajie

Xizhaosi

Guangqumen East

Bagou 10

China International Exhibition Center

Sunhe

Maquanying

Cuigezhuang

Wangjing East

Wangjing

Wangjing West 15

A

Beijing Capital Airport Terminal 2

Taiyanggong

Sanyuanqiao

Liangmaqiao

Agricultural Exhibition Center

13 A

Dongzhimen

Tuanjiehu

Hujialou

Jintaixizhao

Guomao

Shuangjing

10 Jinsong

Fengbo 15

A

Beijing Capital Airport Terminal 3

Dongxiaoying 6

Sihui East 1

Jiaohuachang 7

Shanghai Metro

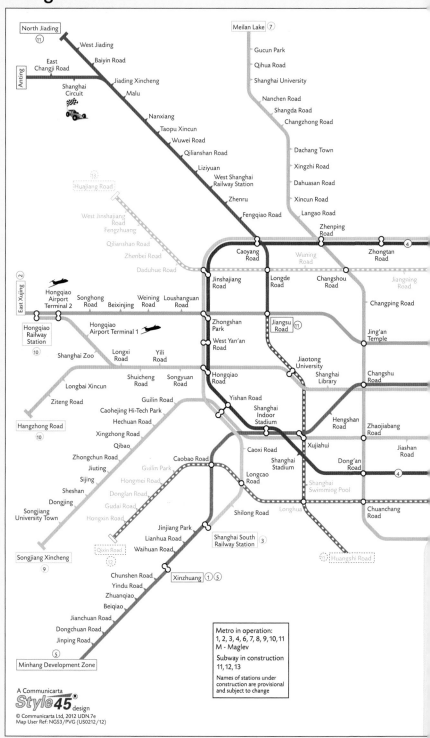

North Jiading ⑪
West Jiading
Baiyin Road
East Changji Road
Anting
Jiading Xincheng
Shanghai Circuit
Malu
Nanxiang
Taopu Xincun
Wuwei Road
Qilianshan Road
Liziyuan
West Shanghai Railway Station
Zhenru
Fengqiao Road

Meilan Lake ⑦
Gucun Park
Qihua Road
Shanghai University
Nanchen Road
Shangda Road
Changzhong Road
Dachang Town
Xingzhi Road
Dahuasan Road
Xincun Road
Langao Road
Zhenping Road
Zhongtan Road

Huajiang Road ③
West Jinshajiang Road
Fengzhuang
Qilianshan Road
Zhenbei Road
Daduhue Road

Caoyang Road
Longde Road
Changshou Road
Wuning Road
④
Jiangning Road

East Xujing ②
Hongqiao Airport Terminal 2
Songhong Road
Beixinjing
Weining Road
Loushanguan Road
Jinshajiang Road
Changping Road

Hongqiao Railway Station ⑩
Hongqiao Airport Terminal 1
Hongqiao Park
Zhongshan Park
West Yan'an Road
Jiangsu Road ⑪
Jing'an Temple

Shanghai Zoo
Longxi Road
Yili Road
Hongqiao Road
Jiaotong University
Shanghai Library
Changshu Road

Longbai Xincun
Shuicheng Road
Songyuan Road
Yishan Road
Shanghai Indoor Stadium
Hengshan Road
Zhaojiabang Road

Ziteng Road
Guilin Road
Caoxi Road
Xujiahui
Jiashan Road

Hangzhong Road ⑩
Caohejing Hi-Tech Park
Hechuan Road
Xingzhong Road
Qibao
Zhongchun Road
Jiuting
Caobao Road
Longcao Road
Shanghai Stadium
Dong'an Road
④

Sijing
Guilin Park
Hongmei Road
Shanghai Swimming Pool

Sheshan
Dongjian Road
Gudai Road
Shilong Road
Longhua
Chuanchang Road

Dongjing
Songjiang University Town
Hongxin Road
Jinjiang Park

Lianhua Road
Shanghai South Railway Station ③
Huangshi Road ⑪

Songjiang Xincheng ⑨
Qixin Road ⑫
Waihuan Road

Chunshen Road
Xinzhuang ① ⑤
Yindu Road
Zhuanqiao
Beiqiao
Jianchuan Road
Dongchuan Road
Jinping Road

Minhang Development Zone ⑤

A Communicarta
Style45® design
© Communicarta Ltd, 2012 UDN.7e
Map User Ref: NGS3/PVG (US0212/12)

Metro in operation:
1, 2, 3, 4, 6, 7, 8, 9, 10, 11
M - Maglev
Subway in construction
11, 12, 13
Names of stations under construction are provisional and subject to change

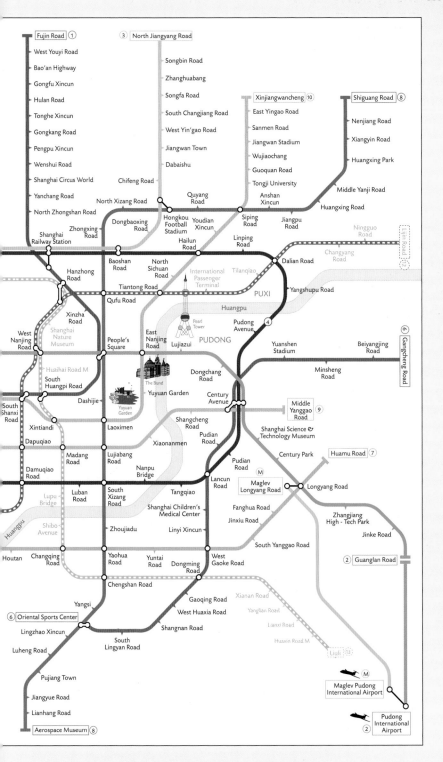

INDEX

Bold page numbers indicate illustrations.
CAPS indicates thematic categories.

A

Affordable Art Beijing 318
Ai Weiwei 47, 50
American Legation, Beijing 105
Ancient Observatory (Guanxiang Tai), Beijing 82
Anting Kite Festival 56
Architecture
    Beijing 18–20, 65
    hutongs 18–19, 74–77, 92–93, **92**, **93**
    Shanghai 20–22, 197, 256–257
    shikumen 207, 210–211, **210**, 241
Arrow Tower (Jian Lou), Beijing 72, 105
Art deco 197
Art Labor, Shanghai 324
Arthur Sackler Museum of Art and Archaeology, Beijing 134
Astor House Hotel, Shanghai 240
ATM machines 291
Automobiles 284, 286

B

Badachu 169
Badaling 148
Baiyun Temple, Shanghai 206, 209
Ballard, J. G. 45
Bamboo Museum (Zhuzi Bowuguan), Moganshan 268
Banque de l'Indochine, Beijing 105
Baochu Pagoda (Baochu Ta), Hangzhou 265
Baoguo Temple (Baoguo Si), Beijing 120, **120**, 317
Bargaining 287
Bars 320–322, 326–327
Beaches 269
Beer 27
Beggars 289
Beidaihe 154
Beihai Park (Beihai Gongyuan), Beijing 50–51, **83**, **84**, 86–87, **86**, 88
Beijing
    architecture 18–20, 65
    Chaoyang District **121**, 122–128, **124**, **126**, 300–302
    Chongwen District 96–106, **96**, **98**, **101**, **102**, **104**, 299
    Dongcheng District **17**, 18–19, **18**, **58–59**, **60**, **61**, 62–82, **62**, **64**, **66–67**, **69**, **70**, **72**, **79**, 88, 295–298

entertainment 318–322
excursions north to the Great Wall 144–156, **144**, **146**, **150–151**, **152**, **155**, 303–304
excursions south **157**, 158–173, **159**, **160**, **162**, **164**, **168**, **171**, **172**, 304–305
food and drink 24–25, 26, **27**
Haidian District **2–3**, **129**, 130–142, **133**, **134**, **140**, **166**, **167**, 302–303
history 16–20, 28–33, 36–39
hotels and restaurants 25, 73, 87, 113, 124, 295–303
shopping 111–113, **122**, 128, 317
Xicheng District **50–51**, **83**, 84–94, **84**, **86**, 298–299
Xuanwu District **52–53**, 108–109, **108**, **110**, **112**, **114**, **118**, 299–300
Beijing Ancient Coins Museum (Gudai Qianbi Zhanlan'guan) 94
Beijing Art Museum 142
Beijing Botanical Garden 141
Beijing Central Academy of Drama, Beijing 77
Beijing Concert Theater 319
Beijing Jazz Festival 57
Beijing Mumingtang Ancient Porcelain Museum (Beijing Mumingtang Guci Biaoben Bowuguan) 106
Beijing Olympic Park 127
Beijing Opera 40, 42
Beijing Planetarium (Beijing Tianwen Guan) 142
Beijing Police Museum 105
Beijing Urban Planning Exhibition Hall (Beijing Chengshi Guihua Zhanlanguan) 106, **106**
Beijing Zoo (Beijing Dongwu Yuan) **13**, 142, **142**
Beijinghua 16
Belgian Embassy, Beijing 103, 104
Bell towers 73, 78, 89
Big Bell Temple (Dazhong Si), Beijing 132
Bing Xin 43
Birthday of Confucius 54
Boya Tower, Beijing 135
Bridge of Nine Turnings (Jiu Qu Qiao), Shanghai 205
Broadway Mansions Hotel, Shanghai 240
Broadway Theatre, Shanghai 242
Bubbling Well Road, Shanghai 252
Buddhism (*fojiao*) 53, 116–117, **116**, 167
Buddhist temples (*simiao*) 167
The Bund 180–184, **180**
Bund History Museum, Shanghai 182
Bund Sightseeing Tunnel, Shanghai 231
Bus 284, 286
Business cards 289

C

Calligraphy 45–46
Cang Bao Lou market, Shanghai 206
Caochangdi Village 50
Capital Museum (Shoudu Bowuguan), Beijing 94
Cathay Theatre (Guotao Dianyingyuan) 218
Cave of the Precious Pearl (Baozhu Dong) 169
Central Plaza (Zhongqu Guangchang), Shanghai 200
Century Avenue (Shiji Dadao), Shanghai 230
Century Park (Shiji Gongyuan), Shanghai 232
Ceramics 247
Chang'an Grand Theater (Chang'an Daxiyuan), Beijing 319
Changfeng Ocean World (Changfeng Haiyang Shijie), Shanghai 254
Changfeng Park, Shanghai 254
Changle Road, Shanghai 219
Changling 153
Changning, Shanghai 254
Changzhou 275
Chaoyang District, Beijing 122–123, 128
    Beijing Olympic Park 127
    Dashanzi Art District (Dashanzi Yishu Qu) 126, **126**
    Dongyue Temple (Dongyue Miao) 125
    hotels and restaurants 300–302
    Ritan Park **121**, 124, **124**
Chaoyang Park (Chaoyang Gongyuan), Beijing 111, 128
Chaoyang Theater (Chaoyang Juchang), Beijing 319
Chen Residence, Zhouzhuang **259**
Chengde Imperial Mountain Resort 155–156, **155**
Chiang Kai-shek **33**, 36–37
China Art Museum 194, **195**, 324
China Film Museum (Zhongguo Dianying Bowuguan), Beijing 128
China Left Wing Writers Museum, Shanghai 241
China National Museum of Fine Arts, Beijing 74
China National Tea Museum, Shuangfeng 264
Chinese lions 119
Chinese New Year/Spring Festival 54, **55**, 111, 282, 285, 289
Chongling 161
Chongwen District, Beijing 96–97, **96**
    hotels and restaurants 299
    Legation Quarter 102–105, **102**, **104**
    Temple of Heaven (Tian Tan) 98–101, **98**, **101**
Christianity 53

Chun Jiang Building, Shanghai 183
CHURCHES
    Hongde Temple (Hongde Tang),
        Shanghai 241
    Mu'en Tang, Shanghai 187
    Northern Cathedral (Bei Tang),
        Beijing 88
    Notre Dame des Victoires Catholic
        Cathedral (Shengmu Desheng
        Tang or Wanghailou Jiaotang),
        Tianjin 162
    Shanghai Community Church 222
    Sheshan Cathedral (Sheshan
        Shengmu Dadian), Shanghai 255
    Southern Cathedral (Nantang),
        Beijing 120
    St. Joseph's Church (Ruose Tang),
        Shanghai 191
    St. Michael's Church, Beijing
        103, 104
    St. Nicholas Church, Shanghai 216
Cinema 51
City Hall (Shanghai Renmin Zhengfu),
    Shanghai 193
Cixi, Empress Dowager 32, 68, 78,
    136, 137, 160–161, **160**
Climate 11, 282, 285
Clothing 282, 285
Commune by the Great Wall
    (Changcheng Jiaoxia De Gongshe)
    152, **152**, 303
Concert Hall of Central Conservatory
    of Music, Beijing 319
Confucian temples (wenmiao) 166
Confucianism (rujia sixiang) 53, 80–81
Confucius 43, 80–81, **80**
Confucius Temple, Beijing 78, **81**
Confucius Temple, Jiading **249**, 258
Confucius Temple (Wen Miao),
    Shanghai **15**, 207, 209
Confucius Temple (Wen Miao),
    Suzhou 270
Confucius Temple (Wen Miao),
    Tianjin 163
Conservatory of Music (Yinyue
    Xueyuan), Shanghai 218
Coward, Noel 45
Credit cards 292
Crime 292
Cuandixia 172–173, **172**
Cultural etiquette 12
Customs 283
Customs House, Shanghai 183
Cycling 88–89, 138, 284, 286

D
Dafosi Dongjie, Beijing 74
Dajing Tower, Shanghai 206–207
Daning Green Land Park (Daning
    Lingshi Gongyuan), Shanghai 248
Dashanzi Art District (Dashanzi Yishu
    Qu), Beijing 50, 126, **126**

Dazanglonghua Temple, Beijing 88–89
Deng Xiaoping 21, 38–39
Ding Dong Ling 160–161
Dingling 153
Disabled travelers 291
Ditan Park, Beijing 82
Dong Mianhua Hutong, Beijing 77
Dongbianmen Watchtower, Beijing 106
Dongcheng District, Beijing **17**,
    62–63, **62**, 82
    Confucius Temple and Imperial
        Academy 78, **81**
    drum and bell towers 73
    Forbidden City (Zijin Cheng)
        18–19, **18**, **58–59**, 64–69, **64**,
        66–67, **69**, 88
    hotels and restaurants 295–298
    hutongs 74–77
    Imperial Granary **60**
    Lama Temple (Yonghe Gong) 79, **79**
    Tiananmen Square (Tiananmen
        Guangchang) **61**, 70–72, **70**,
        72, 88, 105
Dongjiadu Cathedral (Dongjiadu
    Tianzhutang), Shanghai 212
Dongsi Batiao, Beijing 76–77
Dongtai Road Antiques Market,
    Shanghai 212
Dongyue Temple (Dongyue Miao),
    Beijing 125
Dragon Boat Festival (Duan Wu) 54,
    56–57, 289
Driving 284, 286
Drugs 23, 288
Drum towers 73, 78, 89
Dumplings 26, **206**, 207, 258
Duobao Pagoda (Duobao Ta, or Many
    Treasures Pagoda), Putuoshan 269
Duolun Museum of Modern Art,
    Shanghai 241, 325
Duolun Road, Shanghai 241

E
Eaglewood Nunnery (Chenxiangge
    An), Shanghai 209
Eastern Qing Tombs (Qing Dongling)
    160–161
Eastlink, Shanghai 325
Eight Outer Temples (Wai Ba Miao) 156
Electricity 288
Embankment House, Shanghai 240
Emergencies 292
EXPERIENCES
    Buddhist vegetarian cuisine 167
    China's ocean life 128
    culture in the Temple 73
    cycling around and beyond Beijing
        138
    Dashanzi (798) Art District 126
    enjoy early morning tai chi 255
    exploring Shanghai's lilong lanes 257
    following the Art Deco Trail 197

    hiking the hills with Beijing
        hikers 173
    an Imperial river ride 132
    learn how to cook Chinese
        style 26
    learning Mandarin or
        Shanghainese 226
    nature's harmony in Suzhou
        Gardens 272
    ride the Shanghai ferry 232
    sipping cocktails at the Long
        Bar 181
    tea harvest 264
    temple fair tradition 111
    venturing beyond the Wall 149
    voyage in a vintage sidecar 211
    walking in the steps of history
        103

F
Fahai Temple (Fahai Si) 168, **168**
Falun Gong 71
Fang Lijun 47, 50
Fangbang Middle Road, Shanghai
    204, **204**
Fashion 48–49, **48**
Faurschou Gallery, Beijing 318
Fayu Temple (Fayu Si), Putuoshan
    269
Feilai Feng, Hangzhou 265
Feng shui 248
FESTIVALS
    Affordable Art Beijing 318
    Anting Kite Festival 56
    Beijing Jazz Festival 57
    Birthday of Confucius 54
    Chinese New Year/Spring Festival
        54, **55**, 111, 282, 285, 289
    Dragon Boat Festival (Duan Wu)
        54, **56–57**, 289
    International Art Festival 57, 126
    Lantern Festival (Yuanxiao Jie) 54
    May Day 56, 248
    Mid-Autumn Festival 54
    Midi Music Festival 56
    National Day 57, 71, 282,
        285, 289
    Temple Fairs 54, 125
    tomb-sweeping Festival of
        Qingming 54, 289
    Youth Day (Qingnian Jie)
        56–57, 289
Five Dragon Pavilions (Wulong
    Ting), Beijing 87
Flower God Temple (Ciji Si),
    Beijing 135
Food and drink 24–27, **24**, **27**, 329
    Buddhist vegetarian cuisine 167
    xiao long bao **206**, 207, 258
Forbidden City (Zijin Cheng), Beijing
    18–19, **18**, **58–59**, 64–69, **64**,
    66–67, **69**, 88

Forbidden City Concert Hall, Beijing 319
Fragrant Hills Park (Xiangshan Gongyuan), Beijing 141, **166**
French, Paul 45
French Banque de l'Indochine, Shanghai 182
French Hospital, Beijing 105
French Legation, Beijing 104
French Post Office, Beijing 103, 104, **104**
Fuxing Island 234
Fuxing Park, Shanghai 216–219, **216**, 255
Fuxue Hutong, Beijing 77

G

Galerie Paris-Beijing, Beijing 318
Gangcha Hutong, Beijing 74
Gao Xingjian 45
Garden of the Palace of Tranquil Longevity (Ningshou Gong Huayuan), Beijing 69
Garden of the Poet Bai Juyi, Songjiang 258
Gate of Earthly Tranquility (Kunning Men), Beijing 68
Gate of Heavenly Purity (Qianqing Men), Beijing 67, 68
Gate of Imperial Supremacy (Huangji Men), Beijing 69
Gate of Martial Prowess (Shenwu Men), Beijing 68, 69
Gate of Supreme Harmony (Taihe Men), Beijing 65
Glen Line Steamship Building, Shanghai 183
Golden Drum Cave (Jingu Dong), Hangzhou 265
Golf 255
Gongqing Forest Park (Gongqing Senlin Gongyuan), Shanghai 234, 248
Grand Canal (Da Yunhe) 266–267, **266**
Grand Mosque, Tianjin 163
Great Hall of the People (Renmin Dahui Tang), Beijing 72
Great Wall **14**, 144–151, **144**, **146**, **150–151**
Great Wall Museum, Badaling 148
Great Wall Museum, Shanhaiguan 154
Great World (Da Shijie), Shanghai 200
Guangdong Development Bank, Shanghai 190
Guanghua Temple, Beijing 88
Guangxu 36, 136, 137, 161
Guanxi 289
Gubei Flower and Bird Market (Gubei Hua Niao Shichang), Shanghai 253
Guo Moruo 43, 88, 241
Guozi Xue, Beijing 78
Gutzlaff Signal Tower, Shanghai 184

H

Haidian District, Beijing 130–131, 142
Big Bell Temple (Dazhong Si) 132
Fragrant Hills Park (Xiangshan Gongyuan) 141, **166**
hotels and restaurants 302–303
Military Museum of Chinese People's Revolution 140, **140**
Old Summer Palace (Yuanmingyuan) 133, **133**
Peking University 134–135, **134**
Summer Palace (Yihe Yuan) **2–3**, **129**, 136–137, **167**
Hall of Imperial Supremacy (Huangji Dian), Beijing 69
Hall of Joyful Hearts (Yuexin Dian), Beijing 86
Hall of Joyful Longevity (Leshou Tang), Beijing 69
Hall of Literary Glory (Wenhua Dian), Beijing 65
Hall of Martial Valor (Wuying Dian), Beijing 65
Hall of Mental Cultivation (Yangxin Dian), Beijing 67, 68
Hall of Middle Harmony (Zhonghe Dian), Beijing 66
Hall of Nourishing Heavenly Nature (Yangxing Dian), Beijing 69
Hall of Preserving Harmony (Baohe Dian), Beijing 66–67
Hall of Supreme Harmony (Taihe Dian), Beijing 65–66
Hall of the Heavenly Kings (Tianwang Dian), Beijing 87
Hall of the Wheel of the Law (Falun Dian), Beijing 86
Hall of True Enlightenment (Zhengjue Dian), Beijing 86
Hall of Union (Jiaotai Dian), Beijing 67
Hall of Universal Peace (Pu'an Dian), Beijing 86
Hall of Worshipping Ancestors (Fengxian Dian), Beijing 68
Hamilton House, Shanghai 190
Hangzhou 260–267, **262**, 314–315
Hangzhou Botanical Gardens (Hangzhou Zhiwuyuan) 265
Haopu Water Pavilions (Haopu Jian), Beijing 87
Headquarters of the Shanghai Communist Party (Zhonguo Gongchandang Shanghai Shiwei Yuanhui) 222
Health 289, 292
High Court, Beijing 105
Hiking 173
The Himalayas Center, Shanghai 236
History 28–39
Holidays 288–289
Hong Miao (Red Temple), Shanghai 190
Hongde Temple (Hongde Tang), Shanghai 241

Hongdu Tailors, Beijing 104–105
Hongkou 240–241
Hongkou Stadium (Hongkou Tiyuguan), Shanghai 241
Hongqiao, Shanghai 253
Hongqiao Park (Hongqiao Gongyuan), Shanghai 253
Hortensia Isle, Beijing 86–87
Hotels 294
House to Testify One's Heart (Jianxin Zhai), Beijing 141
Huagang Pa, Hangzhou 264
Huaihai Middle Road, Shanghai 218–219
Hualian Department Store, Shanghai 186
Huang Rui 51
Huanghua Cheng 149
Huangpu, Shanghai 190–191
Huangpu Park, Shanghai 182
Huangpu River 188–189, **188**, 234–235, **234**, 287
Huangpu River Ferry 232
Huangshan 279–280, **279**, 316
Huayanjing Pagoda (Huayanjing Ta), Hangzhou 263
Hui Muslims 209
Huiji Temple (Huiji Si), Putuoshan 269
Huoshan Park, Shanghai 242–243
Hutongs 18–19, 74–77, 92–93, **92**, **93**
Huxinting Teahouse, Shanghai 205
Huzhu Pagoda (Huzhu Ta), Shanghai 255

I

Imperial Academy (Guozi Jian), Beijing 78
Imperial civil service exam 78
Imperial Garden (Yuhua Yuan), Beijing 68
Imperial Granary, Beijing **60**, 82
Imperial Granary Theater, Beijing 319
Imperial Kitchen (Yushanfang), Beijing 68
Imperial Palace (Xing Gong) 169
Imperial Wall Ruins Park, Beijing 89
Incense Burner Peak (Xianglu Peak), Beijing 141
Insurance 289
International Art Festival 57, 126
International Friendship Forest, Badaling 148
Internet 288
Ishiguro, Kazuo 45
Islam (*yisilan jiao*) 53

J

Jade Buddha Temple (Yufo Si), Shanghai 245–246, **246**
Jesuit missionaries 222
Jewish Refugees Museum, Shanghai 325
Jews 242–243, 257

Jiading 258
Jiang Qing 38, 51
Jiang Rong 45
Jiao Shan 154
Jingan, Shanghai 252
Jingan Park (Jingan Gongyuan), Shanghai 252, 255
Jingan Temple (Jingan Si), Shanghai 252
Jingdezhen Ceramics Art Center, Shanghai 254
Jingshan Park, Beijing 69
Jinjiang Tower (Xin Jinjiang Dajiudian), Shanghai 219
Jinmao Tower (Jinmao Dasha), Shanghai 233, **233**, **256**
Jinshanling 149
Judaism (*youtai jiao*) 53

K

Karaoke 289
Kong Fuzi. *See* Confucius
Kunqu Opera Museum (Kunchu Bowuguan), Suzhou 270

L

Lama Temple (Yonghe Gong), Beijing **79**, **79**
Language 9, 12, 16, 23, 186, 226, 287–288, 289, 290, 328–329
Lantern Festival (Yuanxiao Jie) 54
Lao Jie (Old Street), Shanghai 206
Lao She 43–44
Lao She Memorial Hall, Beijing 82
Lao She Teahouse (Lao She Chaguan), Beijing 319
Legation Quarter, Beijing 102–105, **102**, **104**
Lei Feng Pagoda, Hangzhou 264
Li Zhisui 72
Ligong Pagoda (Ligong Ta), Hangzhou 265
Lilongs 257
Lines 289–290
Ling Ta Altar Tower, Nanjing 278
Lingyin Temple (Lingyin Si), Hangzhou 265
Literature 43–45, 57, 293
Little Western Heaven (Xiao Xi Tian), Beijing 87
Little Xinjiang, Shanghai 191
Liu Wei 50–51
Liu Xiaodong 50
Liuhe Pagoda (Liuhe Ta), Hangzhou 265
Liulichang 110–111, **110**
Local customs 289–290
Long Bar, Shanghai 181, 184
Longhua Cemetery of Martyrs (Longhua Lieshi Lingyuan), Shanghai 223
Longhua Park, Shanghai 223, **223**

Longhua Temple and Pagoda (Longhua Si and Longhua Ta), Shanghai **213**, 223
Longjing (Dragonwell) 264
Lotus Market (Hehua Shichang), Beijing 90
Lu Xun 43, 45, 240–241
Lu Xun Museum (Beijing Luxun Bowuguan), Beijing **44**, 94
Lu Xun Museum, Shanghai 325
Lu Xun Park (Lu Xun Gongyuan), Shanghai **237**, **240**, 241
Lupu Bridge (Lupu Daqiao Qiao), Shanghai 223
Luzhi 275
Lyceum Theater (Lanxin Daxiyuan), Shanghai 219

M

M50 Art Gallery District, Shanghai 51, 245
Ma Jian 45
Magazines 290
Maglev line (Shanghai Cifu Shifan Yunying Xian) 236
Mandarin 12, 16, 23, 186, 226, 290, 328–329
Mansion of Prince Gong (Gong Wang Fu), Beijing 88, 90
Mao Dun 43
Mao Zedong 37, **37**, 64, 224–225, **224**
Mao Zedong Mausoleum (Mao Zhuxi Jinian Tang), Beijing 72
Marco Polo Bridge (Lugou Qiao), Tianjin 36–37, 164, **164**
Martial arts 45
Mausoleum of Sun Quan, Nanjing 278
Mausoleum of Sun Yat-sen, Nanjing **276**, 277–278
May Day 56, 248
Media 290
Medical emergencies 292
Medicines 288
Mei Lanfang 91, **91**
Mei Lanfang Museum, Beijing 90, 91
Memorial Hall of the Nanjing Massacre (Nanjing Datusha Jinianguan), Nanjing 278
Menlou Hutong, Beijing 77
Meridian Gate (Wu Men), Beijing 65
Metropole Hotel, Shanghai 190
Metropolis Flower Market (Dadu Shixianhua Shichang), Shanghai 194
Mid-Autumn Festival 54
Midi Music Festival 56
Mid-Lake Pavilion Teahouse (Huxinting Chashi), Shanghai 205
Military Museum of Chinese People's Revolution (Zhongguo Renmin Geming Junshi Bowuguan), Beijing 140, **140**

Ming Dynasty City Wall Ruins Park (Ming Chengqiang Yizhi Gongyuan), Beijing 106
Ming Tombs (Ming Shisanling) **143**, 153
Ming Tombs (Ming Xiaoliang), Nanjing 278
Moganshan 268, **268**, 315
Moller House (Male Bieshu), Shanghai 219
Money matters 11, 290–291
Monument to the People's Heroes (Renmin Yingxiong Jinianbei), Beijing 72
Monument to the People's Heroes, Shanghai 182
Mu'en Tang, Shanghai 187
Muling 161
MUSEUMS
Art Labor, Shanghai 324
Arthur Sackler Museum of Art and Archaeology, Beijing 134
Bamboo Museum (Zhuzi Bowuguan), Moganshan 268
Beijing Ancient Coins Museum (Gudai Qianbi Zhanlan'guan) 94
Beijing Art Museum 142
Beijing Mumingtang Ancient Porcelain Museum (Beijing Mumingtang Guci Biaoben Bowuguan) 106
Beijing Police Museum 105
Bund History Museum, Shanghai 182
Capital Museum (Shoudu Bowuguan), Beijing 94
China Art Museum 194, **195**, 324
China Film Museum (Zhongguo Dianying Bowuguan), Beijing 128
China Left Wing Writers Museum, Shanghai 241
China National Museum of Fine Arts, Beijing 74
China National Tea Museum, Shuangfeng 264
Eastlink, Shanghai 325
Faurschou Gallery, Beijing 318
Galerie Paris-Beijing, Beijing 318
Great Wall Museum, Badaling 148
Great Wall Museum, Shanhaiguan 154
Jewish Refugees Museum, Shanghai 325
Kunqu Opera Museum (Kunchu Bowuguan), Suzhou 270
Lu Xun Museum (Beijing Luxun Bowuguan), Beijing 94
Lu Xun Museum, Shanghai 325
M50 Art Gallery District, Shanghai 245

Mei Lanfang Museum, Beijing 90, 91
Military Museum of Chinese People's Revolution (Zhongguo Renmin Geming Junshi Bowuguan), Beijing 140, **140**
Museum of Ancient Architecture (Gudai Jianzhu Bowuguan), Beijing 120
Museum of Contemporary Art/MOCA, Shanghai 325
Museum of Folk Art, Shanghai 212
Museum of Natural History (Ziran Bowuguan), Beijing 106
Museum of Public Art, Shanghai 191
Museum of the First Chinese Communist Party Congress, Shanghai 325
Museum of the War of Resistance Against Japan (Zhongguo Renmin Kangri Zhanzheng Jinianguan) 164
Nanjing Museum for Modern History 276
National Art Museum of China, 318
National Museum of China (Guojia Bowuguan), Beijing 71
Pace Gallery, Beijing 318–319
Pekin Fine Arts, Beijing 318
Pingtan Museum, Suzhou 270–271
Poly Art Museum, Beijing 82
Propaganda Poster Art Center (Xuanchuanhua Nianhua Yishu Zhongxin), Shanghai 226, 325
Redgate Gallery, Beijing 318
Rockbund Art Museum, Shanghai 189
Shanghai Arts & Crafts Museum 218
Shanghai Children's Museum (Shanghai Ertong Bowuguan) 253, **253**
Shanghai Discovery Children's Museum 253
Shanghai Duolun Museum of Modern Art 241
Shanghai Glass Museum 325
Shanghai Jewish Refugees Museum 243
Shanghai Municipal History Museum (Shanghai Chengshi Lishi Fazhan Chenlieguan) 230–231
Shanghai Museum **177**, 193, 196–199, **196**, 325
Shanghai Museum of Contemporary Art (MOCA) 51, 193
Shanghai Museum of Natural History **190**, 191
Shanghai Museum of Public Security (Shanghai Gong An Bowuguan) 226
Shanghai Science and Technology Museum (Shanghai Kexue Keji Bowuguan) 232, 325
ShangHart Gallery, Beijing 318

Shikumen Open House Museum (Wulixiang Shikumen Minju Chenlieguan), Shanghai 220–221
Site of the First National Congress of the Chinese Communist Party, Shanghai 221
Studio Rouge, Shanghai 325–326
Suzhou Museum (Suzhou Bowuguan) 271
Suzhou Silk Museum (Suzhou Sichou Bowuguan), Suzhou 271
Ullens Center for Contemporary Art (UCCA), Beijing 318–319
Vanguard Gallery, Shanghai 326
White Box Museum of Art, Beijing 319
Xintiandi Postal Museum, Shanghai 221
Xu Beihong Museum, Beijing 90
Music 40–43
Muslim Quarter, Beijing 115
Muslims 25, 27, 53, 191, 209
Mutianyu 148

N

Nan Luogu Xiang, Beijing 77, 82, 89
Nanjianzi Xiang, Beijing 74–75
Nanjing **177**, 276–278, **276**, 316
Nanjing East Road, Shanghai **10**, 185–187, **185**
Nanjing Museum for Modern History 276
Nanpu Bridge (Nanpu Daqiao), Shanghai 212, 234
Nanshi, Shanghai 202–203, **202**, 206–207, 212
  Fangbang Middle Road and around 204, **204**
  temples 209
  Yu Yuan Bazaar and Teahouse 205–206, **206**
  Yuyuan Gardens **20–21**, **55**, **201**, 208, **208**
Nanxiang 258
National Art Museum of China, 318
National Center for the Performing Arts, Beijing 319
National Day 57, 71, 282, 285, 289
National Museum of China (Guojia Bowuguan), Beijing 71
Natural Wild Insect Kingdom (Da Ziran Yesheng Kunchong Guan), Shanghai 231
Newspapers 290
Nightclubs 320–322, 326–327
Nine Dragon Pine 170
Nine Dragon Screen (Jiulong Bi), Beijing 68–69
No. 3 Girls Middle School, Shanghai 254

North Temple Pagoda (Bei Si Ta), Suzhou 271
Northern Cathedral (Bei Tang), Beijing 88
Notre Dame des Victoires Catholic Cathedral (Shengmu Desheng Tang or Wanghailou Jiaotang), Tianjin 162
Numbers 186

O

Ohel Moishe Synagogue, Shanghai 243
Ohel Rachel Synagogue (Youtai Jiaotong), Shanghai 252
Okura Garden Hotel (Huayuan Fandian), Shanghai 219
Old Jinjiang Hotel (Lao Jinjiang Fandian), Shanghai 219
Old Shanghai Teahouse 204
Old Summer Palace (Yuanmingyuan), Beijing 133, **133**
Opening times 291
Opera 40, **41**, 42, 319, 324
Opium 31–32, 34–35, **34–35**
Oriental Pearl TV Tower (Dongfang Mingzhu Guangbao Dianshi Ta), Shanghai **227**, 230
Ox Street Mosque, Beijing 115

P

Pace Gallery, Beijing 318
Pagoda of the Buddha's Tooth (Foya Sheli Ta) 169
Palace of Concentrated Beauty (Chuxiu Gong), Beijing 68
Palace of Earthly Tranquility (Kunning Gong), Beijing 67
Palace of Eternal Spring (Changchun Gong), Beijing 68
Palace of Heavenly Purity (Qianqing Gong), Beijing 67
Palace of Tranquil Longevity (Ningshou Gong), Beijing 68
Pandas **13**, 142, **142**
Parkson Department Store, Shanghai 218
Passports 291
Pavilion of Peace and Harmony in Old Age (Yihe Xuan), Beijing 69
Pavilion of Pleasant Sounds (Changyin Ge), Beijing 69
Pavilion of Shared Coolness (Fenliang Ge), Beijing 87
Peace Hotel, Shanghai 183
Peace Park (Heping Gongyuan), Shanghai 248
Peach Orchard Mosque (Xiaotaoyuan Qingzhen), Shanghai 207
Pekin Fine Arts, Beijing 318

Peking Man 28, 165
Peking University (PKU) 134–135, **134**
People's Court, Shanghai 190
People's Park (Renmin Gongyuan), Shanghai 193–194
People's Square (Renmin Guangchang), Shanghai 192–195, **192**
Philosophy 52–53
Pingtan Museum, Suzhou 270–271
Pogue, William 147
Polo, Marco 273
Poly Art Museum, Beijing 82
Post offices 288
Precious Stone Hill, Hangzhou 264–265
Presidential Palace (Zongtong Fu), Nanjing 276
Prince Chun's Mansion, Beijing 89, 90
Propaganda Poster Art Center (Xuanchuanhua Nianhua Yishu Zhongxin), Shanghai 226, 325
Prosperous Kingdom Guesthouse (Xingguo Binguan), Shanghai 254
Pudong, Shanghai **174–175**, **227**, 228–236, **228**, **230**, **233**, **266**, 309–311
Pudong Park (Pudong Gongyuan), Shanghai 230
Puji Temple (Puji Si), Putuoshan 269
Purple Bamboo Park (Zizhuyuan Gongyuan) 142
Purple Cloud Cave (Ziyun Dong), Hangzhou 265
Pushkin, Alexander 218
Putuo Zongcheng Temple (Putuo Zongcheng Zhi Miao) 156
Putuoshan 269, 315
Puyi 32
Puyou Temple (Puyou Si) 156

Q
Qianlong **29**, 31, 73, 79, 98, 100, 137, 155, 156, 160, 267
Qianshi Hutong, Beijing 112
Qiantang River 265
Qinci Yangdian Temple (Qinci Yangdian Si), Shanghai 236
Qing Tombs 160–161, **160**
Qingcaotang Tea Plantation, Moganshan 268
Qipao (long dress) **48**, 49
Qipu Road Market (Qipu Lu Shichang), Shanghai 244–245

R
Radio 290
Rear Lakes, Beijing 90
Red cooking (*hong shao*) 26–27
The Red Theatre (Hong Juchang), Beijing 319
Redgate Gallery, Beijing 318

Religion 52–53
Renmin Road, Shanghai 207
Rest rooms 291
Restaurants 294
Revolutionary Historical Relic Exhibition Hall (Changning Qu Geming Wenwu Chenlie Guan), Shanghai 254
Ricci, Matteo 94, 120, 267
Ritan Park, Beijing **121**, 124, **124**
River cruises 189, 287
River of Crescents (Pan Chi), Beijing 78
RMB (*yuan renminbi*) 11
Rockbund Art Museum, Shanghai 189
Round Castle (Tuancheng), Beijing 86
Ruiguang Pagoda (Ruiguang Ta), Suzhou 273
Russian Consulate, Shanghai 234

S
Safety 287
San Jiao Park (Sanjiao Gongyuan), Shanghai 200
Shanghai
    architecture 20–22, 197, 256–257
    The Bund to People's Square **10**, 178–200, **180**, **185**, **190**, **192**, **195**, **196**, 305–307
    entertainment 219, 324–327
    excursions **259**, 260–280, **262**, **268**, **270**, **272**, **274**, **276**, **279**, 314–316
    food and drink **24**, 25–27
    Fuxing Road to Huaihai Road **213**, 214–226, **216**, **218**, **220**, **223**, 307–309
    history 20–23, 30–39
    hotels and restaurants 189, 305–314
    Nanshi **201**, 202–212, **202**, **204**, **206**, **208**
    North Shanghai **237**, 238–248, **240**, **242**, **244**, **246**, 311
    Pudong **174–175**, **227**, 228–236, **228**, **230**, **233**, **266**, 309–311
    shopping 186–187, 205, 253, 323
    West Shanghai **249**, 250–258, **253**, **254**, 311–314
Shanghai Arts & Crafts Museum 218
Shanghai Center for Jewish Studies (Shanghai Youtai Yanjiu Zhongxin) 218–219, 243
Shanghai Children's Museum (Shanghai Ertong Bowuguan) 253, **253**
Shanghai Circus World (Shanghai Maxi Cheng) 248
Shanghai Club 184
Shanghai Community Church 222
Shanghai Concert Hall (Shanghai Yinyue Ting) 200
Shanghai Conservatory of Music Middle School (Shanghai Yinyue Xueyuan Zhongxueo) 222

Shanghai Discovery Children's Museum 253
Shanghai Duolun Museum of Modern Art 241, 325
Shanghai Fashion Store 186
Shanghai First Provisions Store 187
Shanghai Glass Museum 325
Shanghai Grand Theater 42, 193–194
Shanghai IFC 231
Shanghai Jewish Refugees Museum 243
Shanghai Library Bibliotheca Zikawei 222
Shanghai Mart and Intex 253
Shanghai Municipal History Museum (Shanghai Chengshi Lishi Fazhan Chenlieguan) 230–231
Shanghai Museum **177**, 193, 196–199, **196**, 325
Shanghai Museum of Contemporary Art (MOCA) 51, 193
Shanghai Museum of Natural History **190**, 191
Shanghai Museum of Public Security (Shanghai Gong An Bowuguan) 226
Shanghai No. 1 Department Store 187
Shanghai Ocean Aquarium (Shanghai Haiyang Shuizuguan) **230**, 231
Shanghai Oriental Art Center (Shanghai Dongfang Yishu Zhongxin) 236
Shanghai Post Office 240
Shanghai Pudong Development Bank 184
Shanghai Railway Station (Shanghai Huochezhan) 245
Shanghai Science and Technology Museum (Shanghai Kexue Keji Bowuguan) 232, 325
Shanghai Stock Exchange Building (Shanghai Zhengquan Jiaoyisuo) 236
Shanghai Tower 233
Shanghai Urban Planning Exhibition Center 193
Shanghai Wild Animal Park (Shanghai Yesheng Dongwuyuan) 236
Shanghai World Financial Center (Shanghai Guoji Jinrong Zhongxin) 233
Shanghai Zoo 253
Shanghainese 12, 23, 226
ShangHart Gallery, Beijing 318
Shanhaiguan 154
Shenyandao Antiques Market, Tianjin 163
Sheshan, Shanghai 255
Sheshan Cathedral (Sheshan Shengmu Dadian), Shanghai 255
Sheshan Observatory (Sheshan Tianwentai), Shanghai 255
Shidu 165
Shijin Huayuan Hutong, Beijing 74
Shikumen 207, 210–211, **210**, 241

Shikumen Open House Museum (Wulixiang Shikumen Minju Chenlieguan), Shanghai 220–221

Shimao Plaza Tower, Shanghai 195

Shui xiang (water towns) 274–275, **274**

Shuxiang Temple (Shuxiang Si) 156

Sidecars 211

Sihang Warehouse, Shanghai 245

Silk 273

Silver Ingot Bridge (Yinding Qiao), Beijing 88, 90

Simatai 149

Sinan Mansions, Shanghai 217, 219

Site of the First National Congress of the Chinese Communist Party (Zhonggong Yidahuizhi Jinianguan), Shanghai 217, **218**, 221

Sleeping Dragon Pine (Wolong Song) 170

Small Oceans Island (Xiaoying Zhou), Hangzhou 263–264

Smedley, Agnes 217

Smoking 290

Snow, Edgar 135

Songjiang 258

Soong Qing-ling 89, 90, 253

Soong Qing-ling Exhibition Hall, Shanghai 253

Soong Qing-ling Mausoleum (Soong Qing-ling Ling-yuan), Shanghai 253

Source of Law Temple (Fayuan Si), Beijing **52–53**, **108**, 114, **114**

South Bund Fabric Market (Nanwaitan Mianliao Shichang), Shanghai 212

South Seas Guanyin (Nanhai Guanyin), Putuoshan 269

Southern Cathedral (Nantang), Beijing 120

Spas 322, 327

Spectacles Lake (Yanjing Hu), Beijing 141

Spirit Way (Shen Dao or Ling Dao) 153

Spitting 290

Square Pagoda, Songjiang 258

St. Joseph's Church (Ruose Tang), Shanghai 191

St. Michael's Church, Beijing 103, 104

St. Nicholas Church, Shanghai 216

Staring 290

Strange Stone Corner (Guai Shi Jiao), Moganshan 268

Studio of Quieting the Mind (Jingxin Zhai), Beijing 87

Studio of the Painted House, Beijing 87

Studio Rouge, Shanghai 325–326

Su Tong 45

Subway 8–9, 194, 284, 286–287, 330–331, 332–333

Summer Palace (Yihe Yuan), Beijing **2–3**, **129**, 136–137, **167**

Sun Yat-sen 33, 36, 141, 217, 276, 277

Suzhou 270–273, **270**, 315–316

Suzhou Creek 234, 244–245, **244**

Suzhou Gardens 272, **272**

Suzhou Museum (Suzhou Bowuguan) 271

Suzhou Silk Museum (Suzhou Sichou Bowuguan), Suzhou 271

Sword Pond (Jian Chi), Moganshan 268

T

Taboos 290

Tai chi 255

Tai ji quan 124

Tailing 161

Taipingqiao Park (Taipingqiao Gongyuan), Shanghai 221

Taiyuan Villa, Shanghai 218

Tanzhe Temple (Tanzhe Si) **157**, 171, **171**

Taoism (*daojiao*) 52–53, 117

Taoist temples (*guan*) 166–167

Taxis 284, 287

Tea 27, **112**

Tea harvest 264

Television 290

Temple fairs 54, 125

TEMPLES 166–167

Baiyun Temple, Shanghai 206, 209

Baoguo Temple (Baoguo Si), Beijing 120, **120**, 317

Big Bell Temple (Dazhong Si), Beijing 132

Confucius Temple, Beijing 78, 81

Confucius Temple, Jiading **249**, 258

Confucius Temple (Wen Miao), Shanghai **15**, 207, 209

Confucius Temple (Wen Miao), Suzhou 270

Confucius Temple (Wen Miao), Tianjin 163

Dongyue Temple (Dongyue Miao), Beijing 125

Eight Outer Temples (Wai Ba Miao) 156

Fahai Temple (Fahai Si) 168, **168**

Fayu Temple (Fayu Si), Putuoshan 269

Flower God Temple (Ciji Si), Beijing 135

Guanghua Temple, Beijing 88

Hong Miao (Red Temple), Shanghai 190

Huiji Temple (Huiji Si), Putuoshan 269

Jade Buddha Temple (Yufo Si), Shanghai 245–246, **246**

Jingan Temple (Jingan Si), Shanghai 252

Lama Temple (Yonghe Gong), Beijing 79, **79**

Lingyin Temple (Lingyin Si), Hangzhou 265

Longhua Temple and Pagoda (Longhua Si and Longhua Ta), Shanghai 213, 223

North Temple Pagoda (Bei Si Ta), Suzhou 271

Puji Temple (Puji Si), Putuoshan 269

Putuo Zongcheng Temple (Putuo Zongcheng Zhi Miao) 156

Puyou Temple (Puyou Si) 156

Qinci Yangdian Temple (Qinci Yangdian Si), Shanghai 236

Shuxiang Temple (Shuxiang Si) 156

Source of Law Temple (Fayuan Si), Beijing **52–53**, **108**, 114, 114

Tanzhe Temple (Tanzhe Si) **157**, 171, **171**

Temple of Ancient Monarchs (Lidai Diwang Miao), Beijing 94

Temple of Appeasing the Distant (Anyuan Miao) 156

Temple of Brightness (Zhao Miao), Beijing 141

Temple of Divine Light (Lingguang Si) 169

Temple of Eternal Peace (Chang'an Si) 169

Temple of Eternal Peace (Yong'an Si), Beijing 86

Temple of Extensive Benevolence (Puren Si) 156

Temple of Great Mercy (Dabei Si) 169

Temple of Heaven (Tian Tan) 98–101, **98**, **101**

Temple of Moon (Yuetan Gongyuan), Beijing 94

Temple of Precious Pearls 169

Temple of Sumeru Happiness and Longevity (Xumi Fushou Zhi Miao) 156

Temple of the Azure Clouds (Biyun Si), Beijing 141, **166**

Temple of the Dragon King (Longwang Tang) 169

Temple of the Fragrant World (Xiangjie Si) 169

Temple of the God of Wealth (Caishen Shengdian) 170

Temple of the Ordination Terrace (Jietai Si) 170

Temple of the Reclining Buddha, Beijing 141

Temple of the Sea God (Haishen Miao), Shanhaiguan 154

Temple of the Town God (Chenghuang Miao), Shanghai 209

Temple of the White Dagoba (Baita Si), Beijing 94
Temple of Universal Happiness (Pule Si) 156
Temple of Universal Tranquility (Puning Si) 156
Temple of Yue Fei (Yue Wang Miao), Hangzhou 265
Tianhou Temple (Tianhou Gong), Tianjin 163
Tianning Temple of Heavenly Peace (Tianning Si), Beijing 120
Wen Tianxiang Temple, Beijing 77
White Cloud Temple (Bai Yun Quan), Beijing 111, 118–119, **118**
Xuanmiao Temple (Xuanmiao Guan), Suzhou 273
Yellow Temple (Huang Si), Moganshan 268
Yunxiang Temple, Nanxiang 258
Zhengguo Temple 169
Zhihua Temple, Beijing 82
Theater 319–320, 324
Three Hill Nunnery (Sanshan An) 169
Tiananmen Incident 38, **38–39**, 70–71
Tiananmen Square (Tiananmen Guangchang) **61**, 70–72, **70**, **72**, 88, 105
Tianhou Temple (Tianhou Gong), Tianjin 163
Tianjin 162–163, **162**, 304–305
Tianning Temple of Heavenly Peace (Tianning Si), Beijing 120
Tianqiao Acrobatic Theatre (Tianqiao Zaji Juchang), Beijing 320
Tiger Hill, Suzhou 273
Time differences 291
Tipping 12, 291
Toilets 291
Tomb-sweeping festival of Qingming 54, 289
Tomorrow Square, Shanghai 195
Tongli **274**, 275
Toroni Sutra Stela, Songjiang 258
Tourist offices 291
Tower for Observing the Moon (Wangyue Lou), Beijing 115
Tower Leaning Toward the Blue Sky (Yiqing Lou), Beijing 87
Traditional painting 46–47
Trains 8, 236, **281**, 284
Transportation 8–9, 283–284
Travelers with disabilities 291
Tunxi (Huangshan Shi) 280
Twin Pagodas, Suzhou **270**, 271–273

U

Uighurs 27, 191
Ullens Center for Contemporary Art (UCCA), Beijing 318–319

V

Vanguard Gallery, Shanghai 326
Villa Rouge, Shanghai 222
The Village at Sanlitun, Beijing **122**, 128, 317
Visas 282–283, 291
Visitor information 9

W

Waibaidu Bridge, Shanghai 182, 234, 242
WALKS/DRIVES
  bicycle tour around the Forbidden City 88–89
  cruise the Huangpu River 234–235
  Jewish Shanghai walk 242–243
  Legation Quarter walking tour 104–105
  Qianmen Dajie and Dashilan walk 112–113
  walk among the *hutongs* 74–77
  walk around Peking University 134–135
  walk around Xintiandi 220–221
  walk Shanghai's Old Town 206–207
  walk the Bund 182–184
Wang Meng 44
Wang Shuo 44
Wang Wei 46–47
Wang Zhima Hutong, Beijing 75–76
Wangou Cemetery, Shanghai 253
Wanping Fortress 164
Water towns (*shui xiang*) 274–275, **274**
Wei Hui 45
Weiming Lake, Beijing 134
Well of the Pearl Concubine (Zhenfei Jing), Beijing 69
Wen Tianxiang Temple, Beijing 77
West Lake (Xi Hu) 262–264
Western Qing Tombs (Qing Xiling) 161
Westin Bund Center, Shanghai 190–191
White Box Museum of Art, Beijing 318
White Cloud Castle, Moganshan 268
White Cloud Temple (Bai Yun Quan), Beijing 111, 118–119, **118**
White Dagoba, Beijing 86–87, **86**
White Russians 217
Working People's Culture Palace (Laodong Renmin Wenhuagong), Beijing 65
Wu Guanzhong 50
Wusongkou, Shanghai 234
Wuzhen 275

X

Xiangqi (Chinese chess) **76**
Xiao long bao **206**, 207, 258

Xicheng District, Beijing 84–85, 94
  Beihai Park (Beihai Gongyuan) **50–51**, **83**, **84**, 86–87, **86**, 88
  hotels and restaurants 298–299
  Mei Lanfang Museum 90, 91
  Rear Lakes 90
Xikai Cathedral (Xikai Jiaotang), Tianjin 163
Xilin Pagoda (Xilin Ta), Songjiang 258
Xinchang Ancient Town (Xinchang Gucheng), Shanghai 236
Xintiandi 219–221, **220**
Xintiandi Postal Museum, Shanghai 221
Xintiandi Style, Shanghai 221
Xitang 275
Xiudaozhe Pagoda (Xiudaozhe Ta), Shanghai 255
Xu Beihong Museum, Beijing 90
Xuanmiao Temple (Xuanmiao Guan), Suzhou 273
Xuanwu District, Beijing 108–120, **120**
  hotels and restaurants 299–300
  Liulichang 110–111, **110**
  Ox Street Mosque 115
  Qianmen Dajie and Dashilan Walk 112–113, **112**
  Source of Law Temple (Fayuan Si) **52–53**, **108**, 114, **114**
  White Cloud Temple (Bai Yun Quan) 118–119, **118**
Xujiahui, Shanghai 222
Xujiahui Cathedral, Shanghai 222
Xujiahui Park (Xujiahui Gongyuan), Shanghai 222

Y

Yan'an Road, Shanghai 253
Yandai Xiejie, Beijing 90
Yangge (folk dance) 138–139, **139**
Yangjingbang style 22, 49
Yangpu Bridge, Shanghai 234
Yangtze Great Bridge (Nanjing Yangzi Da Qiao) 278
Yellow Dragon Cave (Huanglong Dong), Hangzhou 265
Yellow Temple (Huang Si), Moganshan 268
Yifu Theater (Yifu Wutai), Shanghai 191
Yixing teapots, Shanghai 205
Yokohama Species Bank, Beijing **102**, 105
Yongle 28–30
Yongzheng (Prince Yong) 79, 132, 160, 161
Youth Day (Qingnian Jie) 56–57, 289
Yu Yuan Bazaar, Shanghai 205, 206, **206**
Yuan renminbi (RMB) 11

Yuan Shikai **31**
Yue Minjun 47, 50
Yuling 160
Yunxiang Temple, Nanxiang 258
Yunyan Pagoda (Yunyan Ta), Suzhou 273
Yuyuan Gardens, Shanghai **20–21**, **55**, **201**, 208, **208**

Z
Zhabei, Shanghai 244–246
Zhabei Park (Zhabei Gongyuan), Shanghai 248

Zhang Jie 44
Zhang Peili 51
Zhang Xiaogang 50
Zhaoling 153
Zhengguo Temple 169
Zhengyang Gate (Qianmen), Beijing 72, 105
Zhenjiao Mosque (Zhenjiao Qingzhensi), Songjiang 258
Zhihua Temple, Beijing 82
Zhongshan Gate (Zhongshan Men), Nanjing 276
Zhongshan Park (Zhongshan Gongyuan), Beijing 65

Zhongshan Park (Zhongshan Gongyuan), Shanghai **254**
Zhou Enlai 70–71, 217–218, 219, 224–225, **224**, 241, 277
Zhoukoudian Peking Man Site (Zhoukoudian Yizhi Bowuguan) 165
Zhouzhuang **259**, 274
Zhu Wei 51
Zhubaoshi Jie, Beijing 112
Zhujiajiao 275
Zijin Shan 276
Zijinshan Observatory (Zijin Shan Tianwentai), Nanjing 278

ILLUSTRATIONS CREDITS

National Geographic
TRAVELER
Beijing & Shanghai

CELEBRATING
◀125▶
YEARS

Published by the National Geographic Society

John M. Fahey, *Chairman of the Board and Chief Executive Officer*

Timothy T. Kelly, *President*

Declan Moore, *Executive Vice President; President, Publishing and Digital Media*

Melina Gerosa Bellows, *Executive Vice President; Chief Creative Officer, Books, Kids, and Family*

Lynn Cutter, *Executive Vice President, Travel*

Keith Bellows, *Senior Vice President and Editor in Chief, National Geographic Travel Media*

Prepared by the Book Division

Hector Sierra, *Senior Vice President and General Manager*

Jonathan Halling, *Design Director, Books and Children's Publishing*

Marianne R. Koszorus, *Design Director, Books*

Barbara A. Noe, *Senior Editor, National Geographic Travel Books*

R. Gary Colbert, *Production Director*

Jennifer A. Thornton, *Director of Managing Editorial*

Susan S. Blair, *Director of Photography*

Meredith C. Wilcox, *Director, Administration and Rights Clearance*

Staff for This Book

Carl Mehler, *Director of Maps*

Michael McNey and Mapping Specialists, *Map Production*

Marshall Kiker, Michael O'Connor, *Associate Managing Editors*

Katie Olsen, *Production Design Assistant*

Manufacturing and Quality Management

Phillip L. Schlosser, *Senior Vice President*

Chris Brown, *Vice President, NG Book Manufacturing*

George Bounelis, *Vice President, Production Services*

Nicole Elliott, *Manager*

Rachel Faulise, *Manager*

Robert L. Barr, *Manager*

KKComm, LLC

Kay Kobor Hankins, *Project Manager/Art Director*

Mary Stephanos/Justin Kavanagh, *Project Editors*

Jane Sunderland, *Contributor*

Cutaway illustrations (pp. 66–67, 101, 182–183, 199) drawn by Maltings Partnership, Derby, England

The National Geographic Society is one of the world's largest nonprofit scientific and educational organizations. Founded in 1888 to "increase and diffuse geographic knowledge," the Society works to inspire people to care about the planet. National Geographic reflects the world through its magazines, television programs, films, music and radio, books, DVDs, maps, exhibitions, live events, school publishing programs, interactive media and merchandise. *National Geographic* magazine, the Society's official journal, published in English and 33 local-language editions, is read by more than 60 million people each month. The National Geographic Channel reaches 435 million households in 37 languages in 173 countries. National Geographic Digital Media receives more than 19 million visitors a month. National Geographic has funded more than 10,000 scientific research, conservation and exploration projects and supports an education program promoting geography literacy. For more information, visit www.nationalgeographic.com.

For more information, please call 1-800-NGS LINE (647-5463) or write to the following address:

National Geographic Society
1145 17th Street N.W.
Washington, D.C. 20036-4688 U.S.A.

For information about special discounts for bulk purchases, please contact National Geographic Books Special Sales: ngspecsales@ngs.org

For rights or permissions inquiries, please contact National Geographic Books Subsidiary Rights: ngbookrights@ngs.org

National Geographic Traveler: Beijing & Shanghai
ISBN: 978-1-4262-1023-5

Printed in Hong Kong
12/THK/1

The information in this book has been carefully checked and to the best of our knowledge is accurate. However, details are subject to change, and the National Geographic Society cannot be responsible for such changes, or for errors or omissions. Assessments of sites, hotels, and restaurants are based on the author's subjective opinions, which do not necessarily reflect the publisher's opinion.

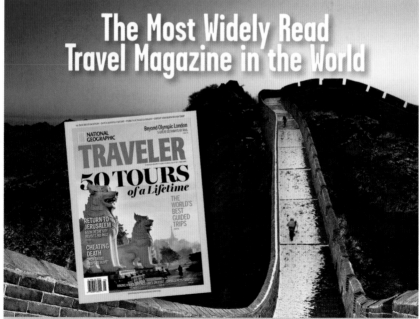